THE
AMERICAN LANGUAGE

OF THE FIRST EDITION OF
THIS BOOK FIFTEEN HUNDRED
COPIES HAVE BEEN PRINTED
AND THE TYPE DISTRIBUTED
THIS IS NUMBER 701

THE
AMERICAN LANGUAGE

A Preliminary Inquiry into the Develop-
ment of English in the United States

BY

H. L. MENCKEN

NEW YORK
ALFRED · A · KNOPF
MCMXIX

PE
2808
M4

PREFACE

The aim of this book is best exhibited by describing its origin. I am, and have been since early manhood, an editor of newspapers, magazines and books, and a critic of the last named. These occupations have forced me into a pretty wide familiarity with current literature, both periodical and within covers, and in particular into a familiarity with the current literature of England and America. It was part of my daily work, for a good many years, to read the principal English newspapers and reviews; it has been part of my work, all the time, to read the more important English novels, essays, poetry and criticism. An American born and bred, I early noted, as everyone else in like case must note, certain salient differences between the English of England and the English of America as practically spoken and written—differences in vocabulary, in syntax, in the shades and habits of idiom, and even, coming to the common speech, in grammar. And I noted too, of course, partly during visits to England but more largely by a somewhat wide and intimate intercourse with English people in the United States, the obvious differences between English and American pronunciation and intonation.

Greatly interested in these differences—some of them so great that they led me to seek exchanges of light with Englishmen—I looked for some work that would describe and account for them with a show of completeness, and perhaps depict the process of their origin. I soon found that no such work existed, either in England or in America—that the whole literature of the subject was astonishingly meagre and unsatisfactory. There were several dictionaries of Americanisms, true enough, but only one of them made any pretension to scientific method, and even that one was woefully narrow and incomplete. The one more general treatise, the work of a man foreign to both Eng-

land and America in race and education, was more than 40
years old, and full of palpable errors. For the rest, there was
only a fugitive and inconsequential literature—an almost useless mass of notes and essays, chiefly by the minor sort of pedagogues, seldom illuminating, save in small details, and often
incredibly ignorant and inaccurate. On the large and important subject of American pronunciation, for example, I could
find nothing save a few casual essays. On American spelling,
with its wide and constantly visible divergences from English
usages, there was little more. On American grammar there was
nothing whatever. Worse, an important part of the poor literature that I unearthed was devoted to absurd efforts to prove that
no such thing as an American variety of English existed—that
the differences I constantly encountered in English and that
my English friends encountered in American were chiefly imag-
inary, and to be explained away by denying them.

Still intrigued by the subject, and in despair of getting any
illumination from such theoretical masters of it, I began a collection of materials for my own information, and gradually it
took on a rather formidable bulk. My interest in it being made
known by various articles in the newspapers and magazines, I
began also to receive contributions from other persons of the
same fancy, both English and American, and gradually my collection fell into a certain order, and I saw the workings of general laws in what, at first, had appeared to be mere chaos. The
present book then began to take form—its preparation a sort
of recreation from other and far different labor. It is anything
but an exhaustive treatise upon the subject; it is not even an
exhaustive examination of the materials. All it pretends to do
is to articulate some of those materials—to get some approach to
order and coherence into them, and so pave the way for a better
work by some more competent man. That work calls for the
equipment of a first-rate philologist, which I am surely not. All
I have done here is to stake out the field, sometimes borrowing
suggestions from other inquirers and sometimes, as in the case
of American grammar, attempting to run the lines myself.

That it should be regarded as an anti-social act to examine

and exhibit the constantly growing differences between English and American, as certain American pedants argue sharply—
this doctrine is quite beyond my understanding. All it indicates, stripped of sophistry, is a somewhat childish effort to gain
the approval of Englishmen—a belated efflorescence of the colonial spirit, often commingled with fashionable aspiration. The
plain fact is that the English themselves are not deceived, nor
do they grant the approval so ardently sought for. On the contrary, they are keenly aware of the differences between the two
dialects, and often discuss them, as the following pages show.
Perhaps one dialect, in the long run, will defeat and absorb the
other; if the two nations continue to be partners in great adventures it may very well happen. But even in that case, something may be accomplished by examining the differences which
exist today. In some ways, as in intonation, English usage is
plainly better than American. In others, as in spelling, American usage is as plainly better than English. But in order to
develop usages that the people of both nations will accept it is
obviously necessary to study the differences now visible. This
study thus shows a certain utility. But its chief excuse is its
human interest, for it prods deeply into national idiosyncrasies
and ways of mind, and that sort of prodding is always entertain-
ing.

I am thus neither teacher, nor prophet, nor reformer, but
merely inquirer. The exigencies of my vocation make me almost
completely bilingual; I can write English, as in this clause, quite
as readily as American, as in this here one. Moreover, I have
a hand for a compromise dialect which embodies the common
materials of both, and is thus free from offense on both sides of
the water—as befits the editor of a magazine published in both
countries. But that compromise dialect is the living speech of
neither. What I have tried to do here is to make a first sketch
of the living speech of These States. The work is confessedly
incomplete, and in places very painfully so, but in such enter-
prises a man must put an arbitrary term to his labors, lest some
mischance, after years of diligence, take him from them too suddenly for them to be closed, and his laborious accumulations, as

Ernest Walker says in his book on English surnames, be "doomed to the waste-basket by harassed executors."

If the opportunity offers in future I shall undoubtedly return to the subject. For one thing, I am eager to attempt a more scientific examination of the grammar of the American vulgar speech, here discussed briefly in Chapter VI. For another thing, I hope to make further inquiries into the subject of American surnames of non-English origin. Various other fields invite. No historical study of American pronunciation exists; the influence of German, Irish-English, Yiddish and other such immigrant dialects upon American has never been investigated; there is no adequate treatise on American geographical names. Contributions of materials and suggestions for a possible revised edition of the present book will reach me if addressed to me in care of the publisher at 220 West Forty-second Street, New York. I shall also be very grateful for the correction of errors, some perhaps typographical but others due to faulty information or mistaken judgment.

In conclusion I borrow a plea in confession and avoidance from Ben Jonson's pioneer grammar of English, published in incomplete form after his death. "We have set down," he said, "that that in our judgment agreeth best with reason and good order. Which notwithstanding, if it seem to any to be too rough hewed, let him plane it out more smoothly, and I shall not only not envy it, but in the behalf of my country most heartily thank him for so great a benefit; hoping that I shall be thought sufficiently to have done my part if in tolling this bell I may draw others to a deeper consideration of the matter; for, touching myself, I must needs confess that after much painful churning this only would come which here we have devised."

MENCKEN.

Baltimore, January 1, 1919.

CONTENTS

I

By Way of Introduction

§ 1

The Diverging Streams—Thomas Jefferson, with his usual prevision, saw clearly more than a century ago that the American people, as they increased in numbers and in the diversity of their national interests and racial strains, would make changes in their mother tongue, as they had already made changes in the political institutions of their inheritance. ("The new circumstances under which we are placed," he wrote to John Waldo from Monticello on August 16, 1813, "call for new words, new phrases, and for the transfer of old words to new objects. An American dialect will therefore be formed.")

Nearly a quarter of a century before this, another great American, and one with an expertness in the matter that the too versatile Jefferson could not muster, had ventured upon a prophecy even more bold and specific. He was Noah Webster, then at the beginning of his stormy career as a lexicographer. In his little volume of "Dissertations on the English Language," printed in 1789 and dedicated to "His Excellency, Benjamin Franklin, Esq., LL.D., F.R.S., late President of the Commonwealth of Pennsylvania," Webster argued that the time for regarding English usage and submitting to English authority had already passed, and that "a future separation of the American tongue from the English" was "necessary and unavoidable." "Numerous local causes," he continued, "such as a new country, new associations of people, new combinations of ideas in arts and sciences, and some intercourse with tribes wholly unknown in Europe, will introduce new words into the American tongue. These causes will produce, in a course of time, a language in

1

North America as different from the future language of England as the modern Dutch, Danish and Swedish are from the German, or from one another.'' [1]

Neither Jefferson nor Webster put a term upon his prophecy. They may have been thinking, one or both, of a remote era, not yet come to dawn, or they may have been thinking, with the facile imagination of those days, of a period even earlier than our own. In the latter case, they allowed far too little (and particularly Webster) for factors that have worked powerfully against the influences they saw so clearly in operation about them. One of these factors, obviously, has been the vast improvement in communications across the ocean, a change scarcely in vision a century ago. It has brought New York relatively nearer to London today than it was to Boston, or even to Philadelphia, during Jefferson's presidency, and that greater proximity has produced a steady interchange of ideas, opinions, news and mere gossip. We latter-day Americans know a great deal more about the everyday affairs of England than the early Americans, for we read more English books, and have more about the English in our newspapers, and meet more Englishmen, and go to England much oftener. The effects of this ceaseless traffic in ideas and impressions, so plainly visible in politics, in ethics and aesthetics, and even in the minutae of social intercourse, are also to be seen in the language. On the one hand there is a swift exchange of new inventions on both sides, so that much of our American slang quickly passes to London and the latest English fashions in pronunciation are almost instantaneously imitated, at least by a minority, in New York; and on the other hand the English, by so constantly having the floor, force upon us, out of their firmer resolution and certitude, a somewhat sneaking respect for their own greater conservatism of speech, so that our professors of the language, in the overwhelming main, combat all signs of differentiation with the utmost diligence, and safeguard the doctrine that the standards of English are the only reputable standards of American.

This doctrine, of course, is not supported by the known laws of

[1] Pp. 22–23.

language, nor has it prevented the large divergences that we shall presently examine, but all the same it has worked steadily toward a highly artificial formalism, and as steadily against the investigation of the actual national speech. Such grammar, so-called, as is taught in our schools and colleges, is a grammar standing four-legged upon the theorizings and false inferences of English Latinists, eager only to break the wild tongue of Shakespeare to a rule; and its frank aim is to create in us a high respect for a book language which few of us ever actually speak and not many of us even learn to write. That language, heavily artificial though it may be, undoubtedly has notable merits. It shows a sonority and a stateliness that you must go to the Latin of the Golden Age to match; its "highly charged and heavy-shotted" periods, in Matthew Arnold's phrase, serve admirably the obscurantist purposes of American pedagogy and of English parliamentary oratory and leader-writing; it is something for the literary artists of both countries to prove their skill upon by flouting it. But to the average American, bent upon expressing his ideas, not stupendously but merely clearly, it must always remain something vague and remote, like Greek history or the properties of the parabola, for he never speaks it or hears it spoken, and seldom encounters it in his everyday reading. If he learns to write it, which is not often, it is with a rather depressing sense of its artificiality. He may master it as a Korean, bred in the colloquial Onmun, may master the literary Korean-Chinese, but he never thinks in it or quite feels it.

This fact, I daresay, is largely responsible for the notorious failure of our schools to turn out students who can put their ideas into words with simplicity and intelligibility. What their professors try to teach is not their mother-tongue at all, but a dialect that stands quite outside their common experience, and into which they have to translate their thoughts, consciously and painfully. Bad writing consists in making the attempt, and failing through lack of practise. Good writing consists, as in the case of Howells, in deliberately throwing overboard the principles so elaborately inculcated, or, as in the case of Lincoln, in standing unaware of them. Thus the study of the language he is supposed to use, to the average American, takes on a sort of bilingual character. On the one hand, he is grounded abominably in a grammar and syntax that have always been largely artificial, even in the country where they are supposed to prevail, and on the other hand he has to pick up the essentials of his actual speech as best he may. "Literary English," says Van Wyck Brooks,[2] "with us is a tradition, just as Anglo-Saxon law with us is a tradition. They persist, not as the normal expressions of a race, . . . but through prestige and precedent and the will and habit of a dominating class largely out of touch with a national fabric unconsciously taking form out of school." What thus goes on out of school does not interest the guardians of our linguistic morals. No attempt to deduce the principles of American grammar, or even of American syntax, from the everyday speech of decently spoken Americans has ever been made. There is no scientific study, general and comprehensive in scope, of the American vocabulary, or of the influences lying at the root of American word-formation. No American philologist, so far as I know, has ever deigned to give the same sober attention to the *sermo plebeius* of his country that he habitually gives to the mythical objective case in theoretical English, or to the pronunciation of Latin, or to the irregular verbs in French.

§ 2

The Academic Attitude—This neglect of the vulgate by those professionally trained to investigate it, and its disdainful dismissal when it is considered at all, are among the strangest phenomena of American scholarship. In all other countries the everyday speech of the people, and even the speech of the illiterate, have the constant attention of philologists, and the laws of their growth and variation are elaborately studied. In France, to name but one agency, there is the Société des Parlers de France, with its diligent inquiries into changing forms; moreover, the Académie itself is endlessly concerned with the

[2] America's Coming of Age; New York, 1915, p. 15. See also the preface to Every-Day English, by Richard Grant White; Boston, 1881, p. xviii.

subject, and is at great pains to observe and note every fluctuation in usage.[3] In Germany, amid many other such works, there are the admirable grammars of the spoken speech by Dr. Otto Bremer. In Sweden there are several journals devoted to the study of the vulgate, and the government has recently granted a subvention of 7500 *kronen* a year to an organization of scholars called the Undersökningen av Svenska Folkmaal, formed to investigate it systematically.[4] In Norway there is a widespread movement to overthrow the official Dano-Norwegian, and substitute a national language based upon the speech of the peasants.[5] In Spain the Academia is constantly at work upon its great Diccionario, Ortografía and Gramática, and revises them at frequent intervals (the last time in 1914), taking in all new words as they appear and all new forms of old ones. And in Latin-America, to come nearer to our own case, the native philologists have produced a copious literature on the matter closest at hand,

[3] The common notion that the Académie combats changes is quite erroneous. In the preface to the first edition of its dictionary (1694) it disclaimed any purpose "to make new words and to reject others at its pleasure." In the preface to the second edition (1718) it confessed that "ignorance and corruption often introduce manners of writing" and that "convenience establishes them." In the preface to the third edition (1740) it admitted that it was "forced to admit changes which the public has made." And so on. Says D. M. Robertson, in A History of the French Academy (London, 1910): "The Academy repudiates any assumption of authority over the language with which the public in its own practise has not first clothed it. So much, indeed, does it confine itself to an interpretation merely of the laws of language that its decisions are sometimes contrary to its own judgment of what is either desirable or expedient."

[4] *Cf. Scandinavian Studies and Notes*, vol. iv, no. 3, Aug. 1917, p. 258.

[5] This movement won official recognition so long ago as 1885, when the Storting passed the first of a series of acts designed to put the two languages on equal footing. Four years later, after a campaign going back to 1874, provision was made for teaching the *landsmaal* in the schools for the training of primary teachers. In 1899 a professorship of the *landsmaal* was established in the University of Christiania. The school boards in the case of primary schools, and the pupils in the case of middle and high schools are now permitted to choose between the two languages, and the *landsmaal* has been given official status by the State Church. The chief impediment to its wider acceptance lies in the fact that it is not, as it stands, a natural language, but an artificial amalgamation of peasant dialects. It was devised in 1848–50 by Ivar Aasen. *Vide* The Language Question, *London Times* Norwegian Supplement, May 18, 1914.

and one finds in it very excellent works upon the Portuguese
dialect of Brazil, and the variations of Spanish in Mexico, the
Argentine, Chili, Peru, Ecuador, Uraguay and even Honduras
and Costa Rica.[6] But in the United States the business has attracted little attention, and less talent. The only existing formal
treatise upon the subject [7] was written by a Swede trained in
Germany and is heavy with errors and omissions. And the only
usable dictionary of Americanisms [8] was written in England, and
is the work of an expatriated lawyer. Not a single volume by a
native philologist, familiar with the language by daily contact
and professionally equipped for the business, is to be found in
the meagre bibliography.

I am not forgetting, of course, the early explorations of Noah
Webster, of which much more anon, nor the labors of our later
dictionary makers, nor the inquiries of the American Dialect Society,[9] nor even the occasional illuminations of such writers as
Richard Grant White, Thomas S. Lounsbury and Brander Matthews. But all this preliminary work has left the main field
almost uncharted. Webster, as we shall see, was far more a
reformer of the American dialect than a student of it. He introduced radical changes into its spelling and pronunciation, but
he showed little understanding of its direction and genius. One
always sees in him, indeed, the teacher rather than the scientific
inquirer; the ardor of his desire to expound and instruct was
only matched by his infinite capacity for observing inaccurately,
and his profound ignorance of elementary philological principles. In the preface to the first edition of his American Dictionary, published in 1828—the first in which he added the quali-
fying adjective to the title—he argued eloquently for the right
of Americans to shape their own speech without regard to Eng-

    [6] A few such works are listed in the bibliography. More of them are men-
tioned in Americanismos, by Miguel de Toro y Gisbert; Paris, n. d.

    [7] Maximilian Schele de Vere: Americanisms: The English of the New
World; New York, 1872.

    [8] Richard H. Thornton: An American Glossary. . . ., 2 vols.; Phila.
and London, 1912.

    [9] Organized Feb. 19, 1889, with Dr. J. J. Child, of Harvard, as its first
president.

lish precedents, but only a year before this he had told Captain Basil Hall [10] that he knew of but fifty genuine Americanisms— a truly staggering proof of his defective observation. Webster was the first American professional scholar, and despite his frequent engrossment in public concerns and his endless public controversies, there was always something sequestered and almost medieval about him. The American language that he described and argued for was seldom the actual tongue of the folks about him, but often a sort of Volapük made up of one part faulty reporting and nine parts academic theorizing. In only one department did he exert any lasting influence, and that was in the department of orthography. The fact that our spelling is simpler and usually more logical than the English we chiefly owe to him. But it is not to be forgotten that the majority of his innovations, even here, were not adopted, but rejected, nor is it to be forgotten that spelling is the least of all the factors that shape and condition a language.

The same caveat lies against the work of the later makers of dictionaries; they have gone ahead of common usage in the matter of orthography, but they have hung back in the far more important matter of vocabulary, and have neglected the most important matter of idiom altogether. The defect in the work of the Dialect Society lies in a somewhat similar circumscription of activity. Its constitution, adopted in 1889, says that "its object is the investigation of the spoken English of the United States and Canada," but that investigation, so far, has got little beyond the accumulation of vocabularies of local dialects, such as they are. Even in this department its work is very far from finished, and the Dialect Dictionary announced years ago has not yet appeared. Until its collections are completed and synchronized, it will be impossible for its members to make any profitable inquiry into the general laws underlying the development of American, or even to attempt a classification of the materials common to the whole speech. The meagreness of the materials accumulated in the five slow-moving volumes of *Dialect Notes* shows clearly, indeed, how little the American philologist is in-

[10] Author of Travels in North America; London, 1829.

terested in the language that falls upon his ears every hour of
the day.   And in *Modern Language Notes* that impression is reinforced, for its bulky volumes contain exhaustive studies of all
the other living languages and dialects, but only an occasional
essay upon American.

Now add to this general indifference a persistent and often
violent effort to oppose any formal differentiation of English and
American, initiated by English purists but heartily supported by
various Americans, and you come, perhaps, to some understanding of the unsatisfactory state of the literature of the subject.
The pioneer dictionary of Americanisms, published in 1816 by
John Pickering, a Massachusetts lawyer,[11] was not only criti-
cized unkindly; it was roundly denounced as something subtly
impertinent and corrupting, and even Noah Webster took a formidable fling at it.[12]   Most of the American philologists of the
early days—Witherspoon, Worcester, Fowler, Cobb and their
like—were uncompromising advocates of conformity, and combatted every indication of a national independence in speech with
the utmost vigilance.   One of their company, true enough, stood
out against the rest.   He was George Perkins Marsh, and in his
"Lectures on the English Language"[13] he argued that "in point
of naked syntactical accuracy, the English of America is not at
all inferior to that of England."   But even Marsh expressed the
hope that Americans would not, "with malice prepense, go about
to republicanize our orthography and our syntax, our grammars
and our dictionaries, our nursery hymns (*sic*) and our Bibles"
to the point of actual separation.[14]   Moreover, he was a philologist only by courtesy; the regularly ordained school-masters were
all against him.   The fear voiced by William C. Fowler, professor of rhetoric at Amherst, that Americans might "break
loose from the laws of the English language"[15] altogether, was

[11] A Vocabulary or Collection of Words and Phrases which Have Been
Supposed to be Peculiar to the United States of America; Boston, 1816.
[12] A Letter to the Hon. John Pickering on the Subject of His Vocabulary; Boston, 1817.
[13] 4th ed., New York, 1870, p. 669.
[14] *Op. cit.* p. 676.
[15] The English Language; New York 1850; rev. ed., 1855. This was
the first American text-book of English for use in colleges. Before its

echoed by the whole fraternity, and so the corrective bastinado was laid on.

It remained, however, for two professors of a later day to launch the doctrine that the independent growth of American was not only immoral, but a sheer illusion. They were Richard Grant White, for long the leading American writer upon language questions, at least in popular esteem, and Thomas S. Lounsbury, for thirty-five years professor of the English language and literature in the Sheffield Scientific School at Yale, and an indefatigable controversialist. Both men were of the utmost industry in research, and both had wide audiences. White's "Words and Their Uses," published in 1872, was a mine of erudition, and his "Everyday English," following eight years later, was another. True enough, Fitzedward Hall, the Anglo-Indian-American philologist, disposed of many of his etymologies and otherwise did execution upon him,[16] but in the main his contentions held water. Lounsbury was also an adept and favorite expositor. His attacks upon certain familiar pedantries of the grammarians were penetrating and effective, and his two books, "The Standard of Usage in English" and "The Standard of Pronunciation in English," not to mention his excellent "History of the English Language" and his numerous magazine articles, showed a profound knowledge of the early development of the language, and an admirable spirit of free inquiry. But both of these laborious scholars, when they turned from English proper to American English, displayed an unaccountable desire to deny its existence altogether, and to the support of that denial they brought a critical method that was anything but unprejudiced. White devoted not less than eight long articles in the *Atlantic Monthly*[17] to a review of the fourth edition of John

publication, according to Fowler himself (rev. ed., p. xi), the language was studied only "superficially" and "in the primary schools." He goes on: "Afterward, when older, in the academy, during their preparation for college, our pupils perhaps despised it, in comparison with the Latin and the Greek; and in the college they do not systematically study the language after they come to maturity."

[16] In Recent Exemplifications of False Philology; London, 1872.

[17] Americanisms, parts I-VIII, April, May, July, Sept., Nov., 1878; Jan., March, May, 1879.

Russell Bartlett's American Glossary,[18] and when he came to the end he had disposed of nine-tenths of Bartlett's specimens and called into question the authenticity of at least half of what remained. And no wonder, for his method was simply that of erecting tests so difficult and so arbitrary that only the exceptional word or phrase could pass them, and then only by a sort of chance. "To stamp a word or a phrase as an Americanism," he said, "it is necessary to show that (1) it is of so-called 'American' origin—that is, that it first came into use in the United States of North America, or that (2) it has been adopted in those States from some language other than English, or has been kept in use there while it has *wholly* passed out of use in England." Going further, he argued that unless "the simple words in compound names" were used in America "in a sense different from that in which they are used in England" the compound itself could not be regarded as an Americanism. The absurdity of all this is apparent when it is remembered that one of his rules would bar out such obvious Americanisms as the use of *sick* in place of *ill*, of *molasses* for *treacle*, and of *fall* for *autumn*, for all of these words, while archaic in England, are by no means wholly extinct; and that another would dispose of that vast category of compounds which includes such unmistakably characteristic Americanisms as *joy-ride*, *rake-off*, *show-down*, *up-lift*, *out-house*, *rubber-neck*, *chair-warmer*, *fire-eater* and *back-talk*.

Lounsbury went even further. In the course of a series of articles in *Harper's Magazine*, in 1913,[19] he laid down the dogma that "cultivated speech . . . affords the only legitimate basis of comparison between the language as used in England and in America," and then went on:

In the only really proper sense of the term, an Americanism is a word or phrase naturally used by an educated American which under similar conditions would not be used by an educated Englishman. The emphasis, it will be seen, lies in the word "educated."

This curious criterion, fantastic as it must have seemed to

---

[18] A Glossary of Words and Phrases Usually Regarded as Peculiar to the United States, 4th ed.; Boston, 1877.
[19] Feb., March, June, July, Sept.

European philologists, was presently reinforced, for in his fourth article Lounsbury announced that his discussion was "restricted to the *written* speech of educated men." The result, of course, was a wholesale slaughter of Americanisms. If it was not impossible to reject a word, like White, on the ground that some stray English poet or other had once used it, it was almost always possible to reject it on the ground that it was not admitted into the vocabulary of a college professor when he sat down to compose formal book-English. What remained was a small company, indeed—and almost the whole field of American idiom and American grammar, so full of interest for the less austere explorer, was closed without even a peek into it.

White and Lounsbury dominated the arena and fixed the fashion. The later national experts upon the national language, with a few somewhat timorous exceptions, pass over its peculiarities without noticing them. So far as I can discover, there is not a single treatise in type upon one of its most salient characters— the wide departure of some of its vowel sounds from those of orthodox English. Marsh, C. H. Grandgent and Robert J. Menner have printed a number of valuable essays upon the subject, but there is no work that co-ordinates their inquiries or that attempts otherwise to cover the field. When, in preparing materials for the following chapters, I sought to determine the history of the *a*-sound in America, I found it necessary to plow through scores of ancient spelling-books, and to make deductions, perhaps sometimes rather rash, from the works of Franklin, Webster and Cobb. Of late the National Council of Teachers of English has appointed a Committee on American Speech and sought to let some light into the matter, but as yet its labors are barely begun and the publications of its members get little beyond preliminaries. Such an inquiry involves a laboriousness which should have intrigued Lounsbury: he once counted the number of times the word *female* appears in "Vanity Fair." But you will find only a feeble dealing with the question in his book on pronunciation. Nor is there any adequate work (for Schele de Vere's is full of errors and omissions) upon the influences felt by American through contact with the languages of our millions of immigrants, nor upon our peculiarly rich and characteristic slang. There are several excellent dictionaries of English slang, and many more of French slang, but I have been able to find but one devoted exclusively to American slang, and that one is a very bad one.

§ 3

The View of Writing Men—But though the native *Gelehrten* thus neglect the vernacular, or even oppose its study, it has been the object of earnest lay attention since an early day, and that attention has borne fruit in a considerable accumulation of materials, if not in any very accurate working out of its origins and principles. The English, too, have given attention to it—often, alas, satirically, or even indignantly. For a long while, as we shall see, they sought to stem its differentiation by heavy denunciations of its vagaries, and so late as the period of the Civil War they attached to it that quality of abhorrent barbarism which they saw as the chief mark of the American people. But in later years they have viewed it with a greater showing of scientific calm, and its definite separation from correct English, at least as a spoken tongue, is now quite frankly admitted. The Cambridge History of English Literature, for example, says that English and American are now ''notably dissimilar'' in vocabulary, and that the latter is splitting off into a distinct dialect.[20] The Eleventh Edition of the Encyclopaedia Britannica, going further, says that the two languages are already so far apart that ''it is not uncommon to meet with [American] newspaper articles of which an untravelled Englishman would hardly be able to understand a sentence.''[21] A great many other academic authorities, including A. H. Sayce and H. W. and F. G. Fowler, bear testimony to the same effect.

On turning to the men actually engaged in writing English, and particularly to those aspiring to an American audience, one finds nearly all of them adverting, at some time or other, to the growing difficulties of intercommunication. William Archer,

[20] Vol. xiv, pp. 484–5; Cambridge, 1917.
[21] Vol. xxv, p. 209.

Arnold Bennett, H. G. Wells, Sidney Low, the Chestertons and Kipling are some of those who have dealt with the matter at length. Low, in an article in the *Westminster Gazette* [22] ironically headed "Ought American to be Taught in our Schools?" has described how the latter-day British business man is "puzzled by his ignorance of colloquial American" and "painfully hampered" thereby in his handling of American trade. He continues:

In the United States of North America the study of the English tongue forms part of the educational scheme. I gather this because I find that they have professors of the English language and literature in the Universities there, and I note that in the schools there are certain hours alloted for "English" under instructors who specialize in that subject. This is quite right. English is still far from being a dead language, and our American kinsfolk are good enough to appreciate the fact.

But I think we should return the compliment. We ought to learn the American language in our schools and colleges. At present it is strangely neglected by the educational authorities. They pay attention to linguistic attainments of many other kinds, but not to this. How many thousands of youths are at this moment engaged in puzzling their brains over Latin and Greek grammar only Whitehall knows. Every well-conducted seminary has some instructor who is under the delusion that he is teaching English boys and girls to speak French with a good Parisian accent. We teach German, Italian, even Spanish, Russian, modern Greek, Arabic, Hindustani. For a moderate fee you can acquire a passing acquaintance with any of these tongues at the Berlitz Institute and the Gouin Schools. But even in these polyglot establishments there is nobody to teach you American. I have never seen a grammar of it or a dictionary. I have searched in vain at the booksellers for "How to Learn American in Three Weeks" or some similar compendium. Nothing of the sort exists. The native speech of one hundred millions of civilized people is as grossly neglected by the publishers as it is by the schoolmasters. You can find means to learn Hausa or Swahili or Cape Dutch in London more easily than the expressive, if difficult, tongue which is spoken in the office, the bar-room, the tram-car, from the snows of Alaska to the mouths of the Mississippi, and is enshrined in a literature that is growing in volume and favor every day.

Low then quotes an extract from an American novel appear-

22 July 18, 1913.

ing serially in an English magazine—an extract including such Americanisms as *side-stepper, saltwater-taffy, Prince-Albert* (coat), *boob, bartender* and *kidding,* and many characteristically American extravagances of metaphor. It might be well argued, he goes on, that this strange dialect is as near to "the tongue that Shakespeare spoke" as "the dialect of Bayswater or Brixton," but that philological fact does not help to its understanding. "You might almost as well expect him [the British business man] to converse freely with a Portuguese railway porter because he tried to stumble through Caesar when he was in the Upper Fourth at school."

In the *London Daily Mail,* W. G. Faulkner lately launched this proposed campaign of education by undertaking to explain various terms appearing in American moving-pictures to English spectators. Mr. Faulkner assumed that most of his readers would understand *sombrero, sidewalk, candy-store, freight-car, boost, elevator, boss, crook* and *fall* (for *autumn*) without help, but he found it necessary to define such commonplace Americanisms as *hoodlum, hobo, bunco-steerer, rubber-neck, drummer, sucker, dive* (in the sense of a thieves' resort), *clean-up, graft* and *to feature.* Curiously enough, he proved the reality of the difficulties he essayed to level by falling into error as to the meanings of some of the terms he listed, among them *dead-beat, flume, dub* and *stag.* Another English expositor, apparently following him, thought it necessary to add definitions of *hold-up, quitter, rube, shack, road-agent, cinch, live-wire* and *scab,*[23] but he, too, mistook the meaning of *dead-beat,* and in addition he misdefined *band-wagon* and substituted *get-out,* seemingly an invention of his own, for *get-away.* Faulkner, somewhat belated in his animosity, seized the opportunity to read a homily upon the vulgarity and extravagance of the American language, and argued that the introduction of its coinages through the moving-picture theatre (*Anglais, cinema*) "cannot be regarded without serious

[23] Of the words cited as still unfamiliar in England, Thornton has traced *hobo* to 1891, *hold-up* and *bunco* to 1887, *dive* to 1882, *dead-beat* to 1877, *hoodlum* to 1872, *road-agent* to 1866, *stag* to 1856, *drummer* to 1836 and *flume* to 1792. All of them are probably older than these references indicate.

misgivings, if only because it generates and encourages mental indiscipline so far as the choice of expressions is concerned.'' In other words, the greater pliability and resourcefulness of American is a fault to be corrected by the English tendency to hold to that which is established.

Cecil Chesterton, in the *New Witness*, recently called attention to the increasing difficulty of intercommunication, not only verbally, but in writing. The American newspapers, he said, even the best of them, admit more and more locutions that puzzle and dismay an English reader. After quoting a characteristic headline he went on:

I defy any ordinary Englishman to say that that is the English language or that he can find any intelligible meaning in it. Even a dictionary will be of no use to him. He must know the language colloquially or not at all. . . . No doubt it is easier for an Englishman to understand American than it would be for a Frenchman to do the same, just as it is easier for a German to understand Dutch than it would be for a Spaniard. But it does not make the American language identical with the English.[24]

Chesterton, however, refrained from denouncing this lack of identity; on the contrary, he allowed certain merits to American. ''I do not want anybody to suppose,'' he said, ''that the American language is in any way inferior to ours. In some ways it has improved upon it in vigor and raciness. In other ways it adheres more closely to the English of the best period.'' Testimony to the same end was furnished before this by William Archer. ''New words,'' he said, ''are begotten by new conditions of life; and as American life is far more fertile of new conditions than ours, the tendency toward neologism cannot but be stronger in America than in England. America has enormously enriched the language, not only with new words, but (since the American mind is, on the whole, quicker and wittier than the English) with apt and luminous colloquial metaphors.''[25]

The list of such quotations might be indefinitely prolonged.

[24] Summarized in *Literary Digest*, June 19, 1915.
[25] America Today, *Scribner's*, Feb. 1899, p. 218.

There is scarcely an English book upon the United States which does not offer some discussion, more or less profound, of American peculiarities of speech, both as they are revealed in spoken discourse (particularly pronunciation and intonation) and as they show themselves in popular literature and in the newspapers, and to this discussion protest is often added, as it very often is by the reviews and newspapers. "The Americans," says a typical critic, "have so far progressed with their self-appointed task of creating an American language that much of their conversation is now incomprehensible to English people." [26] On our own side there is almost equal evidence of a sense of difference, despite the fact that the educated American is presumably trained in orthodox English, and can at least read it without much feeling of strangeness. "The American," says George Ade, in his book of travel, "In Pastures New," "must go to England in order to learn for a dead certainty that he does not speak the English language. . . . This pitiful fact comes home to every American when he arrives in London—that there are two languages, the English and the American. One is correct; the other is incorrect. One is a pure and limpid stream; the other is a stagnant pool, swarming with bacilli." [27] This was written in 1906. Twenty-five years earlier Mark Twain had made the same observation. "When I speak my native tongue in its utmost purity in England," he said, "an Englishman can't understand me at all." [28] The languages, continued Mark, "were identical several generations ago, but our changed conditions and the spread of our people far to the south and far to the west have made many alterations in our pronunciation, and have introduced new words among us and changed the meanings of old ones." Even before this the great humorist had marked and hailed these differences. Already in "Roughing It" he was celebrating "the vigorous new vernacular of the

26 *London Court Journal*, Aug. 28, 1892.

27 In Pastures New; New York, 1906, p. 6.

28 Concerning the American Language, in The Stolen White Elephant; Boston, 1882. A footnote says that the essay is "part of a chapter crowded out of A Tramp Abroad." (Hartford, 1880.)

occidental plains and mountains,'' [29] and in all his writings, even the most serious, he deliberately engrafted its greater liberty and more fluent idiom upon the stem of English, and so lent the dignity of his high achievement to a dialect that was as unmistakably American as the point of view underlying it.

The same tendency is plainly visible in William Dean Howells. His novels are mines of American idiom, and his style shows an undeniable revolt against the trammels of English grammarians. In 1886 he made a plea in *Harper's* for a concerted effort to put American on its own legs. "If we bother ourselves," he said, "to write what the critics imagine to be 'English,' we shall be priggish and artificial, and still more so if we make our Americans talk 'English.' . . . On our lips our continental English will differ more and more from the insular English, and we believe that this is not deplorable but desirable.'' [30] Howells then proceeded to discuss the nature of the difference, and described it accurately as determined by the greater rigidity and formality of the English of modern England. In American, he said, there was to be seen that easy looseness of phrase and gait which characterized the English of the Elizabethan era, and particularly the Elizabethan hospitality to changed meanings and bold metaphors. American, he argued, made new words much faster than English, and they were, in the main, words of much greater daring and savor.

The difference between the two tongues, thus noted by the writers of both, was made disconcertingly apparent to the American troops when they first got to France and came into contact with the English. Fraternizing was made difficult by the wide divergence in vocabulary and pronunciation—a divergence interpreted by each side as a sign of uncouthness. The Y. M. C. A. made a characteristic effort to turn the resultant feeling of strangeness and homesickness among the Americans to account. In the *Chicago Tribune's* Paris edition of July 7, 1917, I find a large advertisement inviting them to make use of the Y. M. C. A.

[29] Hartford, 1872, p. 45.
[30] The Editor's Study, *Harper's Magazine*, Jan. 1886.

clubhouse in the Avenue Montaigue, "where *American* is spoken." Earlier in the war the *Illinoiser Staats Zeitung,* no doubt seeking to keep the sense of difference alive, advertised that it would "publish articles daily in the *American* language."

§ 4

Foreign Observers—What English and American laymen have thus observed has not escaped the notice of continental philologists. The first edition of Bartlett, published in 1848, brought forth a long and critical review in the *Archiv für das Studium der neueren Sprachen und Literaturen* by Prof. Felix Flügel,[21] and in the successive volumes of the *Archiv,* down to our own day, there have been many valuable essays upon Americanisms, by such men as Herrig, Koehler and Koeppel. Various Dutch philologists, among them Barentz, Keijzer and Van der Voort, have also discussed the subject, and a work in French has been published by G. A. Barringer.[32] That, even to the lay Continental, American and English now differ considerably, is demonstrated by the fact that many of the popular German *Sprachführer* appear in separate editions, *Amerikanisch* and *Englisch.* This is true of the "Metoula Sprachführer" published by Prof. F. Langenscheidt[33] and of the "Polyglott Kuntz" books.[34] The American edition of the latter starts off with the doctrine that *"Jeder, der nach Nord-Amerika oder Australien will, muss Englisch können,"* but a great many of the words and phrases that appear in its examples would be unintelligible to many Englishmen—*e. g., free-lunch, real-estate agent, buckwheat, corn* (for *maize*), *conductor, pop-corn* and *drug-store*—and a number of others would suggest false meanings or otherwise puzzle—*e. g., napkin, saloon, wash-stand, water-pitcher* and *apple-pie.*[35] To

[31] Die englische Sprache in Nordamerika, band iv, heft i; Braunschweig, 1848.

[32] Étude sur l'Anglais Parlé aux Etats Unis (la Langue Américaine), *Actes de la Société Philologique de Paris,* March, 1874.

[33] Metoula-Sprachführer. . . . Englisch von Karl Blattner; Ausgabe für Amerika; Berlin-Schöneberg, 1912.

[34] Polyglott Kuntze; Schnellste Erlernung jeder Sprache ohne Lehrer; Amerikanisch; Bonn a. Rh., n. d.

[35] Like the English expositors of American slang, this German falls into

these pedagogical examples must be added that of Baedeker, of guide-book celebrity. In his guide-book to the United States, prepared for Englishmen, he is at pains to explain the meaning of various American words and phrases.

A philologist of Scandinavian extraction, Elias Molee, has gone so far as to argue that the acquisition of correct English, to a people grown so mongrel in blood as the Americans, has become a useless burden. In place of it he proposes a mixed tongue, based on English, but admitting various elements from the other Germanic languages. His grammar, however, is so much more complex than that of English that most Americans would probably find his artificial "American" very difficult of acquirement. At all events it has made no progress.[36]

§ 5

The Characters of American—The characters chiefly noted in American speech by all who have discussed it are, first, its general uniformity throughout the country, so that, dialects, properly speaking, are confined to recent immigrants, to the native whites of a few isolated areas and to the negroes of the South; and, secondly, its impatient disdain of rule and precedent, and hence its large capacity (distinctly greater than that of the English of England) for taking in new 'words and phrases and for manufacturing new locutions out of its own materials. The first of these characters has struck every observer, native and foreign. In place of the local dialects of other countries we have a general *Volkssprache* for the whole nation, and if it is condi-

several errors. For example, he gives *cock* for *rooster*, *boots* for *shoes*, *braces* for *suspenders* and *postman* for *letter-carrier*, and lists *iron-monger*, *joiner* and *linen-draper* as American terms. He also spells *wagon* in the English manner, with two *g's*, and translates *Schweinefüsse* as *pork-feet*. But he spells such words as *color* in the American manner and gives the pronunciation of *clerk* as the American *klörk*, not as the English *klark*.

[36] Molee's notions are set forth in Plea for an American Language . . .; Chicago, 1888; and Tutonish; Chicago, 1902. He announced the preparation of A Dictionary of the American Language in 1888, but so far as I know it has not been published. He was born in Wisconsin, of Norwegian parents, in 1845, and pursued linguistic studies at the University of Wisconsin, where he seems to have taken a Ph. B.

tioned at all it is only by minor differences in pronunciation and by the linguistic struggles of various groups of newcomers. "The speech of the United States," said Gilbert M. Tucker, "is quite unlike that of Great Britain in the important particular that here we have no dialects."[37] "We all," said Mr. Taft during his presidency, "speak the same language and have the same ideas." "Manners, morals and political views," said the *New York World*, commenting upon this dictum, "have all undergone a standardization which is one of the remarkable aspects of American evolution. Perhaps it is in the uniformity of language that this development has been most noteworthy. Outside of the Tennessee mountains and the back country of New England there is no true dialect."[38] "While we have or have had single counties as large as Great Britain," says another American observer, "and in some of our states England could be lost, there is practically no difference between the American spoken in our 4,039,000 square miles of territory, except as spoken by foreigners. We, assembled here, would be perfectly understood by delegates from Texas, Maine, Minnesota, Louisiana, or Alaska, or from whatever walk of life they might come. We can go to any of the 75,000 postoffices in this country and be entirely sure we will be understood, whether we want to buy a stamp or borrow a match."[39] "From Portland, Maine, to Portland, Oregon," agrees an English critic, "no trace of a distinct dialect is to be found. The man from Maine, even though he may be of inferior education and limited capacity, can completely understand the man from Oregon."[40]

No other country can show such linguistic solidarity, nor any approach to it—not even Canada, for there a large part of the population resists learning English altogether. The Little Russian of the Ukraine is unintelligible to the citizen of Petrograd;

[37] American English, *North American Review*, Jan. 1883.
[38] Oct. 1, 1909.
[39] J. F. Healy, general manager of the Davis Colliery Co. at Elkins, W. Va., in a speech before the West Virginia Coal Mining Institute, at Wheeling, Dec. 1910; reprinted as The American Language; Pittsburgh, 1911.
[40] *Westminster Review*, July, 1888, p. 35.

the Northern Italian can scarcely follow a conversation in Sicilian; the Low German from Hamburg is a foreigner in Munich; the Breton flounders in Gascony.   Even in the United Kingdom there are wide divergences.[41]   "When we remember," says the New International Encyclopaedia [42] "that the dialects of the countries (*sic*) in England have marked differences—so marked, indeed that it may be doubted whether a Lancashire miner and a Lincolnshire farmer could understand each other—we may well be proud that our vast country has, strictly speaking, only one language."   This uniformity was noted by the earliest observers; Pickering called attention to it in the preface to his Vocabulary and ascribed it, no doubt accurately, to the restlessness of the Americans, their inheritance of the immigrant spirit, "the frequent removals of people from one part of our country to another."   It is especially marked in vocabulary and grammatical forms—the foundation stones of a living speech.   There may be slight differences in pronunciation and intonation—a Southern softness, a Yankee drawl, a Western burr—but in the words they use and the way they use them all Americans, even the least tutored, follow the same line.   One observes, of course, a polite speech and a common speech, but the common speech is everywhere the same, and its uniform vagaries take the place of the dialectic variations of other lands.   A Boston street-car conductor could go to work in Chicago, San Francisco or New Orleans without running the slightest risk of misunderstanding his new fares.   Once he had picked up half a dozen localisms, he would be, to all linguistic intents and purposes, fully naturalized.

Of the intrinsic differences that separate American from English the chief have their roots in the obvious disparity between the environment and traditions of the American people since the seventeenth century and those of the English.   The latter have lived under a stable social order, and it has impressed upon their souls their characteristic respect for what is customary and of

[41] W. W. Skeat distinguishes no less than 9 dialects in Scotland, 3 in Ireland and 30 in England and Wales.   *Vide* English Dialects From the Eighth Century to the Present Day; Cambridge, 1911, p. 107 *et seq.*
[42] *Art.* Americanisms, 2nd ed.

good report. Until the war brought chaos to their institutions, their whole lives were regulated, perhaps more than those of any other people save the Spaniards, by a regard for precedent. The Americans, though largely of the same blood, have felt no such restraint, and acquired no such habit of conformity. On the contrary, they have plunged to the other extreme, for the conditions of life in their new country have put a high value upon the precisely opposite qualities of curiosity and daring, and so they have acquired that character of restlessness, that impatience of forms, that disdain of the dead hand, which now broadly marks them. From the first, says a recent literary historian, they have been "less phlegmatic, less conservative than the English. There were climatic influences, it may be; there was surely a spirit of intensity everywhere that made for short effort." [43] Thus, in the arts, and thus in business, in politics, in daily intercourse, in habits of mind and speech. The American is not, in truth, lacking in a capacity for discipline; he has it highly developed; he submits to leadership readily, and even to tyranny. But, by a curious twist, it is not the leadership that is old and decorous that fetches him, but the leadership that is new and extravagant. He will resist dictation out of the past, but he will follow a new messiah with almost Russian willingness, and into the wildest vagaries of economics, religion, morals and speech. A new fallacy in politics spreads faster in the United States than anywhere else on earth, and so does a new fashion in hats, or a new revelation of God, or a new means of killing time, or a new metaphor or piece of slang.

Thus the American, on his linguistic side, likes to make his language as he goes along, and not all the hard work of his grammar teachers can hold the business back. A novelty loses nothing by the fact that it is a novelty; it rather gains something, and particularly if it meet the national fancy for the terse, the vivid, and, above all, the bold and imaginative. The characteristic American habit of reducing complex concepts to the starkest abbreviations was already noticeable in colonial times,

[43] F. L. Pattee: A History of American Literature Since 1870; New York, 1916.

and such highly typical Americanisms as *O. K., N. G.,* and *P. D. Q.,* have been traced back to the first days of the republic. Nor are the influences that shaped these early tendencies invisible today, for the country is still in process of growth, and no settled social order has yet descended upon it. Institution-making is still going on, and so is language-making. In so modest an operation as that which has evolved *bunco* from *buncombe* and *bunk* from *bunco* there is evidence of a phenomenon which the philologist recognizes as belonging to the most primitive and lusty stages of speech. The American vulgate is not only constantly making new words, it is also deducing roots from them, and so giving proof, as Prof. Sayce says, that "the creative powers of language are even now not extinct." [44]

But of more importance than its sheer inventions, if only because much more numerous, are its extensions of the vocabulary, both absolutely and in ready workableness, by the devices of rhetoric. The American, from the beginning, has been the most ardent of recorded rhetoricians. His politics bristles with pungent epithets; his whole history has been bedizened with tall talk; his fundamental institutions rest as much upon brilliant phrases as upon logical ideas. And in small things as in large he exercises continually an incomparable capacity for projecting hidden and often fantastic relationships into arresting parts of speech. Such a term as *rubber-neck* is almost a complete treatise on American psychology; it reveals the national habit of mind more clearly than any labored inquiry could ever reveal it. It has in it precisely the boldness and disdain of ordered forms that are so characteristically American, and it has too the grotesque humor of the country, and the delight in devastating opprobriums, and the acute feeling for the succinct and savory. The same qualities are in *rough-house, water-wagon, near-silk, has-been, lame-duck* and a thousand other such racy substantives, and in all the great stock of native verbs and adjectives. There is, indeed, but a shadowy boundary in these new coinages between the various parts of speech. *Corral,* borrowed

[44] A. H. Sayce: Introduction to the Science of Language, 2 vols.; London, 1900. See especially vol. ii, ch. vi.

from the Spanish, immediately becomes a verb and the father of an adjective. *Bust*, carved out of *burst*, erects itself into a noun. *Bum*, coming by way of an earlier *bummer* from the German *bummler*, becomes noun, adjective, verb and adverb. Verbs are fashioned out of substantives by the simple process of prefixing the preposition: *to engineer, to chink, to stump, to hog.* Others grow out of an intermediate adjective, as *to boom.* Others are made by torturing nouns with harsh affixes, as *to burglarize* and *to itemize*, or by groping for the root, as *to resurrect.* Yet others are changed from intransitive to transitive: a sleeping-car *sleeps* thirty passengers. So with the adjectives. They are made of substantives unchanged: *codfish, jitney.* Or by bold combinations: *down-and-out, up-state, flat-footed.* Or by shading down suffixes to a barbaric simplicity: *scary, classy, tasty.* Or by working over adverbs until they tremble on the brink between adverb and adjective: *right* and *near* are examples.

All of these processes, of course, are also to be observed in the English of England; in the days of its great Elizabethan growth they were in the lustiest possible being. They are, indeed, common to all languages; they keep language alive. But if you will put the English of today beside the American of today you will see at once how much more forcibly they are in operation in the latter than in the former. English has been arrested in its growth by its purists and grammarians. It shows no living change in structure and syntax since the days of Anne, and very little modification in either pronunciation or vocabulary. Its tendency is to conserve that which is established; to say the new thing, as nearly as possible, in the old way; to combat all that expansive gusto which made for its pliancy and resilience in the days of Shakespeare. In place of the old loose-footedness there is set up a preciosity which, in one direction, takes the form of unyielding affectations in the spoken language, and in another form shows itself in the heavy Johnsonese of current English writing—the Jargon denounced by Sir Arthur Quiller-Couch in his Cambridge lectures. This "infirmity of speech" Quiller-Couch finds "in parliamentary debates and in the newspapers";

. . . "it has become the medium through which Boards of Government, County Councils, Syndicates, Committees, Commercial Firms, express the processes as well as the conclusions of their thought, and so voice the reason of their being." Distinct from journalese, the two yet overlap, "and have a knack of assimilating each other's vices." [45]

American, despite the gallant efforts of the professors, has so far escaped any such suffocating formalization. We, too, of course, have our occasional practitioners of the authentic English Jargon; in the late Grover Cleveland we produced an acknowledged master of it. But in the main our faults in writing lie in precisely the opposite direction. That is to say, we incline toward a directness of statement which, at its greatest, lacks restraint and urbanity altogether, and toward a hospitality which often admits novelties for the mere sake of their novelty, and is quite uncritical of the difference between a genuine improvement in succinctness and clarity, and mere extravagant raciness. "The tendency," says one English observer, "is . . . to consider the speech of any man, as any man himself, as good as any other." [46] "All beauty and distinction," says another, [47] "are ruthlessly sacrificed to force." Moreover, this strong revolt against conventional bonds is by no means confined to the folk-speech, nor even to the loose conversational English of the upper classes; it also gets into more studied discourse, both spoken and written. I glance through the speeches of Dr. Woodrow Wilson, surely a purist if we have one at all, and find, in a few moments, half a dozen locutions that an Englishman in like position would never dream of using, among them *we must get a move on*, [48] *hog* as a verb, [49] *gum-shoe* as an adjective with

[45] *Cf.* the chapter, Interlude: On Jargon, in Quiller-Couch's On the Art of Writing; New York, 1916. Curiously enough, large parts of the learned critic's book are written in the very Jargon he attacks.

[46] Alexander Francis: Americans: an Impression; New York, 1900.

[47] G. Lowes Dickinson, in the *English Review*, quoted by *Current Literature*, April, 1910.

[48] Speech before the Chamber of Commerce Convention, Washington, Feb. 19, 1916.

[49] Speech at workingman's dinner, New York, Sept. 4, 1912.

verbal overtones,[50] *onery* in place of *ordinary*,[51] and *that is going some.*[52] From the earliest days, indeed, English critics have found this gipsy tendency in our most careful writing. They denounced it in Marshall, Cooper, Mark Twain, Poe, Lossing, Lowell and Holmes, and even in Hawthorne and Thoreau; and it was no less academic a work than W. C. Brownell's "French Traits" which brought forth, in a London literary journal, the dictum that "the language most depressing to the cultured Englishman is the language of the cultured American." Even "educated American English," agrees the chief of modern English grammarians, "is now almost entirely independent of British influence, and differs from it considerably, though as yet not enough to make the two dialects—American English and British English—mutually unintelligible."[53]

American thus shows its character in a constant experimentation, a wide hospitality to novelty, a steady reaching out for new and vivid forms. No other tongue of modern times admits foreign words and phrases more readily; none is more careless of precedents; none shows a greater fecundity and originality of fancy. It is producing new words every day, by trope, by agglutination, by the shedding of inflections, by the merging of parts of speech, and by sheer brilliance of imagination. It is full of what Bret Harte called the "sabre-cuts of Saxon"; it meets Montaigne's ideal of "a succulent and nervous speech, short and compact, not as much delicated and combed out as vehement and brusque, rather arbitrary than monotonous, not pedantic but soldierly, as Suetonius called Caesar's Latin." One pictures the common materials of English dumped into a pot, exotic flavorings added, and the bubblings assiduously and expectantly skimmed. What is old and respected is already in decay the moment it comes into contact with what is new and vivid. Let American confront a novel problem alongside Eng-

50 Wit and Wisdom of Woodrow Wilson, comp. by Richard Linthicum; New York, 1916, p. 54.

51 Speech at Ridgewood, N. J., April 22, 1910.

52 Wit and Wisdom . . ., p. 56.

53 Henry Sweet: A New English Grammar, Logical and Historical, 2 parts; Oxford, 1900–03, part i, p. 224.

lish, and immediately its superior imaginativeness and resourcefulness become obvious. *Movie* is better than *cinema;* it is not only better American, it is better English. *Bill-board* is better than *hoarding*. *Office-holder* is more honest, more picturesque, more thoroughly Anglo-Saxon that *public-servant*. *Stemwinder* somehow has more life in it, more fancy and vividness, than the literal *keyless-watch*. Turn to the terminology of railroading (itself, by the way, an Americanism) : its creation fell upon the two peoples equally, but they tackled the job independently. The English, seeking a figure to denominate the wedge-shaped fender in front of a locomotive, called it a *plough;* the Americans, characteristically, gave it the far more pungent name of *cow-catcher*. So with the casting where two rails join. The English called it a *crossing-plate*. The Americans, more responsive to the suggestion in its shape, called it a *frog*.

This boldness of conceit, of course, makes for vulgarity. Unrestrained by any critical sense—and the critical sense of the professors counts for little, for they cry wolf too often—it flowers in such barbaric inventions as *tasty, alright, no-account, pants, go-aheadativeness, tony, semi-occasional, to fellowship* and *to doxologize*. Let it be admitted: American is not infrequently vulgar; the Americans, too, are vulgar (Bayard Taylor called them "Anglo-Saxons relapsed into semi-barbarism"); America itself is unutterably vulgar. But vulgarity, after all, means no more than a yielding to natural impulses in the face of conventional inhibitions, and that yielding to natural impulses is at the heart of all healthy language-making. The history of English, like the history of American and every other living tongue, is a history of vulgarisms that, by their accurate meeting of real needs, have forced their way into sound usage, and even into the lifeless catalogues of the grammarians. The colonial pedants denounced *to advocate* as bitterly as they ever denounced *to compromit* or *to happify,* and all the English authorities gave them aid, but it forced itself into the American language despite them, and today it is even accepted as English and has got into the Oxford Dictionary. *To donate,* so late as 1870, was dismissed by Richard Grant White as ignorant and

abominable and to this day the English will have none of it, but
there is not an American dictionary that doesn't accept it, and
surely no American writer would hesitate to use it.[54] *Reliable,
gubernatorial, standpoint* and *scientist* have survived opposition
of equal ferocity. The last-named was coined by William
Whewell, an Englishman, in 1840, but was first adopted in
America. Despite the fact that Fitzedward Hall and other eminent philologists used it and defended it, it aroused almost in-
credible opposition in England. So recently as 1890 it was denounced by the *London Daily News* as "an ignoble Americanism," and according to William Archer it was finally accepted
by the English only "at the point of the bayonet."[55]

The purist performs a useful office in enforcing a certain
logical regularity upon the process, and in our own case the
omnipresent example of the greater conservatism of the English
corrects our native tendency to go too fast, but the process itself is as inexorable in its workings as the precession of the
equinoxes, and if we yield to it more eagerly than the English
it is only a proof, perhaps, that the future of what was once the
Anglo-Saxon tongue lies on this side of the water. "The story
of English grammar," says Murison, "is a story of simplification, of dispensing with grammatical forms."[56] And of the
most copious and persistent enlargement of vocabulary and mu-
tation of idiom ever recorded, perhaps, by descriptive philology.
English now has the brakes on, but American continues to leap
in the dark, and the prodigality of its movement is all the indi-

[54] Despite this fact an academic and ineffective opposition to it still goes
on. On the Style Sheet of the *Century Magazine* it is listed among the
"words and phrases to be avoided." It was prohibited by the famous *Index
Expurgatorius* prepared by William Cullen Bryant for the *New York Evening Post*, and his prohibition is still theoretically in force, but the word
is now actually permitted by the *Post*. The *Chicago Daily News* Style
Book, dated July 1, 1908, also bans it.

[55] *Scientist* is now in the Oxford Dictionary. So are *reliable, standpoint*
and *gubernatorial*. But the *Century Magazine* still bans *standpoint* and the
Evening Post (at least in theory) bans both *standpoint* and *reliable*. The
Chicago Daily News accepts *standpoint*, but bans *reliable* and *gubernatorial*.
All of these words, of course, are now quite as good as *ox* or *and*.

[56] *Art.* Changes in the Language Since Shakespeare's Time, Cambridge
History of English Literature, vol. xiv. p. 491.

cation that is needed of its intrinsic health, its capacity to meet the ever-changing needs of a restless and iconoclastic people, constantly fluent in racial composition, and disdainful of hampering traditions. "Language," says Sayce, "is no artificial product, contained in books and dictionaries and governed by the strict rules of impersonal grammarians. It is the living expression of the mind and spirit of a people, ever changing and shifting, whose sole standard of correctness is custom and the common usage of the community. . . . The first lesson to be learned is that there is no intrinsic right or wrong in the use of language, no fixed rules such as are the delight of the teacher of Latin prose. What is right now will be wrong hereafter, what language rejected yesterday she accepts today.'' [57]

§ 6

The Materials of American—One familiar with the habits of pedagogues need not be told that, in their grudging discussions of American, they have spent most of their energies upon vain attempts to classify its materials. White and Lounsbury, as I have shown, carried the business to the limits of the preposterous; when they had finished identifying and cataloguing Americanisms there were no more Americanisms left to study. The ladies and gentlemen of the American Dialect Society, though praiseworthy for their somewhat deliberate industry, fall into a similar fault, for they are so eager to establish minute dialectic variations that they forget the general language almost altogether.

Among investigators of less learning there is a more spacious view of the problem, and the labored categories of White and Lounsbury are much extended. Pickering, the first to attempt a list of Americanisms, rehearsed their origin under the following headings:

1. "We have formed some new words."
2. "To some old ones, that are still in use in England, we have affixed new significations."

[57] Introduction to the Science of Language, vol. ii, pp. 333–4.

3. "Others, which have long been obsolete in England, are still retained in common use among us."

Bartlett, in the second edition of his dictionary, dated 1859, increased these classes to nine;

1. Archaisms, *i. e.*, old English words, obsolete, or nearly so, in England, but retained in use in this country.

2. English words used in a different sense from what they are in England. These include many names of natural objects differently applied.

3. Words which have retained their original meaning in the United States, though not in England.

4. English provincialisms adopted into general use in America.

5. Newly coined words, which owe their origin to the productions or to the circumstances of the country.

6. Words borrowed from European languages, especially the French, Spanish, Dutch and German.

7. Indian words.

8. Negroisms.

9. Peculiarities of pronunciation.

Some time before this, but after the publication of Bartlett's first edition in 1848, William C. Fowler, professor of rhetoric at Amherst, devoted a brief chapter to "American Dialects" in his well-known work on English [58] and in it one finds the following formidable classification of Americanisms:

1. Words borrowed from other languages.

   a. Indian, as *Kennebec, Ohio, Tombigbee; sagamore, quahaug, succotash.*

   b. Dutch, as *boss, kruller, stoop.*

   c. German, as *spuke* (?), *sauerkraut.*

   d. French, as *bayou, cache, chute, crevasse, levee.*

   e. Spanish, as *calaboose, chapparal, hacienda, rancho, ranchero.*

   f. Negro, as *buckra.*

2. Words "introduced from the necessity of our situation, in order to express new ideas."

   a. Words "connected with and flowing from our political institutions," as *selectman, presidential, congressional, caucus, mass-meeting, lynch-law, help* (for *servants*).

   b. Words "connected with our ecclesiastical institutions," as *associational, consociational, to fellowship, to missionate.*

[58] *Op. cit.*, pp. 119–28.

c. Words "connected with a new country," as *lot, diggings, betterments, squatter.*

3. Miscellaneous Americanisms.

a. Words and phrases become obsolete in England, as *talented, offset* (for *set-off*), *back and forth* (for *backward and forward*).

b. Old words and phrases "which are now merely provincial in England," as *hub, whap* (?), *to wilt.*

c. Nouns formed from verbs by adding the French suffix *-ment,* as *publishment, releasement, requirement.*

d. Forms of words "which fill the gap or vacancy between two words which are approved," as *obligate* (between *oblige* and *obligation*) and *variate* (between *vary* and *variation*).

e. "Certain compound terms for which the English have different compounds," as *bank-bill,* (*bank-note*), *book-store* (*book-seller's shop*), *bottom-land* (*interval land*), *clapboard* (*pale*), *sea-board* (*sea-shore*), *side-hill* (*hill-side*).

f. "Certain colloquial phrases, apparently idiomatic, and very expressive," as *to cave in, to flare up, to flunk out, to fork over, to hold on, to let on, to stave off, to take on.*

g. Intensives, "often a matter of mere temporary fashion," as *dreadful, mighty, plaguy, powerful.*

h. "Certain verbs expressing one's state of mind, but partially or timidly," as *to allot upon* (for *to count upon*), *to calculate, to expect* (*to think* or *believe*), *to guess, to reckon.*

i. "Certain adjectives, expressing not only quality, but one's subjective feelings in regard to it," as *clever, grand, green, likely, smart, ugly.*

j. Abridgments, as *stage* (for *stage-coach*), *turnpike* (for *turnpike-road*), *spry* (for *sprightly*), *to conduct* (for *to conduct one's self*).

k. "Quaint or burlesque terms," as *to tote, to yank; humbug, loafer, muss, plunder* (for *baggage*), *rock* (for *stone*).

l. "Low expressions, mostly political," as *slangwhanger, loco foco, hunker; to get the hang of.*

m. "Ungrammatical expressions, disapproved by all," as *do don't, used to could, can't come it, Universal preacher* (for *Universalist*), *there's no two ways about it.*

Elwyn, in 1859, attempted no classification.[59] He confined his glossary to archaic English words surviving in America, and sought only to prove that they had come down "from our remotest ancestry" and were thus undeserving of the reviling lav-

[59] Alfred L. Elwyn, M. D.: Glossary of Supposed Americanisms . . .; Phila., 1859.

ished upon them by English critics. Schele de Vere, in 1872, followed Bartlett, and devoted himself largely to words borrowed from the Indian dialects, and from the French, Spanish and Dutch. But Farmer, in 1889,[60] ventured upon a new classification, prefacing it with the following definition:

An Americanism may be defined as a word or phrase, old or new, employed by general or respectable usage in America in a way not sanctioned by the best standards of the English language. As a matter of fact, however, the term has come to possess a wider meaning, and it is now applied not only to words and phrases which can be so described, but also to the new and legitimately born words adapted to the general needs and usages, to the survivals of an older form of English than that now current in the mother country, and to the racy, pungent vernacular of Western life.

He then proceeded to classify his materials thus:

1. Words and phrases of purely American derivation, embracing words originating in:
      a. Indian and aboriginal life.
      b. Pioneer and frontier life.
      c. The church.
      d. Politics.
      e. Trades of all kinds.
      f. Travel, afloat and ashore.
2. Words brought by colonists, including:
      a. The German element.
      b. The French.
      c. The Spanish.
      d. The Dutch.
      e. The negro.
      f. .The Chinese.
3. Names of American things, embracing:
      a. Natural products.
      b. Manufactured articles.
4. Perverted English words.
5. Obsolete English words still in good use in America.
6. English words, American by inflection and modification.
7. Odd and ignorant popular phrases, proverbs, vulgarisms, and colloquialisms, cant and slang.
8. Individualisms.
9. Doubtful and miscellaneous.

[60] John S. Farmer: Americanisms Old and New . . .; London, 1889.

Clapin, in 1902,[61] reduced these categories to four:

1. Genuine English words, obsolete or provincial in England, and universally used in the United States.
2. English words conveying, in the United States, a different meaning from that attached to them in England.
3. Words introduced from other languages than the English:— French, Dutch, Spanish, German, Indian, etc.
4. Americanisms proper, *i.e.*, words coined in the country, either representing some new idea or peculiar product.

Thornton, in 1912, substituted the following:

1. Forms of speech now obsolete or provincial in England, which survive in the United States, such as *allow, bureau, fall, gotten, guess, likely, professor, shoat.*
2. Words and phrases of distinctly American origin, such as *belittle, lengthy, lightning-rod, to darken one's doors, to bark up the wrong tree, to come out at the little end of the horn, blind tiger, cold snap, gay Quaker, gone coon, long sauce, pay dirt, small potatoes, some pumpkins.*
3. Nouns which indicate quadrupeds, birds, trees, articles of food, etc., that are distinctively American, such as *ground-hog, hang-bird, hominy, live-oak, locust, opossum, persimmon, pone, succotash, wampum, wigwam.*
4. Names of persons and classes of persons, and of places, such as *Buckeye, Cracker, Greaser, Hoosier, Old Bullion, Old Hickory,* the *Little Giant, Dixie, Gotham,* the *Bay State,* the *Monumental City.*
5. Words which have assumed a new meaning, such as *card, clever, fork, help, penny, plunder, raise, rock, sack, ticket, windfall.*

In addition, Thornton added a provisional class of "words and phrases of which I have found earlier examples in American than in English writers; . . . with the *caveat* that further research may reverse the claim"—a class offering specimens in *alarmist, capitalize, eruptiveness, horse of another colour (sic!), the jig's up, nameable, omnibus bill, propaganda* and *whitewash.*

No more than a brief glance at these classifications is needed to show that they hamper the inquiry by limiting its scope—not so much, to be sure, as the ridiculous limitations of White and Lounsbury, but still very seriously. They meet the ends of

---

[61] Sylva Clapin: A New Dictionary of Americanisms, Being a Glossary of Words Supposed to be Peculiar to the United States and the Dominion of Canada; New York, 1902.

purely descriptive lexicography, but largely leave out of account
some of the most salient characters of a living language, for
example, pronunciation and idiom. Only Bartlett and Farmer
establish a separate category of Americanisms produced by
changes in pronunciation, though even Thornton, of course, is
obliged to take notice of such forms as *bust* and *bile*. None of
them, however, goes into the matter at any length, nor even into
the matter of etymology. Bartlett's etymologies are scanty and
often inaccurate; Schele de Vere's are sometimes quite fanciful;
Thornton offers scarcely any at all. The best of these collections of Americanisms, and by long odds, is Thornton's. It
presents an enormous mass of quotations, and they are all very
carefully dated, and it corrects most of the more obvious errors
in the work of earlier inquirers. But its very dependence upon
quotations limits it chiefly to the written language, and so the
enormously richer materials of the spoken language are passed
over, and particularly the materials evolved during the past
twenty years. One searches the two fat volumes in vain for
such highly characteristic forms as *would of, near-accident,* and
buttinski, the use of *sure* as an adverb, and the employment of
well as a sort of general equivalent of the German *also.*

These grammatical and syntactical tendencies are beyond the
scope of Thornton's investigation, but it is plain that they must
be prime concerns of any future student who essays to get at the
inner spirit of the language. Its difference from standard English is not merely a difference in vocabulary, to be disposed of
in an alphabetical list; it is, above all, a difference in pronunciation, in intonation, in conjugation and declension, in metaphor
and idiom, in the whole fashion of using words. A page from
one of Ring W. Lardner's baseball stories contains few words
that are not in the English vocabulary, and yet the thoroughly
American color of it cannot fail to escape anyone who actually
listens to the tongue spoken around him. Some of the elements
which enter into that color will be considered in the following
pages. The American vocabulary, of course, must be given
first attention, for in it the earliest American divergences are
embalmed and it tends to grow richer and freer year after year,

but attention will also be paid to materials and ways of speech that are less obvious, and in particular to certain definite tendencies of the grammar of spoken American, hitherto wholly neglected.

II

The Beginnings of American

§ 1

In Colonial Days—William Gifford, the first editor of the *Quarterly Review*, is authority for the tale that some of the Puritan clergy of New England, during the Revolution, proposed that English be formally abandoned as the national language of America, and Hebrew adopted in its place. An American chronicler, Charles Astor Bristed, makes the proposed tongue Greek, and reports that the change was rejected on the ground that "it would be more convenient for us to keep the language as it is, and make the English speak Greek."[1] The story, though it has the support of the editors of the Cambridge History of American Literature,[2] has an apocryphal smack; one suspects that the savagely anti-American Gifford invented it. But, true or false, it well indicates the temper of those times. The passion for complete political independence of England bred a general hostility to all English authority, whatever its character, and that hostility, in the direction of present concern to us, culminated in the revolutionary attitude of Noah Webster's "Dissertations on the English Language," printed in 1789. Webster harbored no fantastic notion of abandoning English altogether, but he was eager to set up American as a distinct and independent dialect. "Let us," he said, "seize the present moment, and establish a national language as well as a national government. . . . As an independent nation our honor requires

[1] Bristed was a grandson of John Jacob Astor and was educated at Cambridge. He contributed an extremely sagacious essay on The English Language in America to a volume of Cambridge Essays published by a group of young Cambridge men; London, 1855.

[2] Vol. i, p. vi.

us to have a system of our own, in language as well as government.''

Long before this the challenge had been flung. Scarcely two years after the Declaration of Independence Franklin was instructed by Congress, on his appointment as minister to France, to employ ''the language of the United States,'' not simply English, in all his ''replies or answers'' to the communications of the ministry of Louis XVI. And eight years before the Declaration Franklin himself had drawn up a characteristically American scheme of spelling reform, and had offered plenty of proof in it, perhaps unconsciously, that the standards of spelling and pronunciation in the New World had already diverged noticeably from those accepted on the other side of the ocean.[3] In acknowledging the dedication of Webster's ''Dissertations'' Franklin endorsed both his revolt against English domination and his forecast of widening differences in future, though protesting at the same time against certain Americanisms that have since come into good usage, and even migrated to England.[4]

This protest was marked by Franklin's habitual mildness, but in other quarters dissent was voiced with far less urbanity. The growing independence of the colonial dialect, not only in its spoken form, but also in its most dignified written form, had begun, indeed, to attract the attention of purists in both England and America, and they sought to dispose of it in its infancy by *force majeure*. One of the first and most vigorous of the attacks upon it was delivered by John Witherspoon, a Scotch clergyman who came out in 1769 to be president of Princeton *in partibus infidelium*. This Witherspoon brought a Scotch hatred of the English with him, and at once became a leader of the party of independence; he signed the Declaration to the tune of much rhetoric, and was the only clergyman to sit in the Continental Congress. But in matters of learning he was orthodox to the point of hunkerousness, and the strange locutions that

[3] Scheme for a New Alphabet and a Reformed Mode of Spelling; Philadelphia, 1768.
[4] Dec. 26, 1789. The Works of B. Franklin, ed. by A. F. Smyth; New York, 1905, vol. i, p. 40.

he encountered on all sides aroused his pedagogic ire. "I have heard in this country," he wrote in 1781, "in the senate, at the bar, and from the pulpit, and see daily in dissertations from the press, errors in grammar, improprieties and vulgarisms which hardly any person of the same class in point of rank and litera-ture would have fallen into in Great Britain."[5]   It was Wither-spoon who coined the word *Americanism*—and at once the Eng-lish guardians of the sacred vessels began employing it as a general synonym for vulgarism and barbarism.   Another learned immigrant, the Rev. Jonathan Boucher, soon joined him.   This Boucher was a friend of Washington, but was driven back to England by his Loyalist sentiments.   He took revenge by print-ing various charges against the Americans, among them that of "making all the haste they can to rid themselves of the [Eng-lish] language."

After the opening of the new century all the British reviews maintained an eager watchfulness for these abhorrent inven-tions, and denounced them, when found, .with the utmost ve-hemence.   The *Edinburgh*, which led the charge, opened its attack in October, 1804, and the appearance of the five volumes of Chief Justice Marshall's "Life of George Washington," dur-ing the three years following, gave the signal for corrective articles in the *British Critic*, the *Critical Review*, the *Annual*, the *Monthly* and the *Eclectic*.   The *British Critic*, in April, 1808, admitted somewhat despairingly that the damage was already done—that "the common speech of the United States has departed very considerably from the standard adopted in England."   The others, however, sought to stay the flood by invective against Marshall and, later, against his rival biog-rapher, the Rev. Aaron Bancroft.   The *Annual*, in 1808, pro-nounced its high curse and anathema upon "that torrent of bar-barous phraseology" which was pouring across the Atlantic, and which threatened "to destroy the purity of the English language."[6]   In Bancroft's "Life of George Washington"

[5] *The Druid*, No. 5; reprinted in Witherspoon's Collected Works, edited by Ashbel Green, vol. iv; New York, 1800–1.
[6] *Vide*, in addition to the citations in the text, the *British Critic*, Nov.

(1808), according to the *British Critic*, there were gross Americanisms, inordinately offensive to Englishmen, "at almost every page."

The Rev. Jeremy Belknap, long anticipating Elwyn, White and Lounsbury, tried to obtain a respite from this abuse by pointing out the obvious fact that many of the Americanisms under fire were merely survivors of an English that had become archaic in England, but this effort counted for little, for on the one hand the British purists enjoyed the chase too much to give it up, and on the other hand there began to dawn in America a new spirit of nationality, at first very faint, which viewed the differences objected to, not with shame, but with a fierce sort of pride. In the first volume of the *North American Review* William Ellery Channing spoke out boldly for "the American language and literature,"[7] and a year later Pickering published his defiant dictionary of "words and phrases which have been supposed to be peculiar to the United States." This thin collection of 500 specimens set off a dispute which yet rages on both sides of the Atlantic. Pickering, however, was undismayed. He had begun to notice the growing difference between the English and American vocabulary and pronunciation, he said, while living in London from 1799 to 1801, and he had made his collections with the utmost care, and after taking counsel with various prudent authorities, both English and American. Already in the first year of the century, he continued, the English had accused the people of the new republic of a deliberate "design to effect an entire change in the language" and while no such design was actually harbored, the facts were the facts, and he cited the current newspapers, the speeches from pulpit and rostrum, and Webster himself in support of them. This debate over Pickering's list, as I say, still continues. Lounsbury, entrenched behind his grotesque categories, once charged that four-fifths of the words in it had "no business to be there," and

1793; Feb. 1810; the *Critical Review*, July 1807; Sept. 1809; the *Monthly Review*, May 1808; the *Eclectic Review*, Aug. 1813.

[7] 1815, pp. 307–14; reprinted in his Remarks on National Literature, Boston, 1823.

Gilbert M. Tucker [8] has argued that only 70 of them were genuine Americanisms. But a careful study of the list, in comparison with the early quotations recently collected by Thornton, seems to indicate that both of these judgments, and many others no less, have done injustice to Pickering. He made the usual errors of the pioneer, but his sound contributions to the subject were anything but inconsiderable, and it is impossible to forget his diligence and his constant shrewdness. He established firmly the native origin of a number of words now in universal use in America—*e. g., backwoodsman, breadstuffs, caucus, clapboard, sleigh* and *squatter*—and of such familiar derivatives as *gubernatorial* and *dutiable,* and he worked out the genesis of not a few loan-words, including *prairie, scow, rapids, hominy* and *barbecue.* It was not until 1848, when the first edition of Bartlett appeared, that his work was supplanted.

§ 2

Sources of Early Americanisms—The first genuine Americanisms were undoubtedly words borrowed bodily from the Indian dialects—words, in the main, indicating natural objects that had no counterparts in England. We find *opossum,* for example, in the form of *opasum,* in Captain John Smith's "Map of Virginia" (1612), and, in the form of *apossoun,* in a Virginia document two years older. *Moose* is almost as old. The word is borrowed from the Algonquin *musa,* and must have become familiar to the Pilgrim Fathers soon after their landing in 1620, for the woods of Massachusetts then swarmed with the huge quadrupeds and there was no English name to designate them. Again, there are *skunk* (from the Abenaki Indian *seganku*), *hickory, squash, paw-paw, raccoon, chinkapin, porgy, chipmunk, pemmican, terrapin, menhaden, catalpa, persimmon* and *cougar.* Of these, *hickory* and *terrapin* are to be found in Robert Beverley's "History and Present State of Virginia" (1705), and *squash, chinkapin* and *persimmon* are in documents of the preceding century. Many of these words, of course, were short-

[8] American English, *North American Review,* April, 1883.

ened or otherwise modified on being taken into colonial English. Thus *chinkapin* was originally *checkinqumin*, and *squash* appears in early documents as *isquontersquash, askutasquash, isquonkersquash* and *squantersquash*. But William Penn, in a letter dated August 16, 1683, used the latter in its present form. Its variations show a familiar effort to bring a new and strange word into harmony with the language—an effort arising from what philologists call the law of Hobson-Jobson. This name was given to it by Col. Henry Yule and A. C. Burnell, compilers of a standard dictionary of Anglo-Indian terms. They found that the British soldiers in India, hearing strange words from the lips of the natives, often converted them into English words of similar sound, though of widely different meaning. Thus the words *Hassan* and *Hosein*, frequently used by the Mohammedans of the country in their devotions, were turned into *Hobson-Jobson*. The same process is constantly in operation elsewhere. By it the French *route de roi* has become *Rotten Row* in English, *écrevisse* has become *crayfish*, and the English *bowsprit* has become *beau pré* (= *beautiful meadow*) in French. The word *pigeon*, in *Pigeon English*, offers another example; it has no connection with the bird, but merely represents a Chinaman's attempt to pronounce the word *business*. No doubt *squash* originated in the same way. That *woodchuck* did so is practically certain. Its origin is to be sought, not in *wood* and *chuck*, but in the Cree word *otchock*, used by the Indians to designate the animal.

In addition to the names of natural objects, the early colonists, of course, took over a great many Indian place-names, and a number of words to designate Indian relations and artificial objects in Indian use. To the last division belong *hominy, pone, toboggan, canoe, tapioca, moccasin, pow-wow, papoose, tomahawk, wigwam, succotash* and *squaw*, all of which were in common circulation by the beginning of the eighteenth century. Finally, new words were made during the period by translating Indian terms, for example, *war-path, war-paint, pale-face, medicine-man, pipe-of-peace* and *fire-water*. The total number of such borrowings, direct and indirect, was a good deal larger

than now appears, for with the disappearance of the red man
the use of loan-words from his dialects has decreased. In our
own time such words as *papoose, sachem, tepee, wigwam* and
wampum have begun to drop out of everyday use;[9] at an earlier
period the language sloughed off *ocelot, manitee, calumet, su-
pawn, samp* and *quahaug*, or began to degrade them to the estate
of provincialisms.[10] A curious phenomenon is presented by the
case of *maize*, which came into the colonial speech from some
West Indian dialect, went over into orthodox English, and from
English into French, German and other continental languages,
and was then abandoned by the colonists. We shall see other
examples of that process later on.

Whether or not *Yankee* comes from an Indian dialect is still
disputed. An early authority, John G. E. Heckwelder, argued
that it was derived from an Indian mispronunciation of the
word *English*.[11] Certain later etymologists hold that it originated more probably in an Indian mishandling of the French
word *Anglais*. Yet others derive it from the Scotch *yankie*,
meaning a gigantic falsehood. A fourth party derive it from
the Dutch, and cite an alleged Dutch model for "Yankee Doodle," beginning "*Yanker* didee doodle down."[12] Of these
theories that of Heckwelder is the most plausible. But here,
as in other directions, the investigation of American etymology
remains sadly incomplete. An elaborate dictionary of words
derived from the Indian languages, compiled by the late W. R.
Gerard, is in the possession of the Smithsonian Institution, but
on account of a shortage of funds it remains in manuscript.

[9] A number of such Indian words are preserved in the nomenclature of
Tammany Hall and in that of the Improved Order of Red Men, an organization with more than 500,000 members. The Red Men, borrowing from
the Indians, thus name the months, in order: *Cold Moon, Snow, Worm,
Plant, Flower, Hot, Buck, Sturgeon, Corn, Travelers', Beaver and Hunting*.
They call their officers *incohonee, sachem, wampum-keeper*, etc. But such
terms, of course, are not in general use.

[10] A long list of such obsolete Americanisms is given by Clapin in his
Dictionary.

[11] An Account of the History, Manners and Customs of the Indian Nations. . . .; Phila., 1818.

[12] *Cf.* Hans Brinker, by Mary Maples Dodge; New York, 1891.

From the very earliest days of English colonization the language of the colonists also received accretions from the languages of the other colonizing nations. The French word *portage*, for example, was already in common use before the end of the seventeenth century, and soon after came *chowder*, *cache*, *caribou*, *voyageur*, and various words that, like the last-named, have since become localisms or disappeared altogether. Before 1750 *bureau*,[13] *gopher*, *batteau*, *bogus*, and *prairie* were added, and *caboose*, a word of Dutch origin, seems to have come in through the French. *Carry-all* is also French in origin, despite its English quality. It comes, by the law of Hobson-Jobson, from the French *carriole*. The contributions of the Dutch during the half century of their conflicts with the English included *cruller*, *cold-slaw*, *dominie* (for *parson*), *cookey*, *stoop*, *span* (of horses), *pit* (as in *peach-pit*), *waffle*, *hook* (a point of land), *scow*, *boss*, *smearcase* and *Santa Claus*.[14] Schele de Vere credits them with *hay-barrack*, a corruption of *hooiberg*. That they established the use of *bush* as a designation for back-country is very probable; the word has also got into South African English. In American it has produced a number of familiar derivatives, *e. g.*, *bush-whacker* and *bush-league*. Barrère and Leland also credit the Dutch with *dander*, which is commonly assumed to be an American corruption of *dandruff*. They say that it is from the Dutch word *donder* (= *thunder*). *Op donderen*, in Dutch, means to burst into a sudden rage. The chief Spanish contributions to American were to come after the War of 1812, with the opening of the West, but *creole*, *calaboose*, *palmetto*, *peewee*, *key* (a small island), *quadroon*, *octoroon*, *barbecue*, *pickaninny* and *stampede* had already entered the language in colonial days. *Jerked beef* came from the Spanish *charqui* by the law of Hobson-Jobson. The Germans who arrived in Pennsylvania in 1682 also undoubtedly gave a few words to the language, though

[13] (*a*) A chest of drawers, (*b*) a government office. In both senses the word is rare in English, though its use by the French is familiar. In the United States its use in (*b*) has been extended, *e. g.*, in *employment-bureau*.
[14] From *Sint-Klaas—Saint Nicholas*. *Santa Claus* has also become familiar to the English, but the Oxford Dictionary still calls the name an Americanism.

it is often difficult to distinguish their contributions from those of the Dutch. It seems very likely, however, that *sauerkraut* [15] and *noodle* are to be credited to them. Finally, the negro slaves brought in *gumbo, goober, juba* and *voodoo* (usually corrupted to *hoodoo*), and probably helped to corrupt a number of other loan-words, for example *banjo* and *breakdown. Banjo* seems to be derived from *bandore* or *bandurria,* modern French and Spanish forms of *tambour,* respectively. It may, however, be an actual negro word; there is a term of like meaning, *bania,* in Senegambian. Ware says that *breakdown,* designating a riotous negro dance, is a corruption of the French *rigadon.* The word is not in the Oxford Dictionary. Bartlett listed it as an Americanism, but Thornton rejected it, apparently because, in the sense of a collapse, it has come into colloquial use in England. Its etymology is not given in the American dictionaries.

§ 3

New Words of English Material—But of far more importance than these borrowings was the great stock of new words that the colonists coined in English metal—words primarily demanded by the "new circumstances under which they were placed," but also indicative, in more than one case, of a delight in the business for its own sake. The American, even in the early eighteenth century, already showed many of the characteristics that were to set him off from the Englishman later on—his bold and somewhat grotesque imagination, his contempt for authority, his lack of aesthetic sensitiveness, his extravagant humor. Among the first colonists there were many men of education, culture and gentle birth, but they were soon swamped by hordes of the ignorant and illiterate, and the latter, cut off from the corrective influence of books, soon laid their hands upon the language. It is impossible to imagine the austere Puritan divines of Massachusetts inventing such verbs as *to cowhide* and *to logroll,* or such adjectives as *no-account* and *stumped,* or such adverbs as *no-how* and

---

[15] The spelling is variously *sauerkraut, saurkraut, sourkraut* and *sourkrout.*

lickety-split, or such substantives as *bull-frog, hog-wallow* and
hoe-cake; but under their eyes there arose a contumacious proletariat which was quite capable of the business, and very eager
for it.   In Boston, so early as 1628, there was a definite class of
blackguard roisterers, chiefly made up of sailors and artisans; in
Virginia, nearly a decade earlier, John Pory, secretary to Governor Yeardley, lamented that "in these five moneths of my con-
tinuance here there have come at one time or another eleven sails
of ships into this river, but fraighted more with ignorance than
with any other marchansize."   In particular, the generation born
in the New World was uncouth and iconoclastic; [16] the only world
it knew was a rough world, and the virtues that environment en-
gendered were not those of niceness, but those of enterprise and
resourcefulness.

Upon men of this sort fell the task of bringing the wilderness
to the ax and the plow, and with it went the task of inventing a
vocabulary for the special needs of the great adventure.   Out of
their loutish ingenuity came a great number of picturesque names
for natural objects, chiefly boldly descriptive compounds: *bull-
frog, canvas-back, lightning-bug, mud-hen, cat-bird, razor-back,
garter-snake, ground-hog* and so on.   And out of an inventiveness somewhat more urbane came such coinages as *live-oak, po-
tato-bug, turkey-gobbler, poke-weed, copper-head, eel-grass, reed-
bird, egg-plant, blue-grass, pea-nut, pitch-pine, cling-stone*
(peach), *moccasin-snake, June-bug* and *butter-nut. Live-oak*
appears in a document of 1610; *bull-frog* was familiar to Beverley in 1705; so was *James-Town weed* (later reduced to *Jimson
weed,* as the English *hurtleberry* or *whortleberry* was reduced to
huckleberry).   These early Americans were not botanists.   They
were often ignorant of the names of the plants they encountered,
even when those plants already had English names, and so they
exercised their fancy upon new ones.   So arose *Johnny-jump-up*
for the *Viola tricolor,* and *basswood* for the common European
linden or *lime-tree* (*Tilia*), and *locust* for the *Robinia pseuda-
cacia* and its allies.   The *Jimson weed* itself was anything but a

[16] *Cf.* The Cambridge History of American Literature, vol. i, pp. 14 and
22.

novelty, but the pioneers apparently did not recognize it, and so we find them ascribing all sorts of absurd medicinal powers to it, and even Beverley solemnly reporting that "some Soldiers, eating it in a Salad, turn'd natural Fools upon it for several Days." The grosser features of the landscape got a lavish renaming, partly to distinguish new forms and partly out of an obvious desire to attain a more literal descriptiveness. I have mentioned *key* and *hook*, the one borrowed from the Spanish and the other from the Dutch. With them came *run, branch, fork, bluff,* (noun), *neck, barrens, bottoms, underbrush, bottom-land, clearing, notch, divide, knob, riffle, gap, rolling-country* and *rapids,*[17] and the extension of *pond* from artificial pools to small natural lakes, and of *creek* from small arms of the sea to shallow feeders of rivers. Such common English geographical terms as *downs, weald, wold, fen, bog, fell, chase, combe, dell, heath* and *moor* disappeared from the colonial tongue, save as fossilized in a few proper names. So did *bracken.*

With the new landscape came an entirely new mode of life— new foods, new forms of habitation, new methods of agriculture, new kinds of hunting. A great swarm of neologisms thus arose, and, as in the previous case, they were chiefly compounds. *Back-country, back-woods, back-woodsman, back-settlers, back-settlements:* all these were in common use early in the eighteenth century. *Back-log* was used by Increase Mather in 1684. *Log-house* appears in the Maryland Archives for 1669.[18] *Hoe-cake, Johnny-cake, pan-fish, corn-dodger, roasting-ear, corn-crib, corn-cob* and *pop-corn* were all familiar before the Revolution. So were *pine-knot, snow-plow, cold-snap, land-slide, salt-lick, prickly-heat, shell-road* and *cane-brake. Shingle* was a novelty in 1705, but one S. Symonds wrote to John Winthrop, of Ipswich, about a *clapboarded* house in 1637. *Frame-house* seems to have come in with *shingle. Trail, half-breed, Indian-summer* and

[17] The American origin of this last word has been disputed, but the weight of evidence seems to show that it was borrowed from the *rapides* of the French Canadians. It is familiar in the United States and Canada, but seldom met with in England.

[18] *Log-cabin* came in later. Thornton's first quotation is dated 1818. The *Log-Cabin* campaign was in 1840.

Indian-file were obviously suggested by the Red Men. *State-house* was borrowed, perhaps, from the Dutch. *Selectman* is first heard of in 1685, displacing the English *alderman*. *Mush* had displaced *porridge* by 1671. Soon afterward *hay-stack* took the place of the English *hay-cock*, and such common English terms as *byre, mews, weir,* and *wain* began to disappear. *Hired-man* is to be found in the Plymouth town records of 1737, and *hired-girl* followed soon after. So early as 1758, as we find by the diary of Nathaniel Ames, the second-year students at Harvard were already called *sophomores,* though for a while the spelling was often made *sophimores*. *Camp-meeting* was later; it did not appear until 1799. But *land-office* was familiar before 1700, and *side-walk, spelling-bee, bee-line, moss-back, crazy-quilt, mud-scow, stamping-ground* and a hundred and one other such compounds were in daily use before the Revolution. After that great upheaval the new money of the confederation brought in a number of new words. In 1782 Gouverneur Morris proposed to the Continental Congress that the coins of the republic be called, in ascending order, *unit, penny-bill, dollar* and *crown*. Later Morris invented the word *cent*, substituting it for the English *penny*.[19] In 1785 Jefferson proposed *mill, cent, dime, dollar* and *eagle*, and this nomenclature was adopted.

Various nautical terms peculiar to America, or taken into English from American sources, came in during the eighteenth century, among them, *schooner, cat-boat* and *pungy*, not to recall *batteau* and *canoe*. According to a recent historian of the American merchant marine,[20] the first schooner ever seen was launched at Gloucester, Mass., in 1713. The word, it appears, was originally spelled *scooner*. *To scoon* was a verb borrowed by the New Englanders from some Scotch dialect, and meant to skim or skip across the water like a flat stone. As the first schooner left the ways and glided out into Gloucester harbor, an enraptured spectator shouted: "Oh, see how she scoons!" "A *scooner* let her be!" replied Captain Andrew Robinson, her

[19] Theo. Roosevelt: Gouverneur Morris; Boston, 1888, p. 104.
[20] William Brown Meloney: The Heritage of Tyre; New York, 1916, p. 15.

builder—and all boats of her peculiar and novel fore-and-aft rig took the name thereafter. The Dutch mariners borrowed the term and changed the spelling, and this change was soon accepted in America. The Scotch root came from the Norse *skunna*, to hasten, and there are analogues in Icelandic, Anglo-Saxon and Old High German. The origin of *cat-boat* and *pungy* I have been unable to determine. Perhaps the latter is related in some way to *pung*, a one-horse sled or wagon. *Pung* was once widely used in the United States, but of late it has sunk to the estate of a New England provincialism. Longfellow used it, and in 1857 a writer in the *Knickerbocker Magazine* reported that *pungs* filled Broadway, in New York, after a snow-storm.

Most of these new words, of course, produced derivatives, for example, *to stack hay*, *to shingle*, *to shuck* (*i. e.*, corn), *to trail* and *to caucus*. *Backwoods* immediately begat *backwoodsman* and was itself turned into a common adjective. The colonists, indeed, showed a beautiful disregard of linguistic nicety. At an early date they shortened the English law-phrase, *to convey by deed*, to the simple verb, *to deed*. Pickering protested against this as a barbarism, and argued that no self-respecting law-writer would employ it, but all the same it was firmly entrenched in the common speech and it has remained there to this day. *To table*, for *to lay on the table*, came in at the same time, and so did various forms represented by *bindery*, for *bookbinder's shop*. *To tomahawk* appeared before 1650, and *to scalp* must have followed soon after. Within the next century and a half they were reinforced by many other such new verbs, and by such adjectives made of nouns as *no-account* and *one-horse*, and such nouns made of verbs as *carry-all* and *goner*, and such adverbs as *no-how*. In particular, the manufacture of new verbs went on at a rapid pace. In his letter to Webster in 1789, Franklin denounced *to advocate*, *to progress*, and *to oppose*—a vain enterprise, for all of them are now in perfectly good usage. *To advocate*, indeed, was used by Thomas Nashe in 1589, and by John Milton half a century later, but it seems to have been reinvented in America. In 1822 and again in 1838 Robert Southey, then poet laureate, led two belated attacks upon it, as a barbarous Americanism, but its obvious usefulness preserved it, and it remains in good usage on both sides of the Atlantic today—one of the earliest of the English borrowings from America. In the end, indeed, even so ardent a purist as Richard Grant White adopted it, as he did to placate.[21]

Webster, though he agreed with Franklin in opposing to advocate, gave his imprimatur to to appreciate (i. e., to rise in value), and is credited by Sir Charles Lyell [22] with having himself invented to demoralize. He also approved to obligate. To antagonize seems to have been given currency by John Quincy Adams, to immigrate by John Marshall, to eventuate by Gouverneur Morris, and to derange by George Washington. Jefferson, always hospitable to new words, used to belittle in his "Notes on Virginia," and Thornton thinks that he coined it. Many new verbs were made by the simple process of prefixing the preposition to common nouns, e. g., to clerk, to dicker, to dump, to blow, (i. e., to bluster or boast), to cord (i. e., wood) to stump, to room and to shin. Others were made by transforming verbs in the orthodox vocabulary, e. g., to cavort from to curvet, and to snoop from to snook. Others arose as metaphors, e. g., to whitewash (figuratively) and to squat (on unoccupied land). Others were made by hitching suffixes to nouns, e. g., to negative, to deputize, to locate, to legislate, to infract, to compromit and to happify. Yet others seem to have been produced by onomatopoeia, e. g., to fizzle, or to have arisen by some other such spontaneous process, so far unintelligible, e. g., to tote. With them came an endless series of verb-phrases, e. g., to draw a bead, to face the music, to darken one's doors, to take to the woods, to fly off the handle, to go on the war-path and to saw wood—all obvious products of frontier life. Many coinages of the pre-Revolutionary era later disappeared. Jefferson used to ambition but it dropped out nevertheless, and so did to compromit, (i. e., to compromise), to homologize, and to happify. Fierce battles raged 'round some of these words, and they were all violently derided in England. Even so useful a verb as to locate, now in perfectly good usage,

[21] Vide his preface to Every-Day English, pp. xxi and xv, respectively.
[22] Vide Lyell's Travels in North America; London, 1845.

was denounced in the third volume of the *North American Review*, and other purists of the times tried to put down *to legislate.*

The young and tender adjectives had quite as hard a row to hoe, particularly *lengthy*. The *British Critic* attacked it in November, 1793, and it also had enemies at home, but John Adams had used it in his diary in 1759 and the authority of Jefferson and Hamilton was behind it, and so it survived. Years later James Russell Lowell spoke of it as "the excellent adjective," [23] and boasted that American had given it to English. *Dutiable* also met with opposition, and moreover, it had a rival, *customable;* but Marshall wrote it into his historic decisions, and thus it took root. The same anonymous watchman of the *North American Review* who protested against *to locate* pronounced his anathema upon "such barbarous terms as *presidential* and *congressional*," but the plain need for them kept them in the language. *Gubernatorial* had come in long before this, and is to be found in the New Jersey Archives of 1734. *Influential* was denounced by the Rev. Jonathan Boucher and by George Canning, who argued that *influent* was better, but it was ardently defended by William Pinkney, of Maryland, and gradually made its way. *Handy, kinky, law-abiding, chunky, solid* (in the sense of well-to-do), *evincive, complected, judgmatical, underpinned, blooded* and *cute* were also already secure in revolutionary days. So with many nouns. Jefferson used *breadstuffs* in his Report of the Secretary of State on Commercial Restrictions, December 16, 1793. *Balance,* in the sense of remainder, got into the debates of the First Congress. *Mileage* was used by Franklin in 1754, and is now sound English. *Elevator,* in the sense of a storage house for grain, was used by Jefferson and by others before him. *Draw,* for *drawbridge,* comes down from Revolutionary days. So does *slip,* in the sense of a berth for vessels. So does *addition,* in the sense of a suburb. So, finally, does *darkey.*

The history of many of these Americanisms shows how vain is the effort of grammarians to combat the normal processes of lan-

[23] Pref. to the Biglow Papers, 2nd series, 1866.

guage development. I have mentioned the early opposition to *dutiable, influential, presidential, lengthy, to locate, to oppose, to advocate, to legislate* and *to progress. Bogus, reliable* and *standpoint* were attacked with the same academic ferocity. All of them are to be found in Bryant's *Index Expurgatorius* [24] (*circa* 1870), and *reliable* was denounced by Bishop Coxe as "that abominable barbarism" so late as 1886.[25]   Edward S. Gould, another uncompromising purist, said of *standpoint* that it was "the bright particular star . . . of solemn philological blundering" and "the very counterpart of Dogberry's *non-com.*" [26] Gould also protested against *to jeopardize, leniency* and *to demean,* and Richard Grant White joined him in an onslaught upon *to donate.* But all of these words are in good use in the United States today, and some of them have gone over into English.[27]

§ 4

Changed Meanings—A number of the foregoing contributions to the American vocabulary, of course, were simply common English words with changed meanings. *To squat,* in the sense of *to crouch,* had been sound English for centuries; what the colonists did was to attach a figurative meaning to it, and then bring that figurative meaning into wider usage than the literal meaning. In a somewhat similar manner they changed the significance of *pond,* as I have pointed out. So, too, with *creek.* In English it designated (and still designates) a small inlet or arm of a large river or of the sea; in American, so early as 1674, it designated any small stream. Many other such changed·meanings crept into American in the early days. A typical one was the use of *lot* to designate a *parcel* of land. Thornton says, perhaps inaccurately, that it originated in the fact that the land in New England was distributed by lot. Whatever the truth, *lot,*

[24] Reprinted in Helpful Hints in Writing and Reading, comp. by Grenville Kleiser; New York, 1911, pp. 15–17.
[25] A. Cleveland Coxe: Americanisms in England, *Forum,* Oct., 1886.
[26] Edwin S. Gould: Good English, or, Popular Errors in Language; New York, 1867; pp. 25–27.
[27] *Cf.* Ch. I, § 5, and Ch. V, § 1.

to this day, is in almost universal use in the United States, though rare in England. Our conveyancers, in describing real property, always speak of "all that *lot* or *parcel* of land." [28]   Other examples of the application of old words to new purposes are afforded by *freshet, barn* and *team.* A *freshet*, in eighteenth century English, meant any stream of fresh water; the colonists made it signify an inundation. A *barn* was a house or shed for storing crops; in the colonies the word came to mean a place for keeping cattle also. A *team*, in English, was a pair of draft horses; in the colonies it came to mean both horses and vehicle.

The process is even more clearly shown in the history of such words as *corn* and *shoe.* *Corn*, in orthodox English, means grain for human consumption, and especially wheat, *e. g.*, the *Corn* Laws. The earliest settlers, following this usage, gave the name of *Indian corn* to what the Spaniards, following the Indians themselves, had called *maíz.* But gradually the adjective fell off, and by the middle of the eighteenth century *maize* was called simply *corn*, and grains in general were called *breadstuffs.* Thomas Hutchinson, discoursing to George III in 1774, used *corn* in this restricted sense, speaking of "rye and *corn* mixed." "What *corn?*" asked George. "*Indian corn*," explained Hutchinson, "or, as it is called in authors, *maize.*" [29]   So with *shoe.* In English it meant (and still means) a topless article of footwear, but the colonists extended its meaning to varieties covering the ankle, thus displacing the English *boot*, which they reserved for foot coverings reaching at least to the knee. To designate the English *shoe* they began to use the word *slipper.* This distinction between English and American usage still prevails, despite the affectation which has lately sought to revive *boot*, and with it its derivatives, *boot-shop* and *bootmaker.*

Store, shop, lumber, pie, dry-goods, cracker, rock and *partridge* among nouns and *to haul, to jew, to notify* and *to heft* among verbs offer further examples of changed meanings. Down to the

---

[28] *Lott* appears in the Connecticut Code of 1650. *Vide* the edition of Andrus; Hartford, 1822. On page 35 is "their landes, *lotts* and accommodations." On page 46 is "meadow and home *lotts.*"

[29] *Vide* Hutchinson's Diary, vol. i, p. 171; London, 1883–6.

middle of the eighteenth century *shop* continued to designate a retail establishment in America, as it does in England to this day. *Store* was applied only to a large establishment—one showing, in some measure, the character of a warehouse. But in 1774 a Boston young man was advertising in the *Massachusetts Spy* for "a *place* as a *clerk* in a *store*" (three Americanisms in a row!). Soon afterward *shop* began to acquire its special American meaning as a factory, *e. g., machine-shop*. Meanwhile *store* completely displaced *shop* in the English sense, and it remained for a late flowering of Anglomania, as in the case of *boot* and *shoe*, to restore, in a measure, the *status quo ante*. *Lumber*, in eighteenth century English, meant disused furniture, and this is its common meaning in England today. But the colonists early employed it to designate timber, and that use of it is now universal in America. Its familiar derivatives, *e. g., lumber-yard, lumberman, lumberjack*, greatly reinforce this usage. *Pie*, in English, means a meat-pie; in American it means a fruit-pie. The English call a fruit-pie a *tart;* the Americans call a meat-pie a *pot-pie*. *Dry-goods*, in England, means "non-liquid goods, as corn" (*i. e.*, wheat); in the United States the term means "textile fabrics or wares." [30] The difference had appeared before 1725. *Rock*, in English, always means a large mass; in America it may mean a small stone, as in *rock-pile* and *to throw a rock*. The Puritans were putting *rocks* into the foundations of their meeting-houses so early as 1712.[31] *Cracker* began to be used for *biscuit* before the Revolution. *Tavern* displaced *inn* at the same time. As for *partridge*, it is cited by a late authority [32] as a salient example of changed meaning, along with *corn* and *store*. In England the term is applied only to the true partridge (*Perdix perdix*) and its nearly related varieties, but in the United States it is also used to designate the ruffed grouse (*Bonasa umbellus*), the common quail (*Colinus virginianus*) and various

[30] The definitions are from the Concise Oxford Dictionary of Current English (1914) and the Standard Dictionary (1906), respectively.

[31] S. Sewall: Diary, April 14, 1712: "I lay'd a *Rock* in the North-east corner of the Foundation of the Meeting-house."

[32] The Americana, . . . *art.* Americanisms: New York, 1903–6.

other tetraonoid birds. This confusion goes back to colonial times. So with *rabbit*. Properly speaking, there are no native rabbits in the United States; they are all hares. But the early colonists, for some unknown reason, dropped the word *hare* out of their vocabulary, and it is rarely heard in American speech to this day. When it appears it is almost always applied to the so-called Belgian hare, which, curiously enough, is not a hare at all, but a true rabbit.

To haul, in English, means to move by force or violence; in the colonies it came to mean to transport in a vehicle, and this meaning survives in sound American. *To jew*, in English, means to cheat; the colonists made it mean to haggle, and devised *to jew down* to indicate an effort to work a reduction in price. *To heft*, in English, means to lift; the early Americans made it mean to weigh by lifting, and kept the idea of weighing in its derivatives, *e. g., hefty*. Finally, there is the familiar American misuse of *Miss* or *Mis'* for *Mrs.*. It was so widespread by 1790 that on November 17 of that year Webster solemnly denounced it in the *American Mercury*.

§ 5

Archaic English Words—Most of the colonists who lived along the American seaboard in 1750 were the descendants of immigrants who had come in fully a century before; after the first settlements there had been much less fresh immigration than many latter-day writers have assumed. According to Prescott F. Hall, "the population of New England . . . at the date of the Revolutionary War . . . was produced out of an immigration of about 20,000 persons *who arrived before 1640*," [33] and we have Franklin's authority for the statement that the total population of the colonies in 1751, then about 1,000,000, had been

---

[33] Immigration, 2nd ed.; New York, 1913, p. 4. Sir J. R. Seeley says, in The Expansion of England (2nd ed.; London, 1895, p. 84) that the emigration from England to New England, after the meeting of the Long Parliament (1640), was so slight for a full century that it barely balanced "the counter-movement of colonists quitting the colony." Richard Hildreth, in his History of the United States, vol. i, p. 267, says that the departures actually exceeded the arrivals.

produced from an original immigration of less than 80,000.[34]
Even at that early day, indeed, the colonists had begun to feel
that they were distinctly separated, in culture and customs, from
the mother-country,[35] and there were signs of the rise of a new
native aristocracy, entirely distinct from the older aristocracy of
the royal governors' courts.[36] The enormous difficulties of communication with England helped to foster this sense of separation. The round trip across the ocean occupied the better part
of a year, and was hazardous and expensive; a colonist who had
made it was a marked man,—as Hawthorne said, "the *petit-
maitre* of the colonies." Nor was there any very extensive exchange of ideas, for though most of the books read in the colonies
came from England, the great majority of the colonists, down to
the middle of the century, seem to have read little save the Bible
and biblical commentaries, and in the native literature of the
time one seldom comes upon any reference to the English authors
who were glorifying the period of the Restoration and the reign
of Anne. Moreover, after 1760 the colonial eyes were upon
France rather than upon England, and Rousseau, Montesquieu,
Voltaire and the Encyclopedists began to be familiar names to
thousands who were scarcely aware of Addison and Steele, or
even of the great Elizabethans.[37]

The result of this isolation, on the one hand, was that proliferation of the colonial speech which I have briefly reviewed, and on
the other hand, the preservation of many words and phrases that
gradually became obsolete in England. The Pilgrims of 1620
brought over with them the English of James I and the Revised *? 1888*

[34] Works, ed. by Sparks: vol. ii, p. 319.
[35] *Cf.* Pehr Kalm: Travels into N. America, tr. by J. R. Forster, 3 vols.;
London, 1770–71.
[36] Sydney George Fisher: The True Story of the American Revolution;
Phila. and London, 1902, p. 27. See also John T. Morse's Life of Thomas
Jefferson in the American Statesmen series (Boston and New York, 1898),
p. 2. Morse points out that Washington, Jefferson and Madison belonged
to this new aristocracy, not to the old one.
[37] *Cf.* the Cambridge History of American Literature, vol. i, p. 119.
Francis Jeffrey, writing on Franklin in the *Edinburgh Review* for July,
1806, hailed him as a prodigy who had arisen "in a society where there
was no relish and no encouragement for literature."

Version, and their descendants of a century later, inheriting it, allowed its fundamentals to be little changed by the academic overhauling that the mother tongue was put to during the early part of the eighteenth century. In part they were ignorant of this overhauling, and in part they were indifferent to it. Whenever the new usage differed from that of the Bible they were inclined to remain faithful to the Bible, not only because of its pious authority but also because of the superior pull of its imminent and constant presence. Thus when an artificial prudery in English ordered the abandonment of the Anglo-Saxon *sick* for the Gothic *ill*, the colonies refused to follow, for *sick* was in both the Old Testament and the New; [38] and that refusal remains in force to this day.

A very large number of words and phrases, many of them now exclusively American, are similar survivals from the English of the seventeenth century, long since obsolete or merely provincial in England. Among nouns Thornton notes *fox-fire, flap-jack, jeans, molasses, beef* (to designate the live animal), *chinch, cord-wood, homespun, ice-cream, julep* and *swingle-tree;* Halliwell [39] adds *andiron, bay-window, cesspool, clodhopper, cross-purposes, greenhorn, loophole, ragamuffin, riff-raff, rigmarole* and *trash;* and other authorities cite *stock* (for cattle), *fall* (for autumn), *offal, din, underpinning* and *adze. Bub,* used in addressing a boy, is very old English, but survives only in American. *Flap-jack* goes back to Piers Plowman, but has been obsolete in England for two centuries. *Muss,* in the sense of a row, is also obsolete over there, but it is to be found in "Anthony and Cleopatra." *Char,* as a noun, disappeared from English a long time ago, but it survives in American as *chore.* Among the adjectives similarly preserved are *to whittle, to wilt* and *to approbate. To guess,* in the American sense of *to suppose,* is to be found in "Henry VI":

[38] Examples of its use in the American sense, considered vulgar and even indecent in England, are to be found in Gen. xlviii, 1; II Kings viii, 7; John xi, 1, and Acts ix, 37.

[39] J. O. Halliwell (Phillips): A Dictionary of Archaisms and Provincialisms, Containing Words now Obsolete in England All of Which are Familiar and in Common Use in America, 2nd ed.; London, 1850.

> Not all together; better far, I *guess,*
> That we do make our entrance several ways.

In "Measure for Measure" Escalus says "I *guess* not" to Angelo. The New English Dictionary offers examples much older—from Chaucer, Wyclif and Gower. *To interview* is in Dekker. *To loan,* in the American sense of to lend, is in 34 and 35 Henry VIII, but it dropped out of use in England early in the eighteenth century, and all the leading dictionaries, both English and American, now call it an Americanism.[40] *To fellowship,* once in good American use but now reduced to a provincialism, is in Chaucer. Even *to hustle,* it appears, is ancient. Among adjectives, *homely,* which means only homelike or unadorned in England, was used in its American sense of plain-featured by both Shakespeare and Milton. Other such survivors are *burly, catty-cornered, likely, deft, copious, scant* and *ornate.* Perhaps *clever* also belongs to this category, that is, in the American sense of amiable.

"Our ancestors," said James Russell Lowell, "unhappily could bring over no English better than Shakespeare's." Shakespeare died in 1616; the Pilgrims landed four years later; Jamestown was founded in 1607. As we have seen, the colonists, saving a few superior leaders, were men of small sensitiveness to the refinements of life and speech: soldiers of fortune, amateur theologians, younger sons, neighborhood "advanced thinkers," bankrupts, jobless workmen, decayed gentry, and other such fugitives from culture—in brief, Philistines of the sort who join tin-pot fraternal orders today, and march in parades, and whoop for the latest mountebanks in politics. There was thus a touch of rhetoric in Lowell's saying that they spoke the English of Shakespeare; as well argue that the London grocers of 1885 spoke the English of Pater. But in a larger sense he said truly, for these men at least brought with them the vocabulary of Shakespeare—or a part of it,—even if the uses he made of it were beyond their comprehension, and they also brought with

[40] An interesting discussion of this verb appeared in the *New York Sun,* Nov. 27, 1914.

them that sense of ease in the language, that fine disdain for formality, that bold experimentalizing in words, which was so peculiarly Elizabethan. There were no grammarians in that day; there were no purists that anyone listened to; it was a case of saying your say in the easiest and most satisfying way. In remote parts of the United States there are still direct and almost pure-blooded descendants of those seventeenth century colonists. Go among them, and you will hear more words from the Shakespearean vocabulary, still alive and in common service, than anywhere else in' the world, and more of the loose and brilliant syntax of that time, and more of its gipsy phrases.[41]

§ 6

Colonial Pronunciation—The debate that long raged over the pronunciation of classical Latin exhibits the difficulty of determining with exactness the shades of sound in the speech of a people long departed from earth. The American colonists, of course, are much nearer to us than the Romans, and so we should have relatively little difficulty in determining just how they pronounced this or that word, but against the fact of their nearness stands the neglect of our philologists, or, perhaps more accurately, our lack of philologists. What Sweet did to clear up the history of English pronunciation,[42] and what Wilhelm Corssen did for Latin, no American professor has yet thought to attempt for American. The literature is almost, if not quite a blank. But here and there we may get a hint of the facts, and though the sum of them is not large, they at least serve to set at rest a number of popular errors.

One of these errors, chiefly prevalent in New England, is that the so-called Boston pronunciation, with its broad *a*'s (making *last, path* and *aunt* almost assonant with *bar*) comes down unbrokenly from the day of the first settlements, and that it is in consequence superior in authority to the pronunciation of the

[41] *Cf.* J. H. Combs: Old, Early and Elizabethan English in the Southern Mountains, *Dialect Notes*, vol. iv, pt. iv, pp. 283–97.
[42] Henry Sweet: A History of English Sounds; London, 1876; Oxford, 1888.

rest of the country, with its flat *a*'s (making the same words assonant with *ban*). A glance through Webster's "Dissertations" is sufficient to show that the flat *a* was in use in New England in 1789, for the pronunciation of such words as *wrath*, *bath* and *path*, as given by him, makes them rhyme with *hath*.[43] Moreover, he gives *aunt* the same *a*-sound. From other sources come indications that the *a* was likewise flattened in such words as *plant, basket, branch, dance, blast, command* and *castle*, and even in *balm* and *calm*. Changes in the sound of the letter have been going on in English ever since the Middle English period,[44] and according to Lounsbury [45] they have moved toward the disappearance of the Continental *a*, "the fundamental vowel-tone of the human voice." Grandgent, another authority,[46] says that it became flattened "by the sixteenth century" and that "until 1780 or thereabouts the standard language had no broad *a*." Even in such words as *father, car* and *ask* the flat *a* was universally used. Sheridan, in the dictionary he published in 1780,[47] actually gave no *ah*-sound in his list of vowels. This habit of flatting the *a* had been brought over, of course, by the early colonists, and was as general in America, in the third quarter of the eighteenth century, as in England. Benjamin Franklin, when he wrote his "Scheme for a New Alphabet and a Reformed Mode of Spelling," in 1768, apparently had no suspicion that any other *a* was possible. But between 1780 and 1790, according to Grandgent, a sudden fashion for the broad *a* (not the *aw*-sound, as in *fall*, but the Continental sound as in *far*) arose in England,[48] and this fashion soon found servile imitation in Boston. But it was as much an affectation in those

[43] P. 124.

[44] *Cf. Art.* Changes in the Language Since Shakespeare's Time, by W. Murison, in The Cambridge History of English Literature, vol. xiv, p. 485.

[45] English Spelling and Spelling Reform; New York, 1909.

[46] C. H. Grandgent: Fashion and the Broad *A*, *Nation*, Jan. 7, 1915.

[47] Thomas Sheridan: A Complete Dictionary of the English Language; London, 1780.

[48] It first appeared in Robert Nares' Elements of Orthography; London, 1784. In 1791 it received full approbation in John Walker's Critical Pronouncing Dictionary.

days as it is today, and Webster indicated the fact pretty plainly in his "Dissertations." How, despite his opposition, the broad *a* prevailed East of the Connecticut river, and how, in the end, he himself yielded to it, and even tried to force it upon the whole nation—this will be rehearsed in the next chapter.

The colonists remained faithful much longer than the English to various other vowel-sounds that were facing change in the eighteenth century, for example, the long *e*-sound in *heard*. Webster says that the custom of rhyming *heard* with *bird* instead of with *feared* came in at the beginning of the Revolution. "To most people in this country," he adds, "the English pronunciation appears like affectation." He also argues for rhyming *deaf* with *leaf*, and protests against inserting a *y*-sound before the *u* in such words as *nature*. Franklin's authority stands behind *git* for *get*. This pronunciation, according to Menner,[49] was correct in seventeenth century England, and perhaps down to the middle of the next century. So was the use of the Continental *i*-sound in *oblige*, making it *obleege*. It is probable that the colonists clung to these disappearing usages much longer than the English. The latter, according to Webster, were unduly responsive to illogical fashions set by the exquisites of the court and by popular actors. He blames Garrick, in particular, for many extravagant innovations, most of them not followed in the colonies. But Garrick was surely not responsible for the use of a long *i*-sound in such words as *motive*, nor for the corruption of *mercy* to *marcy*. Webster denounced both of these barbarisms. The second he ascribed somewhat lamely to the fact that the letter *r* is called *ar*, and proposed to dispose of it by changing the *ar* to *er*.

As for the consonants, the colonists seem to have resisted valiantly that tendency to slide over them which arose in England after the Restoration. Franklin, in 1768, still retained the sound of *l* in such words as *would* and *should*, a usage not met with in England after the year 1700. In the same way, according to Menner, the *w* in *sword* was sounded in America "for

[49] Robert J. Menner; The Pronunciation of English in America, *Atlantic Monthly*, March, 1915.

some time after Englishmen had abandoned it.'' The sensitive ear of Henry James detected an unpleasant *r*-sound in the speech of Americans, long ago got rid of by the English, so late as 1905; he even charged that it was inserted gratuitously in innocent words.[50] The obvious slurring of the consonants by Southerners is explained by a recent investigator [51] on the ground that it began in England during the reign of Charles II, and that most of the Southern colonists came to the New World at that time. The court of Charles, it is argued, was under French influence, due to the king's long residence in France and his marriage to Henrietta Marie. Charles ''objected to the inharmonious contractions *will'nt* (or *wolln't*) and *wasn't* and *weren't* . . . and set the fashion of using the softly euphonious *won't* and *wan't*, which are used in speaking to this day by the best class of Southerners.'' A more direct French influence upon Southern pronunciation is also pointed out. ''With full knowledge of his *g's* and his *r's*, . . . [the Southerner] sees fit to glide over them, . . . and he carries over the consonant ending one word to the vowel beginning the next, just as the Frenchman does.'' The political importance of the South, in the years between the Mecklenburg Declaration and the adoption of the Constitution, tended to force its provincialisms upon the common language. Many of the acknowledged leaders of the nascent nation were Southerners, and their pronunciation, as well as their phrases, must have become familiar everywhere. Pickering gives us a hint, indeed, at the process whereby their usage influenced that of the rest of the people.[52]

The Americans early dropped the *h*-sound in such words as *when* and *where*, but so far as I can determine they never elided it at the beginning of words, save in the case of *herb*, and a few others. This elision is commonly spoken of as a cockney vulgarism, but it has extended to the orthodox English speech. In *ostler* the initial *h* is openly left off; in *hotel* and *hospital* it is

[50] The Question of Our Speech; Boston and New York, 1906, pp. 27–29.
[51] Elizabeth H. Hancock: Southern Speech, *Neale's Monthly*, Nov., 1913, pp. 606–7.
[52] *Vide* his remarks on *balance* in his Vocabulary. See also Marsh, p. 671.

seldom sounded, even by the most careful Englishmen. Certain English words in *h*, in which the *h* is now sounded, betray its former silence by the fact that not *a* but *an* is still put before them. It is still good English usage to write *an hotel* and *an historical;* it is the American usage to write *a hotel* and *a historical.*

The great authority of Webster was sufficient to establish the American pronunciation of *schedule.* In England the *sch* is always given the soft sound, but Webster decided for the hard sound, as in *scheme.* The variance persists to this day. The name of the last letter of the alphabet, which is always *zed* in English, is usually made *zee* in the United States. Thornton shows that this Americanism arose in the eighteenth century.

III

The Period of Growth

§ 1

The New Nation—The American language thus began to be
recognizably differentiated from English in both vocabulary and
pronunciation by the opening of the nineteenth century, but as
yet its growth was hampered by two factors, the first being the
lack of a national literature of any pretentions and the second
being an internal political disharmony which greatly conditioned and enfeebled the national consciousness. During the
actual Revolution common aims and common dangers forced
the Americans to show a united front, but once they had
achieved political independence they developed conflicting interests, and out of those conflicting interests came suspicions and
hatreds which came near wrecking the new confederation more
than once. Politically, their worst weakness, perhaps, was an
inability to detach themselves wholly from the struggle for domination still going on in Europe. The surviving Loyalists of
the revolutionary era—estimated by some authorities to have
constituted fully a third of the total population in 1776—were
ardently in favor of England, and such patriots as Jefferson
were as ardently in favor of France. This engrossment in the
quarrels of foreign nations was what Washington warned against
in his Farewell Address. It was at the bottom of such bitter
animosities as that between Jefferson and Hamilton. It in-
spired and perhaps excused the pessimism of such men as Burr.
Its net effect was to make it difficult for the people of the new
nation to think of themselves, politically, as Americans. Their
state of mind, vacillating, uncertain, alternately timorous and

pugnacious, has been well described by Henry Cabot Lodge in his essay on "Colonialism in America."[1]   Soon after the Treaty of Paris was signed, someone referred to the late struggle, in Franklin's hearing, as the War for Independence. "Say, rather, the War of the Revolution," said Franklin. "The War for Independence is yet to be fought."

"That struggle," adds Lossing, "occurred, and that independence was won, by the Americans in the War of 1812."[2] In the interval the new republic had passed through a period of *Sturm und Drang* whose gigantic perils and passions we have begun to forget—a period in which disaster ever menaced, and the foes within were no less bold and pertinacious than the foes without.   Jefferson, perhaps, carried his fear of "monocrats" to the point of monomania, but under it there was undoubtedly a body of sound fact.   The poor debtor class (including probably a majority of the veterans of the Revolution) had been fired by the facile doctrines of the French Revolution to demands which threatened the country with bankruptcy and anarchy, and the class of property-owners, in reaction, went far to the other extreme.   On all sides, indeed, there flourished a strong British party, and particularly in New England, where the so-called codfish aristocracy (by no means extinct, even today) exhibited an undisguised Anglomania, and looked forward confidently to a *rapprochement* with the mother country.[3]   This Anglomania showed itself, not only in ceaseless political agitation, but also in an elaborate imitation of English manners.   We have already seen, on Noah Webster's authority, how it even extended to the pronunciation of the language.

The first sign of the dawn of a new national order came with the election of Thomas Jefferson to the Presidency in 1800. The issue in the campaign was a highly complex one, but under it lay a plain conflict between democratic independence and the

[1] In Studies in History; Boston, 1884.

[2] Benson J. Lossing: Our Country. . . .; New York, 1879.

[3] The thing went, indeed, far beyond mere hope.   In 1812 a conspiracy was unearthed to separate New England from the republic and make it an English colony.   The chief conspirator was one John Henry, who acted under the instructions of Sir John Craig, Governor-General of Canada.

old doctrine of dependence and authority; and with the Alien
and Sedition Laws about his neck, so vividly reminiscent of the
issues of the Revolution itself, Adams went down to defeat.
Jefferson was violently anti-British and pro-French; he saw all
the schemes of his political opponents, indeed, as English plots;
he was the man who introduced the bugaboo into American politics. His first acts after his inauguration were to abolish all
ceremonial at the court of the republic, and to abandon spoken
discourses to Congress for written messages. That ceremonial,
which grew up under Washington, was an imitation, he believed, of the formality of the abhorrent Court of St. James;
as for the speeches to Congress, they were palpably modelled
upon the speeches from the throne of the English kings. Both
reforms met with wide approval; the exactions of the English,
particularly on the high seas, were beginning to break up the
British party. But confidence in the solidarity and security
of the new nation was still anything but universal. The surviving doubts, indeed, were strong enough to delay the ratifica-
tion of the Twelfth Amendment to the Constitution, providing
for more direct elections of President and Vice-President, until
the end of 1804, and even then three of the five New England
states rejected it,[4] and have never ratified it, in fact, to this
day. Democracy was still experimental, doubtful, full of gun-
powder. In so far as it had actually come into being, it had
come as a boon conferred from above. Jefferson, its protag-
onist, was the hero of the populace, but he was not of the populace himself, nor did he ever quite trust it.

It was reserved for Andrew Jackson, a man genuinely of the
people, to lead and visualize the rise of the lower orders. Jackson, in his way, was the archetype of the new American—ignorant, pushful, impatient of restraint and precedent, an iconoclast, a Philistine, an Anglophobe in every fibre. He came
from the extreme backwoods and his youth was passed amid
surroundings but little removed from downright savagery.[5]

[4] Maine was not separated from Massachusetts until 1820.

[5] Vide Andrew Jackson. . . ., by William Graham Sumner; Boston, 1883,
pp. 2–10.

Thousands of other young Americans like him were growing up at the same time—youngsters filled with a vast impatience of all precedent and authority, revilers of all that had come down from an elder day, incorrigible libertarians. They swarmed across the mountains and down the great rivers, wrestling with the naked wilderness and setting up a casual, impromptu sort of civilization where the Indian still menaced. Schools were few and rudimentary; there was not the remotest approach to a cultivated society; any effort to mimic the amenities of the East, or of the mother country, in manner or even in speech, met with instant derision. It was in these surroundings and at this time that the thorough-going American of tradition was born: blatant, illogical, elate, "greeting the embarrassed gods" uproariously and matching "with Destiny for beers." Jackson was unmistakably of that company in his every instinct and idea, and it was his fate to give a new and unshakable confidence to its aspiration at the Battle of New Orleans. Thereafter all doubts began to die out; the new republic was turning out a success. And with success came a vast increase in the national egoism. The hordes of pioneers rolled down the western valleys and on to the great plains.[6] America began to stand for something quite new in the world—in government, in law, in public and private morals, in customs and habits of mind, in the minutia of social intercourse. And simultaneously the voice of America began to take on its characteristic twang, and the speech of America began to differentiate itself boldly and unmistakably from the speech of England. The average Philadelphian or Bostonian of 1790 had not the slightest difficulty in making himself understood by a visiting Englishman. But the average Ohio boatman of 1810 or plainsman of 1815 was already speaking a dialect that the Englishman would have shrunk from as barbarous and unintelligible, and before long it began to leave

[6] Indiana and Illinois were erected into territories during Jefferson's first term, and Michigan during his second term. Kentucky was admitted to the union in 1792, Tennessee in 1796, Ohio in 1803. Lewis and Clarke set out for the Pacific in 1804. The Louisiana Purchase was ratified in 1803, and Louisiana became a state in 1812.

its mark upon and to get direction and support from a distinctively national literature.

That literature, however, was very slow in coming to a dignified, confident and autonomous estate. Down to Jefferson's day it was almost wholly polemical, and hence lacking in the finer values; he himself, an insatiable propagandist and controversialist, was one of its chief ornaments. "The novelists and the historians, the essayists and the poets, whose names come to mind when American literature is mentioned," says a recent literary historian, "have all flourished since 1800." [7] Pickering, so late as 1816, said that "in this country we can hardly be said to have any authors by profession." It was a true saying, though the new day was about to dawn; Bryant had already written "Thanatopsis" and was destined to publish it the year following. Difficulties of communication hampered the circulation of the few native books that were written; it was easier for a man in the South to get books from London than to get them from Boston or New York, and the lack of a copyright treaty with England flooded the country with cheap English editions. "It is much to be regretted," wrote Dr. David Ramsay, of Charleston, S. C., to Noah Webster in 1806, "that there is so little intercourse in a literary way between the states. As soon as a book of general utility comes out in any state it should be for sale in all of them." Ramsay asked for little; the most he could imagine was a sale of 2,000 copies for an American work in America. But even that was far beyond the possibilities of the time.

An external influence of great potency helped to keep the national literature scant and timorous during those early and perilous days. It was the extraordinary animosity of the English critics, then at the zenith of their pontifical authority, to all books of American origin or flavor. This animosity, culminating in Sydney Smith's famous sneer,[8] was but part of a

---

[7] Barrett Wendell: A Literary History of America; New York, 1900.

[8] "In the four quarters of the globe, who reads an American book? or goes to an American play? or looks at an American picture or statue?" *Edinburgh Review*, Jan., 1820.

larger hostility to all things American, from political theories to table manners. The American, after the war of 1812, became the pet abomination of the English, and the chief butt of the incomparable English talent for moral indignation. There was scarcely an issue of the *Quarterly Review,* the *Edinburgh,* the *Foreign Quarterly,* the *British Review* or *Blackwood's,* for a generation following 1814, in which he was not stupendously assaulted. Gifford, Sydney Smith and the poet Southey became specialists in this business; it took on the character of a holy war; even such mild men as Wordsworth were recruited for it. It was argued that the Americans were rogues and swindlers, that they lived in filth and squalor, that they were boors in social intercourse, that they were poltroons and savages in war, that they were depraved and criminal, that they were wholly devoid of the remotest notion of decency or honor. The *Foreign Quarterly,* summing up in January, 1844, pronounced them "horn-handed and pig-headed, hard, persevering, unscrupulous, carnivorous, with a genius for lying." Various Americans went to the defense of their countrymen, among them, Irving, Cooper, Timothy Dwight, J. K. Paulding, John Neal, Edward Everett and Robert Walsh. Paulding, in "John Bull in America, or, the New Munchausen," published in 1825, attempted satire. Even an Englishman, James Sterling, warned his fellow-Britons that, if they continued their intolerant abuse, they would "turn into bitterness the last drops of good-will toward England that exist in the United States." But the avalanche of denunciation kept up, and even down to a few years ago it was very uncommon for an Englishman to write of American politics, or manners, or literature without betraying his dislike. Not, indeed, until the Prussian began monopolizing the whole British talent for horror and invective did the Yankee escape the lash.[9]

This gigantic pummelling, in the long run, was destined to encourage an independent spirit in the national literature, if

[9] *Cf.* As Others See Us, by John Graham Brooks; New York, 1908, ch. vii. Also, The Cambridge History of American Literature, vol. i, pp. 205–8.

only by a process of mingled resentment and despair, but for some time its chief effect was to make American writers of a more delicate aspiration extremely self-conscious and diffident. The educated classes, even against their will, were influenced by the torrent of abuse; they could not help finding in it an occasional reasonableness, an accidental true hit. The result, despite the efforts of Channing, Knapp and other such valiant defenders of the native author, was uncertainty and skepticism in native criticism. "The first step of an American entering upon a literary career," says Lodge, writing of the first quarter of the century, "was to pretend to be an Englishman in order that he might win the approval, not of Englishmen, but of his own countrymen." Cooper, in his first novel, "Precaution," chose an English scene, imitated English models, and obviously hoped to placate the critics thereby. Irving, too, in his earliest work, showed a considerable discretion, and his "History of New York," as everyone knows, was first published anonymously. But this puerile spirit did not last long. The English onslaughts were altogether too vicious to be received lying down; their very fury demanded that they be met with a united and courageous front. Cooper, in his second novel, "The Spy," boldly chose an American setting and American characters, and though the influence of his wife, who came of a Loyalist family, caused him to avoid any direct attack upon the English, he attacked them indirectly, and with great effect, by opposing an immediate and honorable success to their derisions. "The Spy" ran through three editions in four months; it was followed by his long line of thoroughly American novels; in 1834 he formally apologized to his countrymen for his early truancy in "Precaution." Irving, too, soon adopted a bolder tone, and despite his English predilections, he refused an offer of a hundred guineas for an article for the *Quarterly Review*, made by Gifford in 1828, on the ground that "the *Review* has been so persistently hostile to our country that I cannot draw a pen in its service."

The same year saw the publication of the first edition of Web-

ster's American Dictionary of the English language, and a
year later followed Samuel L. Knapp's "Lectures on American
Literature," the first history of the national letters ever attempted. Knapp, in his preface, thought it necessary to prove,
first of all, that an American literature actually existed, and
Webster, in his introduction, was properly apologetic, but there
was no real need for timorousness in either case, for the American attitude toward the attack of the English was now definitely
changing from uneasiness to defiance. The English critics, in
fact, had overdone the thing, and though their clatter was to
keep up for many years more, they no longer spread terror
or had much influence. Of a sudden, as if in answer to them,
doubts turned to confidence, and then into the wildest sort of
optimism, not only in politics and business, but also in what
passed for the arts. Knapp boldly defied the English to produce a "tuneful sister" surpassing Mrs. Sigourney; more, he
argued that the New World, if only by reason of its superior
scenic grandeur, would eventually hatch a poetry surpassing
even that of Greece and Rome. "What are the Tibers and
Scamanders," he demanded, "measured by the Missouri and the
Amazon? Or what the loveliness of Illysus or Avon by the
Connecticut or the Potomack?"

In brief, the national feeling, long delayed at birth, finally
leaped into being in amazing vigor. "One can get an idea of
the strength of that feeling," says R. O. Williams, "by glancing
at almost any book taken at random from the American publications of the period. Belief in the grand future of the United
States is the key-note of everything said and done. All things
American are to be grand—our territory, population, products,
wealth, science, art—but especially our political institutions and
literature. The unbounded confidence in the material development of the country which now characterizes the extreme northwest of the United States prevailed as strongly throughout the
eastern part of the Union during the first thirty years of the
century; and over and above a belief in, and concern for, ma-
terialistic progress, there were enthusiastic anticipations of
achievements in all the moral and intellectual fields of national

greatness.'' [10] Nor was that vast optimism wholly without warrant. An American literature was actually coming into being, and with a wall of hatred and contempt shutting in England, the new American writers were beginning to turn to the Continent for inspiration and encouragement. Irving had already drunk at Spanish springs; Emerson and Bayard Taylor were to receive powerful impulses from Germany, following Ticknor, Bancroft and Everett before them; Bryant was destined to go back to the classics. Moreover, Cooper and John P. Kennedy had shown the way to native sources of literary material, and Longfellow was making ready to follow them; novels in imitation of English models were no longer heard of; the ground was preparing for ''Uncle Tom's Cabin.'' Finally, Webster himself, as Williams demonstrated, worked better than he knew. His American Dictionary was not only thoroughly American: it was superior to any of the current dictionaries of the English, so much so that for a good many years it remained ''a sort of mine for British lexicography to exploit.''

Thus all hesitations disappeared, and there arose a national consciousness so soaring and so blatant that it began to dismiss all British usage and opinion as puerile and idiotic. William L. Marcy, when Secretary of State under Pierce (1853–57), issued a circular to all American diplomatic and consular officers, loftily bidding them employ only ''the American language'' in communicating with him. The Legislature of Indiana, in an act approved February 15, 1838, establishing the state university at Bloomington,[11] provided that it should instruct the youth of the new commonwealth (it had been admitted to the Union in 1816) ''in the American, learned and foreign languages . . . and literature.'' Such grandiose pronuncia-

[10] Our Dictionaries and Other English Language Topics; New York, 1890, pp. 30–31.

[11] It is curious to note that the center of population of the United States, according to the last census, is now ''in southern Indiana, in the western part of Bloomington city, Monroe county.'' Can it be that this early declaration of literary independence laid the foundation for Indiana's recent pre-eminence in letters? Cf. The Language We Use, by Alfred Z. Reed, New York Sun, March 13, 1918.

mentos well indicate and explain the temper of the era.[12] It was a time of expansion and braggadocia. The new republic would not only produce a civilization and a literature of its own; it would show the way for all other civilizations and literatures. Rufus Wilmot Griswold, the enemy of Poe, rose from his decorous Baptist pew to protest that so much patriotism amounted to insularity and absurdity, but there seems to have been no one to second the motion. It took, indeed, the vast shock of the Civil War to unhorse the optimists. While the Jackson influence survived, it was the almost unanimous national conviction that "he who dallies is a dastard, and he who doubts is damned."

§ 2

The Language in the Making—All this jingoistic bombast, however, was directed toward defending, not so much the national vernacular as the national beautiful letters. True enough, an English attack upon a definite American locution always brought out certain critical minute-men, but in the main they were anything but hospitable to the racy neologisms that kept crowding up from below, and most of them were eager to be accepted as masters of orthodox English and very sensitive to the charge that their writing was bestrewn with Americanisms. A glance through the native criticism of the time will show how ardently even the most uncompromising patriots imitated the Johnsonian jargon then fashionable in England. Fowler and Griswold followed pantingly in the footsteps of Macaulay; their prose is extraordinarily ornate and self-conscious, and one searches it in vain for any concession to colloquialism. Poe, the master of them all, achieved a style so elephantine that many an English leader-writer must have studied it with envy. A few bolder spirits, as we have seen, spoke out for national freedom in language as well as in letters—among them, Channing— but in the main the Brahmins of the time were conservatives in

[12] Support also came from abroad. Czar Nicholas I, of Russia, smarting under his defeat in the Crimea, issued an order that his own state papers should be prepared in Russian and American — not English.

that department, and it is difficult to imagine Emerson or Irving or Bryant sanctioning the innovations later adopted so easily by Howells. Lowell and Walt Whitman, in fact, were the first men of letters, properly so called, to give specific assent to the great changes that were firmly fixed in the national speech during the half century between the War of 1812 and the Civil War. Lowell did so in his preface to the second series of "The Biglow Papers." Whitman made his declaration in "An American Primer." In discussing his own poetry, he said: "It is an attempt to give the spirit, the body and the man, new words, new potentialities of speech—an American, a cosmopolitan (for the best of America is the best cosmopolitanism) range of self-expression." And then: "The Americans are going to be the most fluent and melodious-voiced people in the world—and the most perfect users of words. The new times, the new people, the new vistas need a new tongue according—yes, and what is more, they will have such a new tongue." To which, as everyone knows, Whitman himself forthwith contributed many daring (and still undigested) novelties, e. g., *camerado*, *romanza*, *Adamic* and *These States*.

Meanwhile, in strong contrast to the lingering conservatism above there was a wild and lawless development of the language below, and in the end it forced itself into recognition, and profited by the literary declaration of independence of its very opponents. "The *jus et norma loquendi*," says W. R. Morfill, the English philologist, "do not depend upon scholars." Particularly in a country where scholarship is still new and wholly cloistered, and the overwhelming majority of the people are engaged upon novel and highly exhilarating tasks, far away from schools and with a gigantic cockiness in their hearts. The remnants of the Puritan civilization had been wiped out by the rise of the proletariat under Jackson, and whatever was fine and sensitive in it had died with it. What remained of an urbane habit of mind and utterance began to be confined to the narrowing feudal areas of the south, and to the still narrower refuge of the Boston Brahmins, now, for the first time, a definitely recognized caste of *intelligentsia*, self-charged with carrying the torch of culture through a new Dark Age. The typical American, in Paulding's satirical phrase, became "a bundling, gouging, impious" fellow, without either "morals, literature, religion or refinement." Next to the savage struggle for land and dollars, party politics was the chief concern of the people, and with the disappearance of the old leaders and the entrance of pushing upstarts from the backwoods, political controversy sank to an incredibly low level. Bartlett, in the introduction to the second edition of his Glossary, describes the effect upon the language. First the enfranchised mob, whether in the city wards or along the western rivers, invented fantastic slang-words and turns of phrase; then they were "seized upon by stump-speakers at political meetings "; then they were heard in Congress; then they got into the newspapers; and finally they came into more or less good usage. Much contemporary evidence is to the same effect. Fowler, in listing "low expressions" in 1850, described them as "chiefly political." "The vernacular tongue of the country," said Daniel Webster, "has become greatly vitiated, depraved and corrupted by the style of the congressional debates." Thornton, in the appendix to his Glossary, gives some astounding specimens of congressional oratory between the 20's and 60's, and many more will reward the explorer who braves the files of the *Congressional Globe*. This flood of racy and unprecedented words and phrases beat upon and finally penetrated the retreat of the *literati,* but the purity of speech cultivated there had little compensatory influence upon the vulgate. The newspaper was now enthroned, and *belles lettres* were cultivated almost in private, and as a mystery. It is probable, indeed, that "Uncle Tom's Cabin" and "Ten Nights in a Bar-room," both published in the early 50's, were the first contemporary native books, after Cooper's day, that the American people, as a people, ever read. Nor did the pulpit, now fast falling from its old high estate, lift a corrective voice. On the contrary, it joined the crowd, and Bartlett denounces it specifically for its bad example, and cites, among its crimes against the language, such inventions as *to doxologize* and *to funeralize.*

To these novelties, apparently without any thought of their uncouthness, Fowler adds *to missionate* and *consociational.*

As I say, the pressure from below broke down the defenses
of the purists, and literally forced a new national idiom upon
them. Pen in hand, they might still achieve laborious imitations of Johnson and Macaulay, but their mouths began to betray them. "When it comes to talking," wrote Charles Astor
Bristed for Englishmen in 1855, "the most refined and best
educated American, who has habitually resided in his own country, the very man who would write, on some serious topic, volumes in which no peculiarity could be detected, will, in half a
dozen sentences, use at least as many words that cannot fail to
strike the inexperienced Englishman who hears them for the
first time." Bristed gave a specimen of the American of that
time, calculated to flabbergast his inexperienced Englishman;
you will find it in the volume of Cambridge Essays, already cited.
His aim was to explain and defend Americanisms, and so shut
off the storm of English reviling, and he succeeded in producing
one of the most thoughtful and persuasive essays on the subject
ever written. But his purpose failed and the attack kept up,
and eight years afterward the Very Rev. Henry Alford, D.D.,
dean of Canterbury, led a famous assault. "Look at those
phrases," he said, "which so amuse us in their speech and
books; at their reckless exaggeration and contempt for con-
gruity; and then compare the character and history of the nation—its blunted sense of moral obligation and duty to man;
its open disregard of conventional right where aggrandizement
is to be obtained; and I may now say, its reckless and fruitless
maintenance of the most cruel and unprincipled war in the history of the world." [13] In his American edition of 1866 Dr.
Alford withdrew this reference to the Civil War and somewhat
ameliorated his indignation otherwise, but he clung to the main
counts in his indictment, and most Englishmen, I daresay, still
give them a certain support. The American is no longer a

[13] A Plea for the Queen's English; London, 1863; 2nd ed., 1864; American ed., New York, 1866.

"vain, egotistical, insolent, rodomontade sort of fellow "; America is no longer the "brigand confederation" of the *Foreign Quarterly* or "the loathsome creature, . . . maimed and lame, full of sores and ulcers" of Dickens; but the Americanism is yet regarded with a bilious eye, and pounced upon viciously when found. Even the friendliest English critics seem to be daunted by the gargantuan copiousness of American inventions in speech. Their position, perhaps, was well stated by Capt. Basil Hall, author of the celebrated "Travels in North America," in 1827. When he argued that "surely such innovations are to be deprecated," an American asked him this question: "If a word becomes universally current in America, why should it not take its station in the language?" "Because," replied Hall in all seriousness, "there are words enough in our language already."

§ 3

The Expanding Vocabulary—A glance at some of the characteristic coinages of the time, as they are revealed in the *Congressional Globe*, in contemporary newspapers and political tracts, and in that grotesque small literature of humor which began with Judge Thomas C. Haliburton's "Sam Slick" in 1835, is almost enough to make one sympathize with Dean Alford. Bartlett quotes *to doxologize* from the *Christian Disciple*, a quite reputable religious paper of the 40's. *To citizenize* was used and explained by Senator Young, of Illinois, in the Senate on February 1, 1841, and he gave Noah Webster as authority for it. *To funeralize* and *to missionate*, along with *consociational*, were contributions of the backwoods pulpit; perhaps it also produced *hell-roaring* and *hellion*, the latter of which was a favorite of the Mormons and even got into a sermon by Henry Ward Beecher. *To deacon*, a verb of decent mien in colonial days, signifying to read a hymn line by line, responded to the rough humor of the time, and began to mean to swindle or adulterate, *e. g.*, to put the largest berries at the top of the box, to extend one's fences *sub rosa*, or to mix sand with sugar. A great rage for extending the vocabulary by the use of suffixes seized upon the corn-fed etymologists, and they produced a formidable new vocabulary in -*ize*, -*ate*, -*ify*, -*acy*, -*ous* and -*ment*. Such inventions as *to obligate*, *to concertize*, *to questionize*, *retiracy*, *savagerous*, *coatee* (a sort of diminutive for *coat*) and *citified* appeared in the popular vocabulary, and even got into more or less good usage. Fowler, in 1850, cited *publishment* and *releasement* with no apparent thought that they were uncouth. And at the same time many verbs were made by the simple process of back formation, as, *to resurrect*, *to excurt*, *to resolute*, *to burgle* [14] and *to enthuse*.[15]

Some of these inventions, after flourishing for a generation or more, were retired with blushes during the period of aesthetic consciousness following the Civil War, but a large number have survived to our own day, and are in good usage. Not even the most bilious purist would think of objecting to *to affiliate*, *to itemize*, *to resurrect* or *to Americanize* today, and yet all of them gave grief to the judicious when they first appeared in the debates of Congress, brought there by statesmen from the backwoods. Nor to such simpler verbs of the period as *to corner* (*i. e.*, the market), *to boss* and *to lynch*.[16] Nor perhaps to *to boom*, *to boost*, *to kick* (in the sense of to protest), *to coast* (on a sled), *to engineer*, *to collide*, *to chink* (*i.e.*, logs), *to feaze*, *to splurge*, *to aggravate* (in the sense of to anger), *to yank* and *to crawfish*. These verbs have entered into the very fibre of the American vulgate, and so have many nouns derived from them, *e. g.*, *boomer*, *boom-town*, *bouncer*, *kicker*, *kick*, *splurge*, *rollercoaster*. A few of them, *e. g.*, *to collide* and *to feaze*, were

14 J. R. Ware, in Passing English of the Victorian Era, says that *to burgle* was introduced to London by W. S. Gilbert in The Pirates of Penzance (April 3, 1880). It was used in America 30 years before.

15 This process, of course, is philologically respectable, however uncouth its occasional products may be. By it we have acquired many everyday words, among them, *to accept* (from *acceptum*), *to exact* (from *exactum*), *to darkle* (from *darkling*), and *pea* (from *pease* = *pois*).

16 All authorities save one seem to agree that this verb is a pure Americanism, and that it is derived from the name of Charles Lynch, a Virginia justice of the peace, who jailed many Loyalists in 1780 without warrant in law. The dissentient, Bristed, says that *to linch* is in various northern English dialects, and means to beat or maltreat.

archaic English terms brought to new birth; a few others, *e. g.*, *to holler*[17] and *to muss*, were obviously mere corruptions. But a good many others, *e. g.*, *to bulldoze*, *to hornswoggle* and *to scoot*, were genuine inventions, and redolent of the soil.

With the new verbs came a great swarm of verb-phrases, some of them short and pithy and others extraordinarily elaborate, but all showing the true national talent for condensing a complex thought, and often a whole series of thoughts, into a vivid and arresting image. Of the first class are *to fill the bill*, *to fizzle out*, *to make tracks*, *to peter out*, *to plank down*, *to go back on*, *to keep tab*, *to light out* and *to back water*. Side by side with them we have inherited such common coins of speech as *to make the fur fly*, *to cut a swath*, *to know him like a book*, *to keep a stiff upper lip*, *to cap the climax*, *to handle without gloves*, *to freeze on to*, *to go it blind*, *to pull wool over his eyes*, *to know the ropes*, *to get solid with*, *to spread one's self*, *to run into the ground*, *to dodge the issue*, *to paint the town red*, *to take a back seat* and *to get ahead of*. These are so familiar that we use them and hear them without thought; they seem as authentically parts of the English idiom as *to be left at the post*. And yet, as the labors of Thornton have demonstrated, all of them are of American nativity, and the circumstances surrounding the origin of some of them have been accurately determined. Many others are palpably the products of the great movement toward the West, for example, *to pan out*, *to strike it rich*, *to jump* or *enter a claim*, *to pull up stakes*, *to rope in*, *to die with one's boots on*, *to get the deadwood on*, *to get the drop*, *to back and fill* (a steamboat phrase used figuratively) and *to get the bulge on*. And in many others the authentic American is no less plain, for example, in *to kick the bucket*, *to put a bug in his*

---

[17] The correct form of this appears to be *halloo* or *holloa*, but in America it is pronounced *holler* and usually represented in print by *hollo* or *hollow*. I have often encountered *holloed* in the past tense. But the Public Printer frankly accepts *holler*. *Vide* the *Congressional Record*, May 12, 1917, p. 2309. The word, in the form of *hollering*, is here credited to "Hon." John L. Burnett, of Alabama. There can be no doubt that the hon. gentleman said *hollering*, and not *holloaing*, or *halloeing*, or *hollowing*, or *hallooing*. *Hello* is apparently a variation of the same word.

ear, to see the elephant, to crack up, to do up brown, to bark up the wrong tree, to jump on with both feet, to go the whole hog, to make a kick, to buck the tiger, to let it slide and *to come out at the little end of the horn. To play possum* belongs to this list. To it Thornton adds *to knock into a cocked hat*, despite its English sound, and *to have an ax to grind. To go for*, both in the sense of belligerency and in that of partisanship, is also American, and so is *to go through* (*i. e.*, to plunder).

Of adjectives the list is scarcely less long. Among the coinages of the first half of the century that are in good use today are *non-committal, highfalutin, well-posted, down-town, played-out, flat-footed, whole-souled* and *true-blue.* The first appears in a Senate debate of 1841; *highfalutin* in a political speech of the same decade. Both are useful words; it is impossible, not employing them, to convey the ideas behind them without circumlocution. The use of *slim* in the sense of meagre, as in *slim chance, slim attendance* and *slim support*, goes back still further. The English use *small* in place of it. Other, and less respectable contributions of the time are *brash, brainy, peart, locoed, pesky, picayune, scary, well-heeled, hardshell* (*e. g.*, Baptist), *low-flung, codfish* (to indicate opprobrium) and *go-to-meeting.* The use of *plumb* as an adjective, as in *plumb crazy*, is an English archaism that was revived in the United States in the early years of the century. In the more orthodox adverbial form of *plump* it still survives, for example, in "she fell *plump* into his arms." But this last is also good English.

The characteristic American substitution of *mad* for *angry* goes back to the eighteenth century, and perhaps denotes the survival of an English provincialism. Witherspoon noticed it and denounced it in 1781, and in 1816 Pickering called it "low" and said that it was not used "except in very familiar conversation." But it got into much better odor soon afterward, and by 1840 it passed unchallenged. Its use is one of the peculiarities that Englishmen most quickly notice in American colloquial speech today. In formal written discourse it is less often encountered, probably because the English marking of it has so conspicuously singled it out. But it is constantly met with in the newspapers and in the *Congressional Record*, and it is not infrequently used by such writers as Howells and Dreiser. In the familiar simile, *as mad as a hornet*, it is used in the American sense. But *as mad as a March hare* is English, and connotes insanity, not mere anger. The English meaning of the word is preserved in *mad-house* and *mad-dog*, but I have often noticed that American rustics, employing the latter term, derive from it a vague notion, not that the dog is demented, but that it is in a simple fury. From this notion, perhaps, comes the popular belief that dogs may be thrown into hydrophobia by teasing and badgering them.

It was not, however, among the verbs and adjectives that the American word-coiners of the first half of the century achieved their gaudiest innovations, but among the substantives. Here they had temptation and excuse in plenty, for innumerable new objects and relations demanded names, and here they exercised their fancy without restraint. Setting aside loan words, which will be considered later, three main varieties of new nouns were thus produced. The first consisted of English words rescued from obsolescence or changed in meaning, the second of compounds manufactured of the common materials of the mother tongue, and the third of entirely new inventions. Of the first class, good specimens are *deck* (of cards), *gulch, gully* and *billion*, the first three old English words restored to usage in America and the last a sound English word changed in meaning. Of the second class, examples are offered by *gum-shoe, mortgage-shark, dug-out, shot-gun, stag-party, wheat-pit, horse-sense, chipped-beef, oyster-supper, buzz-saw, chain-gang* and *hell-box*. And of the third there are instances in *buncombe, greaser, conniption, bloomer, campus, galoot, maverick, roustabout, bugaboo* and *blizzard*.

Of these coinages, perhaps those of the second class are most numerous and characteristic. In them American exhibits one of its most marked tendencies: a habit of achieving short cuts in speech by a process of agglutination. Why explain laboriously, as an Englishman might, that the notes of a new bank (in a day of innumerable new banks) are insufficiently secure? Call them *wild-cat* notes and have done! Why describe a gigantic rain storm with the lame adjectives of everyday? Call it a *cloud-burst* and immediately a vivid picture of it is conjured up. *Rough-neck* is a capital word; it is more apposite and savory than the English *navvy*, and it is overwhelmingly more American.[18] *Square-meal* is another. *Fire-eater* is yet another. And the same instinct for the terse, the eloquent and the picturesque is in *boiled-shirt, blow-out, big-bug, claim-jumper, spread-eagle, come-down, back-number, claw-hammer* (coat), *bottom-dollar, poppy-cock, cold-snap, back-talk, back-taxes, calamity-howler, cut-off, fire-bug, grab-bag, grip-sack, grub-stake, pay-dirt, tender-foot, stocking-feet, ticket-scalper, store-clothes, small-potatoes, cake-walk, prairie-schooner, round-up, snake-fence, flat-boat, under-the-weather, on-the-hoof,* and *jumping-off-place.* These compounds (there must be thousands of them) have been largely responsible for giving the language its characteristic tang and color. Such specimens as *bell-hop, semi-occasional, chair-warmer* and *down-and-out* are as distinctively American as baseball or the quick-lunch.

The spirit of the language appears scarcely less clearly in some of the coinages of the other classes. There are, for example, the English words that have been extended or restricted in meaning, e. g., *docket* (for court calendar), *betterment* (for improvement to property), *collateral* (for security), *crank* (for fanatic), *jumper* (for tunic), *tickler* (for memorandum or reminder),[19] *carnival* (in such phrases as *carnival of crime*), *scrape* (for fight or difficulty),[20] *flurry* (of snow, or in the market), *suspenders, diggings* (for habitation) and *range*. Again, there are the new assemblings of English materials, e. g., *doggery, rowdy, teetotaler, goatee, tony* and *cussedness*. Yet again, there are the purely artificial words, e. g., *sockdolager, hunkydory, scalawag, guyascutis, spondulix, slumgullion, rambunctious, scrumptious,*

---

[18] *Rough-neck* is often cited, in discussions of slang, as a latter-day invention, but Thornton shows that it was used in Texas in 1836.

[19] This use goes back to 1839.

[20] Thornton gives an example dated 1812. Of late the word has lost its final *e* and shortened its vowel, becoming *scrap*.

to skedaddle, to absquatulate and *to exfluncticate.*[21]   In the use of the last-named coinages fashions change.   In the 40's *to absquatulate* was in good usage, but it has since disappeared. Most of the other inventions of the time, however, have to some extent survived, and it would be difficult to find an American of today who did not know the meaning of *scalawag* and *rambunctious* and who did not occasionally use them.   A whole series of artificial American words groups itself around the prefix *ker,* for example, *ker-flop, ker-splash, ker-thump, ker-bang, ker-plunk, ker-slam* and *ker-flummux.*   This prefix and its onomatopoeic daughters have been borrowed by the English, but Thornton and Ware agree that it is American.   Its origin has not been determined.   As Sayce says, "the native instinct of language breaks out wherever it has the chance, and coins words which can be traced back to no ancestors."

In the first chapter I mentioned the superior imaginativeness revealed by Americans in meeting linguistic emergencies, whereby, for example, in seeking names for new objects introduced by the building of railroads, they surpassed the English *plough* and *crossing-plate* with *cow-catcher* and *frog.*   That was in the 30's.   Already at that early day the two languages were so differentiated that they produced wholly distinct railroad nomenclatures.   Such commonplace American terms as *box-car, caboose, air-line* and *ticket-agent* are still quite unknown in England.   So are *freight-car, flagman, towerman, switch, switching-engine, switch-yard, switchman, track-walker, engineer, baggage-room, baggage-check, baggage-smasher, accommodation-train, baggage-master, conductor, express-car, flat-car, hand-car, way-bill, expressman, express-office, fast-freight, wrecking-crew, jerk-water, commutation-ticket, commuter, round-trip, mileage-book, ticket-scalper, depot, limited, hot-box, iron-horse, stop-over, tie, rail, fish-plate, run, train-boy, chair-car, club-car, diner, sleeper, bumpers, mail-clerk, passenger-coach, day-coach, excursionist,*

---

[21] *Cf.* Terms of Approbation and Eulogy. . . . by Elise L. Warnock, *Dialect Notes,* vol. iv, part 1, 1913.   Among the curious recent coinages cited by Miss Warnock are *scallywampus, supergobosnoptious, hyperfirmatious, scrumdifferous* and *swellellegous.*

excursion-train, railroad-man, ticket-office, truck and *right-of-way,* not to mention the verbs, *to flag, to derail, to express, to dead-head, to side-swipe, to stop-over, to fire* (*i. e.,* a locomotive), *to switch, to side-track, to railroad, to commute, to telescope* and *to clear the track.* These terms are in constant use in America; their meaning is familiar to all Americans; many of them have given the language everyday figures of speech.[22] But the majority of them would puzzle an Englishman, just as the English *luggage-van, permanent-way, goods-waggon, guard, carrier, booking-office, return-ticket, railway-rug,* R. S. O. (railway sub-office), *tripper, line, points, shunt, metals* and *bogie* would puzzle the average untravelled American.

In two other familiar fields very considerable differences between English and American are visible; in both fields they go back to the era before the Civil War. They are politics and that department of social intercourse which has to do with drinking. Many characteristic American political terms originated in revolutionary days, and have passed over into English. Of such sort are *caucus* and *mileage.* But the majority of those in common use today were coined during the extraordinarily exciting campaigns following the defeat of Adams by Jefferson. Charles Ledyard Norton has devoted a whole book to their etymology and meaning;[23] the number is far too large for a list of them to be attempted here. But a few characteristic specimens may be recalled, for example, the simple agglutinates: *omnibus-bill, banner-state, favorite-son, anxious-bench, gag-rule, office-seeker* and *straight-ticket;* the humorous metaphors: *pork-barrel, pie-counter, wire-puller, land-slide, carpet-bagger, lame-duck* and *on the fence;* the old words put to new uses: *plank, platform, machine, precinct, slate, primary, floater, repeater, bolter, stalwart, filibuster, regular* and *fences;* the new coinages: *gerrymander, heeler, buncombe, roorback, mugwump* and *to bulldoze;* the new derivatives: *abolitionist, candidacy, boss-*

[22] *E.g., single-track mind, to jump the rails, to collide head-on, broad-gauge man, to walk the ties, blind-baggage, underground-railroad, tank-town.*

[23] Political Americanisms. . . .; New York and London, 1890.

rule, per-diem, to lobby and *boodler;* and the almost innumerable verbs and verb-phrases: *to knife, to split a ticket, to go up Salt River, to bolt, to eat crow, to boodle, to divvy, to grab* and *to run.* An English candidate never *runs;* he *stands.* To *run,* according to Thornton, was already used in America in 1789; it was universal by 1820. *Platform* came in at the same time. *Machine* was first applied to a political organization by Aaron Burr. The use of *mugwump* is commonly thought to have originated in the Blaine campaign of 1884, but it really goes back to the 30's. *Anxious-bench* (or *anxious-seat*) at first designated only the place occupied by the penitent at revivals, but was used in its present political sense in Congress so early as 1842. *Banner-state* appears in *Niles' Register* for December 5, 1840. *Favorite-son* appears in an ode addressed to Washington on his visit to Portsmouth, N. H., in 1789, but it did not acquire its present ironical sense until it was applied to Martin Van Buren. Thornton has traced *bolter* to 1812, *filibuster* to 1863, *roorback* to 1844, and *split-ticket* to 1842. *Regularity* was an issue in Tammany Hall in 1822.[24] There were *primaries* in New York city in 1827, and hundreds of *repeaters* voted. In 1829 there were *lobby-agents* at Albany, and they soon became *lobbyists;* in 1832 *lobbying* had already extended to Washington. All of these terms are now as firmly imbedded in the American vocabulary as *election* or *congressman.*

In the department of conviviality the imaginativeness of Americans has been shown in both the invention and the naming of new and often highly complex beverages. So vast has been the production of novelties, in fact, that England has borrowed many of them, and their names with them. And not only England: one buys *cocktails* and *gin-fizzes* in "American bars" that stretch from Paris to Yokohama. *Cocktail, stone-fence* and *sherry-cobbler* were mentioned by Irving in 1809;[25] by Thackeray's day they were already well-known in England. Thornton traces the *sling* to 1788, and the *stinkibus* and *anti-fogmatic,*

24 Gustavus Myers: The History of Tammany Hall; 2nd ed.; New York, 1917, ch. viii.
25 Knickerbocker's History of New York; New York, 1809, p. 241.

both now extinct, to the same year. The origin of the *rickey,
fizz, sour, cooler, skin, shrub* and *smash*, and of such curious
American drinks as the *horse's neck, Mamie Taylor, Tom-and-
Jerry, Tom-Collins, John-Collins, bishop, stone-wall, gin-fix,
brandy-champarelle, golden-slipper, hari-kari, locomotive, whis-
key-daisy, blue-blazer, black-stripe, white-plush* and *brandy-
crusta* is quite unknown; the historians of alcoholism, like the
philologists, have neglected them.[26] But the essentially American character of most of them is obvious, despite the fact that
a number have gone over into English. The English, in naming their drinks, commonly display a far more limited imagination. Seeking a name, for example, for a mixture of whiskey
and soda-water, the best they could achieve was *whiskey-and-
soda.* The Americans, introduced to the same drink, at once
gave it the far more original name of *high-ball.* So with *ginger-
ale* and *ginger-pop.* So with *minerals* and *soft-drinks.* Other
characteristic Americanisms (a few of them borrowed by the
English) are *red-eye, corn-juice, eye-opener, forty-rod, squirrel-
whiskey, phlegm-cutter, moon-shine, hard-cider, apple-jack* and
corpse-reviver, and the auxiliary drinking terms, *speak-easy,
sample-room, blind-pig, barrel-house, bouncer, bung-starter, dive,
doggery, schooner, shell, stick, duck, straight, saloon, finger,
pony* and *chaser.* Thornton shows that *jag, bust, bat* and *to
crook the elbow* are also Americanisms. So are *bartender* and
saloon-keeper. To them might be added a long list of common
American synonyms for *drunk,* for example, *piffled, pifflicated,
awry-eyed, tanked, snooted, stewed, ossified, slopped, fiddled,
edged, loaded, het-up, frazzled, jugged, soused, jiggered, corned,
jagged* and *bunned.* Farmer and Henley list *corned* and *jagged*
among English synonyms, but the former is obviously an Americanism derived from *corn-whiskey* or *corn-juice,* and Thornton
says that the latter originated on this side of the Atlantic also.

[26] Extensive lists of such drinks, with their ingredients, are to be
found in the Hoffman House Bartender's Guide, by Charles Mahoney, 4th
ed.; New York, 1916; in The Up-to-date Bartenders' Guide, by Harry
Montague; Baltimore, 1913; and in Wehman Brothers' Bartenders' Guide;
New York, 1912. An early list, from the *Lancaster (Pa.) Journal* of Jan.
26, 1821, is quoted by Thornton, vol. ii, p. 985.

§ 4

Loan-Words—The Indians of the new West, it would seem, had little to add to the contributions already made to the American vocabulary by the Algonquins of the Northeast. The American people, by the beginning of the second quarter of the nineteenth century, knew almost all they were destined to know of the aborigine, and they had names for all the new objects that he had brought to their notice and for most of his peculiar implements and ceremonies. A few translated Indian terms, *e. g., squaw-man, big-chief, great-white-father* and *happy-hunting ground,* represent the meagre fresh stock that the western pioneers got from him. Of more importance was the suggestive and indirect effect of his polysynthetic dialects, and particularly of his vivid proper names, *e. g., Rain-in-the-Face, Young-Man-Afraid-of-His-Wife* and *Voice-Like-Thunder.* These names, and other word-phrases like them, made an instant appeal to American humor, and were extensively imitated in popular slang. One of the surviving coinages of that era is *Old-Stick-in-the-Mud,* which Farmer and Henley note as having reached England by 1823.

Contact with the French in Louisiana and along the Canadian border, and with the Spanish in Texas and further West, brought many more new words. From the Canadian French, as we have already seen, *prairie, batteau, portage* and *rapids* had been borrowed during colonial days; to these French contributions *bayou, picayune, levee, chute, butte, crevasse,* and *lagniappe* were now added, and probably also *shanty* and *canuck.* The use of *brave* to designate an Indian warrior, almost universal until the close of the Indian wars, was also of French origin.

From the Spanish, once the Mississippi was crossed, and particularly after the Mexican war, in 1846, there came a swarm of novelties, many of which have remained firmly imbedded in the language. Among them were numerous names of strange objects: *lariat, lasso, ranch, loco* (weed), *mustang, sombrero, canyon, desperado, poncho, chapparel, corral, broncho, plaza, peon, cayuse, burro, mesa, tornado, sierra* and *adobe*. To them, as soon as gold was discovered, were added *bonanza, eldorado, placer* and *vigilante*. *Cinch* was borrowed from the Spanish *cincha* in the early Texas days, though its figurative use did not come in until much later. *Ante*, the poker term, though the etymologists point out its obvious origin in the Latin, probably came into American from the Spanish. Thornton's first example of its use in its current sense is dated 1857, but Bartlett reported it in the form of *anti* in 1848. *Coyote* came from the Mexican dialect of Spanish; its first parent was the Aztec *coyotl*. *Tamale* had a similar origin, and so did *frijole* and *tomato*. None of these is good Spanish.[27] As usual, derivatives quickly followed the new-comers, among them *peonage, broncho-buster, ranchman* and *ranch-house,* and the verbs *to ranch, to lasso, to corral, to ante up,* and *to cinch. To vamose* (from the Spanish *vamos,* let us go), came in at the same time. So did *sabe.* So did *gazabo.*

This was also the period of the first great immigrations, and the American people now came into contact, on a large scale, with peoples of divergent race, particularly Germans, Irish Catholics from the South of Ireland (the Irish of colonial days "were descendants of Cromwell's army, and came from the North of Ireland "),[28] and, on the Pacific Coast, Chinese. So early as the 20's the immigration to the United States reached 25,000 in a year; in 1824 the Legislature of New York, in alarm, passed a restrictive act.[29] The Know-Nothing movement of the 50's need not concern us here. Suffice it to recall that the immigration of 1845 passed the 100,000 mark, and that that of 1854 came within sight of 500,000. These new Americans, most of them Germans and Irish, did not all remain in the East; a great many spread through the West and Southwest with the other pioneers. Their effect upon the language was not large,

[27] Many such words are listed in Félix Ramos y Duarte's Diccionaro de Mejicanismos, 2nd ed. Mexico City, 1898; and in Miguel de Toro y Gisbert's Americanismos; Paris, n. d.

[28] Prescott F. Hall: Immigration. . . . New York, 1913, p. 5.

[29] Most of the provisions of this act, however, were later declared unconstitutional. Several subsequent acts met the same fate.

perhaps, but it was still very palpable, and not only in the vocabulary. Of words of German origin, *saurkraut* and *noodle*, as we have seen, had come in during the colonial period, apparently through the so-called Pennsylvania Dutch, *i. e.*, a mixture, much debased, of the German dialects of Switzerland, Suabia and the Palatinate. The new immigrants now contributed *pretzel*, *pumpernickel*, *hausfrau*, *lager-beer*, *pinocle*, *wienerwurst*, *dumb* (for stupid), *frankfurter*, *bock-beer*, *schnitzel*, *leberwurst*, *blutwurst*, *rathskeller*, *schweizer* (cheese), *delicatessen*, *hamburger* (*i. e.*, steak), *kindergarten* and *katzenjammer*.[30] From them, in all probability, there also came two very familiar Americanisms, *loafer* and *bum*. The former, according to the Standard Dictionary, is derived from the German *laufen;* another authority says that it originated in a German mispronounciation of *lover*, *i. e.*, as *lofer*.[31] Thornton shows that the word was already in common use in 1835. *Bum* was originally *bummer*, and apparently derives from the German *bummler*.[32] Both words have produced derivatives: *loaf* (noun), *to loaf*, *corner-loafer*, *common-loafer*, *to bum*, *bum* (adj.) and *bummery*, not to mention *on the*

[30] The majority of these words, it will be noted, relate to eating and drinking. They mirror the profound effect of German immigration upon American drinking habits and the American cuisine. It is a curious fact that loan-words seldom represent the higher aspirations of the creditor nation. French and German have borrowed from English, not words of lofty significance, but such terms as *beefsteak*, *roast-beef*, *pudding*, *grog*, *jockey*, *tourist*, *sport*, *five-o'clock-tea*, *cocktail* and *sweepstakes*. "The contributions of England to European civilization, as tested by the English words in Continental languages," says L. P. Smith, "are not, generally, of a kind to cause much national self-congratulation." Nor would a German, I daresay, be very proud of the German contributions to American.

[31] *Vide* a paragraph in *Notes and Queries*, quoted by Thornton, vol. i, p. 248.

[32] Thornton offers examples of this form ranging from 1856 to 1885 During the Civil War the word acquired the special meaning of looter. The Southerners thus applied it to Sherman's men. *Vide* Southern Historical Society Papers, vol. xii, p. 428; Richmond, 1884. Here is a popular rhyme that survived until the early 90's:

> Isidor, psht, psht!
> Vatch de shtore, psht, psht!
> Vhile I ketch de *bummer*
> Vhat shtole de suit of clothes!

Bummel-zug is common German slang for slow train.

bum. *Loafer* has migrated in England, but *bum* is still unknown there in the American sense. In English, indeed, *bum* is used to designate an unmentionable part of the body and is thus not employed in polite discourse.

Another example of debased German is offered by the American *Kriss Kringle*. It is from *Christkindlein*, or *Christkind'l*, and properly designates, of course, not the patron saint of Christmas, but the child in the manger. A German friend tells me that the form *Kriss Kringle*, which is that given in the Standard Dictionary, and the form *Krisking'l*, which is that most commonly used in the United States, are both quite unknown in Germany. Here, obviously, we have an example of a loan-word in decay. Whole phrases have gone through the same process, for example, *nix come erous* (from *nichts kommt heraus*) and *'rous mit 'im* (from *heraus mit ihm*). These phrases, like *wie geht's* and *ganz gut*, are familiar to practically all Americans, no matter how complete their ignorance of correct German. Most of them know, too, the meaning of *gesundheit, kümmel, seidel, wanderlust, stein, speck, maennerchor, schützenfest, sängerfest, turnverein, hoch, yodel, zwieback,* and *zwei* (as in *zwei bier*). I have found *snitz* (= *schnitz*) in *Town Topics*.[33] *Prosit* is in all American dictionaries.[34] *Bower*, as used in cards, is an Americanism derived from the German *bauer*, meaning the jack. The exclamation, *ouch!* is classed as an Americanism by Thornton, and he gives an example dated 1837. The New English Dictionary refers it to the German *autsch*, and Thornton says that "it may have come across with the Dunkers or the Mennonites." *Ouch* is not heard in English, save in the sense of a clasp or buckle set with precious stones (= OF *nouche*), and even in that sense it is archaic. *Shyster* is very probably German also; Thornton has traced it back to the 50's.[35] *Rum-dumb* is grounded upon the

33 Jan. 24, 1918, p. 4.

34 Nevertheless, when I once put it into a night-letter a Western Union office refused to accept it, the rules requiring all night-letters to be in "plain English." Meanwhile, the English have borrowed it from American, and it is actually in the Oxford Dictionary.

35 The word is not in the Oxford Dictionary, but Cassell gives it and says that it is German and an Americanism. The Standard Dictionary does

meaning of *dumb* borrowed from the German; it is not listed in the English slang dictionaries.[36] Bristed says that the American meaning of *wagon*, which indicates almost any four-wheeled, horse-drawn vehicle in this country but only the very heaviest in England, was probably influenced by the German *wagen*. He also says that the American use of *hold on* for *stop* was suggested by the German *halt an*, and White says that the substitution of *standpoint* for *point of view*, long opposed by all purists, was first made by an American professor who sought "an Anglicized form" of the German *standpunkt*. The same German influence may be behind the general facility with which American forms compound nouns. In most other languages, for example, Latin and French, the process is rare, and even English lags far behind American. But in German it is almost unrestricted. "It is," says L. P. Smith, "a great step in advance toward that ideal language in which meaning is expressed, not by terminations, but by the simple method of word position."

The immigrants from the South of Ireland, during the period under review, exerted an influence upon the language that was vastly greater than that of the Germans, both directly and indirectly, but their contributions to the actual vocabulary were probably less. They gave American, indeed, relatively few new words; perhaps *shillelah*, *colleen*, *spalpeen*, *smithereens* and *poteen* exhaust the unmistakably Gaelic list. *Lallapalooza* is also probably an Irish loan-word, though it is not Gaelic. It apparently comes from *allay-foozee*, a Mayo provincialism, signifying a sturdy fellow. *Allay-foozee*, in its turn, comes from the French *Allez-fusil*, meaning "Forward the muskets!"—a memory, ac-

---

not give its etymology. Thornton's first example, dated 1856, shows a variant spelling, *shuyster*, thus indicating that it was then recent. All subsequent examples show the present spelling. It is to be noted that the suffix *-ster* is not uncommon in English, and that it usually carries a deprecatory significance, as in *trickster*, *punster*, *gamester*, etc.

[36] The use of *dumb* for stupid is widespread in the United States. *Dumbhead*, obviously from the German *dummkopf*, appears in a list of Kansas words collected by Judge J. C. Ruppenthal, of Russell, Kansas. (*Dialect Notes*, vol. iv, pt. v, 1916, p. 322.) It is also noted in Nebraska and the Western Reserve, and is very common in Pennsylvania. *Uhrgucker* (= *uhr-gucken*) is also on the Kansas list of Judge Ruppenthal.

cording to P. W. Joyce,[37] of the French landing at Killala in
1798. Such phrases as *Erin go bragh* and such expletives as
begob and *begorry* may perhaps be added: they have got into
American, though they are surely not distinctive Americanisms.
But of far more importance than these few contributions to the
vocabulary were certain speech habits that the Irish brought with
them—habits of pronunciation, of syntax and even of grammar.
These habits were, in part, the fruit of efforts to translate the
idioms of Gaelic into English, and in part borrowings from the
English of the age of James I. The latter, preserved by Irish
conservatism in speech,[38] came into contact in America with
habits surviving, with more or less change, from the same time,
and so gave those American habits an unmistakable reinforcement. The Yankees, so to speak, had lived down such Jacobean
pronunciations as *tay* for *tea* and *desave* for *deceive*, and these
forms, on Irish lips, struck them as uncouth and absurd, but they
still clung, in their common speech, to such forms as *h'ist* for
hoist, *bile* for *boil*, *chaw* for *chew*, *jine* for *join*,[39] *sass* for *sauce*,
heighth for *height* and *rench* for *rinse* and *lep* for *leap*, and the
employment of precisely the same forms by the thousands of
Irish immigrants who spread through the country undoubtedly
gave them a certain support, and so protected them, in a measure, from the assault of the purists. And the same support was
given to *drownded* for *drowned*, *oncet* for *once*, *ketch* for *catch*,
ag'in for *against* and *onery* for *ordinary*.

[37] English As We Speak It in Ireland, 2nd ed.; London and Dublin, 1910,
pp. 179–180.

[38] "Our people," says Dr. Joyce, "are very conservative in retaining old
customs and forms of speech. Many words accordingly that are discarded
as old-fashioned—or dead and gone—in England, are still flourishing—alive
and well, in Ireland. [They represent] . . . the classical English of
Shakespeare's time," pp. 6–7.

[39] Pope rhymed *join* with *mine*, *divine* and *line;* Dryden rhymed *toil*
with *smile*. William Kenrick, in 1773, seems to have been the first English lexicographer to denounce this pronunciation. *Tay* survived in England
until the second half of the eighteenth century. Then it fell into disrepute,
and certain purists, among them Lord Chesterfield, attempted to change the
ea-sound to *ee* in all words, including even *great*. *Cf.* the remarks under
boil in A Desk-Book of Twenty-Five Thousand Words Frequently Mispronounced, by Frank H. Vizetelly; New York, 1917. Also, The Standard of
Pronunciation in English, by T. S. Lounsbury; New York, 1904, pp. 98–103.

Certain usages of Gaelic, carried over into the English of Ireland, fell upon fertile soil in America. One was the employment of the definite article before nouns, as in French and German. An Irishman does not say "I am good at Latin," but "I am good at *the* Latin." In the same way an American does not say "I had measles," but "I had *the* measles." There is, again, the use of the prefix *a* before various adjectives and gerunds, as in *a-going* and *a-riding*. This usage, of course, is native to English, as *aboard* and *afoot* demonstrate, but it is much more common in the Irish dialect, on account of the influence of the parallel Gaelic form, as in *a-n-aice = a-near*, and it is also much more common in American. There is, yet again, a use of intensifying suffixes, often set down as characteristically American, which was probably borrowed from the Irish. Examples are *no-siree* and *yes-indeedy*, and the later *kiddo* and *skiddoo*. As Joyce shows, such suffixes, in Irish-English, tend to become whole phrases. The Irishman is almost incapable of saying plain yes or no; he must always add some extra and gratuitous asseveration.[40] The American is in like case. His speech bristles with intensives: *bet your life, not on your life, well I guess, and no mistake*, and so on. The Irish extravagance of speech struck a responsive chord in the American heart. The American borrowed, not only occasional words, but whole phrases, and some of them have become thoroughly naturalized. Joyce, indeed, shows the Irish origin of scores of locutions that are now often mistaken for native Americanisms, for example, *great shakes, dead* (as an intensive), *thank you kindly, to split one's sides* (*i. e.*, laughing), and *the tune the old cow died of*, not to mention many familiar similes and proverbs. Certain Irish pronunciations, Gaelic rather than archaic English, got into American during the nineteenth century. Among them, one recalls *bhoy*, which entered our political slang in the middle 40's and survived into our own time. Again, there is the very characteristic American word *ballyhoo*, signifying

[40] Amusing examples are to be found in Donlevy's Irish Catechism. To the question, "Is the Son God?" the answer is not simply "Yes," but "Yes, certainly He is." And to the question, "Will God reward the good and punish the wicked?", the answer is "Certainly; there is no doubt He will."

the harangue of a *ballyhoo-man,* or *spieler* (that is, barker) before a cheap show, or, by metaphor, any noisy speech. It is from *Ballyhooly,* the name of a village in Cork, once notorious for its brawls. Finally, there is *shebang.* Schele de Vere derives it from the French *cabane,* but it seems rather more likely that it is from the Irish *shebeen.*

The propagation of Irishisms in the United States was helped, during many years, by the enormous popularity of various dramas of Irish peasant life, particularly those of Dion Boucicault. So recently as 1910 an investigation made by the *Dramatic Mirror* showed that some of his pieces, notably "Kathleen Mavourneen," "The Colleen Bawn" and "The Shaugraun," were still among the favorites of popular audiences. Such plays, at one time, were presented by dozens of companies, and a number of Irish actors, among them Andrew Mack, Chauncey Olcott and Boucicault himself, made fortunes appearing in them. An influence also to be taken into account is that of Irish songs, once in great vogue. But such influences, like the larger matter of American borrowings from Anglo-Irish, remain to be investigated. So far as I have been able to discover, there is not a single article in print upon the subject. Here, as elsewhere, our philologists have wholly neglected a very interesting field of inquiry.

From other languages the borrowings during the period of growth were naturally less. Down to the last decades of the nineteenth century, the overwhelming majority of immigrants were either Germans or Irish; the Jews, Italians and Slavs were yet to come. But the first Chinese appeared in 1848, and soon their speech began to contribute its inevitable loan-words. These words, of course, were first adopted by the miners of the Pacific Coast, and a great many of them have remained California localisms, among them such verbs as *to yen* (to desire strongly, as a Chinaman desires opium) and *to flop-flop* (to lie down), and such nouns as *fun,* a measure of weight. But a number of others have got into the common speech of the whole country, e. g., *fan-tan, kow-tow, chop-suey, ginseng, joss, yok-a-mi* and *tong.* Contrary to the popular opinion, *dope* and *hop* are not from the Chinese.

Neither, in fact, is an Americanism, though the former has one meaning that is specially American, *i. e.*, that of information or formula, as in *racing-dope* and *to dope out*. Most etymologists derive the word from the Dutch *doop*, a sauce. In English, as in American, it signifies a thick liquid, and hence the viscous cooked opium. *Hop* is simply the common name of the *Humuluslupulus*. The belief that hops have a soporific effect is very ancient, and hop-pillows were brought to America by the first English colonists.

The derivation of *poker*, which came into American from California in the days of the gold rush, has puzzled etymologists. It is commonly derived from *primero*, the name of a somewhat similar game, popular in England in the sixteenth century, but the relation seems rather fanciful. It may possibly come, indirectly, from the Danish word *pokker*, signifying the devil. *Pokerish*, in the sense of alarming, was a common adjective in the United States before the Civil War; Thornton gives an example dated 1827. Schele de Vere says that *poker*, in the sense of a hobgoblin, was still in use in 1871, but he derives the name of the game from the French *poche* (= *pouche, pocket*). He seems to believe that the bank or pool, in the early days, was called the *poke*. Barrère and Leland, rejecting all these guesses, derive *poker* from the Yiddish *pochger*, which comes in turn from the verb *pochgen*, signifying to conceal winnings or losses. This *pochgen* is obviously related to the German *pocher* (= *boaster, braggart*). There were a good many German Jews in California in the early days, and they were ardent gamblers. If Barrère and Leland are correct, then *poker* enjoys the honor of being the first loanword taken into American from the Yiddish.

§ 5

Pronunciation—Noah Webster, as we saw in the last chapter, sneered at the broad *a*, in 1789, as an Anglomaniac affectation. In the course of the next 25 years, however, he seems to have suffered a radical change of mind, for in ''The American Spelling Book,'' published in 1817, he ordained it in *ask, last, mass, aunt, grant, glass* and their analogues, and in his 1829 revision he clung to this pronunciation, beside adding *master, pastor, amass, quaff, laugh, craft,* etc., and even *massive*. There is some difficulty, however, in determining just what sound he proposed to give the *a,* for there are several *a*-sounds that pass as broad, and the two main ones differ considerably. One appears in *all,* and may be called the *aw*-sound. The other is in *art,* and may be called the *ah*-sound. A quarter of a century later Richard Grant White distinguished between the two, and denounced the former as ''a British peculiarity.'' Frank H. Vizetelly, writing in 1917, still noted the difference, particularly in such words as *daunt, saunter* and *laundry.* It is probable that Webster, in most cases, intended to advocate the *ah*-sound, as in *father,* for this pronunciation now prevails in New England. Even there, however, the *a* often drops to a point midway between *ah* and *aa,* though never actually descending to the flat *aa,* as in *an, at* and *anatomy.*

But the imprimatur of the Yankee Johnson was not potent enough to stay the course of nature, and, save in New England, the flat *a* swept the country. He himself allowed it in *stamp* and *vase.* His successor and rival, Lyman Cobb, decided for it in *pass, draft, stamp* and *dance,* though he kept to the *ah*-sound in *laugh, path, daunt* and *saunter.* By 1850 the flat *a* was dominant everywhere West of the Berkshires and South of New Haven, and had even got into such proper names as *Lafayette* and *Nevada.*[41]

Webster failed in a number of his other attempts to influence American pronunciation. His advocacy of *deef* for *deaf* had popular support while he lived, and he dredged up authority for it out of Chaucer and Sir William Temple, but the present pronunciation gradually prevailed, though *deef* remains familiar in the common speech. Joseph E. Worcester and other rival lexicographers stood against many of his pronunciations, and he took the field against them in the prefaces to the successive editions of his spelling-books. Thus, in that to ''The Elementary Spelling

[41] Richard Meade Bache denounced it, in *Lafayette,* during the 60's. *Vide* his Vulgarisms and Other Errors of Speech, 2nd ed., Philadelphia, 1869, p. 65.

Book," dated 1829, he denounced the "affectation" of inserting a *y*-sound before the *u* in such words as *gradual* and *nature,* with its compensatory change of *d* into a French *j* and of *t* into *ch*. The English lexicographer, John Walker, had argued for this "affectation" in 1791, but Webster's prestige, while he lived, remained so high in some quarters that he carried the day, and the older professors at Yale, it is said, continued to use *natur* down to 1839.[42] He favored the pronunciation of *either* and *neither* as *ee-ther* and *nee-ther,* and so did most of the English authorities of his time. The original pronunciation of the first syllable, in England, probably made it rhyme with *bay,* but the *ee*-sound was firmly established by the end of the eighteenth century. Toward the middle of the following century, however, there arose a fashion of an *ai*-sound, and this affectation was borrowed by certain Americans. Gould, in the 50's, put the question, "Why do you say *i*-ther and *ni*-ther?" to various Americans. The reply he got was: "The words are so pronounced by the best-educated people in England." This imitation still prevails in the cities of the East. "All of us," says Lounsbury, "are privileged in these latter days frequently to witness painful struggles put forth to give to the first syllable of these words the sound of *i* by those who have been brought up to give it the sound of *e*. There is apparently an impression on the part of some that such a pronunciation establishes on a firm foundation an otherwise doubtful social standing."[43] But the vast majority of Americans continue to say *ee-ther* and not *eye-ther*. White and Vizetelly, like Lounsbury, argue that they are quite correct in so doing. The use of *eye-ther,* says White, is no more than "a copy of a second-rate British affectation."

[42] R. J. Menner: The Pronunciation of English in America, *Atlantic Monthly,* March, 1915, p. 361.
[43] The Standard of Pronunciation in English, pp. 109–112.

IV

American and English Today

§ 1

The Two Vocabularies—By way of preliminary to an examination of the American of today I offer a brief list of terms in common use that differ in American and English. Here are 200 of them, all chosen from the simplest colloquial vocabularies and without any attempt at plan or completeness:

American	English
ash-can	dust-bin
baby-carriage	pram
backyard	garden
baggage	luggage
baggage-car	luggage-van
ballast (railroad)	metals
bath-tub	bath
beet	beet-root
bid (noun)	tender
bill-board	hoarding
boarder	paying-guest
boardwalk (seaside)	promenade
bond (finance)	debenture
boot	Blucher, or Wellington
brakeman	brakesman
bucket	pail
bumper (car)	buffer
bureau	chest of drawers
calendar (court)	cause-list
campaign (political)	canvass
can (noun)	tin
candy	sweets
cane	stick
canned-goods	tinned-goods

American	English
car (railroad)	carriage, van or waggon
checkers (game)	draughts
chicken-yard	fowl-run
chief-clerk	head-clerk
city-editor	chief-reporter
city-ordinance	by-law
clipping (newspaper)	cutting
coal-oil	paraffin
coal-scuttle	coal-hod
commission-merchant	factor
conductor (of a train)	guard
corn	maize, or Indian corn
corner (of a street)	crossing
corset	stays
counterfeiter	coiner
cow-catcher	plough
cracker	biscuit
cross-tie	sleeper
delicatessen-store	Italian-warehouse
department-store	stores
Derby (hat)	bowler
dime-novel	shilling-shocker
druggist	chemist
drug-store	chemist's-shop
drummer	bagman
dry-goods-store	draper's-shop
editorial	leader, or leading-article
elevator	lift
elevator-boy	lift-man
excursionist	tripper
express-company	carrier
filing-cabinet	nest-of-drawers
fire-department	fire-brigade
fish-dealer	fishmonger
floor-walker	shop-walker
fraternal-order	friendly-society
freight	goods
freight-agent	goods-manager
freight-car	goods-waggon
frog (railway)	crossing-plate
garters (men's)	sock-suspenders
gasoline	petrol
grade (railroad)	gradient

American	English
grain	corn
grain-broker	corn-factor
grip	hold-all
groceries	stores
hardware-dealer	ironmonger
haystack	haycock
headliner	topliner
hod-carrier	hodman
hog-pen	piggery
hospital (private)	nursing-home
huckster	coster(monger)
hunting	shooting
Indian	Red Indian
Indian Summer	St. Martin's Summer
instalment-business	credit-trade
instalment-plan	hire-purchase plan
janitor	caretaker
legal-holiday	bank-holiday
letter-box	pillar-box
letter-carrier	postman
livery-stable	mews [1]
locomotive engineer	engine-driver
lumber	deals
mad	angry
Methodist	Wesleyan
molasses	treacle
monkey-wrench	spanner
moving-picture-theatre	cinema
napkin (dinner)	serviette
necktie	tie, or cravat
news-dealer	news-agent
newspaper-man	pressman, or journalist
oatmeal	porridge
officeholder	public-servant
orchestra (seats in a theatre)	stalls
overcoat	great-coat
package	parcel
parlor	drawing-room
parlor-car	saloon-carriage
patrolman (police)	constable

[1] It should be noted that *mews* is used only in the larger cities. In the small towns *livery-stable* is commoner. *Mews* is quite unknown in America save as an occasional archaism.

American	English
pay-day	wage-day
peanut	monkey-nut
pie (fruit)	tart
pitcher	jug
poorhouse	workhouse
post-paid	post-free
potpie	pie
prepaid	carriage-paid
press (printing)	machine
program (of a meeting)	agenda
proof-reader	corrector-of-the-press
public-school	board-school
quotation-marks	inverted-commas
railroad	railway
railroad-man	railway-servant
rails	line
rare (of meat)	underdone
receipts (in business)	takings
Rhine-wine	Hock
road-bed (railroad)	permanent-way
road-repairer	road-mender
roast	joint
roll-call	division
rooster	cock
round-trip-ticket	return-ticket
rutabaga	mangel-wurzel
saleswoman	shop-assistant
saloon	public-house
scarf-pin	tie-pin
scow	lighter
sewer	drain
shirtwaist	blouse
shoe	boot
shoemaker	bootmaker
shoestring	bootlace
shoe-tree	boot-form
sick	ill
sidewalk	pavement
silver (collectively)	plate
sled	sledge
sleigh	sledge
soft-drinks	minerals
spigot	tap

American	English
squash	vegetable-marrow
stem-winder	keyless-watch
stockholder	shareholder
stocks	shares
store-fixtures	shop-fittings
street-cleaner	crossing-sweeper
street-railway	tramway
subway	tube, or underground
suspenders (men's)	braces
sweater	jersey
switch (noun, railway)	points
switch (verb, railway)	shunt
taxes (municipal)	rates
taxpayer (local)	ratepayer
tenderloin (of beef)	under-cut
ten-pins	nine-pins
thumb-tack	drawing-pin
ticket-office	booking-office
tinner	tinker
tin-roof	leads
track (railroad)	line
trained-nurse	hospital-nurse
transom (of door)	fanlight
trolley-car	tramcar
truck (vehicle)	lorry
truck (of a railroad car)	bogie
trunk	box
typewriter (operator)	typist
typhoid-fever	enteric
undershirt	vest
vaudeville-theatre	music-hall
vegetables	greens
vest	waistcoat
warden (of a prison)	governor
warehouse	stores
wash-rag	face-cloth
wash-stand	wash-hand-stand
wash-wringer	mangle
waste-basket	waste-paper-basket
whipple-tree [2]	splinter-bar
witness-stand	witness-box
wood-alcohol	methylated-spirits

[2] Sometimes *whiffle-tree.*

§ 2

Differences in Usage—The differences here listed, most of them between words in everyday employment, are but examples of a divergence in usage which extends to every department of daily life. In his business, in his journeys from his home to his office, in his dealings with his family and servants, in his sports and amusements, in his politics and even in his religion the American uses, not only words and phrases, but whole syntactical constructions, that are unintelligible to the Englishman, or intelligible only after laborious consideration. A familiar anecdote offers an example in miniature. It concerns a young American woman living in a region of prolific orchards who is asked by a visiting Englishman what the residents do with so much fruit. Her reply is a pun: "We eat all we can, and what we can't we can." This answer would mystify nine Englishmen out of ten, for in the first place it involves the use of the flat American *a* in *can't* and in the second place it applies an unfamiliar name to the vessel that every Englishman knows as a *tin*, and then adds to the confusion by deriving a verb from the substantive. There are no such things as *canned-goods* in England; over there they are *tinned*. The *can* that holds them is a *tin; to can* them is *to tin* them. . . . And they are counted, not as *groceries*, but as *stores*, and advertised, not on *bill-boards* but on *hoardings*.[3] And the cook who prepares them for the table is not *Nora* or *Maggie*, but *Cook*, and if she does other work in addition she is not a *girl for general housework*, but a *cook-general*, and not *help*, but a *servant*. And the boarder who eats them is not a *boarder* at all, but a *paying-guest*, though he is said *to board*. And the grave of the tin, once it is emptied, is not the *ash-can*, but the *dust-bin*, and the man who carries it away is not the *garbage-man* or the *ash-man* or the *white-wings*, but the *dustman*.

An Englishman, entering his home, does not walk in upon the

[3] The latter has crept into American of late. I find it on p. 58 of The United States at War, a pamphlet issued by the Library of Congress, 1917. The compiler of this pamphlet is a savant bearing the fine old British name of Herman H. B. Meyer.

first floor, but upon the *ground floor.* What he calls the *first floor* (or, more commonly, *first storey,* not forgetting the penultimate *e!*) is what we call the *second floor,* and so on up to the roof—which is covered not with *tin,* but with *slate, tiles* or *leads.* He does not *take* a paper; he *takes in* a paper. He does not ask his servant, "is there any *mail* for me?" but, "are there any *letters* for me?" for *mail,* in the American sense, is a word that he seldom uses, save in such compounds as *mail-van* and *mail-train.* He always speaks of it as *the post.* The man who brings it is not a *letter-carrier,* but a *postman.* It is *posted,* not *mailed,* at a *pillar-box,* not at a *mail-box.* It never includes *postal-cards,* but only *post-cards;* never *money-orders,* but only *postal-orders.* The Englishman dictates his answers, not to a *typewriter,* but to a *typist;* a *typewriter* is merely the machine. ¶If he desires the recipient to call him by telephone he doesn't say, *"phone me* at a quarter *of* eight," but *"ring me up* at a quarter *to* eight." And when the call comes he says *"are you there?"* When he gets home, he doesn't find his wife waiting for him in the *parlor* or *living-room,*[4] but in the *drawing-room* or in her *sitting-room,* and the tale of domestic disaster that she has to tell does not concern the *hired-girl* but the *slavey* and the *scullery-maid.* He doesn't bring her a box of *candy,* but a box of *sweets.* He doesn't leave a *derby* hat in the hall, but a *bowler.* His wife doesn't wear *shirtwaists* but *blouses.* When she buys one she doesn't say *"charge it"* but *"put it down."* When she orders a *tailor-made suit,* she calls it a *coat-and-skirt.* When she wants a *spool of thread* she asks for a *reel of cotton.* Such things are bought, not in the *department-stores,* but at the *stores,* which are substantially the same thing. In these stores *calico* means a plain cotton cloth; in the United States it means a printed cotton cloth. Things bought on the instalment plan in England are said to be bought on the *hire-purchase* plan or system; the instalment business itself is the *credit-trade.* Goods ordered by *post* (not mail) on which the dealer pays the cost of transportation are said to be sent, not *postpaid* or *prepaid,* but *post-free* or *carriage-paid.*

apparently suggested, in America, by the German *wohnzimmer.*
[4] *Living-room,* however, is gradually making its way in England. It was

An Englishman does not wear *suspenders* and *neckties*, but *braces* and *cravats*. *Suspenders* are his wife's garters; his own are *sock-suspenders*. The family does not seek sustenance in a rare *tenderloin* and *squash*, but in *underdone under-cut* and *vegetable marrow*. It does not eat *beets*, but *beet-roots*. The wine on the table, if miraculously German, is not *Rhine wine*, but *Hock*. . . . The maid who laces the stays of the mistress of the house is not *Maggie* but *Robinson*. The nurse-maid is not *Lizzie* but *Nurse*. So, by the way, is a trained nurse in a hospital, whose full style is not *Miss Jones*, but *Nurse Jones*. And the hospital itself, if private, is not a hospital at all, but a *nursing-home*, and its trained nurses are plain *nurses*, or *hospital nurses*, or maybe *nursing sisters*. And the white-clad young gentlemen who make love to them are not *studying medicine* but *walking the hospitals*. Similarly, an English law student does not study law, but *the* law.

If an English boy goes to a *public school*, it is not a sign that he is getting his education free, but that his father is paying a good round sum for it and is accepted as a gentleman. A *public school* over there corresponds to our *prep school;* it is a place maintained chiefly by endowments, wherein boys of the upper classes are prepared for the universities. What we know as a *public school* is called a *board school* in England, not because the pupils are boarded but because it is managed by a school board. English school-boys are divided, not into *classes*, or *grades*, but into *forms*, which are numbered, the lowest being the *first form*. The benches they sit on are also called *forms*. The principal of an English school is a *head-master* or *head-mistress;* the lower pedagogues used to be *ushers*, but are now *assistant masters* (or *mistresses*). The head of a university is a *chancellor*. He is always some eminent public man, and a *vice-chancellor* performs his duties. The head of a mere college may be a *president, principal, rector, dean* or *provost*. At the universities the students are not divided into *freshmen, sophomores, juniors* and *seniors*, as with us, but are simply *first-year men, second-year men*, and so on. Such distinctions, however, are not as important in England as in America; members of the university (they are called *mem-*

bers, not *students*) do not flock together according to seniority. An English university man does not *study;* he *reads.* He knows nothing of *frats, class-days, senior-proms* and such things; save at Cambridge and Dublin he does not even have a *commencement.* On the other hand his daily speech is full of terms unintelligible to an American student, for example, *wrangler, tripos, head, pass-degree* and *don.*

The upkeep of board-schools in England comes out of the *rates,* which are local taxes levied upon householders. For that reason an English municipal taxpayer is called a *ratepayer.* The functionaries who collect and spend his money are not *office-holders* but *public-servants.* The head of the local police is not a *chief of police,* but a *chief constable.* The fire *department* is the fire *brigade.* The *street-cleaner* is a *crossing-sweeper.* The parish *poorhouse* is a *workhouse.* If it is maintained by two or more parishes jointly it becomes a *union.* A pauper who accepts its hospitality is said to be *on the rates.* A policeman is a *bobby* familiarly and *constable* officially. He is commonly mentioned in the newspapers, not by his surname, but as *P. C. 643a—i. e.,* Police Constable No. 643a. The *fire laddie,* the *ward executive,* the *roundsman,* the *strong-arm squad* and other such objects of American devotion are unknown in England. An English saloon-keeper is officially a licensed *victualler.* His saloon is a *public house,* or, colloquially, a *pub.* He does not sell beer by the *bucket* or *can* or *growler* or *schooner,* but by the *pint.* He and his brethren, taken together, are the *licensed trade.* His back-room is a *parlor.* If he has a few upholstered benches in his place he usually calls it a *lounge.* He employs no *bartenders* or *mixologists.* *Barmaids* do the work, with maybe a *barman* to help.

The American language, as we have seen, has begun to take in the English *boot* and *shop,* and it is showing hospitality to *head-master, haberdasher* and *week-end,* but *subaltern, civil servant, porridge, moor, draper, treacle, tram* and *mufti* are still strangers in the United States, as *bleachers, picayune, air-line, campus, chore, scoot, stogie* and *hoodoo* are in England. A *subaltern* is a commissioned officer in the army, under the rank of captain. A *civil servant* is a public servant in the national civil service; if he is of high rank, he is usually called a *permanent official. Porridge, moor, scullery, draper, treacle* and *tram,* though unfamiliar, still need no explanation. *Mufti* means ordinary male clothing; an army officer out of uniform is said to be in *mufti.* To this officer a sack-suit or business-suit is a *lounge-suit.* He carries his clothes, not in a *trunk* or *grip* or *suit-case,* but in a *box.* He does not *miss* a train; he *loses* it. He does not ask for a *round-trip* ticket, but for a *return* ticket. If he proposes to go to the theatre he does not *reserve* or *engage* seats; he *books* them, and not at the *box-office,* but at the *booking-office.* If he sits downstairs, it is not in the *orchestra,* but in the *stalls.* If he likes vaudeville, he goes to a *music-hall,* where the *head-liners* are *top-liners.* If he has to stand in line, he does it, not in a *line,* but in a *queue.*

In England a corporation is a *public company* or *limited liability company.* The term *corporation,* over there, is applied to the mayor, aldermen and sheriffs of a city, as in *the London corporation.* An Englishman writes *Ltd.* after the name of an incorporated bank or trading company as we write *Inc.* He calls its president its *chairman* or *managing director.* Its stockholders are its *shareholders,* and hold *shares* instead of *stock* in it. Its bonds are *debentures.* The place wherein such companies are floated and looted—the Wall Street of England—is called the *City,* with a capital *C.* Bankers, stock-jobbers, promoters, directors and other such leaders of its business are called *City* men. The financial editor of a newspaper is its *City* editor. Government bonds are *consols,* or *stocks,* or the *funds.*[5] To have *money in the stocks* is to own such bonds. Promissory notes are *bills.* An Englishman hasn't a *bank-account,* but a *banking-account.* He draws *cheques* (not *checks*), not on his *bank,* but on his *bankers.*[6] In England there is a rigid distinction between a *broker* and a *stock-broker.* A *broker* means, not a dealer in

[5] This form survives in the American term *city-stock,* meaning the bonds of a municipality. But government securities are always called *bonds.*

[6] *Cf.* A Glossary of Colloquial Slang and Technical Terms in Use in the Stock Exchange and in the Money Market, by A. J. Wilson, London, 1895.

securities, as in our *Wall Street broker*, but a dealer in second-hand furniture. *To have the brokers* [7] *in the house* means to be bankrupt, with one's very household goods in the hands of one's creditors.

Tariff reform, in England, does not mean a movement toward free trade, but one toward protection. The word *Government*, meaning what we call the administration, is always capitalized and plural, *e.g.*, "The Government *are* considering the advisability, etc." *Vestry, committee, council, ministry* and even *company* are also plural, though sometimes not capitalized. A member of Parliament does not *run* for office; he *stands*.[8] He does not make a *campaign*, but a *canvass*. He does not represent a *district*, but a *division* or *constituency*. He never makes a *stumping trip*, but always a *speaking tour*. When he looks after his fences he calls it *nursing the constituency*. At a political meeting (they are often rough in England) the *bouncers* are called *stewards;* the suffragettes used to delight in stabbing them with hatpins. A member of Parliament is not afflicted by the numerous bugaboos that menace an American congressman. He knows nothing of *lame ducks, pork barrels, gag-rule, junkets, gerrymanders, omnibus bills, snakes, niggers in the woodpile, Salt river, crow, bosses, ward heelers, men higher up, silk-stockings, repeaters, ballot-box stuffers* and *straight* and *split tickets* (he always calls them *ballots* or *voting papers*). He has never heard of *direct primaries*, the *recall* or the *initiative and referendum*. A *roll-call* in Parliament is a *division*. A member speaking is said to be *up* or *on his legs*. When the house adjourns it is said to *rise*. A member referring to another in the course of a debate does not say "the gentleman from Manchester," but "the *honorable* gentleman" (written *hon. gentleman*) or, if he happens to be a privy councillor, "the *right honorable* gentleman," or, if he is a member for one of the universities, "the *honorable and learned* gentleman." If the speaker chooses to be intimate or facetious, he may say "my honorable *friend*."

7 Or *bailiffs*.

8 But he is *run* by his party organization. *Cf*. The Government of England, by A. Lawrence Lowell; New York, 1910, vol. ii, p. 29.

In the United States a *pressman* is a man who runs a printing press; in England he is a newspaper reporter, or, as the English usually say, a *journalist*.[9] This journalist works, not at *space* rates, but at *lineage* rates. A printing press is a *machine*. An editorial in a newspaper is a *leading article* or *leader*. An editorial paragraph is a *leaderette*. A newspaper clipping is a *cutting*. A proof-reader is a *corrector of the press*. A pass to the theatre is an *order*. The room-clerk of a hotel is the *secretary*. A real-estate agent or dealer is an *estate-agent*. The English keep up most of the old distinctions between physicians and surgeons, barristers and solicitors. A surgeon is often plain *Mr.*, and not *Dr.* Neither he nor a doctor has an *office*, but always a *surgery* or *consulting room*. A barrister is greatly superior to a solicitor. He alone can address the higher courts and the parliamentary committees; a solicitor must keep to office work and the courts of first instance. A man with a grievance goes first to his solicitor, who then *instructs* or *briefs* a barrister for him. If that barrister, in the course of the trial, wants certain evidence removed from the record, he moves that it be *struck out*, not *stricken out*, as an American lawyer would say. Only barristers may become judges. An English barrister, like his American brother, takes a *retainer* when he is engaged. But the rest of his fee does not wait upon the termination of the case: he expects and receives a *refresher* from time to time. A barrister is never admitted to the bar, but is always *called*. If he becomes a *King's Counsel*, or *K. C.* (a purely honorary appointment), he is said to have *taken silk*.

The common objects and phenomena of nature are often differently named in English and American. As we saw in a previous chapter, such Americanisms as *creek* and *run*, for small streams, are practically unknown in England, and the English *moor* and *downs* early disappeared from American. The Englishman knows the meaning of *sound* (*e. g.*, Long Island *Sound*), but he

---

[9] Until very recently no self-respecting American newspaper reporter would call himself a *journalist*. He always used *newspaper man*, and referred to his vocation, not as a profession, but as the newspaper *business*. This old prejudice, however, now seems to be breaking down. *Cf.* Don't Shy at *Journalist, the Editor and Publisher and Journalist*, June 27, 1914.

nearly always uses *channel* in place of it. In the same way the American knows the meaning of the English *bog*, but rejects the English distinction between it and *swamp*, and almost always uses *swamp*, or *marsh* (often elided to *ma'sh*). The Englishman seldom, if ever, describes a severe storm as a *hurricane*, a *cyclone*, a *tornado* or a *blizzard*. He never uses *cold-snap*, *cloudburst* or *under the weather*. He does not say that the temperature is *29 degrees* (Fahrenheit) or that the thermometer or the mercury is at 29 degrees, but that there are *three degrees of frost*. He calls ice water *iced-water*. He knows nothing of *blue-grass* country or of *pennyr'yal*. What we call the *mining regions* he knows as the *black country*. He never, of course, uses *down-East* or *up-State*. Many of our names for common fauna and flora are unknown to him save as strange Americanisms, *e. g.*, *terrapin*, *moose*, *persimmon*, *gumbo*, *egg-plant*, *alfalfa*, *sweet-corn*, *sweet-potato* and *yam*. Until lately he called the *grapefruit* a *shaddock*. He still calls the *beet* a *beet-root* and the *rutabaga* a *mangel-wurzel*. He is familiar with many fish that we seldom see, *e. g.*, the *turbot*. He also knows the *hare*, which is seldom heard of in America. But he knows nothing of *devilled-crabs*, *crab-cocktails*, *clam-chowder* or *oyster-stews*, and he never goes to *oyster-suppers*, *clam-bakes* or *burgoo-picnics*. He doesn't buy *peanuts* when he goes to the circus. He calls them *monkey-nuts*, and to eat them publicly is *infra dig*. The common American use of *peanut* as an adjective of disparagement, as in *peanut politics*, is incomprehensible to him.

In England a *hack* is not a public coach, but a horse let out at hire, or one of similar quality. A life insurance policy is usually not an insurance policy at all, but an *assurance* policy. What we call the normal income tax is the *ordinary* tax; what we call the surtax is the *supertax*.[10] An Englishman never lives *on* a street, but always *in* it. He never lives in a *block* of houses, but in a *row;* it is never in a *section* of the city, but always in a *district*. Going home by train he always takes the *down-train*, no matter whether he be proceeding southward to Wimbleton,

<hr>

[10] *Cf.* a speech of Senator La Follette, *Congressional Record*, Aug. 27, 1917, p. 6992.

westward to Shepherd's Bush, northward to Tottenham or eastward to Noak's Hill. A train headed toward London is always an *up-train*, and the track it runs on is the *up-line*. *Eastbound* and *westbound* tracks and trains are unknown in England. When an Englishman boards a bus it is not at a *street-corner*, but at a *crossing*, though he is familiar with such forms as Hyde Park *Corner*. The place he is bound for is not three *squares* or *blocks* away, but three *turnings*. *Square*, in England, always means a small park. A backyard is a *garden*. A subway is always a *tube*, or the *underground*, or the *Metro*. But an underground passage for pedestrians is a *subway*. English streets have no *sidewalks;* they always call them *pavements* or *footways*. An automobile is always a *motor-car* or *motor*. *Auto* is almost unknown, and with it the verb *to auto*. So is *machine*. So is *joy-ride*.

An Englishman always calls russet, yellow or tan shoes *brown* shoes (or, if they cover the ankle, *boots*). He calls a pocketbook a *purse*, and gives the name of *pocketbook* to what we call a *memorandum-book*. His walking-stick is always a *stick*, never a *cane*. By *cord* he means something strong, almost what we call *twine;* a thin cord he always calls a *string;* his *twine* is the lightest sort of *string*. When he applies the adjective *homely* to a woman he means that she is simple and home-loving, not necessarily that she is plain. He uses *dessert*, not to indicate the whole last course at dinner, but to designate the fruit only; the rest is *ices* or *sweets*. He uses *vest*, not in place of *waistcoat*, but in place of *undershirt*. Similarly, he applies *pants*, not to his trousers, but to his drawers. An Englishman who inhabits bachelor quarters is said to live in *chambers;* if he has a flat he calls it a *flat*, and not an *apartment;* [11] *flat-houses* are often *mansions*. The janitor or superintendent thereof is a *care-taker*. The scoundrels who snoop around in search of divorce evidence are not *private detectives*, but *private enquiry agents*.

[11] According to the New International Encyclopedia, 2nd ed. (*Art. Apartment House*), the term *flat* "is usually in the United States restricted to apartments in houses having no elevator or hall service." In New York such apartments are commonly called *walk-up apartments*. Even with the qualification, *apartment* is better than *flat*.

The Englishman is naturally unfamiliar with baseball, and in consequence his language is bare of the countless phrases and metaphors that it has supplied to American. Many of these phrases and metaphors are in daily use among us, for example, *fan, rooter, bleachers, batting-average, double-header, pennant-winner, gate-money, busher, minor-leaguer, glass-arm, to strike out, to foul, to be shut out, to coach, to play ball, on the bench, on to his curves* and *three strikes and out*. The national game of draw-poker has also greatly enriched American with terms that are either quite unknown to the Englishman, or known to him only as somewhat dubious Americanisms, among them *cold-deck, kitty, full-house, divvy, a card up his sleeve, three-of-a-kind, to ante up, to pony up, to hold out, to cash in, to go it one better, to chip in* and *for keeps*. But the Englishman uses many more racing terms and metaphors than we do, and he has got a good many phrases from other games, particularly cricket. The word *cricket* itself has a definite figurative meaning. It indicates, in general, good sportsmanship. To take unfair advantage of an opponent is not *cricket*. The sport of boating, so popular on the Thames, has also given colloquial English some familiar terms, almost unknown in the United States, *e. g., punt* and *weir*. Contrariwise, *pungy, batteau* and *scow* are unheard of in England, and *canoe* is not long emerged from the estate of an Americanism.[12] The game known as *ten-pins* in America is called *nine-pins* in England, and once had that name over here. The Puritans forbade it, and its devotees changed its name in order to evade the prohibition.[13] Finally, there is *soccer*, a form of football quite unknown in the United States. What we call simply football is *Rugby* or *Rugger* to the Englishman. The word *soccer* is derived from *association;* the rules of the game were

[12] Canoeing was introduced into England by John MacGregor in 1866, and there is now a Royal Canoe Club. In America the canoe has been familiar from the earliest times, and in Mme. Sarah Kemble Knight's diary (1704) there is much mention of *cannoos*. The word itself is from an Indian dialect, probably the Haitian, and came into American through the Spanish, in which it survives as *canoa*.

[13] "An act was passed to prohibit playing *nine-pins;* as soon as the law was put in force, it was notified everywhere, '*Ten-pins* played here.' "— Capt. Marryat: Diary in America, vol. iii, p. 195.

established by the London Football Association. *Soccer* is one of the relatively few English experiments in ellipsis. Another is to be found in *Bakerloo*, the name of one of the London underground lines, from *Baker-street* and *Waterloo*, its termini.

The English have an ecclesiastical vocabulary with which we are almost unacquainted, and it is in daily use, for the church bulks large in public affairs over there. Such terms as *vicar, canon, verger, prebendary, primate, curate, non-conformist, dissenter, convocation, minster, chapter, crypt, living, presentation, glebe, benefice, locum tenens, suffragan, almoner, dean* and *pluralist* are to be met with in the English newspapers constantly, but on this side of the water they are seldom encountered. Nor do we hear much of *matins, lauds, lay-readers, ritualism* and the *liturgy*. The English use of *holy orders* is also strange to us. They do not say that a young man is *studying for the ministry*, but that he is *reading for holy orders*. They do not say that he is *ordained*, but that he *takes orders*. Save he be in the United Free Church of Scotland, he is never a *minister;* save he be a nonconformist, he is never a *pastor;* a clergyman of the Establishment is always either a *rector*, a *vicar* or a *curate*, and colloquially a *parson*.

In American *chapel* simply means a small church, usually the branch of some larger one; in English it has the special sense of a place of worship unconnected with the establishment. Though three-fourths of the people of Ireland are Catholics (in Munster and Connaught, more than nine-tenths), and the Protestant Church of Ireland has been disestablished since 1871, a Catholic place of worship in the country is still a *chapel* and not a *church*.[14] So is a Methodist wailing-place in England, however large it may be, though now and then *tabernacle* is substituted. In the same way the English Catholics sometimes vary *chapel* with *oratory*, as in *Brompton Oratory*. A Methodist, in Great

[14] "The term *chapel*," says Joyce, in English as We Speak It in Ireland, has so ingrained itself in my mind that to this hour the word instinctively springs to my lips when I am about to mention a Catholic place of worship; and I always feel some sort of hesitation or reluctance in substituting the word *church*. I positively could not bring myself to say, 'Come, it is time now to set out for *church*.' It must be either *mass* or chapel."

Britain, is not a *Methodist*, but a *Wesleyan*. Contrariwise, what the English call simply a *churchman* is an *Episcopalian* in the United States, what they call the *Church* (always capitalized!) is the *Protestant Episcopal* Church,[15] what they call a *Roman Catholic* is simply a *Catholic,* and what they call a *Jew* is usually softened (if he happens to be an advertiser) to a *Hebrew.* The English Jews have no such idiotic fear of the plain name as that which afflicts the more pushing and obnoxious of the race in America.[16] "News of *Jewry*" is a common head-line in the *London Daily Telegraph,* which is owned by Lord Burnham, a Jew, and has had many Jews on its staff, including Judah P. Benjamin, the American. The American language, of course, knows nothing of *dissenters.* Nor of such gladiators of dissent as the *Plymouth Brethren,* nor of the *nonconformist conscience,* though the United States suffers from it even more damnably than England. The English, to make it even, get on without *circuit-riders, holy-rollers, Dunkards, Seventh Day Adventists* and other such American *ferae naturae,* and are born, live, die and go to heaven without the aid of either the *uplift* or the *chautauqua.*

In music the English cling to an archaic and unintelligible nomenclature, long since abandoned in America. Thus they call a double whole note a *breve,* a whole note a *semibreve,* a half note a *minim,* a quarter note a *crotchet,* an eighth note a *quaver,* a sixteenth note a *semi-quaver,* a thirty-second note a *demisemiquaver,* and a sixty-fourth note a *hemidemisemiquaver,* or *semi-demisemiquaver.* If, by any chance, an English musician should write a one-hundred-and-twenty-eighth note he probably wouldn't know what to call it. This clumsy terminology goes back to the days of plain chant, with its *longa, brevis, semi-brevis, minima* and *semiminima.* The French and Italians cling to a system almost as confusing, but the Germans use *ganze, halbe, viertel,*

15 Certain dissenters, of late, show a disposition to borrow the American usage. Thus the *Christian World,* organ of the English Congregationalists, uses *Episcopal* to designate the Church of England.

16 So long ago as the 70's certain Jews petitioned the publishers of Webster's and Worcester's dictionaries to omit their definitions of the verb *to jew,* and according to Richard Grant White, the publisher of Worcester's complied. Such a request, in England, would be greeted with derision.

achtel, etc. I have been unable to discover the beginnings of the American system, but it would seem to be borrowed from the German. Since the earliest times the majority of music teachers in the United States have been Germans, and most of the rest have had German training.

In the same way the English hold fast to a clumsy and inaccurate method of designating the sizes of printers' types. In America the simple point system makes the business easy; a line of *14-point* type occupies exactly the vertical space of two lines of *7-point.* But the English still indicate differences in size by such arbitrary and confusing names as *brilliant, diamond, small pearl, pearl, ruby, ruby-nonpareil, nonpareil, minion-nonpareil, emerald, minion, brevier, bourgeois, long primer, small pica, pica, English, great primer* and *double pica.* They also cling to a fossil system of numerals in stating ages. Thus, an Englishman will say that he is *seven-and-forty,* not that he is *forty-seven.* This is probably a direct survival, preserved by more than a thousand years of English conservatism, of the Anglo-Saxon *seofan-and-feowertig.* He will also say that he weighs eleven *stone* instead of 154 pounds. A *stone* is 14 pounds, and it is always used in stating the heft of a man. Finally, he employs such designations of time as *fortnight* and *twelvemonth* a great deal more than we do, and has certain special terms of which we know nothing, for example, *quarter-day, bank holiday, long vacation, Lady Day* and *Michaelmas. Per contra,* he knows nothing whatever of our *Thanksgiving, Arbor, Labor* and *Decoration Days,* or of *legal holidays,* or of *Yom Kippur.*

In English usage, to proceed, the word *directly* is always used to signify *immediately;* in American a contingency gets into it, and it may mean no more than *soon.* In England *quite* means "completely, wholly, entirely, altogether, to the utmost extent, nothing short of, in the fullest sense, positively, absolutely"; in America it is conditional, and means only nearly, approximately, substantially, as in "he sings *quite* well." An Englishman does not say "I will pay you *up*" for an injury, but "I will pay you *back.*" He doesn't look *up* a definition in a dictionary; he looks it *out.* He doesn't say, being ill, "I am *getting* on well," but

"I am *going* on well." He doesn't use the American "different *from*" or "different *than*"; he uses "different *to*." He never adds the pronoun in such locutions as "it hurts *me*," but says simply "it hurts." He never "catches *up with you*" on the street; he "catches *you up*." He never says "are you through?" but "have you finished?" He never uses *to notify* as a transitive verb; an official act may be *notified*, but not a person. He never uses *gotten* as the perfect participle of *get;* he always uses plain *got*.[17] An English servant never washes the *dishes;* she always washes the *dinner* or *tea things*. She doesn't *live out*, but *goes into service*. She smashes, not the *mirror*, but the *looking-glass*. Her beau is not her *fellow*, but her *young man*. She does not *keep company* with him but *walks out* with him.

That an Englishman always calls out "*I say!*", and not simply "say!" when he desires to attract a friend's attention or register a protestation of incredulity—this perhaps is too familiar to need notice. His "*hear, hear!*" and "*oh, oh!*" are also well known. He is much less prodigal with *good-bye* than the American; he uses *good-day* and *good-afternoon* far more often. A shop-assistant would never say *good-bye* to a customer. To an Englishman it would have a subtly offensive smack; *good-afternoon* would be more respectful. Another word that makes him flinch is *dirt*. He never uses it, as we do, to describe the soil in the garden; he always says *earth*. Various very common American phrases are quite unknown to him, for example, *over his signature, on time* and *planted to corn*. The first-named he never uses, and he has no equivalent for it; an Englishman who issues a signed statement simply makes it *in writing*. He knows nothing of our common terms of disparagement, such as *kike, wop, yap* and *rube*. His pet-name for a tiller of the soil is not *Rube* or *Cy*, but *Hodge*. When he goes gunning he does not call it *hunting*, but *shooting; hunting* is reserved for the chase of the fox.

An intelligent Englishwoman, coming to America to live, told me that the two things which most impeded her first communications with untravelled Americans, even above the gross differ-

[17] But nevertheless he uses *begotten*, not *begot*.

ences between England and American pronunciation and intonation, were the complete absence of the general utility adjective
jolly from the American vocabulary, and the puzzling omnipres-
ence and versatility of the American verb *to fix*. In English
colloquial usage *jolly* means almost anything; it intensifies all
other adjectives, even including *miserable* and *homesick*. An
Englishman is *jolly* tired, *jolly* hungry or *jolly well* tired; his
wife is *jolly* sensible; his dog is *jolly* keen; the prices he pays for
things are *jolly dear* (never *steep* or *stiff* or *high:* all Americanisms). But he has no noun to match the American *proposition*,
meaning proposal, business, affair, case, consideration, plan,
theory, solution and what not: only the German *zug* can be
ranged beside it.[18] And he has no verb in such wide practise as
to fix. In his speech it means only to make fast or to determine.
In American it may mean to repair, as in "the plumber *fixed*
the pipe"; to dress, as in "Mary *fixed* her hair"; to prepare, as
in "the cook is *fixing* the gravy"; to bribe, as in "the judge was
fixed"; to settle, as in "the quarrel was *fixed* up"; to heal, as in
"the doctor *fixed* his boil"; to finish, as in "Murphy *fixed*
Sweeney in the third round"; to be well-to-do, as in "John is
well-*fixed*"; to arrange, as in "I *fixed* up the quarrel"; to be
drunk, as in "the whiskey *fixed* him"; to punish, as in "I'll *fix*
him"; and to correct, as in "he *fixed* my bad Latin." Moreover, it is used in all its English senses. An Englishman never
goes to a dentist to have his teeth *fixed*. He does not *fix* the
fire; he *makes it up*, or *mends* it. He is never *well-fixed*, either
in money or by liquor.[19]

The English use *quite* a great deal more than we do, and,
as we have seen, in a different sense. *Quite rich,* in American,

---

[18] This specimen is from the *Congressional Record* of Dec. 11, 1917: "I
do not like to be butting into this *proposition*, but I look upon this post-
office business as a purely business *proposition*." The speaker was "Hon"
Homer P. Snyder, of New York. In the *Record* of Jan. 12, 1918, p. 8294,
proposition is used as a synonym for state of affairs.

[19] Already in 1855 Bristed was protesting that *to fix* was having "more
than its legitimate share of work all over the Union." "In English
conversation," he said, "the panegyrical adjective of all work is *nice;*
in America it is *fine.*" This was before the adoption of *jolly* and its
analogues, *ripping, stunning, rattling,* etc.

means tolerably rich, richer than most; *quite so,* in English, is identical in meaning with *exactly so.* In American *just* is almost equivalent to the English *quite,* as in *just lovely.* Thornton shows that this use of *just* goes back to 1794. The word is also used in place of *exactly* in other ways, as in *just in time, just how many* and *just what do you mean?*

§ 3

Honorifics—Among the honorifics and euphemisms in everyday use one finds many notable divergences between the two languages. On the one hand the English are almost as diligent as the Germans in bestowing titles of honor upon their men of mark, and on the other hand they are very careful to withhold such titles from men who do not legally bear them. In America every practitioner of any branch of the healing art, even a chiropodist or an osteopath, is a doctor *ipso facto,* but in England, as we have seen, a good many surgeons lack the title and it is not common in the lesser ranks. Even graduate physicians may not have it, but here there is a yielding of the usual meticulous exactness, and it is customary to address a physician in the second person as *Doctor,* though his card may show that he is only *Medicinae Baccalaureus,* a degree quite unknown in America. Thus an Englishman, when he is ill, always sends for the *doctor,* as we do. But a surgeon is usually plain *Mr.*[20] An English veterinarian or dentist or druggist or masseur is never *Dr.*

Nor *Professor.* In all save a few large cities of America every male pedagogue is a professor, and so is every band leader, dancing master and medical consultant. But in England the title is very rigidly restricted to men who hold chairs in the universities, a necessarily small body. Even here a superior title

---

[20] In the Appendix to the Final Report of the Royal Commission on Venereal Diseases, London, 1916, p. iv., I find the following: "*Mr.* C. J. Symonds, F.R.C.S., M.D.; *Mr.* F. J. McCann, F.R.C.S., M.D.; *Mr.* A. F. Evans, F.R.C.S. *Mr.* Symonds is consulting surgeon to Guy's Hospital, *Mr.* McCann is an eminent London gynecologist, and *Mr.* Evans is a general surgeon in large practise. All would be called *Doctor* in the United States.

always takes precedence. Thus, it used to be *Professor* Almroth Wright, but now it is always *Sir* Almroth Wright. Huxley was always called *Professor* Huxley until he was appointed to the Privy Council. This appointment gave him the right to have *Right Honourable* put before his name, and thereafter it was customary to call him simply *Mr.* Huxley, with the *Right Honourable,* so to speak, floating in the air. The combination, to an Englishman, was more flattering than *Professor,* for the English always esteem political dignities far more than the dignities of learning. This explains, perhaps, why their universities distribute so few honorary degrees. In the United States every respectable Protestant clergyman is a D.D., and it is almost impossible for a man to get into the papers without becoming an LL.D.,[21] but in England such honors are granted only grudgingly. So with military titles. To promote a war veteran from sergeant to colonel by acclamation, as is often done in the United States, is unknown over there. The English have nothing equivalent to the gaudy tin soldiers of our governors' staffs, nor to the bespangled colonels and generals of the Knights Templar and Patriarchs Militant, nor to the nondescript captains and majors of our country towns. An English railroad conductor (*railway guard*) is never *Captain,* as he always is in the United States. Nor are military titles used by the police. Nor is it the custom to make every newspaper editor a colonel, as is done south of the Potomac. Nor is an attorney-general or postmaster-general called *General.* Nor are the glories of public office, after they have officially come to an end, embalmed in such clumsy quasi-titles as *ex-United States Senator, ex-Judge of the Circuit Court of Appeals, ex-Federal Trade Commissioner* and *former Chief of the Fire Department.*

But perhaps the greatest difference between English and American usage is presented by *the Honorable.* In the United States the title is applied loosely to all public officials of apparent respectability, from senators and ambassadors to the mayors of

---

[21] Among the curious recipients of this degree have been Gumshoe Bill Stone, Uncle Joe Cannon and Josephus Daniels. Billy Sunday, the evangelist, is a D.D.

fifth-rate cities and the members of state legislatures, and with some show of official sanction to many of them, especially congressmen. But it is questionable whether this application has any actual legal standing, save perhaps in the case of certain judges. Even the President of the United States, by law, is not *the Honorable*, but simply *the President*. In the First Congress the matter of his title was exhaustively debated; some members wanted to call him *the Honorable* and others proposed *His Excellency* and even *His Highness*. But the two Houses finally decided that it was "not proper to annex any style or title other than that expressed by the Constitution." Congressmen themselves are not *Honorables*. True enough, the *Congressional Record*, in printing a set speech, calls it "Speech of *Hon.* John Jones" (without the *the* before the *Hon.*—a characteristic Americanism), but in reporting the ordinary remarks of a member it always calls him plain *Mr.* Nevertheless, a country congressman would be offended if his partisans, in announcing his appearance on the stump, did not prefix *Hon.* to his name. So would a state senator. So would a mayor or governor. I have seen the sergeant-at-arms of the United States Senate referred to as *Hon.* in the records of that body.[22] More, the prefix is actually usurped by the Superintendent of State Prisons of New York.[23]

In England the thing is more carefully ordered, and bogus *Hons.* are unknown. The prefix is applied to both sexes and belongs by law, *inter alia*, to all present or past maids of honor, to all justices of the High Court during their terms of office, to the Scotch Lords of Session, to the sons and daughters of viscounts and barons, to the younger sons and (all daughters) of earls, and to the members of the legislative and executive councils of the colonies. But *not* to members of Parliament, though each is, in debate, an *hon. gentleman*. Even a member of the cabinet is not an *Hon.*, though he is a *Right Hon.* by virtue of membership in the Privy Council, of which the Cabinet is legally merely a committee. This last honorific belongs, not only to

[22] *Congressional Record*, May 16, 1918, p. 7147.
[23] *Vide* his annual reports, printed at Sing Sing Prison.

privy councillors, but also to all peers lower than marquesses (those above are *Most Hon.*), to Lord Mayors during their terms of office, to the Lord Advocate and to the Lord Provosts of Edinburgh and Glasgow. Moreover, a peeress whose husband is a *Right Hon.* is a *Right Hon.* herself.

The British colonies follow the jealous usage of the mother-country. Even in Canada the lawless American example is not imitated. I have before me a ''Table of Titles to be Used in Canada,'' laid down by royal warrant, which lists those who are *Hons.* and those who are not *Hons.* in the utmost detail. Only privy councillors of Canada (not to be confused with imperial privy councillors) are permitted to retain the prefix after going out of office, though ancients who were legislative councillors at the time of the union, July 1, 1867, may still use it by a sort of courtesy, and former speakers of the Dominion Senate and House of Commons and various retired judges may do so on application to the King, countersigned by the governor-general. The following are lawfully *the Hon.*, but only during their tenure of office: the solicitor-general, the speaker of the House of Commons, the presidents and speakers of the provincial legislatures, members of the executive councils of the provinces, the chief justice, the judges of the Supreme and Exchequer Courts, the judges of the Supreme Courts of Ontario, Nova Scotia, New Brunswick, British Columbia, Prince Edward Island, Saskatchewan and Alberta, the judges of the Courts of Appeal of Manitoba and British Columbia, the Chancery Court of Prince Edward Island, and the Circuit Court of Montreal—these, and no more. A lieutenant-governor of a province is not *the Hon.*, but *His Honor*. The governor-general is *His Excellency*, and so is his wife, but in practise they usually have superior honorifics, and do not forget to demand their use.

But though an Englishman, and, following him, a colonial, is thus very careful to restrict *the Hon.* to proper uses, he always insists, when he serves without pay as an officer of any organization, to indicate his volunteer character by writing *Hon.* before the name of his office. If he leaves it off it is a sign that he is a hireling. Thus, the agent of the New Zealand government in London, a paid officer, is simply the *agent*, but the agents at Brisbane and Adelaide, in Australia, who serve for the glory of it, are *hon. agents.* In writing to a Briton one must be careful to put *Esq.*, behind his name, and not *Mr.*, before it. The English make a clear distinction between the two forms. *Mr.*, on an envelope, indicates that the sender holds the receiver to be his inferior; one writes to *Mr.* John Jackson, one's greengrocer, but to James Thompson, *Esq.*, one's neighbor. Any man who is entitled to the *Esq.* is a *gentleman*, by which an Englishman means a man of sound connections and dignified occupation—in brief, of ponderable social position. Thus a dentist, a shop-keeper or a clerk can never be a gentleman in England, even by courtesy, and the qualifications of an author, a musical conductor, a physician, or even a member of Parliament have to be established. But though he is thus enormously watchful of masculine dignity, an Englishman is quite careless in the use of *lady.* He speaks glibly of *lady-clerks, lady-typists, lady-doctors* and *lady-inspectors.* In America there is a strong disposition to use the word less and less, as is revealed by the substitution of *saleswoman* and *salesgirl* for the *saleslady* of yesteryear. But in England *lady* is still invariably used instead of woman in such compounds as *lady-golfer, lady-secretary* and *lady-champion.* The *women's singles*, in England tennis, are always *ladies' singles; women's wear*, in English shops, is always *ladies' wear.* Perhaps the cause of this distinction between *lady* and *gentleman* has been explained by Price Collier in "England and the English." In England, according to Collier, the male is always first. His comfort goes before his wife's comfort, and maybe his dignity also. *Gentleman-clerk* or *gentleman-author* would make an Englishman howl, though he uses *gentleman-rider.* So would the growing American custom of designating the successive heirs of a private family by the numerals proper to royalty. John Smith *3rd* and William Simpson *IV* are gravely received at Harvard; at Oxford they would be ragged unmercifully.

An Englishman, in speaking or writing of public officials, avoids those long and clumsy combinations of title and name which figure so copiously in American newspapers. Such locutions as *Assistant Secretary of the Interior* Jones, *Fourth Assistant Postmaster-General* Brown, *Inspector of Boilers* Smith, *Judge of the Appeal Tax Court* Robinson, *Chief Clerk of the Treasury* Williams and *Collaborating Epidermologist* White [24] are quite unknown to him. When he mentions a high official, such as the Secretary for Foreign Affairs, he does not think it necessary to add the man's name; he simply says "the Secretary for Foreign Affairs" or "the Foreign Secretary." And so with the Lord Chancellor, the Chief Justice, the Prime Minister, the Bishop of Carlisle, the Chief Rabbi, the First Lord (of the Admiralty), the Master of Pembroke (College), the Italian Ambassador, and so on. Certain ecclesiastical titles are sometimes coupled to surnames in the American manner, as in *Dean Stanley*, and *Canon Wilberforce*, but *Prime Minister Lloyd-George* would seem heavy and absurd. But in other directions the Englishman has certain clumsinesses of his own. Thus, in writing a letter to a relative stranger, he sometimes begins it, not *My dear Mr. Jones* but *My dear John Joseph Jones*. He may even use such a form as *My dear Secretary for War* in place of the American *My dear Mr. Secretary*. In English usage, incidentally, *My dear* is more formal than simply *Dear*. In America, of course, this distinction is lost, and such forms as *My dear John Joseph Jones* appear only as conscious imitations of English usage.

I have spoken of the American custom of dropping the definite article before *Hon.* It extends to *Rev.* and the like, and has the authority of very respectable usage behind it. The opening sentence of the *Congressional Record* is always: "The Chaplain, *Rev.* ―― ――, D.D., offered the following prayer." When chaplains for the army or navy are confirmed by the Senate they always appear in the *Record* as *Revs.*, never as *the Revs.* I also find the honorific without the article in the New International Encyclopaedia, in the *World* Almanac, and in a widely-

---

[24] I encountered this gem in *Public Health Reports*, a government publication, for April 26, 1918, p. 610.

popular American grammar-book.[25]   So long ago as 1867, Gould protested against this elision as barbarous and idiotic, and drew up the following *reductio ad absurdum:*

At last annual meeting of Black Book Society, honorable John Smith took the chair, assisted by reverend John Brown and venerable John White. The office of secretary would have been filled by late John Green, but for his decease, which rendered him ineligible. His place was supplied by inevitable John Black. In the course of the evening eulogiums were pronounced on distinguished John Gray and notorious Joseph Brown. Marked compliment was also paid to able historian Joseph White, discriminating philosopher Joseph Green, and learned professor Joseph Black. But conspicuous speech of the evening was witty Joseph Gray's apostrophe to eminent astronomer Jacob Brown, subtle logician Jacob White, etc., etc.[26]

Richard Grant White, a year or two later, joined the attack in the New York *Galaxy,* and William Cullen Bryant included the omission of the article in his *Index Expurgatorius,* but these anathemas were as ineffective as Gould's irony. The more careful American journals, of course, incline to the *the,* and I note that it is specifically ordained on the Style-sheet of the *Century Magazine,* but the overwhelming majority of American newspapers get along without it, and I have often noticed its omission on the sign-boards at church entrances.[27]   In England it is never omitted.

---

[25] For the *Record* see the issue of Dec. 14, 1917, p. 309. For the New International Encyclopaedia see the article on Brotherhood of Andrew and Philip. For the *World* Almanac see the article on Young People's Society of Christian Endeavor, ed. of 1914. The grammar-book is Longman's Briefer Grammar; New York, 1908, p. 160. The editor is George J. Smith, a member of the board of examiners of the New York City Department of Education.

[26] Edwin S. Gould: Good English; New York, 1867, pp. 56–57.

[27] Despite the example of Congress, however, the Department of State inserts the *the. Vide* the *Congressional Record,* May 4, 1918, p. 6552. But the War Department, the Treasury and the Post Office omit it. *Vide* the *Congressional Record,* May 11, 1918, p. 6895 and p. 6914 and May 14, p. 7004, respectively. So, it appears, does the White House. *Vide* the *Congressional Record,* May 10, 1918, p. 6838, and June 12, 1918, p. 8293.

§ 4

Euphemisms and Forbidden Words—But such euphemisms as *lady-clerk* are, after all, much rarer in English than in American usage. The Englishman seldom tries to gloss menial occupations with sonorous names; on the contrary, he seems to delight in keeping their menial character plain. He says *servants*, not *help*. Even his railways and banks have *servants;* the chief trades-union of the English railroad men is the Amalgamated Society of Railway *Servants*. He uses *employé* in place of *clerk, workman* or *laborer* much less often than we do. True enough he calls a boarder a *paying-guest*, but that is probably because even a boarder may be a gentleman. Just as he avoids calling a fast train the *limited*, the *flier* or the *cannon-ball*, so he never calls an *undertaker* a *funeral director* or *mortician*,[28] or a *dentist* a *dental surgeon* or *ontologist*, or an *optician* an *optometrist*, or a *barber shop* (he always makes it *barber's shop*) a *tonsorial parlor*, or a common public-house a *café*, a *restaurant*, an *exchange*, a *buffet* or a *hotel*, or a tradesman a *storekeeper* or *merchant*, or a fresh-water college a *university*. A *university*, in England, always means a collection of colleges.[29] He avoids displacing terms of a disparaging or disagreeable significance with others less brutal, or thought to be less brutal, *e. g.*, *ready-to-wear* or *ready-tailored* for *ready-made, used* or *slightly-used* for *second-hand, mahoganized* for *imitation-mahogany, aisle manager* for *floor-walker* (he makes it *shop-walker*), *loan-office* for *pawn-shop*. Also, he is careful not to use such words as *rector, deacon* and *baccalaureate* in merely rhetorical senses.[30]

[28] In the 60's an undertaker was often called an *embalming surgeon* in America.

[29] In a list of American "universites" I find the Christian of Canton, Mo., with 125 students; the Lincoln, of Pennsylvania, with 184; the Southwestern Presbyterian, of Clarksville, Tenn., with 86; and the Newton Theological, with 77. Most of these, of course, are merely country high-schools.

[30] The Rev. John C. Stephenson in the *New York Sun*, July 10, 1914: . . . "that empty courtesy of addressing every clergyman as *Doctor*. . . . And let us abolish the abuse of . . . *baccalaureate* sermons for sermons before graduating classes of high schools and the like."

When we come to words, that, either intrinsically or by usage, are improper, a great many curious differences between English and American reveal themselves. The Englishman, on the whole, is more plain-spoken than the American, and such terms as *bitch, mare* and *in foal* do not commonly daunt him, largely, perhaps, because of his greater familiarity with country life; but he has a formidable index of his own, and it includes such essentially harmless words as *sick, stomach, bum* and *bug*. The English use of *ill* for *sick* I have already noticed, and the reasons for the English avoidance of *bum*. *Sick*, over there, means nauseated, and when an Englishman says that he was *sick* he means that he vomited, or, as an American would say, was *sick at the stomach*. The older (and still American) usage, however, survives in various compounds. *Sick-list*, for example, is official in the Navy,[31] and *sick-leave* is known in the Army, though it is more common to say of a soldier that he is *invalided home*. *Sick-room* and *sick-bed* are also in common use, and *sick-flag* is used in place of the American *quarantine-flag*. But an Englishman hesitates to mention his stomach in the presence of ladies, though he discourses freely about his liver. To avoid the necessity he employs such euphemisms as *Little Mary*. As for *bug*, he restricts its use very rigidly to the *Cimex lectularius*, or common bed-bug, and hence the word has a highly impolite connotation. All other crawling things he calls *insects*. An American of my acquaintance once greatly offended an English friend by using *bug* for *insect*. The two were playing billiards one summer evening in the Englishman's house, and various flying things came through the window and alighted on the cloth. The American, essaying a shot, remarked that he had killed a *bug* with his cue. To the Englishman this seemed a slanderous reflection upon the cleanliness of his house.[32]

[31] *Cf.* Dardanelles Commission Report; London, 1916, p. 58, § 47.
[32] Edgar Allan Poe's "The Gold *Bug*" is called "The Golden *Beetle*" in England. Twenty-five years ago an Enlishman named *Buggey*, laboring under the odium attached to the name, had it changed to *Norfolk-Howard*, a compound made up of the title and family name of the Duke of Norfolk. The wits of London at once doubled his misery by adopting *Norfolk-Howard* as a euphemism for *bed-bug*.

The Victorian era saw a great growth of absurd euphemisms in England, including *second wing* for the leg of a fowl, but it was in America that the thing was carried farthest. Bartlett hints that *rooster* came into use in place of *cock* as a matter of delicacy, the latter word having acquired an indecent significance, and tells us that, at one time, even *bull* was banned as too vulgar for refined ears. In place of it the early purists used *cow-creature, male-cow* and even *gentleman-cow*.[33] *Bitch, ram, buck* and *sow* went the same way, and there was a day when even *mare* was prohibited. Bache tells us that *pismire* was also banned, *antmire* being substituted for it. In 1847 the word *chair* was actually barred out and *seat* was adopted in its place.[34] These were the palmy days of euphemism. The delicate *female* was guarded from all knowledge, and even from all suspicion, of evil. "To utter aloud in her presence the word *shirt*," says one historian, "was an open insult."[35] Mrs. Trollope, writing in 1832, tells of "a young German gentleman of perfectly good manners" who "offended one of the principal families . . . by having pronounced the word *corset* before the ladies of it."[36] The word *woman*, in those sensitive days, became a term of reproach, comparable to the German *mensch;* the uncouth *female* took its place.[37] In the same way the legs of the fair became *limbs* and their breasts *bosoms*, and *lady* was substituted for *wife*. *Stomach*, under the ban in England, was transformed, by some unfathomable magic, into a euphemism denoting the whole region from the nipples to the pelvic arch. It was during

[33] A recent example of the use of *male-cow* was quoted in the *Journal* of the American Medical Association, Nov. 17, 1917, advertising page 24.

[34] *New York Organ* (a *"family journal* devoted to temperance, morality, education and general literature"), May 29, 1847. One of the editors of this delicate journal was T. S. Arthur, author of Ten Nights in a Bar-room.

[35] John Graham Brooks: As Others See Us; New York, 1908, p. 11.

[36] Domestic Manners of the Americans, 2 vols.; London, 1832; vol. i, p. 132.

[37] *Female*, of course, was epidemic in England too, but White says that it was "not a Briticism," and so early as 1839 the Legislature of Maryland expunged it from the title of a bill "to protect the reputation of unmarried *females*," substituting *women*, on the ground that *female* "was an Americanism in that application."

this time that the newspapers invented such locutions as *interesting* (or *delicate*) *condition, criminal operation, house of ill* (or *questionable*) *repute, disorderly-house, sporting-house, statutory offense, fallen woman* and *criminal assault*. Servant girls ceased to be seduced, and began to be *betrayed*. Various French terms, *enceinte* and *accouchement* among them, were imported to conceal the fact that lawful wives occasionally became pregnant and had lyings-in.

White, between 1867 and 1870, launched various attacks upon these ludicrous gossamers of speech, and particularly upon *enceinte, limb* and *female*, but only *female* succumbed. The passage of the notorious Comstock Postal Act, in 1873, greatly stimulated the search for euphemisms. Once that act was upon the statute-books and Comstock himself was given the amazingly inquisitorial powers of a post-office inspector, it became positively dangerous to print certain ancient and essentially decent English words. To this day the effects of that old reign of terror are still visible. We yet use *toilet* and *public comfort station* in place of better terms,[38] and such idiotic forms as *red-light district, disorderly-house, blood-poison, social-evil, social disease* and *white slave* ostensibly conceal what every flapper is talking about. The word *cadet*, having a foreign smack and an innocent native meaning, is preferred to the more accurate *procurer;* even prostitutes shrink from the forthright *pimp*, and employ a characteristic American abbreviation, *P. I.*—a curious brother to *S. O. B.* and *2 o'clock*. Nevertheless, a movement toward honesty is getting on its legs. The vice crusaders, if they have accomplished nothing else, have at least forced the newspapers to use the honest terms, *syphilis, prostitute, brothel* and *venereal disease*, albeit somewhat gingerly. It is, perhaps, significant of the change going on that the *New York Evening Post*

---

[38] The French *pissoir*, for instance, is still regarded as indecent in America, and is seldom used in England, but it has gone into most of the Continental languages. It is curious to note, however, that these languages also have their pruderies. Most of them, for example, use *W. C.*, an abbreviation of the English *water-closet*, as a euphemism. The whole subject of national pruderies, in both act and speech, remains to be investigated.

recently authorized its reporters to use *street-walker*.[39]   But in certain quarters the change is viewed with alarm, and curious traces of the old prudery still survive.   The Department of Health of New York City, in April, 1914, announced that its efforts to diminish venereal disease were much handicapped because "in most newspaper offices the words *syphilis* and *gonorrhea* are still tabooed, and without the use of these terms it is almost impossible to correctly state the problem."   The Army Medical Corps, in the early part of 1918, encountered the same difficulty: most newspapers refused to print its bulletins regarding venereal disease in the army.   One of the newspaper trade journals thereupon sought the opinions of editors upon the subject, and all of them save one declared against the use of the two words.   One editor put the blame upon the Post-office, which still cherishes the Comstock tradition.   Another reported that "at a recent conference of the Scripps Northwest League editors" it was decided that "the use of such terms as *gonorrhea, syphilis,* and even *venereal diseases* would not add to the tone of the papers, and that the term *vice diseases* can be readily substituted."[40]   The Scripps papers are otherwise anything but distinguished for their "tone," but in this department they yield to the Puritan habit.   An even more curious instance of prudery came to my notice in Philadelphia several years ago. A one-act play of mine, "The Artist," was presented at the Little Theatre there, and during its run, on February 26, 1916, the *Public Ledger* reprinted some of the dialogue.   One of the characters in the piece is *A Virgin*.   At every occurrence a change was made to *A Young Girl*.   Apparently, even *virgin* is still regarded as too frank in Philadelphia.[41]   Fifty years

[39] Even the *Springfield Republican*, the last stronghold of Puritan *Kultur*, printed the word on Oct. 11, 1917, in a review of New Adventures, by Michael Monahan.

[40] *Pep*, July, 1918, p. 8.

[41] Perhaps the Quaker influence is to blame.   At all events, Philadelphia is the most pecksniffian of American cities, and thus probably leads the world.   Early in 1918, when a patriotic moving-picture entitled "To Hell with the Kaiser" was sent on tour under government patronage, the word *hell* was carefully toned down, on the Philadelphia billboards, to *h——*.

ago the very word *decent* was indecent in the South: no respectable woman was supposed to have any notion of the difference between *decent* and *indecent*.

In their vocabularies of opprobrium and profanity English and Americans diverge sharply. The English *rotter* and *blighter* are practically unknown in America, and there are various American equivalents that are never heard in England. A *guy*, in the American vulgate, simply signifies a man; there is not necessarily any disparaging significance. But in English, high or low, it means one who is making a spectacle of himself. The derivative verb, *to guy*, is unknown in English; its nearest equivalent is *to spoof*, which is unknown in American. The average American, I believe, has a larger vocabulary of profanity than the average Englishman, and swears a good deal more, but he attempts an amelioration of many of his oaths by softening them to forms with no apparent meaning. *Darn* (= *dern* = *durn*) for *damn* is apparently of English origin, but it is heard ten thousand times in America to once in England. So is *dog-gone*. Such euphemistic written forms as *damphool* and *damfino* are also far more common in this country. *All-fired* for *hell-fired*, *gee-whiz* for *Jesus*, *tarnal* for *eternal*, *tarnation* for *damnation*, *cuss* for *curse*, *goldarned* for *Goddamned*, *by gosh* for *by God* and *great Scott* for *great God* are all Americanisms; Thornton has traced *all-fired* to 1835, *tarnation* to 1801 and *tarnal* to 1790. *By golly* has been found in English literature so early as 1843, but it probably originated in America; down to the Civil War it was the characteristic oath of the negro slaves. Such terms as *bonehead*, *pinhead* and *boob* have been invented, perhaps, to take the place of the English *ass*, which has a flavor of impropriety in America on account of its identity in sound with the American pronunciation of *arse*.[42] At an earlier day *ass* was always differentiated by making it *jackass*. Another word that is improper in America but not in England is *tart*. To an Englishman the word connotes sweetness, and so, if he be of the lower orders, he may apply

[42] *Cf.* R. M. Bache: Vulgarisms and Other Errors of Speech; Phila., 1869, p. 34 *et seq.*

it to his sweetheart. But to the American it signifies a prostitute, or, at all events, a woman of too ready an amiability.

But the most curious disparity between the profane vocabulary of the two tongues is presented by *bloody*. This word is
entirely without improper significance in America, but in England it is regarded as the vilest of indecencies. The sensation
produced in London when George Bernard Shaw put it into the
mouth of a woman character in his play, "Pygmalion," will
be remembered. "The interest in the first English performance," said the *New York Times*,[43] "centered in the heroine's
utterance of this banned word. It was waited for with trembling, heard shudderingly, and presumably, when the shock
subsided, interest dwindled." But in New York, of course, it
failed to cause any stir. Just why it is regarded as profane
and indecent by the English is one of the mysteries of the language. The theory that it has some blasphemous reference to
the blood of Christ is disputed by many etymologists. It came
in during the latter half of the seventeenth century, and at the
start it apparently meant no more than "in the manner of a
blood," *i. e.,* a rich young roisterer of the time. Thus, *bloody
drunk* was synonymous with *as drunk as a lord*. The adjective
remained innocuous for 200 years. Then it suddenly acquired its
present abhorrent significance. It is regarded with such aversion by the English that even the lower orders often substitute
bleeding as a euphemism.

So far no work devoted wholly to the improper terms of English and American has been published, but this lack may be soon
remedied by a compilation made by a Chicago journalist. It is
entitled "The Slang of Venery and Its Analogues," and runs
to two large volumes. A small edition, mimeographed for private circulation, was issued in 1916. I have examined this work
and found it of great value. If the influence of comstockery is
sufficient to prevent its publication in the United States, as seems
likely, it will be printed in Switzerland.

[43] April 14, 1914.

V

Tendencies in American

§ 1

International Exchanges—More than once, during the preceding chapters, we encountered Americanisms that had gone over into English, and English locutions that had begun to get a foothold in the United States. Such exchanges are made very frequently and often very quickly, and though the guardians of English still attack every new Americanism vigorously, even when, as in the case of *scientist*, it is obviously sound and useful, they are often routed by public pressure, and have to submit in the end with the best grace possible. For example, consider *caucus*. It originated in Boston at some indeterminate time before 1750, and remained so peculiarly American for more than a century following that most of the English visitors before the Civil War remarked its use. But, according to J. Redding Ware,[1] it began to creep into English political slang about 1870, and in the 80's it was lifted to good usage by the late Joseph Chamberlain. Ware, writing in the first years of the present century, said that the word had become "very important" in England, but was "not admitted into dictionaries." But in the Concise Oxford Dictionary, dated 1914, it is given as a sound English word, though its American origin is noted. The English, however, use it in a sense that has become archaic in America, thus preserving an abandoned American meaning in the same way that many abandoned British meanings have been preserved on this side. In the United States the word means, and has meant for years, a meeting of some division,

<hr>

[1] In Passing English of the Victorian Era; London, n. d., p. 68.

large or small, of a political or legislative body for the purpose
of agreeing upon a united course of action in the main assembly.
In England it means the managing committee of a party or frac-
tion—something corresponding to our national committee, or
state central committee, or steering committee, or to the half-
forgotten congressional caucuses of the 20's. It has a disparaging significance over there, almost equal to that of our words
organization and *machine*. Moreover, it has given birth to two
derivatives of like quality, both unknown in America—*caucus-
dom*, meaning machine control, and *caucuser*, meaning a machine
politician.[2]

A good many other such Americanisms have got into good
usage in England, and new ones are being exported constantly.
Farmer describes the process of their introduction and assimilation. American books, newspapers and magazines, especially
the last, circulate in England in large number, and some of their
characteristic locutions pass into colloquial speech. Then they
get into print, and begin to take on respectability. "The phrase,
'as the Americans say,'" he continues, "might in some cases
be ordered from the type foundry as a logotype, so frequently
does it do introduction duty."[3] Ware shows another means of
ingress: the argot of sailors. Many of the Americanisms he
notes as having become naturalized in England, *e. g., boodle,
boost* and *walk-out*, are credited to Liverpool as a sort of half-
way station. Travel brings in still more: England swarms
with Americans, and Englishmen themselves, visiting America,
bring home new and racy phrases. Bishop Coxe says[4] that

---

[2] The Oxford Dictionary, following the late J. H. Trumbull, the well-
known authority on Indian languages, derives the word from the Algonquin
cau-cau-as-u, one who advises. But most other authorities, following
Pickering, derive it from *caulkers*. The first caucuses, it would appear,
were held in a caulkers' shop in Boston, and were called *caulkers' meetings*.
The Rev. William Gordon, in his History of the Rise and Independence of
the United States, Including the Late War, published in London in 1788,
said that "more than fifty years ago Mr. Samuel Adams' father and twenty
others, one or two from the north end of the town [Boston], where the
ship business is carried on, used to meet, make a *caucus*, and lay their
plans for introducing certain persons into places of trust and power."

[3] Americanisms Old and New; p. vii.

[4] A. Cleveland Coxe: Americanisms in England, *Forum*, Oct. 1886.

Dickens, in his "American Notes," gave English currency to *reliable, influential, talented* and *lengthy.* Bristed, writing in 1855, said that *talented* was already firmly fixed in the English vocabulary by that time. All four words are in the Concise Oxford Dictionary, and only *lengthy* is noted as "originally an Americanism." Finally, there is the influence of the moving pictures. Hundreds of American films are shown in England every week, and the American words and phrases appearing in their titles, sub-titles and other explanatory legends thus become familiar to the English. "The patron of the picture palace," says W. G. Faulkner, in an article in the *London Daily Mail,* "learns to think of his railway station as a *depot;* he has alternatives to one of our newest words, *hooligan,* in *hoodlum* and *tough;* he watches a *dive,* which is a thieves' kitchen or a room in which bad characters meet, and whether the villain talks of *dough* or *sugar* he knows it is money to which he is referring. The musical ring of the word *tramp* gives way to the stodgy *hobo* or *dead-beat.* It may be that the plot reveals an attempt to deceive some simple-minded person. If it does, the innocent one is spoken of as a *sucker,* a *come-on,* a *boob,* or a *lobster* if he is stupid into the bargain."

Mr. Faulkner goes on to say that a great many other Americanisms are constantly employed by Englishmen "who have not been affected by the avalanche . . . which has come upon us through the picture palace." "Thus today," he says, "we hear people speak of the *fall* of the year, a *stunt* they have in hand, their desire to *boost* a particular business, a *peach* when they mean a pretty girl, a *scab*—a common term among strikers,—the *glad-eye, junk* when they mean worthless material, their efforts *to make good,* the *elevator* in the hotel or office, the *boss* or manager, the *crook* or swindler; and they will tell you that they have the *goods*—that is, they possess the requisite qualities for a given position." The venerable Frederic Harrison, writing in the *Fortnightly Review* in the Spring of 1918, denounced this tendency with a vigor recalling the classical anathemas of Dean Alford and Sydney Smith.[5] "Stale American phrases, . . ."

[5] Reprinted, in part, in the *New York Sun,* May 12, 1918.

he said, "are infecting even our higher journalism and our parliamentary and platform oratory. . . . A statesman is now *out*
for victory; he is *up against* pacificism. . . . He has *a card up
his sleeve*, by which the enemy are at last to be *euchred*. Then
a fierce fight in which hundreds of noble fellows are mangled
or drowned is a *scrap*. . . . To criticise a politician is to call
for his *scalp*. . . . The other fellow is beaten to a *frazzle*."
And so on. "Bolshevism," concluded Harrison sadly, "is ruin-
ing language as well as society."

But though there are still many such alarms by constables of
the national speech, the majority of Englishmen continue to
make borrowings from the tempting and ever-widening American vocabulary. What is more, some of these loan-words take
root, and are presently accepted as sound English, even by the
most watchful. The two Fowlers, in "The King's English,"
separate Americanisms from other current vulgarisms, but many
of the latter on their list are actually American in origin, though
they do not seem to know it—for example, *to demean* and *to
transpire*. More remarkable still, the Cambridge History of
English Literature lists *backwoodsman, know-nothing* and *yel-
low-back* as English compounds, apparently in forgetfulness of
their American origin, and adds *skunk, squaw* and *toboggan* as
direct importations from the Indian tongues, without noting that
they came through American, and remained definite Americanisms for a long while.[6] It even adds *musquash*, a popular name
for the *Fiber zibethicus*, borrowed from the Algonquin *musk-
wessu* but long since degenerated to *musk-rat* in America.
Musquash has been in disuse in this country, indeed, since the
middle of the last century, save as a stray localism, but the
English have preserved it, and it appears in the Oxford Dictionary.[7]

A few weeks in London or a month's study of the London

[6] Vol. xiv. pp. 507, 512.

[7] In this connection it is curious to note that, though the raccoon is an
animal quite unknown in England, there was, until lately, a destroyer called
the *Raccoon* in the British Navy. This ship was lost with all hands off the
Irish coast, Jan. 9, 1918.

newspapers will show a great many other American pollutions of the well of English. The argot of politics is full of them. Many beside *caucus* were introduced by Joseph Chamberlain, a politician skilled in American campaign methods and with an American wife to prompt him. He gave the English their first taste of *to belittle,* one of the inventions of Thomas Jefferson. *Graft* and *to graft* crossed the ocean in their nonage. *To bluff* has been well understood in England for 30 years. It is in Cassell's and the Oxford Dictionaries, and has been used by no less a magnifico than Sir Almroth Wright.[8] *To stump,* in the form of *stump-oratory,* is in Carlyle's "Latter-Day Pamphlets," *circa* 1850, and *caucus* appears in his "Frederick the Great,"[9] though, as we have seen on the authority of Ware, it did not come into general use in England until ten years later. *Buncombe* (usually spelled *bunkum*) is in all the later English dictionaries. In the London stock market and among English railroad men various characteristic Americanisms have got a foothold. The meaning of *bucket-shop* and *to water,* for example, is familiar to every London broker's clerk. English trains are now *telescoped* and carry *dead-heads,* and in 1913 a rival to the Amalgamated Order of Railway *Servants* was organized under the name of the National Union of *Railway Men.* The beginnings of a movement against the use of *servant* are visible in other directions, and the American *help* threatens to be substituted; at all events, *Help Wanted* advertisements are now occasionally encountered in English newspapers. But it is American verbs that seem to find the way into English least difficult, particularly those compounded with prepositions and adverbs, such as *to pan out* and *to swear off.* Most of them, true enough,

---

[8] The Unexpurgated Case Against Woman Suffrage; London, 1913, p. 9. *To bluff* has also gone into other languages, notably the Spanish. During the Cuban revolution of March, 1917, the newspapers of Havana, objecting to the dispatches sent out by American correspondents, denounced the latter as *los blofistas.* Meanwhile, *to bluff* has been shouldered out in the country of its origin, at least temporarily, by a verb borrowed from the French, *to camouflage.* This first appeared in the Spring of 1917.

[9] Book iv, ch. iii. The first of the six volumes was published in 1858 and the last in 1865.

are still used as conscious Americanisms, but used they are, and with increasing frequency. The highly typical American verb *to loaf* is now naturalized, and Ware says that *The Loaferies* is one of the common nicknames of the Whitechapel workhouse.

It is curious, reading the fulminations of American purists of the last generation, to note how many of the Americanisms they denounced have not only got into perfectly good usage at home but even broken down all guards across the ocean. *To placate* and *to antagonize* are examples. The Oxford Dictionary distinguishes between the English and American meanings of the latter: in England a man may antagonize only another man, in America he may antagonize a mere idea or thing. But, as the brothers Fowler show, even the English meaning is of American origin, and no doubt a few more years will see the verb completely naturalized in Britain. *To placate*, attacked vigorously by all native grammarians down to (but excepting) White, now has the authority of the *Spectator*, and is accepted by Cassell. *To donate* is still under the ban, but *to transpire* has been used by the *London Times*. Other old bugaboos that have been embraced are *gubernatorial, presidential* and *standpoint*. White labored long and valiantly to convince Americans that the adjective derived from *president* should be without the *i* in its last syllable, following the example of *incidental, regimental, monumental, governmental, oriental, experimental* and so on; but in vain, for *presidential* is now perfectly good English. *To demean* is still questioned, but English authors of the first rank have used it, and it will probably lose its dubious character very soon.

The flow of loan-words in the opposite direction meets with little impediment, for social distinction in America is still largely dependent upon English recognition, and so there is an eager imitation of the latest English fashions in speech. This emulation is most noticeable in the large cities of the East, and particularly in what Schele de Vere called "Boston and the Boston dependencies." New York is but little behind. The small stores there, if they are of any pretentions, are now almost invariably called *shops*. Shoes for the well-to-do are no longer *shoes,* but *boots,* and they are sold in *bootshops.* One encounters, too, in the side-streets off Fifth avenue, a multitude of *gift-shops, tea-shops* and *haberdashery-shops.* In Fifth avenue itself there are several *luggage-shops.* In August, 1917, signs appeared in the New York surface cars in which the conductors were referred to as *guards.* This effort to be English and correct was exhibited over the sign manual of Theodore P. Shonts, president of the Interborough, a gentleman of Teutonic name, but evidently a faithful protector of the king's English. On the same cars, however, painted notices, surviving from some earlier régime, mentioned the guards as *conductors. To Let* signs are now as common in all our cities as *For Rent* signs. We all know the *charwoman,* and have begun to forget our native modification of *char,* to wit, *chore.* Every apartment-house has a *tradesmen's-entrance.* In Charles street, in Baltimore, some time ago, the proprietor of a fashionable stationery store directed me, not to the elevator, but to the *lift.*

Occasionally, some uncompromising patriot raises his voice against these importations, but he seldom shows the vigorous indignation of the English purists, and he seldom prevails. White, in 1870, warned Americans against the figurative use of *nasty* as a synonym for *disagreeable.*[10] This use of the word was then relatively new in England, though, according to White, the *Saturday Review* and the *Spectator* had already succumbed. His objections to it were unavailing; *nasty* quickly got into American and has been there ever since. In 1883 Gilbert M. Tucker protested against *good-form, traffic* (in the sense of travel), *to bargain* and *to tub* as Briticisms that we might well do without, but all of them took root and are perfectly sound American today. There is, indeed, no intelligible reason why such English inventions and improvements should not be taken in, even though the motive behind the welcome to them may occasionally cause a smile. English, after all, is the mother of American, and the child, until lately, was still at nurse. The English, confronted by some of our fantastic innovations, may well regard them as impudences to be put down, but what they

[10] Words and Their Use, new ed.; New York, 1876, p. 198.

offer in return often fits into our vocabulary without offering it any outrage. American, indeed, is full of lingering Briticisms, all maintaining a successful competition with native forms. If we take back *shop* it is merely taking back something that *store* has never been able to rid us of: we use *shop-worn, shoplifter, shopping, shopper, shop-girl* and *to shop* every day. In the same way the word *penny* has survived among us, despite the fact that there has been no American coin of that name for more than 125 years. We have *nickel-in-the-slot* machines, but when they take a cent we call them *penny-in-the-slot* machines. We have *penny-arcades* and *penny-whistles*. We do not play *cent*-ante, but *penny*-ante. We still "turn an honest *penny*" and say "a *penny* for your thoughts." The pound and the shilling became extinct a century ago, but the penny still binds us to the mother tongue.

§ 2

Points of Difference—These exchanges and coalescences, however, though they invigorate each language with the blood of the other and are often very striking in detail, are neither numerous enough nor general enough to counteract the centrifugal force which pulls them apart. The simple fact is that the spirit of English and the spirit of American have been at odds for nearly a century, and that the way of one is not the way of the other. The loan-words that fly to and fro, when examined closely, are found to be few in number both relatively and absolutely: they do not greatly affect the larger movements of the two languages. Many of them, indeed, are little more than temporary borrowings; they are not genuinely adopted, but merely momentarily fashionable. The class of Englishmen which affects American phrases is perhaps but little larger, taking one year with another, than the class of Americans which affects English phrases. This last class, it must be plain, is very small. Leave the large cities and you will have difficulty finding any members of it. It is circumscribed, not because there is any very formidable prejudice against English locutions as such, but simply because recognizably English locutions, in a good many cases, do not fit into the American language. The American thinks in American and the Englishman in English, and it requires a definite effort, usually but defectively successful, for either to put his thoughts into the actual idiom of the other.

The difficulties of this enterprise are well exhibited, though quite unconsciously, by W. L. George in a chapter entitled "Litany of the Novelist" in his book of criticism, "Literary Chapters." [11] This chapter, it is plain by internal evidence, was written, not for Englishmen, but for Americans. A good part of it, in fact, is in the second person—we are addressed and argued with directly. And throughout there is an obvious endeavor to help out comprehension by a studied use of purely American phrases and examples. One hears, not of the *East End*, but of the *East Side;* not of the *City*, but of *Wall Street;* not of *Belgravia* or the *West End*, but of *Fifth avenue;* not of *bowler* hats, but of *Derbys;* not of idlers in *pubs*, but of *saloon loafers;* not of *pounds*, *shillings* and *pence*, but of *dollars* and *cents*. In brief, a gallant attempt upon a strange tongue, and by a writer of the utmost skill—but a hopeless failure none the less. In the midst of his best American, George drops into Briticism after Briticism, some of them quite as unintelligible to the average American reader as so many Gallicisms. On page after page they display the practical impossibility of the enterprise: *back-garden* for *back-yard*, *perambulator* for *baby-carriage*, *corn*-market for *grain*-market, coal-*owner* for coal-*operator*, *post* for *mail*, and so on. And to top them there are English terms that have no American equivalents at all, for example, *kitchen-fender*.

The same failure, perhaps usually worse, is displayed every time an English novelist or dramatist essays to put an American into a novel or a play, and to make him speak American. However painstakingly it is done, the Englishman invariably falls into capital blunders, and the result is derided by Americans as Mark Twain derided the miners' lingo of Bret Harte, and for the same reason. The thing lies deeper than vocabulary and

[11] Boston, 1918, pp. 1–43.

even than pronunciation and intonation; the divergences show themselves in habits of speech that are fundamental and almost indefinable. And when the transoceanic gesture is from the other direction they become even plainer. An Englishman, in an American play, seldom shows the actual speech habit of the Sassenach; what he shows is the speech habit of an American actor trying to imitate George Alexander. "There are not five playwrights in America," said Channing Pollock one day, "who can write English"—that is, the English of familiar discourse. "Why should there be?" replied Louis Sherwin. "There are not five thousand people in America who can *speak* English." [12]

The elements that enter into the special character of American have been rehearsed in the first chapter: a general impatience of rule and restraint, a democratic enmity to all authority, an extravagant and often grotesque humor, an extraordinary capacity for metaphor [13]—in brief, all the natural marks of what Van Wyck Brooks calls "a popular life which bubbles with energy and spreads and grows and slips away ever more and more from the control of tested ideas, a popular life with the lid off." [14] This is the spirit of America, and from it the American language is nourished. Brooks, perhaps, generalizes a bit too lavishly. Below the surface there is also a curious conservatism, even a sort of timorousness; in a land of manumitted peasants the primary trait of the peasant is bound to show itself now and then; as Wendell Phillips once said, "more than any other people, we Americans are afraid of one another"—that is, afraid of opposition, of derision, of all the consequences of singularity. But in the field of language, as in that of politics, this suspicion of the new is often transformed into a suspicion of the merely unfamiliar, and so its natural tendency toward conservatism is overcome. It is of the essence of democracy that it remain a government by amateurs, and under a government by amateurs it is precisely the expert who is most questioned—and it is the expert

---

[12] *Green Book Magazine*, Nov., 1913, p. 768.

[13] An interesting note on this characteristic is in College Words and Phrases, by Eugene H. Babbitt, *Dialect Notes*, vol. ii, pt. i, p. 11.

[14] America's Coming of Age; p. 15.

who commonly stresses the experience of the past. And in a democratic society it is not the iconoclast who seems most revolutionary, but the purist. The derisive designation of *high-brow* is thoroughly American in more ways than one. It is a word put together in an unmistakably American fashion, it reflects an habitual American attitude of mind, and its potency in debate is peculiarly national too.

I daresay it is largely a fear of the weapon in it—and there are many others of like effect in the arsenal—which accounts for the far greater prevalence of idioms from below in the formal speech of America than in the formal speech of England. There is surely no English novelist of equal rank whose prose shows so much of colloquial looseness and ease as one finds in the prose of Howells: to find a match for it one must go to the prose of the neo-Celts, professedly modelled upon the speech of peasants, and almost proudly defiant of English grammar and syntax, and to the prose of the English themselves before the Restoration. Nor is it imaginable that an Englishman of comparable education and position would ever employ such locutions as those I have hitherto quoted from the public addresses of Dr. Wilson—that is, innocently, seriously, as a matter of course. The Englishman, when he makes use of coinages of that sort, does so in conscious relaxation, and usually with a somewhat heavy sense of doggishness. They are proper to the paddock or even to the dinner table, but scarcely to serious scenes and occasions. But in the United States their use is the rule rather than the exception; it is not the man who uses them, but the man who doesn't use them, who is marked off. Their employment, if high example counts for anything, is a standard habit of the language, as their diligent avoidance is a standard habit of English.

A glance through the *Congressional Record* is sufficient to show how small is the minority of purists among the chosen leaders of the nation. Within half an hour, turning the pages at random, I find scores of locutions that would paralyze the stenographers in the House of Commons, and they are in the speeches, not of wild mavericks from the West, but of some of the chief men of the two Houses. Surely no Senator occupied a more conspicuous position, during the first year of the war, than Lee S. Overman, of North Carolina, chairman of the Committee on Rules, and commander of the administration forces on the floor. Well, I find Senator Overman using *to enthuse* in a speech of the utmost seriousness and importance, and not once, but over and over again.[15] I turn back a few pages and encounter it again—this time in the mouth of General Sherwood, of Ohio. A few more, and I find a fit match for it, to wit, *to biograph.*[16] The speaker here is Senator L. Y. Sherman, of Illinois. In the same speech he uses *to resolute.* A few more, and various other characteristic verbs are unearthed: *to demagogue,*[17] *to dope out,*[18] *to fall down* [19] (in the sense of to fail), *to jack up,*[20] *to phone,*[21] *to peeve,*[22] *to come across,*[23] *to hike, to butt in,*[24] *to back pedal, to get solid with, to hooverize, to trustify, to feature, to insurge, to haze, to reminisce, to camouflage, to play for a sucker,* and so on, almost *ad infinitum.* And with them, a large number of highly American nouns, chiefly compounds, all pressing upward for recognition: *tin-Lizzie, brain-storm, come-down, pin-head, trustification, porkbarrel, buck-private, dough-boy, cow-country.* And adjectives: *jitney, bush* (for rural), *balled-up,*[25] *dolled-up, phoney, taxpaid.*[26] And phrases: *dollars to doughnuts, on the job, that gets me, one best bet.* And back-formations: *ad, movie, photo.* And

---

[15] March 26, 1918, pp. 4376–7.

[16] Jan. 14, 1918, p. 903.

[17] Mr. Campbell, of Kansas, in the House, Jan. 19, 1918, p. 1134.

[18] Mr. Hamlin, of Missouri, in the House, Jan. 19, 1918, p. 1154.

[19] Mr. Kirby, of Arkansas, in the Senate, Jan. 24, 1918, p. 1291; Mr. Lewis, of Illinois, in the Senate, June 6, 1918, p. 8024.

[20] Mr. Weeks of Massachusetts, in the Senate, Jan. 17, 1918, p. 988.

[21] Mr. Smith, of South Carolina, in the Senate, Jan. 17, 1918, p. 991.

[22] Mr. Borland, of Missouri, in the House, Jan. 29, 1918, p. 1501.

[23] May 4, 1917, p. 1853.

[24] Mr. Snyder, of New York, Dec. 11, 1917.

[25] *Balled-up* and its verb, *to ball up,* were originally somewhat improper, no doubt on account of the slang significance of *ball,* but of late they have made steady progress toward polite acceptance.

[26] After the passage of the first War Revenue Act cigar-boxes began to bear this inscription: "The contents of this box have been *taxed paid* as cigars of Class B as indicated by the Internal Revenue stamp affixed." Even *tax-paid,* which was later substituted, is obviously better than this clumsy double inflection.

various substitutions and Americanized inflections: *over* for *more than*, *gotten* for *got* in the present perfect,[27] *rile* for *roil*, *bust* for *burst*. This last, in truth, has come into a dignity that even grammarians will soon hesitate to question. Who, in America, would dare to speak of *bursting* a broncho, or of a *trust-burster?* [28]

§ 3

Lost Distinctions—This general iconoclasm reveals itself especially in a disdain for most of the niceties of modern English. The American, like the Elizabethan Englishman, is usually quite unconscious of them and even when they have been instilled into him by the hard labor of pedagogues he commonly pays little heed to them in his ordinary discourse. The English distinction between *will* and *shall* offers a salient case in point. This distinction, it may be said at once, is far more a confection of the grammarians than a product of the natural forces shaping the language. It has, indeed, little etymological basis, and is but imperfectly justified logically. One finds it disregarded in the Authorized Version of the Bible, in all the plays of Shakespeare, in the essays of the reign of Anne, and in some of the best examples of modern English literature. The theory behind it is so inordinately abstruse that the Fowlers, in ''The King's English,''[29] require 20 pages to explain it, and even then they come to the resigned conclusion that the task is hopeless. ''The idiomatic use [of the two auxiliaries],'' they say, ''is so complicated that those who are not to the manner born can hardly acquire it.'' [30] Well, even those who are to the manner born seem to find

---

[27] Mr. Bankhead, of Alabama, in the Senate, May 14, 1918, p. 6995.

[28] *Bust* seems to be driving out *burst* completely when used figuratively. Even in a literal sense it creeps into more or less respectable usage. Thus I find ''a *busted* tire'' in a speech by Gen. Sherwood, of Ohio, in the House, Jan. 24, 1918. The familiar American derivative, *buster,* as in *Buster Brown,* is unknown to the English.

[29] Pp. 133–154.

[30] L. Pearsall Smith, in The English Language, p. 20, says that ''the differentiation is . . . so complicated that it can hardly be mastered by those born in parts of the British Islands in which it has not yet been established''—*e. g.,* all of Ireland and most of Scotland.

it difficult, for at once the learned authors cite blunder in the writings of Richardson, Stevenson, Gladstone, Jowett, Oscar Wilde, and even Henry Sweet, author of the best existing grammar of the English language. In American the distinction is almost lost. No ordinary American, save after the most laborious reflection, would detect anything wrong in this sentence from the *London Times*, denounced as corrupt by the Fowlers: "We must reconcile what we would like to do with what we can do." Nor in this by W. B. Yeats: "The character who delights us may commit murder like Macbeth . . . and yet we will rejoice in every happiness that comes to him." Half a century ago, impatient of the effort to fasten the English distinction upon American, George P. Marsh attacked it as of "no logical value or significance whatever," and predicted that "at no very distant day this verbal quibble will disappear, and one of the auxiliaries will be employed, with all persons of the nominative, exclusively as the sign of the future, and the other only as an expression of purpose or authority."[31] This prophecy has been substantially verified. *Will* is sound American "with all persons of the nominative," and *shall* is almost invariably an "expression of purpose or authority."[32]

And so, though perhaps not to the same extent, with *who* and *whom*. Now and then there arises a sort of panicky feeling that *whom* is being neglected, and so it is trotted out,[33] but in the

[31] Quoted by White, in Words and Their Uses, pp. 264–5. White, however, dissented vigorously and devoted 10 pages to explaining the difference between the two auxiliaries. Most of the other authorities of the time were also against Marsh—for example, Richard Meade Bache (See his Vulgarisms and Other Errors of Speech, p. 92 *et seq.*). Sir Edmund Head, governor-general of Canada from 1854 to 1861, wrote a whole book upon the subject: *Shall* and *Will*, or Two Chapters on Future Auxiliary Verbs; London, 1856.

[32] The probable influence of Irish immigration upon the American usage is not to be overlooked. Joyce says flatly (English As We Speak It in Ireland, p. 77) that, "like many another Irish idiom this is also found in American society chiefly through the influence of the Irish." At all events, the Irish example must have reinforced it. In Ireland "*Will* I light the fire, ma'am?" is colloquially sound.

[33] Often with such amusing results as "*whom* is your father?" and "*whom* spoke to me?" The exposure of excesses of that sort always attracts the wits, especially Franklin P. Adams.

main the American language tends to dispense with it, at least in its least graceful situations. Noah Webster, always the pragmatic reformer, denounced it so long ago as 1783. Common sense, he argued, was on the side of *"who* did he marry?"* To-day such a form as *"whom* are you talking to?"* would seem somewhat affected in ordinary discourse in America; *"who* are you talking to?"* is heard a thousand times oftener—and is doubly American, for it substitutes *who* for *whom* and puts a preposition at the end of a sentence: two crimes that most English purists would seek to avoid. It is among the pronouns that the only remaining case inflections in English are to be found, if we forget the possessive, and even here these survivors of an earlier day begin to grow insecure. Lounsbury's defense of "it is *me,"* [34] as we shall see in the next chapter, has support in the history and natural movement of the language, and that movement is also against the preservation of the distinction between *who* and *whom.* The common speech plays hob with both of the orthodox inflections, despite the protests of grammarians, and in the long run, no doubt, they will be forced to yield to its pressure, as they have always yielded in the past. Between the dative and accusative on the one side and the nominative on the other there has been war in the English language for centuries, and it has always tended to become a war of extermination. Our now universal use of *you* for *ye* in the nominative shows the dative and accusative swallowing the nominative, and the practical disappearance of *hither, thither* and *whither,* whose place is now taken by *here, there* and *where,* shows a contrary process. In such wars a *posse comitatus* marches ahead of the disciplined army. American stands to English in the relation of that posse to that army. It is incomparably more enterprising, more contemptuous of precedent and authority, more impatient of rule.

A shadowy line often separates what is currently coming into sound usage from what is still regarded as barbarous. No self-respecting American, I daresay, would defend *ain't* as a substi-

[34] "It is *I"* is quite as unsound historically. The correct form would be "it *am* I" or "I am it." Compare the German: "ich *bin* es," not, "es *ist* ich."

tute for *isn't*, say in "he *ain't* the man," and yet *ain't* is already tolerably respectable in the first person, where English countenances the even more clumsy *aren't*. *Aren't* has never got a foothold in the American first person; when it is used at all, which is very rarely, it is always as a conscious Briticism. Facing the alternative of employing the unwieldy "am I not in this?" the American turns boldly to "*ain't* I in this?" It still grates a bit, perhaps, but *aren't* grates even more. Here, as always, the popular speech is pulling the exacter speech along, and no one familiar with its successes in the past can have much doubt that it will succeed again, soon or late. In the same way it is breaking down the inflectional distinction between adverb and adjective, so that "I feel *bad*" begins to take on the dignity of a national idiom, and *sure, to go big* and *run slow* [35] become almost respectable. When, on the entrance of the United States into the war, the Marine Corps chose "treat 'em *rough*" as its motto, no one thought to raise a grammatical objection, and the clipped adverb was printed upon hundreds of thousands of posters and displayed in every town in the country, always with the imprimatur of the national government. So, again, American, in its spoken form, tends to obliterate the distinction between nearly related adjectives, *e. g.*, *healthful* and *healthy*, *tasteful* and *tasty*. And to challenge the somewhat absurd textbook prohibition of terminal prepositions, so that "where are we *at?*" loses its old raciness. And to dally with the double negative, as in "I have no doubt *but* that." [36]

But these tendencies, or at least the more extravagant of them, belong to the next chapter. How much influence they exert, even

[35] A common direction to motormen and locomotive engineers. The English form is "slow down." I note, however, that "drive slow*ly*" is in the taxicab shed at the Pennsylvania Station, in New York.

[36] I quote from a speech made by Senator Sherman, of Illinois, in the United States Senate on June 20, 1918. *Vide Congressional Record* for that day, p. 8743. Two days later, "There is no question *but* that" appeared in a letter by John Lee Coulter, A.M., Ph.D., dean of West Virginia University. It was read into the *Record* of June 22 by Mr. Ashwell, one of the Louisiana representatives. Even the pedantic Senator Henry Cabot Lodge, oozing Harvard from every pore, uses *but that*. *Vide* the *Record* for May 14, 1918, p. 6996.

indirectly, is shown by the American disdain of the English precision in the use of the indefinite pronoun. I turn to the *Saturday Evening Post,* and in two minutes find: *"one* feels like an atom when *he* begins to review *his* own life and deeds."[37] The error is very rare in English; the Fowlers, seeking examples of it, could get them only from the writings of a third-rate woman novelist, Scotch to boot. But it is so common in American that it scarcely attracts notice. Neither does the appearance of a redundant *s* in such words as *towards, downwards, afterwards* and *heavenwards.* In England this *s* is used relatively seldom, and then it usually marks a distinction in meaning, as it does on both sides of the ocean between *beside* and *besides.* "In modern standard English," says Smith,[38] "though not in the English of the United States, a distinction which we feel, but many of us could not define, is made between *forward* and *forwards; forwards* being used in definite contrast to any other direction, as 'if you move at all, you can only move *forwards,*' while *forward* is used where no such contrast is implied, as in the common phrase 'to bring a matter forward.'"[39] This specific distinction, despite Smith, probably retains some force in the United States too, but in general our usage allows the *s* in cases where English usage would certainly be against it. Gould, in the 50's, noted its appearance at the end of such words as *somewhere* and *anyway,* and denounced it as vulgar and illogical. Thornton has traced *anyways* back to 1842 and shown that it is an archaism, and to be found in the Book of Common Prayer (*circa* 1560); perhaps it has been preserved by analogy with *sideways.* Henry James, in "The Question of Our Speech," attacked "such forms of impunity as *somewheres else* and *nowheres else, a good ways on* and *a good ways off*" as "vulgarisms with what a great deal of general credit for what we good-naturedly call 'refinement' appears so able to coexist."[40] *Towards* and *afterwards,* though frowned upon in England, are now quite sound in American. I

---

[37] June 15, 1918, p. 62.

[38] The English Language, p. 79.

[39] This phrase, of course, is a Briticism, and seldom used in America. The American form is "to take a matter up."

[40] P. 30.

find the former in the title of an article in *Dialect Notes*, which plainly gives it scholastic authority.[41] More (and with no little humor), I find it in the deed of a fund given to the American Academy of Arts and Letters to enable the gifted philologs of that sanhedrin "to consider its duty *towards* the conservation of the English language in its beauty and purity." [42] Both *towards* and *afterwards*, finally, are included in the *New York Evening Post's* list of "words no longer disapproved when in their proper places," along with *over* for *more than*, and *during* for *in the course of.*

In the last chapter we glanced at several salient differences between the common coin of English and the common coin of American—that is, the verbs and adjectives in constant colloquial use—the rubber-stamps, so to speak, of the two languages. America has two adverbs that belong to the same category. They are *right* and *good*. Neither holds the same place in English. Thornton shows that the use of *right*, as in *right away, right good* and *right now,* was already widespread in the United States early in the last century; his first example is dated 1818. He believes that the locution was "possibly imported from the southwest of Ireland." Whatever its origin, it quickly attracted the attention of English visitors. Dickens noted *right away* as an almost universal Americanism during his first American tour, in 1842, and poked fun at it in the second chapter of "American Notes." *Right* is used as a synonym for *directly*, as in *right away, right off, right now* and *right on time;* for *moderately*, as in *right well, right smart, right good* and *right often*, and in place of *precisely*, as in *right there.* Some time ago, in an article on Americanisms, an English critic called it "that most distinctively American word," and concocted the following dialogue to instruct the English in its use:

How do I get to ——?
Go *right* along, and take the first turning (*sic*) on the *right*, and you are *right* there.

41 A Contribution *Towards*, etc., by Prof. H. Tallichet, vol. 1, pt. iv.
42 *Yale Review*, April, 1918, p. 545.

Right?
Right.
Right! [43]

Like W. L. George, this Englishman failed in his attempt to write correct American despite his fine pedagogical passion. No American would ever say "take the first turning"; he would say "turn at the first corner." As for *right away*, R. O. Williams argues that "so far as analogy can make good English, it is as good as one could choose." [44] Nevertheless, the Oxford Dictionary admits it only as an Americanism, and avoids all mention of the other American uses of *right* as an adverb. *Good* is almost as protean. It is not only used as a general synonym for all adjectives and adverbs connoting satisfaction, as in *to feel good, to be treated good, to sleep good*, but also as a reinforcement to other adjectives and adverbs, as in "I hit him *good* and hard" and "I am *good* and tired." Of late *some* has come into wide use as an adjective-adverb of all work, indicating special excellence or high degree, as in *some girl, some sick, going some*, etc. It is still below the salt, but threatens to reach a more respectable position. One encounters it in the newspapers constantly and in the *Congressional Record*, and not long ago a writer in the *Atlantic Monthly* [45] hymned it ecstatically as "*some* word—a true super-word, in fact" and argued that it could be used "in a sense for which there is absolutely no synonym in the dictionary." Basically, it appears to be an adjective, but in many of its common situations the grammarians would probably call it an adverb. It gives no little support to the growing tendency, already noticed, to break down the barrier between the two parts of speech.

§ 4

Foreign Influences Today—No other great nation of today supports so large a foreign population as the United States,

---

[43] I Speak United States, *Saturday Review*, Sept. 22, 1894.
[44] Our Dictionaries, pp. 84–86.
[45] Should Language Be Abolished? by Harold Goddard, *Atlantic Monthly*, July, 1918, p. 63.

either relatively or absolutely; none other contains so many foreigners forced to an effort, often ignorant and ineffective, to master the national language. Since 1820 nearly 35,000,000 immigrants have come into the country, and of them probably not 10,000,000 brought any preliminary acquaintance with English with them. The census of 1910 showed that nearly 1,500,000 persons then living permanently on American soil could not speak it at all; that more than 13,000,000 had been born in other countries, chiefly of different language; and that nearly 20,000,-000 were the children of such immigrants, and hence under the influence of their speech habits. Altogether, there were probably at least 25,000,000 whose house language was not the vulgate, and who thus spoke it in competition with some other language. No other country houses so many aliens. In Great Britain the alien population, for a century past, has never been more than 2 per cent of the total population, and since the passage of the Alien Act of 1905 it has tended to decline steadily. In Germany, in 1910, there were but 1,259,873 aliens in a population of more than 60,000,000, and of these nearly a half were German-speaking Austrians and Swiss. In France, in 1906, there were 1,000,000 foreigners in a population of 39,000,000 and a third of them were French-speaking Belgians, Luxembourgeois and Swiss. In Italy, in 1911, there were but 350,000 in a population of 35,000,000.

This large and constantly reinforced admixture of foreigners has naturally exerted a constant pressure upon the national language, for the majority of them, at least in the first generation, have found it quite impossible to acquire it in any purity, and even their children have grown up with speech habits differing radically from those of correct English. The effects of this pressure are obviously two-fold; on the one hand the foreigner, struggling with a strange and difficult tongue, makes efforts to simplify it as much as possible, and so strengthens the native tendency to disregard all niceties and complexities, and on the other hand he corrupts it with words and locutions from the language he has brought with him, and sometimes with whole idioms and grammatical forms. We have seen, in earlier chapters, how the

Dutch and French of colonial days enriched the vocabulary of the colonists, how the German immigrants of the first half of the nineteenth century enriched it still further, and how the Irish of the same period influenced its everyday usages. The same process is still going on. The Italians, the Slavs, and, above all, the Russian Jews, make steady contributions to the American vocabulary and idiom, and though these contributions are often concealed by quick and complete naturalization their foreignness to English remains none the less obvious. *I should worry*,[46] in its way, is correct English, but in essence it is as completely Yiddish as *kosher, ganof, schadchen, oi-yoi, matzoh* or *mazuma*.[47] *Black-hand*, too, is English in form, but it is nevertheless as plainly an Italian loan-word as *spaghetti, mafia* or *padrone*.

The extent of such influences upon American, and particularly upon spoken American, remains to be studied; in the whole literature I can find but one formal article upon the subject. That article [48] deals specifically with the suffix *-fest*, which came into American from the German and was probably suggested by familiarity with *sängerfest*. There is no mention of it in any of the dictionaries of Americanisms, and yet, in such forms as *talk-fest* and *gabfest* it is met with almost daily. So with *-heimer, -inski* and *-bund*. Several years ago *-heimer* had a great vogue in slang, and was rapidly done to death. But *wiseheimer* re-

[46] In Yiddish, *ish ka bibble*. The origin and meaning of the phrase have been variously explained. The prevailing notion seems to be that it is a Yiddish corruption of the German *nicht gefiedelt* (= *not fiddled* = *not flustered*). But this seems to me to be fanciful. To the Jews *ish* is obviously the first personal pronoun and *kaa* probably corruption of *kann*. As for *bibble* I suspect that it is the offspring of *bedibbert* (= *embarrassed, intimidated*). The phrase thus has an ironical meaning, *I should be embarrassed*, almost precisely equivalent to *I should worry*.

[47] All of which, of course, are coming into American, along with many other Yiddish words. These words tend to spread far beyond the areas actually settled by Jews. Thus I find *mazuma* in A Word-List from Kansas, from the collectanea of Judge J. C. Ruppenthal, of Russell, Kansas, *Dialect Notes*, vol. iv. pt. v, 1916, p. 322.

[48] Louise Pound: Domestication of the Suffix *-fest*, *Dialect Notes*, vol. iv, pt. v, 1916. Dr. Pound, it should be mentioned, has also printed a brief note on *-inski*. Her observation of American is peculiarly alert and accurate.

mains in colloquial use as a facetious synonym for *smart-aleck,* and after awhile it may gradually acquire dignity. Far lowlier words, in fact, have worked their way in. *Buttinski,* perhaps, is going the same route. As for the words in *-bund,* many of them are already almost accepted. *Plunder-bund* is now at least as good as *pork-barrel* and *slush-fund,* and *money-bund* is frequently heard in Congress.[49]   Such locutions creep in stealthily, and are secure before they are suspected. Current slang, out of which the more decorous language dredges a large part of its raw materials, is full of them. *Nix* and *nixy,* for *no,* are debased forms of the German *nichts; aber nit,* once as popular as *camouflage,* is obviously *aber nicht.* And a steady flow of nouns, all needed to designate objects introduced by immigrants, enriches the vocabulary. The Hungarians not only brought their national condiment with them; they also brought its name, *paprika,* and that name is now thoroughly American.[50]   In the same way the Italians brought in *camorra, padrone, spaghetti* and a score of other substantives, and the Jews made contributions from Yiddish and Hebrew and greatly reinforced certain old borrowings from German. Once such a loan-word gets in it takes firm root. During the first year of American participation in the World War an effort was made, on patriotic grounds, to substitute *liberty-cabbage* for *sour-kraut,* but it quickly failed, for the name had become as completely Americanized as the thing itself, and so *liberty-cabbage* seemed affected and absurd. In the same way a great many other German words survived the passions of the time. Nor could all the influence of the professional patriots obliterate that German influence which has fastened upon the American *yes* something of the quality of *ja.*

Constant familiarity with such contributions from foreign languages and with the general speech habits of foreign peoples has made American a good deal more hospitable to loan-words than English, even in the absence of special pressure. Let the same

[49] For example, see the *Congressional Record* for April 3, 1918, p. 4928.

[50] *Paprika* is in the Standard Dictionary, but I have been unable to find it in any English dictionary. Another such word is *kimono,* from the Japanese.

word knock at the gates of the two languages, and American will admit it more readily, and give it at once a wider and more intimate currency. Examples are afforded by *café, vaudeville, employé, boulevard, cabaret, toilette, exposé, kindergarten, dépôt, fête* and *menu. Café,* in American, is a word of much larger and more varied meaning than in English and is used much more frequently, and by many more persons. So is *employé,* in the naturalized form of *employee.* So is *toilet:* we have even seen it as a euphemism for native terms that otherwise would be in daily use. So is *kindergarten:* I read lately of a *kindergarten* for the elementary instruction of conscripts. Such words are not unknown to the Englishman, but when he uses them it is with a plain sense of their foreignness. In American they are completely naturalized, as is shown by the spelling and pronunciation of most of them. An American would no more think of attempting the French pronunciation of *depot* or of putting the French accents upon it than he would think of spelling *toilet* with the final *te* or of essaying to pronounce *Anheuser* in the German manner. Often curious battles go on between such loanwords and their English equivalents, and with varying fortunes. In 1895 Weber and Fields tried to establish *music-hall* in New York, but it quickly succumbed to *vaudeville-theatre,* as *variety* had succumbed to *vaudeville* before it. In the same way *lawn-fete* (without the circumflex accent, and commonly pronounced *feet*) has elbowed out the English *garden-party.* But now and then, when the competing loan-word happens to violate American speech habits, a native term ousts it. The French *crèche* offers an example; it has been entirely displaced by *day-nursery.*

The English, in this matter, display their greater conservatism very plainly. Even when a loan-word enters both English and American simultaneously a sense of foreignness lingers about it on the other side of the Atlantic much longer than on this side, and it is used with far more self-consciousness. The word *matinée* offers a convenient example. To this day the English commonly print it in italics, give it its French accent, and pronounce it with some attempt at the French manner. But in America it is entirely naturalized, and the most ignorant man uses it without any feeling that it is strange. The same lack of any sense of linguistic integrity is to be noticed in many other directions—for example, in the freedom with which the Latin *per* is used with native nouns. One constantly sees *per day, per dozen, per hundred, per mile,* etc., in American newspapers, even the most careful, but in England the more seemly *a* is almost always used, or the noun itself is made Latin, as in *per diem. Per,* in fact, is fast becoming an everyday American word. Such phrases as "as *per* your letter (or order) of the 15th inst." are incessantly met with in business correspondence. The same greater hospitality is shown by the readiness with which various un-English prefixes and affixes come into fashion, for example, *super-* and *-itis.* The English accept them gingerly; the Americans take them in with enthusiasm, and naturalize them instanter.[51]

The same deficiency in reserve is to be noted in nearly all other colonialized dialects. The Latin-American variants of Spanish, for example, have adopted a great many words which appear in true Castilian only as occasional guests. Thus in Argentina *matinée, menu, début, toilette* and *femme de chambre* are perfectly good Argentine, and in Mexico *sandwich* and *club* have been thoroughly naturalized. The same thing is to be noted in the French of Haiti, in the Portuguese of Brazil, and even in the Danish of Norway. Once a language spreads beyond the country of its origin and begins to be used by people born, in the German phrase, to a different *Sprachgefühl,* the sense of loyalty to its vocabulary is lost, along with the instinctive feeling for its idiomatic habits. How far this destruction of its forms may go in the absence of strong contrary influences is exhibited by the rise of the Romance languages from the vulgar Latin of the Roman provinces, and, here at home, by the decay of foreign languages in competition with English. The Yiddish that the Jews from Russia bring in is German debased with Russian, Polish and He-

---

[51] *Cf.* Vogue Affixes in Present-Day Word-Coinage, by Louise Pound, *Dialect Notes,* vol. v, pt. i, 1918. Dr. Pound ascribes the vogue of *super-* to German influences, and is inclined to think that *-dom* may be helped by the German *-thum.*

brew; in America, it quickly absorbs hundreds of words and idioms from the speech of the streets. Various conflicting German dialects, among the so-called Pennsylvania Dutch and in the German areas of the Northwest, combine in a patois that, in its end forms, shows almost as much English as German. Classical examples of it are "es giebt gar kein *use*," "Ich kann es nicht *ständen*" and "mein *stallion* hat über die *fenz gescheumpt* und dem nachbar sein *whiet* abscheulich *gedämätscht.*"[52] The use of *gleiche* for *to like*, by false analogy from *gleich* (= *like, similar*) is characteristic. In the same way the Scandinavians in the Northwest corrupt their native Swedish and Dano-Norwegian. Thus, American-Norwegian is heavy with such forms as *strit-kar, reit-evé, nekk-töi* and *staits-pruessen*, for *street-car, right away, necktie* and *states-prison*, and admits such phrases as "det *meka* ingen *difrens.*"[53]

The changes that Yiddish has undergone in America, though rather foreign to the present inquiry, are interesting enough to be noticed. First of all, it has admitted into its vocabulary a large number of everyday substantives, among them *boy, chair, window, carpet, floor, dress, hat, watch, ceiling, consumption, property, trouble, bother, match, change, party, birthday, picture, paper* (only in the sense of *newspaper*), *gambler, show, hall, kitchen, store, bedroom, key, mantelpiece, closet, lounge, broom, tablecloth, paint, landlord, fellow, tenant, shop, wages, foreman, sleeve, collar, cuff, button, cotton, thimble, needle, pocket, bargain, sale, remnant, sample, haircut, razor, waist, basket, school, scholar, teacher, baby, mustache, butcher, grocery, dinner, street* and *walk*. And with them many characteristic Americanisms,

[52] *Vide* Pennsylvania Dutch, by S. S. Haldeman; Philadelphia, 1872. Also, The Pennsylvania German Dialect, by M. D. Learned; Baltimore, 1889. Also Die Zukunft deutscher Bildung in Amerika, by O. E. Lessing, *Monatshefte für deutsche Sprache und Pedagogik*, Dec., 1916. Also, Where Do You Stand? by Herman Hagedorn; New York, 1918, pp. 106–7. Also, On the German Dialect Spoken in the Valley of Virginia, by H. M. Hays, *Dialect Notes*, vol. iii, pt. iv, 1908, pp. 263–78.

[53] *Vide* Notes on American-Norwegian, by Nils Flaten, *Dialect Notes*, vol. ii, 1900. Also, for similar corruptions, The Jersey Dutch Dialect, by J. Dyneley Prince, *ibid.*, vol. iii, pt. vi, 1910, pp. 461–84. Also, see under Hempl, Flom, Bibaud, Buies and A. M. Elliott in the bibliography.

for example, *bluffer, faker, boodler, grafter, gangster, crook, guy, kike, piker, squealer, bum, cadet, boom, bunch, pants, vest, loafer, jumper, stoop, saleslady, ice-box* and *raise*, with their attendant verbs and adjectives. These words are used constantly; many of them have quite crowded out the corresponding Yiddish words. For example, *ingel*, meaning *boy* (it is a Slavic loan-word in Yiddish), has been obliterated by the English word. A Jewish immigrant almost invariably refers to his son as his *boy*, though strangely enough he calls his daughter his *meidel*. "Die *boys* mit die *meidlach* haben a good time" is excellent American Yiddish. In the same way *fenster* has been completely displaced by *window*, though *tür* (= *door*) has been left intact. *Tisch* (= *table*) also remains, but *chair* is always used, probably because few of the Jews had chairs in the old country. There the *beinkel*, a bench without a back, was in use; chairs were only for the well-to-do. *Floor* has apparently prevailed because no invariable corresponding word was employed at home: in various parts of Russia and Poland a floor is a *dill*, a *podlogé*, or a *bricke*. So with *ceiling*. There were six different words for it.

Yiddish inflections have been fastened upon most of these loan-words. Thus, "er hat ihm *abgefaked*" is "he cheated him," *zubumt* is the American *gone to the bad, fix'n* is to *fix, usen* is *to use*, and so on. The feminine and diminutive suffix *-ké* is often added to nouns. Thus *bluffer* gives rise to *blufferké* (= hypocrite), and one also notes *dresské, katké, watchké* and *bummerké*. "Oi! is sie a *blufferké!*" is good American Yiddish for "isn't she a hypocrite!" The suffix *-nick*, signifying agency, is also freely applied. *Allrightnick* means an upstart, an offensive boaster, one of whom his fellows would say "He is all right" with a sneer. Similarly, *consumptionick* means a victim of tuberculosis. Other suffixes are *-chick* and *-ige*, the first exemplified in *boychick*, a diminutive of *boy*, and the second in *next-doorige*, meaning the woman next-door, an important person in ghetto social life. Some of the loan-words, of course, undergo changes on Yiddish-speaking lips. Thus, *landlord* becomes *lendler, lounge* becomes *lunch, tenant* becomes *tenner*, and *whiskers* loses its final *s*. "Wie gefällt dir sein *whisker?*" (= how do you like his beard?) is good Yiddish, ironically intended. *Fellow*, of course, changes to the American *feller*, as in "Rosie hat schon a *feller*" (= Rosie has got a *feller*, *i. e.*, a sweetheart). *Show*, in the sense of *chance*, is used constantly, as in "git ihm a *show*" (= give him a chance). *Bad boy* is adopted bodily, as in "er is a *bad boy*." *To shut up* is inflected as one word, as in "er hat nit gewolt *shutup'n* (= he wouldn't shut up). *To catch* is used in the sense of to obtain, as in "*catch'n* a gmilath chesed" (= to raise a loan). Here, by the way, *gmilath chesed* is excellent Biblical Hebrew. *To bluff*, unchanged in form, takes on the new meaning of to lie: a *bluffer* is a liar. Scores of American phrases are in constant use, among them, *all right, never mind, I bet you, no sir* and *I'll fix you.* It is curious to note that *sure Mike*, borrowed by the American vulgate from Irish English, has gone over into American Yiddish. Finally, to make an end, here are two complete and characteristic American Yiddish sentences: "Sie wet *clean'n* die *rooms, scrub'n* dem *floor, wash'n* die *windows, dress'n* dem *boy* und gehn in *butcher-store* und in *grocery.* Dernoch vet sie machen *dinner* und gehn in *street* für a *walk.*[54]

American itself, in the Philippines, and to a lesser extent in Porto Rico and on the Isthmus, has undergone similar changes under the influence of Spanish and the native dialects. Maurice P. Dunlap[55] offers the following specimen of a conversation between two Americans long resident in Manila:

Hola, amigo.
Komusta kayo.
Porque were you hablaing with ese señorita?
She wanted a job as lavandera.
Cuanto?
Ten cents, conant, a piece, so I told her no kerry.
Have you had chow? Well, spera till I sign this chit and I'll take a paseo with you.

[54] For all these examples of American Yiddish I am indebted to the kindness of Abraham Cahan, editor of the *Jewish Daily Forward.* Mr. Cahan is not only editor of the chief Yiddish newspaper of the United States, but also an extraordinarily competent writer of English, as his novel, The Rise of David Levinsky, demonstrates.

[55] What Americans Talk in the Philippines, *American Review of Reviews*, Aug., 1913.

Here we have an example of Philippine American that shows all the tendencies of American Yiddish. It retains the general forms of American, but in the short conversation, embracing but 41 different words, there are eight loan-words from the Spanish (*hola, amigo, porque, ese, señorita, lavandera, cuanto* and *paseo*), two Spanish locutions in a debased form (*spera* for *espera* and *no kerry* for *no quiro*), two loan-words from the Taglog (*komusta* and *kayo*), two from Pigeon English (*chow* and *chit*), one Philippine-American localism (*conant*), and a Spanish verb with an English inflection (*hablaing*).

The immigrant in the midst of a large native population, of course, exerts no such pressure upon the national language as that exerted upon an immigrant language by the native, but nevertheless his linguistic habits and limitations have to be reckoned with in dealing with him, and the concessions thus made necessary have a very ponderable influence upon the general speech. In the usual sense, as we have seen, there are no dialects in American; two natives, however widely their birthplaces may be separated, never have any practical difficulty understanding each other. But there are at least quasi-dialects among the immigrants—the Irish, the German, the Scandinavian, the Italian, the Jewish, and so on—and these quasi-dialects undoubtedly leave occasional marks, not only upon the national vocabulary, but also upon the general speech habits of the country, as in the case, for example, of the pronunciation of *yes*, already mentioned, and in that of the substitution of the diphthong *oi* for the *ur*-sound in such words as *world, journal* and *burn*—a Yiddishism now almost universal among the lower classes of New York, and threatening to spread.[56] More important, however, is the support given to a native tendency by the foreigner's incapacity for employing (or even comprehending) syntax of any complexity, or words not of the simplest. This is the tendency toward succinct-

[56] *Cf.* The English of the Lower Classes in New York City and Vicinity, *Dialect Notes*, vol. i, pt. ix, 1896. It is curious to note that the same corruption occurs in the Spanish spoken in Santo Domingo. The Dominicans thus change *porque* into *poique*. *Cf.* Santo Domingo, by Otto Schoenrich; New York, 1918, p. 172. See also High School Circular No. 17, Dept. of Education, City of New York, June 19, 1912, p. 6.

ness and clarity, at whatever sacrifice of grace. One English observer, Sidney Low, puts the chief blame for the general explosiveness of American upon the immigrant, who must be communicated with in the plainest words available, and is not socially worthy of the suavity of circumlocution anyhow.[57] In his turn the immigrant seizes upon these plainest words as upon a sort of convenient Lingua Franca—his quick adoption of *damn* as a universal adjective is traditional—and throws his influence upon the side of the underlying speech habit when he gets on in the vulgate. Many characteristic Americanisms of the sort to stagger lexicographers—for example, *near-silk*—have come from the Jews, whose progress in business is a good deal faster than their progress in English. Others, as we have seen, have come from the German immigrants of half a century ago, from the so-called Pennsylvania Dutch (who are notoriously ignorant and uncouth), and from the Irish, who brought with them a form of English already very corrupt. The same and similar elements greatly reinforce the congenital tendencies of the dialect—toward the facile manufacture of compounds, toward a disregard of the distinctions between parts of speech, and, above all, toward the throwing off of all etymological restraints.

§ 5

Processes of Word Formation—Some of these tendencies, it has been pointed out, go back to the period of the first growth of American, and were inherited from the English of the time. They are the products of a movement which, reaching its height in the English of Elizabeth, was dammed up at home, so to speak, by the rise of linguistic self-consciousness toward the end of the reign of Anne, but continued almost unobstructed in the colonies. For example, there is what philologists call the habit of backformation—a sort of instinctive search, etymologically unsound, for short roots in long words. This habit, in Restoration days, precipitated a quasi-English word, *mobile*, from the Latin *mobile*

[57] The American People, 2 vols.; New York, 1909–11, vol. ii, pp. 449–50. For a discussion of this effect of contact with foreigners upon a language see also Beach-la-Mar, by William Churchill; Washington, 1911, p. 11 *et seq.*

vulgus, and in the days of William and Mary it went a step further by precipitating *mob* from *mobile.* *Mob* is now sound English, but in the eighteenth century it was violently attacked by the new sect of purists,[58] and though it survived their onslaught they undoubtedly greatly impeded the formation and adoption of other words of the same category. But in the colonies the process went on unimpeded, save for the feeble protests of such stray pedants as Witherspoon and Boucher. *Rattler* for *rattlesnake, pike* for *turnpike, draw* for *drawbridge, coon* for *raccoon, possum* for *opossum, cuss* for *customer, cute* for *acute, squash* for *askutasquash*—these American back-formations are already antique; *Sabbaday* for *Sabbath-day* has actually reached the dignity of an archaism. To this day they are formed in great numbers; scarcely a new substantive of more than two syllables comes in without bringing one in its wake. We have thus witnessed, within the past two years, the genesis of scores now in wide use and fast taking on respectability; *phone* for *telephone, gas* for *gasoline, co-ed* for *co-educational, pop* for *populist, frat* for *fraternity, gym* for *gymnasium, movie* for *moving-picture, prep-school* for *preparatory-school, auto* for *automobile, aero* for *aeroplane.* Some linger on the edge of vulgarity: *pep* for *pepper, flu* for *influenza, plute* for *plutocrat, pen* for *penitentiary, con* for *confidence* (as in *con-man, con-game* and *to con*), *convict* and *consumption, defi* for *defiance, beaut* for *beauty, rep* for *reputation, stenog* for *stenographer, ambish* for *ambition, vag* for *vagrant, champ* for *champion, pard* for *partner, coke* for *cocaine, simp* for *simpleton, diff* for *difference.* Others are already in perfectly good usage: *smoker* for *smoking-car, diner* for *dining-car, sleeper* for *sleeping-car, oleo* for *oleomargarine, hypo* for *hyposulphite of soda, Yank* for *Yankee, confab* for *confabulation, memo* for *memorandum, pop-concert* for *popular-concert. Ad* for *advertisement* is struggling hard for recognition; some of its compounds, *e. g., ad-writer, want-ad, display-ad, ad-card, ad-rate, column-ad* and *ad-man,* are already accepted in technical terminology. *Boob* for *booby* promises to become sound American in a few years; its synonyms are no more respectable than it is. At

[58] *Vide* Lounsbury: The Standard of Usage in English, pp. 65–7.

its heels is *bo* for *hobo,* an altogether fit successor to *bum* for *bummer.*[59]

A parallel movement shows itself in the great multiplication of common abbreviations. "Americans, as a rule," says Farmer, "employ abbreviations to an extent unknown in Europe. . . . This trait of the American character is discernible in every department of the national life and thought."[60] *O. K., C. O. D., N. G., G. O. P.* (get out and push) and *P. D. Q.,* are almost national hall-marks; the immigrant learns them immediately after *damn* and *go to hell.* Thornton traces *N. G.* to 1840; *C. O. D.* and *P. D. Q.* are probably as old. As for *O. K.,* it was in use so early as 1790, but it apparently did not acquire its present significance until the 20's; originally it seems to have meant "ordered recorded."[11] During the presidential campaign of 1828 Jackson's enemies, seeking to prove his illiteracy, alleged that he used it for "oll korrect." Of late the theory has been put forward that it is derived from an Indian word, *okeh,* signifying "so be it," and Dr. Woodrow Wilson is said to support this theory and to use *okeh* in endorsing government papers, but I am unaware of the authority upon which the etymology is based. Bartlett says that the figurative use of *A No. 1,* as in *an A No. 1 man,* also originated in America, but this may not be true. There can be little doubt, however, about *T. B.* (for *tuberculosis*), *G. B.* (for *grand bounce*), *23, on the Q. T.,* and *D. & D.* (*drunk and disorderly*). The language breeds such short forms of speech prodigiously; every trade and profession has a host of them; they are innumerable in the slang of sport.[61]

What one sees under all this, account for it as one will, is a double habit, the which is, at bottom, sufficient explanation of the gap which begins to yawn between English and American, particularly on the spoken plane. On the one hand it is a habit of verbal economy—a jealous disinclination to waste two words on what can be put into one, a natural taste for the brilliant and

[59] For an exhaustive discussion of these formations *cf.* Clipped Words, by Elizabeth Wittman, *Dialect Notes,* vol. iv, pt. ii, 1914.
[60] Americanisms Old and New, p. 1.
[61] *Cf.* Semi-Secret Abbreviations, by Percy W. Long, *Dialect Notes,* vol. iv, pt. iii, 1915.

succinct, a disdain of all grammatical and lexicographical dainti-
ness, born partly, perhaps, of ignorance, but also in part of a
sound sense of their imbecility.   And on the other hand there is
a high relish and talent for metaphor—in Brander Matthews'
phrase, "a figurative vigor that the Elizabethans would have
realized and understood."   Just as the American rebels instinctively against such parliamentary circumlocutions as "I am not
prepared to say" and "so much by way of being," [62] just as he
would fret under the forms of English journalism, with its reporting empty of drama, its third-person smothering of speeches
and its complex and unintelligible jargon,[63] just so, in his daily
speech and writing he chooses terseness and vividness whenever
there is any choice, and seeks to make one when it doesn't exist.
There is more than mere humorous contrast between the famous
placard in the wash-room of the British Museum: "These Basins
Are For Casual Ablutions Only," and the familiar sign at American railroad-crossings: "Stop! Look! Listen!"   Between the
two lies an abyss separating two cultures, two habits of mind,
two diverging tongues.   It is almost unimaginable that Englishmen, journeying up and down in elevators, would ever have
stricken the teens out of their speech, turning *sixteenth* into
simple *six* and *twenty-fourth* into *four;* the clipping is almost as
far from their way of doing things as the climbing so high in the
air.   Nor have they the brilliant facility of Americans for making
new words of grotesque but penetrating tropes, as in *corn-fed,*
tight-wad, bone-head, bleachers and *juice* (for *electricity*); when
they attempt such things the result is often lugubrious; two hundred years of schoolmastering has dried up their inspiration.
Nor have they the fine American hand for devising new verbs;
to maffick and *to limehouse* are their best specimens in twenty
years, and both have an almost pathetic flatness.   Their business
with the language, indeed, is not in this department.   They are

---

[62] The classical example is in a parliamentary announcement by Sir
Robert Peel: "When that question is made to me in a proper time, in a
proper place, under proper qualifications, and with proper motives, I
will hesitate long before I will refuse to take it into consideration."

[63] *Cf.* On the Art of Writing, by Sir Arthur Quiller-Couch; p. 100 *et seq.*

not charged with its raids and scoutings, but with the organization of its conquests and the guarding of its accumulated stores.

For the student interested in the biology of language, as opposed to its paleontology, there is endless material in the racy neologisms of American, and particularly in its new compounds and novel verbs. Nothing could exceed the brilliancy of such inventions as *joy-ride, high-brow, road-louse, sob-sister, nature-faker, stand-patter, lounge-lizard, hash-foundry, buzz-wagon, has-been, end-seat-hog, shoot-the-chutes* and *grape-juice-diplomacy.* They are bold; they are vivid; they have humor; they meet genuine needs. *Joy-ride,* I note, is already going over into English, and no wonder. There is absolutely no synonym for it; to convey its idea in orthodox English would take a whole sentence. And so, too, with certain single words of metaphorical origin: *barrel* for large and illicit wealth, *pork* for unnecessary and dishonest appropriations of public money, *joint* for illegal liquor-house, *tenderloin* for gay and dubious neighborhood.[64] Most of these, and of the new compounds with them, belong to the vocabulary of disparagement. Here an essential character of the American shows itself: his tendency to combat the disagreeable with irony, to heap ridicule upon what he is suspicious of or doesn't understand.

The rapidity with which new verbs are made in the United States is really quite amazing. Two days after the first regulations of the Food Administration were announced, *to hooverize* appeared spontaneously in scores of newspapers, and a week later it was employed without any visible sense of its novelty in the debates of Congress and had taken on a respectability equal to that of *to bryanize, to fletcherize* and *to oslerize. To electrocute* appeared inevitably in the first public discussion of capital pun-

---

[64] This use of *tenderloin* is ascribed to Alexander (alias "Clubber") Williams, a New York police captain. *Vide* the *New York Sun,* July 11, 1913. Williams, in 1876, was transferred from an obscure precinct to West Thirtieth Street. "I've been having chuck steak ever since I've been on the force," he said, "and now I'm going to have a bit of tenderloin." "The name," says the *Sun,* "has endured more than a generation, moving with the changed amusement geography of the city, and has been adopted in all parts of the country."

ishment by electricity; *to taxi* came in with the first taxi-cabs; *to commute* no doubt accompanied the first commutation ticket; *to insurge* attended the birth of the Progressive balderdash. Of late the old affix *-ize*, once fecund of such monsters as *to funeralize*, has come into favor again, and I note, among its other products, *to belgiumize, to vacationize, to picturize* and *to scenarioize*. In a newspaper headline I even find *to s o s*, in the form of its gerund.[65] Many characteristic American verbs are compounds of common verbs and prepositions or adverbs, with new meanings imposed. Compare, for example, *to give* and *to give out, to go back* and *to go back on, to beat* and *to beat it, to light* and *to light out, to butt* and *to butt in, to turn* and *to turn down, to show* and *to show up, to put* and *to put over, to wind* and *to wind up*. Sometimes, however, the addition seems to be merely rhetorical, as in *to start off, to finish up, to open up* and *to hurry up*. *To hurry up* is so commonplace in America that everyone uses it and no one notices it, but it remains rare in England. *Up* seems to be essential to many of these latter-day verbs, *e. g.*, *to pony up, to doll up, to ball up*; without it they are without significance. Nearly all of them are attended by derivative adjectives or nouns; *cut-up, show-down, kick-in, come-down, hangout, start-off, run-in, balled-up, dolled-up, wind-up, bang-up, turn-down, jump-off*.

In many directions the same prodigal fancy shows itself—for example, in the free interchange of parts of speech, in the bold inflection of words not inflected in sound English, and in the invention of wholly artificial words. The first phenomenon has already concerned us. Would an English literary critic of any pretensions employ such a locution as "all by her *lonesome*"? I have a doubt of it—and yet I find that phrase in a serious book by the critic of the *New Republic*.[66] Would an English M. P. use "he has another *think* coming" in debate? Again I doubt it—but even more anarchistic dedications of verbs and adjectives to substantival use are to be found in the *Congressional Record* every day. *Jitney* is an old American substantive lately

---

[65] *New York Evening Mail*, Feb. 2, 1918, p. 1.
[66] Horizons, by Francis Hackett; New York, 1918, p. 53.

revived; a month after its revival it was also an adjective, and before long it may also be a verb and even an adverb. *To lift up* was turned tail first and made a substantive, and is now also an adjective and a verb. *Joy-ride* became a verb the day after it was born as a noun. And what of *livest?* An astounding inflection, indeed—but with quite sound American usage behind it. The *Metropolitan Magazine*, of which Col. Roosevelt is an editor, announces on its letter paper that it is "the *livest* magazine in America," and *Poetry*, the organ of the new poetry movement, prints at the head of its contents page the following encomium from the *New York Tribune:* "the *livest* art in America today is poetry, and the *livest* expression of that art is in this little Chicago monthly."

Now and then the spirit of American shows a transient faltering, and its inventiveness is displaced by a banal extension of meaning, so that a single noun comes to signify discrete things. Thus *laundry,* meaning originally a place where linen is washed, has come to mean also the linen itself. So, again, *gun* has come to mean fire-arms of all sorts, and has entered into such compounds as *gun-man* and *gun-play.* And in the same way *party* has been borrowed from the terminology of the law and made to do colloquial duty as a synonym for *person.* But such evidences of poverty are rare and abnormal; the whole movement of the language is toward the multiplication of substantives. A new object gets a new name, and that new name enters into the common vocabulary at once. *Sundae* and *hokum* are late examples; their origin is dubious and disputed, but they met genuine needs and so they seem to be secure. A great many more such substantives are deliberate inventions, for example, *kodak, protectograph, conductorette, bevo, klaxon, vaseline, jap-a-lac, resinol, autocar, postum, crisco, electrolier, addressograph, alabastine, orangeade, pianola, victrola, dictagraph, kitchenette, crispette, cellarette, uneeda, triscuit* and *peptomint.* Some of these indicate attempts at description: *oleomargarine, phonograph* and *gasoline* are older examples of that class. Others represent efforts to devise designations that will meet the conditions of advertising psychology and the trade-marks law, to wit, that they be (*a*) new, (*b*) easily remembered, and (*c*) not directly descriptive. Probably the most successful invention of this sort is *kodak*, which was devised by George Eastman, inventor of the portable camera so called. *Kodak* has so far won acceptance as a common noun that Eastman is often forced to assert his proprietary right to it.[67] *Vaseline* is in the same position. The annual crop of such inventions in the United States is enormous.[68] The majority die, but a hearty few always survive.

Of analogous character are artificial words of the *scalawag* and *rambunctious* class, the formation of which constantly goes on. Some of them are shortened compounds: *grandificent* (from *grand* and *magnificent*), *sodalicious* (from *soda* and *delicious*) and *warphan(age)* (from *war* and *orphan(age)*).[69] Others are made up of common roots and grotesque affixes: *swelldoodle*, *splendiferous* and *peacharino*. Yet others are mere extravagant inventions: *scallywampus*, *supergobsloptious* and *floozy*. Most of these are devised by advertisement writers or college students, and belong properly to slang, but there is a steady movement of selected specimens into the common vocabulary. The words in *-doodle* hint at German influences, and those in *-ino* owe something to Italian, or at least to popular burlesques of what is conceived to be Italian.

§ 6

Pronunciation—"Language," said Sayce, in 1879, "does not consist of letters, but of sounds, and until this fact has been brought home to us our study of it will be little better than an

[67] It has even got into the Continental languages. In October, 1917, the Verband Deutscher Amateurphotographen-Vereine was moved to issue the following warning: "Es gibt kein deutschen *Kodaks*. *Kodak*, als Sammelname für photographische Erzeugnisse ist falsch und bezeichnet nur die Fabrikate der Eastman-*Kodak*-Company. Wer von einem *Kodak* spricht und nur allgemein eine photographische Kamera meint, bedenkt nicht, dass er mit der Weiterverbreitung dieses Wortes die deutsche Industrie sugunsten der amerikanisch-englischen schädigt."

[68] *Cf.* Word-Coinage and Modern Trade Names, by Louise Pound, *Dialect Notes*, vol. iv, pt. i, 1913, pp. 29–41. Most of these coinages produce derivatives, *e. g., bevo-officer, to kodak, kodaker.*

[69] This conscious shortening, of course, is to be distinguished from the shortening that goes on in words by gradual decay, as in *Christmas* (from *Christ's mass*) and *daisy* (from *day's eye*).

exercise of memory." [70] The theory, at that time, was somewhat strange to English grammarians and etymologists, despite the investigations of A. J. Ellis and the massive lesson of Grimm's law; their labors were largely wasted upon deductions from the written word. But since then, chiefly under the influence of Continental philologists, and particularly of the Dane, J. O. H. Jespersen, they have turned from orthographical futilities to the actual sounds of the tongue, and the latest and best grammar of it, that of Sweet, is frankly based upon the spoken English of educated Englishmen—not, remember, of conscious purists, but of the general body of cultivated folk. Unluckily, this new method also has its disadvantages. The men of a given race and time usually write a good deal alike, or, at all events, attempt to write alike, but in their oral speech there are wide variations. "No two persons," says a leading contemporary authority upon English phonetics,[71] "pronounce exactly alike." Moreover, "even the best speaker commonly uses more than one style." The result is that it is extremely difficult to determine the prevailing pronunciation of a given combination of letters at any time and place. The persons whose speech is studied pronounce it with minute shades of difference, and admit other differences according as they are conversing naturally or endeavoring to exhibit their pronunciation. Worse, it is impossible to represent a great many of these shades in print. Sweet, trying to do it,[72] found himself, in the end, with a preposterous alphabet of 125 letters. Prince L.-L. Bonaparte more than doubled this number, and Ellis brought it to 390.[73] Other phonologists, English and Continental, have gone floundering into the same bog. The dictionary-makers, forced to a far greater economy of means, are brought into obscurity. The difficulties of the enterprise, in fact, are probably unsurmountable. It is, as White says, "almost impossible for one person to express to another by signs the

[70] The Science of Language, vol. ii, p. 339.

[71] Daniel Jones: The Pronunciation of English, 2nd ed.; Cambridge, 1914, p. 1. Jones is lecturer in phonetics at University College, London.

[72] Vide his Handbook of Phonetics, p. xv, et seq.

[73] It is given in Ellis' Early English Pronunciation, p. 1293 et seq. and in Sayce's The Science of Language, vol. i, p. 353 et seq.

sound of any word." "Only the voice," he goes on, "is capable of that; for the moment a sign is used the question arises, What is the value of that sign? The sounds of words are the most delicate, fleeting and inapprehensible things in nature. . . . Moreover, the question arises as to the capability to apprehend and distinguish sounds on the part of the person whose evidence is given." [74] Certain German orthoepists, despairing of the printed page, have turned to the phonograph, and there is a Deutsche Grammophon-Gesellschaft in Berlin which offers records of specimen speeches in a great many languages and dialects, including English. The phonograph has also been put to successful use in language teaching by various American correspondence schools.

In view of all this it would be hopeless to attempt to exhibit in print the numerous small differences between English and American pronunciation, for many of them are extremely delicate and subtle, and only their aggregation makes them plain. According to a recent and very careful observer,[75] the most important of them do not lie in pronunciation at all, properly so called, but in intonation. In this direction, he says, one must look for the true characters "of the English accent." I incline to agree with White,[76] that the pitch of the English voice is somewhat higher than that of the American, and that it is thus more penetrating. The nasal twang which Englishmen observe in the *vox Americana*, though it has high overtones, is itself not high pitched, but rather low pitched, as all constrained and muffled tones are apt to be. The causes of that twang have long engaged phonologists, and in the main they agree that there is a physical basis for it— that our generally dry climate and rapid changes of temperature produce an actual thickening of the membranes concerned in the production of sound.[77] We are, in brief, a somewhat snuffling

[74] Every-Day English, p. 29.

[75] Robert J. Menner: The Pronunciation of English in America, *Atlantic Monthly*, March, 1915, p. 366.

[76] Words and Their Uses, p. 58.

[77] The following passage from Kipling's American Notes, ch. i, will be recalled: "Oliver Wendell Holmes says that the Yankee schoolmarm, the cider and the salt codfish of the Eastern states are responsible for what

people, and much more given to catarrhs and coryzas than the inhabitants of damp Britain. Perhaps this general impediment to free and easy utterance, subconsciously apprehended, is responsible for the American tendency to pronounce the separate syllables of a word with much more care than an Englishman bestows upon them; the American, in giving *extraordinary* six distinct syllables instead of the Englishman's grudging four, may be seeking to make up for his natural disability. Marsh, in his "Lectures on the English Language,"[78] sought two other explanations of the fact. On the one hand, he argued that the Americans of his day read a great deal more than the English, and were thus much more influenced by the spelling of words, and on the other hand he pointed out that "our flora shows that the climate of even our Northern States belongs . . . to a more Southern type than that of England," and that "in Southern latitudes . . . articulation is generally much more distinct than in Northern regions." In support of the latter proposition he cited the pronunciation of Spanish, Italian and Turkish, as compared with that of English, Danish and German—rather unfortunate examples, for the pronunciation of German is at least as clear as that of Italian. Swedish would have supported his case far better: the Swedes debase their vowels and slide over their consonants even more markedly than the English. Marsh believed that there was a tendency among Southern peoples to throw the accent back, and that this helped to "bring out all the syllables." One finds a certain support for this notion in various American peculiarities of stress. *Advertisement* offers an example. The prevailing American pronunciation, despite incessant pedagogical counterblasts, puts the accent on the penult, whereas the English pronunciation stresses the second syllable. *Paresis* illustrates the same tendency. The English accent the first syllable, but, as Krapp says, American usage clings to the

he calls a nasal accent. I know better. They stole books from across the water without paying for 'em, and the snort of delight was fixed in their nostrils for ever by a just Providence. That is why they talk a foreign tongue today."

[78] Lecture xxx. The English Language in America.

accent on the second syllable.[79]   There are, again, *pianist, primarily* and *telegrapher*.   The English accent the first syllable of each; we commonly accent the second.   In *temporarily* they also accent the first; we accent the third.   Various other examples might be cited.   But when one had marshalled them their significance would be at once set at naught by four very familiar words, *mamma, papa, inquiry* and *ally*.   Americans almost invariably accent each on the first syllable; Englishmen stress the second.   For months, during 1918, the publishers of the Standard Dictionary, advertising that work in the street-cars, explained that *ally* should be accented on the second syllable, and pointed out that owners of their dictionary were safeguarded against the vulgarism of accenting it on the first.   Nevertheless, this free and highly public instruction did not suffice to exterminate *al'ly*.   I made note of the pronunciations overheard, with the word constantly on all lips.   But one man of my acquaintance regularly accented the second syllable, and he was an eminent scholar, professionally devoted to the study of language.

Thus it is unsafe, here as elsewhere, to generalize too facilely, and particularly unsafe to exhibit causes with too much assurance.   "Man frage nicht warum," says Philipp Karl Buttmann.   "Der Sprachgebrauch lässt sich nur beobachten."[80]   But the greater distinctness of American utterance, whatever its genesis and machinery, is palpable enough in many familiar situations.   "The typical American accent," says Vizetelly, "is often harsh and unmusical, but it sounds all of the letters to be sounded, and slurs, but does not distort, the rest."[81]   An American, for example, almost always sounds the first *l* in *fulfill;* an Englishman makes the first syllable *foo*.   An American sounds every syllable in *extraordinary, literary, military, secretary* and the other words of the -*ary*-group; an Englishman never pronounces the *a* of the penultimate syllable.   *Kindness*, with the *d* silent, would attract notice in the United States; in England, according to

[79] Modern English, p. 166.   *Cf.* A Desk-Book of 25,000 Words Frequently Mispronounced, by Frank H. Vizetelly, p. 652.

[80] Lexilogus, 2nd ed.; Berlin, 1860, p. 239.   An English translation was published in London in 1846.

[81] A Desk-Book of 25,000 Words Frequently Mispronounced, p. xvi.

Jones,[82] the *d* is "very commonly, if not usually" omitted. *Often*, in America, commonly retains a full *t;* in England it is actually and officially *offen*. Let an American and an Englishman pronounce *program(me)*. Though the Englishman retains the long form of the last syllable in writing, he reduces it in speaking to a thick triple consonant, *grm;* the American enunciates it clearly, rhyming it with *damn.* Or try the two with any word ending in -*g*, say *sporting* or *ripping*. Or with any word having *r* before a consonant, say *card, harbor, lord* or *preferred*. "The majority of Englishmen," says Menner, "certainly do not pronounce the *r* . . .; just as certainly the majority of educated Americans pronounce it distinctly."[83] Henry James, visiting the United States after many years of residence in England, was much harassed by this persistent *r*-sound, which seemed to him to resemble "a sort of morose grinding of the back teeth."[84] So sensitive to it did he become that he began to hear where it was actually non-existent, save as an occasional barbarism, for example, in *Cuba-r, vanilla-r* and *California-r*. He put the blame for it, and for various other departures from the strict canon of contemporary English, upon "the American common school, the American newspaper, and the American Dutchman and Dago." Unluckily for his case, the full voicing of the *r* came into American long before the appearance of any of these influences. The early colonists, in fact, brought it with them from England, and it still prevailed there in Dr. Johnson's day, for he protested publicly against the "rough snarling sound" and led the movement which finally resulted in its extinction.[85] Today, extinct, it is mourned by English purists, and the Poet Laureate denounces the clergy of the Established Church for saying "the *sawed* of the *Laud*" instead of "the sword of the Lord."[86]

But even in the matter of elided consonants American is not always the conservator. We cling to the *r*, we preserve the final

<hr />

[82] The Pronunciation of English, p. 17.
[83] The Pronunciation of English in America, op. cit., p. 362.
[84] The Question of Our Speech, p. 29 *et seq.*
[85] *Cf.* The Cambridge History of English Literature, vol. xiv, p. 487.
[86] Robert Bridges: A Tract on the Present State of English Pronunciation; Oxford, 1913.

g, we give *nephew* a clear *f*-sound instead of the clouded English *v*-sound, and we boldly nationalize *trait* and pronounce its final *t*, but we drop the second *p* from *pumpkin* and change the *m* to *n*, we change the *ph*(= *f*)-sound to plain *p* in *diphtheria, diphthong* and *naphtha*,[87] we relieve *rind* of its final *d*, and, in the complete sentence, we slaughter consonants by assimilation. I have heard Englishmen say *brand-new*, but on American lips it is almost invariably *bran-new*. So nearly universal is this nasalization in the United States that certain American lexicographers have sought to found the term upon *bran* and not upon *brand*. Here the national speech is powerfully influenced by Southern dialectical variations, which in turn probably derive partly from French example and partly from the linguistic limitations of the negro. The latter, even after two hundred years, has great difficulties with our consonants, and often drops them. A familiar anecdote well illustrates his speech habit. On a train stopping at a small station in Georgia a darkey threw up a window and yelled "Wah ee?" The reply from a black on the platform was "Wah oo?" A Northerner aboard the train, puzzled by this inarticulate dialogue, sought light from a Southern passenger, who promptly translated the first question as "Where is he?" and the second as "Where is who?" A recent viewer with alarm [88] argues that this conspiracy against the consonants is spreading, and that English printed words no longer represent the actual sounds of the American language. "Like the French," he says, "we have a marked *liaison*—the borrowing of a letter from the preceding word. We invite one another to 'c'meer' (= come here) . . . 'Hoo-zat?' (= who is that?) has as good a *liaison* as the French *vois avez*." This critic believes that American tends to abandon *t* for *d*, as in *Sadd'y* (= Saturday) and *siddup* (= sit up), and to get rid of *h*, as in "ware-zee?" (= where is he?). But here we invade the vulgar speech, which belongs to the next chapter.

[87] An interesting discussion of this peculiarity is in Some Variant Pronunciations in the New South, by William A. Read, *Dialect Notes*, vol. iii, pt. vii, 1911, p. 504 *et seq.*

[88] Hugh Mearns: Our Own, Our Native Speech, *McClure's Magazine*, Oct., 1916.

Among the vowels the most salient difference between English and American pronunciation, of course, is marked off by the flat American *a*. This flat *a*, as we have seen, has been under attack at home for nearly a century. The New Englanders, very sensitive to English example, substitute a broad *a* that is even broader than the English, and an *a* of the same sort survives in the South in a few words, *e. g., master, tomato* and *tassel,* but everywhere else in the country the flat *a* prevails. Fashion and the example of the stage oppose it,[89] and it is under the ban of an active wing of schoolmasters, but it will not down. To the average American, indeed, the broad *a* is a banner of affectation, and he associates it unpleasantly with spats, Harvard, male tea-drinking, wrist watches and all the other objects of his social suspicion. He gets the flat sound, not only into such words as *last, calf, dance* and *pastor,* but even into *piano* and *drama. Drama* is sometimes *drayma* west of Connecticut, but almost never *drahma* or *drawma. Tomato* with the *a* of *bat,* may sometimes borrow the *a* of *plate,* but *tomahto* is confined to New England and the South. *Hurrah,* in American, has also borrowed the *a* of *plate;* one hears *hurray* much oftener than *hurraw.* Even *amen* frequently shows that *a,* though not when sung. Curiously enough, it is displaced in *patent* by the true flat *a.* The English rhyme the first syllable of the word with *rate;* in America it always rhymes with *rat.*

The broad *a* is not only almost extinct outside of New England; it begins to show signs of decay even there. At all events, it has gradually disappeared from many words, and is measurably less sonorous in those in which it survives than it used to be. A century ago it appeared, not only in *dance, aunt, glass, past,* etc., but also in *Daniel, imagine, rational* and *travel.*[90] And in 1857 Oliver Wendell Holmes reported it in *matter, handsome, caterpillar, apple* and *satisfaction.* It has been displaced in virtually all of these, even in the most remote reaches of the back country,

[89] The American actor imitates, not only English pronunciation in all its details, but also English dress and bearing. His struggles with such words as *extraordinary* are often very amusing.

[90] *Cf.* Duncan Mackintosh: Essai Raissoné dur la Grammaire et la Prononciation Anglais; Boston, 1797.

by the national flat *a*. Grandgent [91] says that the broad *a* is now restricted in New England to the following situations:

1. when followed by *s* or *ns*, as in *last* and *dance*.
2. when followed by *r* preceding another consonant, as in *cart*.
3. when followed by *lm*, as in *calm*.
4. when followed by *f, s* or *th*, as in *laugh, pass* and *path*.

The *u*-sound also shows certain differences between English and American usage. The English reduce the last syllable of *figure* to *ger;* the educated American preserves the *u*-sound as in *nature*. The English make the first syllable of *courteous* rhyme with *fort;* the American standard rhymes it with *hurt*. The English give an *oo*-sound to the *u* of *brusque;* in America the word commonly rhymes with *tusk*. A *u*-sound, as everyone knows, gets into the American pronunciation of *clerk*, by analogy with *insert;* the English cling to a broad *a*-sound, by analogy with *hearth*. Even the latter, in the United States, is often pronounced to rhyme with *dearth*. The American, in general, is much less careful than the Englishman to preserve the shadowy *y*-sound before *u* in words of the *duke*-class. He retains it in *few*, but surely not in *new*. Nor in *duke, blue, stew, due, duty* and *true*. Nor even in *Tuesday*. Purists often attack the simple *oo*-sound. In 1912, for example, the Department of Education of New York City warned all the municipal high-school teachers to combat it.[92] But it is doubtful that one pupil in a hundred was thereby induced to insert the *y* in *induced*. Finally there is *lieutenant*. The Englishman pronounces the first syllable *left;* the American invariably makes it *loot*. White says that the prevailing American pronunciation is relatively recent. "I never heard it," he reports, "in my boyhood." [93] He was born in New York in 1821.

The *i*-sound presents several curious differences. The English make it long in all words of the *hostile*-class; in America it is commonly short, even in *puerile*. The English also lengthen it in *sliver;* in America the word usually rhymes with *liver*. The

[91] Fashion and the Broad *A*, *Nation*, Jan 7, 1915.
[92] High School Circular No. 17, June 19, 1912.
[93] Every-Day English, p. 243.

short *i*, in England, is almost universally substituted for the *e* in *pretty,* and this pronunciation is also inculcated in most American schools, but I often hear an unmistakable *e*-sound in the United States, making the first syllable rhyme with *bet.* Contrariwise, most Americans put the short *i* into *been,* making it rhyme with *sin.* In England it shows a long *e*-sound, as in *seen.* A recent poem by an English poet makes the word rhyme with *submarine, queen* and *unseen.*[94] The *o*-sound, in American, tends to convert itself into an *aw*-sound. *Cog* still retains a pure *o,* but one seldom hears it in *log* or *dog.* Henry James denounces this "flatly-drawling group" in "The Question of Our Speech,"[95] and cites *gawd, dawg, sawft, lawft, gawne, lawst* and *frawst* as horrible examples. But the English themselves are not guiltless of the same fault. Many of the accusations that James levels at American, in truth, are echoed by Robert Bridges in "A Tract on the Present State of English Pronunciation." Both spend themselves upon opposing what, at bottom, are probably natural and inevitable movements—for example, the gradual decay of all the vowels to one of neutral color, represented by the *e* of *danger,* the *u* of *suggest,* the second *o* of *common* and the *a* of *prevalent.* This decay shows itself in many languages. In both English and High German, during their middle periods, all the terminal vowels degenerated to *e*—now sunk to the aforesaid neutral vowel in many German words, and expunged from English altogether. The same sound is encountered in languages so widely differing otherwise as Arabic, French and Swedish. "Its existence," says Sayce, "is a sign of age and decay; meaning has become more important than outward form, and the educated intelligence no longer demands a clear pronunciation in order to understand what is said."[96]

All these differences between English and American pronunciation, separately considered, seem slight, but in the aggregate they are sufficient to place serious impediments between mutual

[94] Open Boats, by Alfred Noyes, New York, 1917, pp. 89–91.
[95] P. 30.
[96] The Science of Language, vol. i, p. 259.

comprehension. Let an Englishman and an American (not of New England) speak a quite ordinary sentence, "My aunt can't answer for my dancing the lancers even passably," and at once the gap separating the two pronunciations will be manifest. Here only the *a* is involved. Add a dozen everyday words—*military, schedule, trait, hostile, been, lieutenant, patent, nephew, secretary, advertisement,* and so on—and the strangeness of one to the other is augmented. "Every Englishman visiting the States for the first time," said an English dramatist some time ago, "has a difficulty in making himself understood. He often has to repeat a remark or a request two or three times to make his meaning clear, especially on railroads, in hotels and at bars. The American visiting England for the first time has the same trouble."[97] Despite the fact that American actors imitate English pronunciation to the best of their skill, this visiting Englishman asserted that the average American audience is incapable of understanding a genuinely English company, at least "when the speeches are rattled off in conversational style." When he presented one of his own plays with an English company, he said, many American acquaintances, after witnessing the performance, asked him to lend them the manuscript, "that they might visit it again with some understanding of the dialogue."[98]

[97] B. MacDonald Hastings, *New York Tribune,* Jan. 19, 1913.
[98] Various minor differences between English and American pronunciation, not noted here, are discussed in British and American Pronunciation, by Louise Pound, *School Review,* vol. xxiii, no. 6, June, 1915.

VI

The Common Speech

§ 1

Grammarians and Their Ways—So far, in the main, the language examined has been of a relatively pretentious and self-conscious variety—the speech, if not always of formal discourse, then at least of literate men. Most of the examples of its vocabulary and idiom, in fact, have been drawn from written documents or from written reports of more or less careful utterances, for example, the speeches of members of Congress and of other public men. The whole of Thornton's excellent material is of this character. In his dictionary there is scarcely a locution that is not supported by printed examples.

It must be obvious that such materials, however lavishly set forth, cannot exhibit the methods and tendencies of a living speech with anything approaching completeness, nor even with accuracy. What men put into writing and what they say when they take sober thought are very far from what they utter in everyday conversation. All of us, no matter how careful our speech habits, loosen the belt a bit, so to speak, when we speak familiarly to our fellows, and pay a good deal less heed to precedents and proprieties, perhaps, than we ought to. It was a sure instinct that made Ibsen put "bad grammar" into the mouth of Nora Helmar in "A Doll's House." She is a general's daughter and the wife of a professor, but even professor's wives are not above occasional bogglings of the cases of pronouns and the conjugations of verbs. The professors themselves, in truth, must have the same habit, for sometimes they show plain signs of it in print. More than once, plowing through profound and interminable treatises of grammar and syntax in

177

preparation for the present work, I have encountered the cheering spectacle of one grammarian exposing, with contagious joy, the grammatical lapses of some other grammarian. And nine times out of ten, a few pages further on, I have found the enchanted purist erring himself.[1] The most funereal of the sciences is saved from utter horror by such displays of human malice and fallibility. Speech itself, indeed, would become almost impossible if the grammarians could follow their own rules unfailingly, and were always right.

But here we are among the learned; and their sins, when detected and exposed, are at least punished by conscience. What are of more importance, to those interested in language as a living thing, are the offendings of the millions who are not conscious of any wrong. It is among these millions, ignorant of regulation and eager only to express their ideas clearly and forcefully, that language undergoes its great changes and constantly renews its vitality. These are the genuine makers of grammar, marching miles ahead of the formal grammarians. Like the Emperor Sigismund, each man among them may well say: *"Ego sum . . . super grammaticam."* It is competent for any individual to offer his contribution—his new word, his better idiom, his novel figure of speech, his short cut in grammar or syntax—and it is by the general vote of the whole body, not by the verdict of a small school, that the fate of the innovation is decided. As Brander Matthews says, there is not even representative government in the matter; the *posse comitatus* decides directly, and despite the sternest protest, finally. The ignorant, the rebellious and the daring come forward with their brilliant barbarisms; the learned and conservative bring up their objections. "And when both sides have been heard, there is a show of hands; and by this the irrevocable decision of the community itself is rendered."[2] Thus it was that the Romance languages were fashioned out of the wreck of Latin, the vast in-

[1] Sweet, perhaps the abbot of the order, makes almost indecent haste to sin. See the second paragraph on the very first page of vol. i of his New English Grammar.

[2] *Yale Review*, April, 1918, p. 548.

fluence of the literate minority to the contrary notwithstanding. Thus it was, too, that English lost its case inflections and many of its old conjugations, and that our *yes* came to be substituted for the *gea-se* (= *so be it*) of an earlier day, and that we got rid of *whom* after *man* in *the man I saw*, and that our stark pronoun of the first person was precipitated from the German *ich*. And thus it is that, in our own day, the language faces forces in America which, not content with overhauling and greatly enriching its materials, now threaten to work changes in its very structure.

Where these tendencies run strongest, of course, is on the plane of the vulgar spoken language. Among all classes the everyday speech departs very far from orthodox English, and even very far from any recognizable spoken English, but among those lower classes which make up the great body of the people it gets so far from orthodox English that it gives promise, soon or late, of throwing off its old bonds altogether, or, at any rate, all save the loosest of them. Behind it is the gigantic impulse that I have described in earlier chapters: the impulse of an egoistic and iconoclastic people, facing a new order of life in highly self-conscious freedom, to break a relatively stable language, long since emerged from its period of growth, to their novel and multitudinous needs, and, above all, to their experimental and impatient spirit. This impulse, it must be plain, would war fiercely upon any attempt at formal regulation, however prudent and elastic; it is often rebellious for the mere sake of rebellion. But what it comes into conflict with, in America, is nothing so politic, and hence nothing so likely to keep the brakes upon it. What it actually encounters here is a formalism that is artificial, illogical and almost unintelligible—a formalism borrowed from English grammarians, and by them brought into English, against all fact and reason, from the Latin. "In most of our grammars, perhaps in all of those issued earlier than the opening of the twentieth century," says Matthews, "we find linguistic laws laid down which are in blank contradiction with the genius of the language."[3] In brief, the American

[3] *Yale Review, op. cit.,* p. 560.

school-boy, hauled before a pedagogue to be instructed in the structure and organization of the tongue he speaks, is actually instructed in the structure and organization of a tongue that he never hears at all, and seldom reads, and that, in more than one of the characters thus set before him, does not even exist.

The effects of this are two-fold. On the one hand he conceives an antipathy to a subject so lacking in intelligibility and utility. As one teacher puts it, "pupils tire of it; often they see nothing in it, because there *is* nothing in it." [4] And on the other hand, the school-boy goes entirely without sympathetic guidance in the living language that he actually speaks, in and out of the classroom, and that he will probably speak all the rest of his life. All he hears in relation to it is a series of sneers and prohibitions, most of them grounded, not upon principles deduced from its own nature, but upon its divergences from the theoretical language that he is so unsuccessfully taught. The net result is that all the instruction he receives passes for naught. It is not sufficient to make him a master of orthodox English and it is not sufficient to rid him of the speech-habits of his home and daily life. Thus he is thrown back upon these speech-habits without any helpful restraint or guidance, and they make him a willing ally of the radical and often extravagant tendencies which show themselves in the vulgar tongue. In other words, the very effort to teach him an excessively tight and formal English promotes his use of a loose and rebellious English. And so the grammarians, with the traditional fatuity of their order, labor for the destruction of the grammar they defend, and for the decay of all those refinements of speech that go with it.

The folly of this system, of course, has not failed to attract the attention of the more intelligent teachers, nor have they failed to observe the causes of its failure. "Much of the fruitlessness of the study of English grammar," says Wilcox,[5] "and

[4] The Difficulties Created by Grammarians Are to be Ignored, by W. H. Wilcox, *Atlantic Educational Journal*, Nov., 1912, p. 8. The title of this article is quoted from ministerial instructions of 1909 to the teachers of French *lycées*.

[5] *Op cit.* p. 7. Mr. Wilcox is an instructor in the Maryland State Normal School.

many of the obstacles encountered in its study are due to 'the difficulties created by the grammarians.' These difficulties arise chiefly from three sources—excessive classification, multiplication of terms for a single conception, and the attempt to treat the English language as if it were highly inflected.'' So long ago as the 60's Richard Grant White began an onslaught upon all such punditic stupidities. He saw clearly that "the attempt to treat English as if it were highly inflected" was making its intelligent study almost impossible, and proposed boldly that all English grammar-books be burned.[6] Of late his ideas have begun to gain a certain acceptance, and as the literature of denunciation has grown [7] the grammarians have been constrained to overhaul their texts. When I was a school-boy, during the penultimate decade of the last century, the chief American grammar was "A Practical Grammar of the English Language," by Thomas W. Harvey.[8] This formidable work was almost purely synthetical: it began with a long series of definitions, wholly unintelligible to a child, and proceeded into a maddening maze of pedagogical distinctions, puzzling even to an adult. The latter-day grammars, at least those for the elementary schools, are far more analytical and logical. For example, there is "Longmans' Briefer Grammar," by George J. Smith,[9] a text now in very wide use. This book starts off, not with page after page of abstractions, but with a well-devised examination of the complete sentence, and the characters and relations of the parts of speech are very simply and clearly developed. But before the end the author begins to succumb to precedent, and on page 114 I find

[6] See especially chapters ix and x of Words and Their Uses and chapters xvii, xviii and xix of Every-Day English; also the preface to the latter, p. xi et seq. The study of other languages has been made difficult by the same attempt to force the characters of Greek and Latin grammar upon them. One finds a protest against the process, for example, in E. H. Palmer's Grammar of Hindustani, Persian and Arabic; London, 1906. In all ages, indeed, grammarians appear to have been fatuous. The learned will remember Aristophanes' ridicule of them in The Clouds, 660–690.

[7] The case is well summarized in Simpler English Grammar, by Patterson Wardlaw, *Bull. of the University of S. Carolina*, No. 38, pt. iii, July, 1914.

[8] Cincinnati, 1868; rev. ed., 1878.

[9] New York, 1903; rev. ed., 1915.

paragraph after paragraph of such dull, flyblown pedantry as this:

> Some Intransitive Verbs are used to link the Subject and some Adjective or Noun. These Verbs are called Copulative Verbs, and the Adjective or Noun is called the Attribute.
>
> The Attribute always describes or denotes the person or thing denoted by the Subject.
>
> Verbals are words that are derived from Verbs and express action or being without asserting it. Infinitives and Participles are Verbals.

And so on. Smith, in his preface, says that his book is intended, "not so much to 'cover' the subject of grammar as to *teach* it," and calls attention to the fact, somewhat proudly, that he has omitted "the rather hard subject of gerunds," all mention of conjunctive adverbs, and even the conjugation of verbs. Nevertheless, he immerses himself in the mythical objective case of nouns on page 108, and does not emerge until the end.[10] "The New-Webster-Cooley Course in English,"[11] another popular text, carries reform a step further. The subject of case is approached through the personal pronouns, where it retains its only surviving intelligibility, and the more lucid *object form* is used in place of *objective case*. Moreover, the pupil is plainly informed, later on, that "a noun has in reality but two case-forms: a possessive and a common case-form." This is the best concession to the facts yet made by a text-book grammarian. But no one familiar with the habits of the pedagogical mind need be told that its interior pull is against even such mild and obvious reforms. Defenders of the old order are by no means silent; a fear seems to prevail that grammar, robbed of its imbecile classifications, may collapse entirely. Wilcox records how the Council of English Teachers of New Jersey, but a few years ago, spoke out boldly for the recognition of no less than five cases

[10] Even Sweet, though he bases his New English Grammar upon the spoken language and thus sets the purists at defiance, quickly succumbs to the labelling mania. Thus his classification of tenses includes such fabulous monsters as these: continuous, recurrent, neutral, definite, indefinite, secondary, incomplete, inchoate, short and long.

[11] By W. F. Webster and Alice Woodworth Cooley; Boston, 1903; rev. eds., 1905 and 1909. The authors are Minneapolis teachers.

in English. "Why five?" asks Wilcox. "Why not eight, or ten, or even thirteen? Undoubtedly because there are five cases in Latin."[12] Most of the current efforts at improvement, in fact, tend toward a mere revision and multiplication of classifications; the pedant is eternally convinced that pigeon-holing and relabelling are contributions to knowledge. A curious proof in point is offered by a pamphlet entitled "Reorganization of English in Secondary Schools," compiled by James Fleming Hosic and issued by the National Bureau of Education.[13] The aim of this pamphlet is to rid the teaching of English, including grammar, of its accumulated formalism and ineffectiveness—to make it genuine instruction instead of a pedantic and meaningless routine. And how is this revolutionary aim set forth? By a meticulous and merciless splitting of hairs, a gigantic manufacture of classifications and sub-classifications, a colossal display of professorial bombast and flatulence.

I could cite many other examples. Perhaps, after all, the disease is incurable. What such laborious stupidity shows at bottom is simply this: that the sort of man who is willing to devote his life to teaching grammar to children, or to training schoolmarms to do it, is not often the sort of man who is intelligent enough to do it competently. In particular, he is not often intelligent enough to grapple with the fluent and ever-amazing permutations of a living and rebellious speech. The only way he can grapple with it at all is by first reducing it to a fixed and formal organization—in brief, by first killing it and embalming it. The difference in the resultant proceedings is not unlike that between a gross dissection and a surgical operation. The difficulties of the former are quickly mastered by any student of normal sense, but even the most casual of laparotomies calls for a man of special skill and address. Thus the elementary study of the national language, at least in America, is almost monopolized by dullards. Children are taught it by men and women who observe it inaccurately and expound it ignorantly. In most other fields the pedagogue meets a certain corrective competition and

[12] *Op. cit.* p. 8.
[13] Bulletin No. 2; Washington, 1917.

criticism. The teacher of any branch of applied mathematics, for example, has practical engineers at his elbow and they quickly expose and denounce his defects; the college teacher of chemistry, however limited his equipment, at least has the aid of text-books written by actual chemists. But English, even in its most formal shapes, is chiefly taught by those who cannot write it decently and who get no aid from those who can. One wades through treatise after treatise on English style by pedagogues whose own style is atrocious. A Huxley or a Stevenson might have written one of high merit and utility—but Huxley and Stevenson had other fish to fry, and so the business was left to Prof. Balderdash. Consider the standard texts on prosody—vast piles of meaningless words—hollow babble about spondees, iambics, trochees and so on—idiotic borrowings from dead languages. Two poets, Poe and Lanier, blew blasts of fresh air through that fog, but they had no successors, and it has apparently closed in again. In the department of prose it lies wholly unbroken; no first-rate writer of English prose has ever written a text-book upon the art of writing it.

§ 2

Spoken American As It Is—But here I wander afield. The art of prose has little to do with the stiff and pedantic English taught in grammar-schools and a great deal less to do with the loose and lively English spoken by the average American in his daily traffic. The thing of importance is that the two differ from each other even more than they differ from the English of a Huxley or a Stevenson. The school-marm, directed by grammarians, labors heroically, but all her effort goes for naught. The young American, like the youngster of any other race, inclines irresistibly toward the dialect that he hears at home, and that dialect, with its piquant neologisms, its high disdain of precedent, its complete lack of self-consciousness, is almost the antithesis of the hard and stiff speech that is expounded out of books. It derives its principles, not from the subtle logic of learned and stupid men, but from the rough-and-ready logic of every day. It has a vocabulary of its own, a syntax of its own, even a grammar of its own. Its verbs are conjugated in a way that defies all the injunctions of the grammar books; it has its contumacious rules of tense, number and case; it has boldly re-established the double negative, once sound in English; it admits double comparatives, confusions in person, clipped infinitives; it lays hands on the vowels, changing them to fit its obscure but powerful spirit; it disdains all the finer distinctions between the parts of speech.

This highly virile and defiant dialect, and not the fossilized English of the school-marm and her books, is the speech of the Middle American of Joseph Jacobs' composite picture—the mill-hand in a small city of Indiana, with his five years of common schooling behind him, his diligent reading of newspapers, and his proud membership in the Order of Foresters and the Knights of the Maccabees.[14] Go into any part of the country, North, East, South or West, and you will find multitudes of his brothers—car conductors in Philadelphia, immigrants of the second generation in the East Side of New York, iron-workers in the Pittsburgh region, corner grocers in St. Louis, holders of petty political jobs in Atlanta and New Orleans, small farmers in Kansas or Kentucky, house carpenters in Ohio, tinners and plumbers in Chicago,—genuine Americans all, hot for the home team, marchers in parades, readers of the yellow newspapers, fathers of families, sheep on election day, undistinguished norms of the *Homo Americanus*. Such typical Americans, after a fashion, know English. They can read it—all save the "hard" words, *i. e.*, all save about 90 per cent of the words of Greek and Latin origin.[15] They can understand perhaps two-thirds of it as it comes from the lips of a political orator or clergyman. They have a feeling that it is, in some recondite sense, superior to the common speech of their kind. They recognize a fluent command of it as the salient mark of a "smart" and "edu-

[14] The Middle American, *American Magazine*, March, 1907.
[15] *Cf.* White: Every-Day English, p. 367 *et seq.*

cated'' man, one with "the gift of gab." But they themselves
never speak it or try to speak it, nor do they look with approbation on efforts in that direction by their fellows.

In no other way, indeed, is the failure of popular education
made more vividly manifest. Despite a gigantic effort to en-
force certain speech habits, universally in operation from end
to end of the country, the masses of the people turn almost
unanimously to very different speech habits, nowhere advocated
and seldom so much as even accurately observed. The literary
critic, Francis Hackett, somewhere speaks of "the enormous gap
between the literate and unliterate American." He is apparently the first to call attention to it. It is the national assumption that no such gap exists—that all Americans, at least if they
be white, are so outfitted with sagacity in the public schools that
they are competent to consider any public question intelligently
and to follow its discussion with understanding. But the truth
is, of course, that the public school accomplishes no such magic.
The inferior man, in America as elsewhere, remains an inferior
man despite the hard effort made to improve him, and his
thoughts seldom if ever rise above the most elemental concerns.
What lies above not only does not interest him; it actually ex-
cites his derision, and he has coined a unique word, *high-brow*,
to express his view of it. Especially in speech is he suspicious
of superior pretension. The school-boy of the lower orders would
bring down ridicule upon himself, and perhaps criticism still
more devastating, if he essayed to speak what his teachers con-
ceive to be correct English, or even correct American, outside
the school-room. On the one hand his companions would laugh
at him as a prig, and on the other hand his parents would probably cane him as an impertinent critic of their own speech.
Once he has made his farewell to the school-marm, all her diligence in this department goes for nothing.[16] The boys with
whom he plays baseball speak a tongue that is not the one taught
in school, and so do the youths with whom he will begin learning a trade tomorrow, and the girl he will marry later on, and
the saloon-keepers, star pitchers, vaudeville comedians, business

[16] *Cf.* Sweet: New English Grammar, vol. i, p. 5.

sharpers and political mountebanks he will look up to and try to imitate all the rest of his life.

So far as I can discover, there has been but one attempt by a competent authority to determine the special characters of this general tongue of the *mobile vulgus*. That authority is Dr. W. W. Charters, now head of the School of Education at the University of Illinois. In 1914 Dr. Charters was dean of the faculty of education and professor of the theory of teaching in the University of Missouri, and one of the problems he was engaged upon was that of the teaching of grammar. In the course of this study he encountered the theory that such instruction should be confined to the rules habitually violated—that the one aim of teaching grammar was to correct the speech of the pupils, and that it was useless to harass them with principles which they already instinctively observed. Apparently inclining to this somewhat dubious notion, Dr. Charters applied to the School Board of Kansas City for permission to undertake an examination of the language actually used by the children in the elementary schools of that city, and this permission was granted. The materials thereupon gathered were of two classes. First, the teachers of grades III to VII inclusive in all the Kansas City public-schools were instructed to turn over to Dr. Charters all the written work of their pupils, "ordinarily done in the regular order of school work" during a period of four weeks. Secondly, the teachers of grades II to VII inclusive were instructed to make note of "all oral errors in grammar made in the school-room and around the school-building" during the five school-days of one week, by children of any age, and to dispatch these notes to Dr. Charters also. The result was an accumulation of material so huge that it was unworkable with the means at hand, and so the investigator and his assistants reduced it. Of the oral reports, two studies were made, the first of those from grades III and VII and the second of those from grades VI and VII. Of the written reports, only those from grades VI and VII of twelve typical schools were examined.

The ages thus covered ran from nine or ten to fourteen or fifteen, and perhaps five-sixths of the material studied came from

children above twelve. Its examination threw a brilliant light
upon the speech actually employed by children near the end
of their schooling in a typical American city, and, *per corollary*,
upon the speech employed by their parents and other older associates. If anything, the grammatical and syntactical habits
revealed were a bit less loose than those of the authentic *Volkssprache*, for practically all of the written evidence was gathered
under conditions which naturally caused the writers to try to
write what they conceived to be correct English, and even the
oral evidence was conditioned by the admonitory presence of the
teachers. Moreover, it must be obvious that a child of the lower
classes, during the period of its actual study of grammar, probably speaks better English than at any time before or afterward,
for it is only then that any positive pressure is exerted upon it
to that end. But even so, the departures from standard usage
that were unearthed were numerous and striking, and their
tendency to accumulate in definite groups showed plainly the
working of general laws.[17]

Thus, no less than 57 per cent of the oral errors reported by
the teachers of grades III and VII involved the use of the verb,
and nearly half of these, or 24 per cent, of the total, involved
a confusion of the past tense form and the perfect participle.
Again, double negatives constituted 11 per cent of the errors, and
the misuse of adjectives or of adjectival forms for adverbs ran
to 4 per cent. Finally, the difficulties of the objective case
among the pronouns, the last stronghold of that case in English,
were responsible for 7 per cent, thus demonstrating a clear tendency to get rid of it altogether. Now compare the errors of
these children, half of whom, as I have just said, were in grade
III, and hence wholly uninstructed in formal grammar, with the
errors made by children of the second oral group—that is, children of grades VI and VII, in both of which grammar is studied.
Dr. Charters' tabulations show scarcely any difference in the

[17] Dr. Charters' report appears as Vol. XVI, No. 2, *University of Missouri Bulletin*, Education Series No. 9, Jan., 1915. He was aided in his
inquiry by Edith Miller, teacher of English in one of the St. Louis high-
schools.

character and relative rank of the errors discovered. Those in the use of the verb drop from 57 per cent of the total to 52 per cent, but the double negatives remain at 7 per cent and the errors in the case of pronouns at 11 per cent.

In the written work of grades VI and VII, however, certain changes appear, no doubt because of the special pedagogical effort against the more salient oral errors. The child, pen in hand, has in mind the cautions oftenest heard, and so reveals something of that greater exactness which all of us show when we do any writing that must bear critical inspection. Thus, the relative frequency of confusions between the past tense forms of verbs and the perfect participles drops from 24 per cent to 5 per cent, and errors based on double negatives drop to 1 per cent. But this improvement in one direction merely serves to unearth new barbarisms in other directions, concealed in the oral tables by the flood of errors now remedied. It is among the verbs that they are still most numerous; altogether, the errors here amount to exactly 50 per cent of the total. Such locutions as *I had went* and *he seen* diminish relatively and absolutely, but in all other situations the verb is treated with the lavish freedom that is so characteristic of the American common speech. Confusions of the past and present tenses jump from 2 per cent to 19 per cent, thus eloquently demonstrating the tenacity of the error. And mistakes in the forms of nouns and pronouns increase from 2 per cent to 16: a shining proof of a shakiness which follows the slightest effort to augment the vocabulary of everyday.

The materials collected by Dr. Charters and his associates are not, of course, presented in full, but his numerous specimens must strike familiar chords in every ear that is alert to the sounds and ways of the *sermo vulgus*. What he gathered in Kansas City might have been gathered just as well in San Francisco, or New Orleans, or Chicago, or New York, or in Youngstown, O., or Little Rock, Ark., or Waterloo, Iowa. In each of these places, large or small, a few localisms might have been noted—*oi* substituted for *ur* in New York, *you-all* in the South, a few Germanisms in Pennsylvania and in the upper Mississippi

Valley, a few Spanish locutions in the Southwest, certain peculiar vowel-forms in New England—but in the main the report would have been identical with the report he makes. That vast uniformity which marks the people of the United States, in political doctrine, in social habit, in general information, in reaction to ideas, in prejudices and enthusiasms, in the veriest details of domestic custom and dress, is nowhere more marked than in language. The incessant neologisms of the national speech sweep the whole country almost instantly, and the iconoclastic changes which its popular spoken form are undergoing show themselves from coast to coast. "He hurt *hisself*," cited by Dr. Charters, is surely anything but a Missouri localism; one hears it everywhere. And so, too, one hears "she invited *him* and *I*," and "it hurt *terrible*," and "I *set* there," and "this *here* man," and "no, I *never, neither,* and "he *ain't* here," and "where is he *at?*" and "it seems *like* I remember," and "if I *was* you," and *"us* fellows," and "he *give* her hell." And "he *taken* and kissed her," and "he *loaned* me a dollar," and "the man was *found* two dollars," and "the bee *stang* him," and "I *wouldda* thought," and *"can* I have one?" and "he got *hisn*," and "the boss *left* him off," and "the baby *et* the soap," and *"them* are the kind I like," and "he *don't* care," and "no one has *their* ticket," and "how *is* the folks?" and "if you would *of gotten* in the car you could *of rode* down."

Curiously enough, this widely dispersed and highly savory dialect—already, as I shall show, come to a certain grammatical regularity—has attracted the professional writers of the country almost as little as it has attracted the philologists. There are foreshadowings of it in "Huckleberry Finn," in "The Biglow Papers" and even in the rough humor of the period that began with J. C. Neal and company and ended with Artemus Ward and Josh Billings, but in those early days it had not yet come to full flower; it wanted the influence of the later immigrations to take on its present character. The enormous dialect literature of twenty years ago left it almost untouched. Localisms were explored diligently, but the general dialect went virtually unobserved. It is not in "Chimmie Fadden"; it is not in

"David Harum"; it is not even in the pre-fable stories of George Ade, perhaps the most acute observer of average, undistinguished American types, urban and rustic, that American literature has yet produced. The business of reducing it to print had to wait for Ring W. Lardner, a Chicago newspaper reporter. In his grotesque tales of base-ball players, so immediately and so deservedly successful and now so widely imitated,[18] Lardner reports the common speech not only with humor, but also with the utmost accuracy. The observations of Charters and his associates are here reinforced by the sharp ear of one specially competent, and the result is a mine of authentic American.

In a single story by Lardner, in truth, it is usually possible to discover examples of almost every logical and grammatical peculiarity of the emerging language, and he always resists very stoutly the temptation to overdo the thing. Here, for example, are a few typical sentences from "The Busher's Honeymoon":[19]

I and Florrie *was* married the day before yesterday just *like* I told you we *was* going to be. . . . You *was* wise to get married in Bedford, where *not nothing* is nearly half so dear. . . . The sum of what I have *wrote* down is $29.40. . . . Allen told me I *should ought* to give the priest $5. . . . I never *seen* him before. . . . I didn't used to eat *no* lunch in the playing season except when I *knowed* I was not going to work. . . . I guess the meals *has* cost me all together about $1.50, and I have *eat* very little myself. . . .

I was willing to tell her all about *them* two poor girls. . . . They must not be *no* mistake about who is the boss in my house. Some men *lets* their *wife* run all over them. . . . Allen has *went* to a college football game. One of the reporters *give* him a pass. . . . He called up and said he *hadn't* only the one pass, but he was not hurting my feelings *none*. . . . The flat across the hall from this *here* one is for rent. . . . If we should *of boughten* furniture it would cost us in the neighborhood of $100, even without *no* piano. . . . I consider myself lucky to *of* found out about this before it was too late and somebody else had *of* gotten the tip. . . . It will always be *ourn*, even when we move away. . . . Maybe you could *of did* better if you had *of went* at it in a different way. . . . Both *her* and you *is* welcome at my house. . . . I never *seen* so much wine *drank* in my life. . . .

[18] You Know Me Al: New York, 1916.
[19] *Saturday Evening Post*, July 11, 1914.

Here are specimens to fit into most of Charters' categories—
verbs confused as to tense, pronouns confused as to case, double
and even triple negatives, nouns and verbs disagreeing in number, *have* softened to *of*, *n* marking the possessive instead of *s*,
like used in place of *as*, and the personal pronoun substituted
for the demonstrative adjective. A study of the whole story
would probably unearth all the remaining errors noted in Kansas
City. Lardner's baseball player, though he has pen in hand
and is on his guard, and is thus very careful to write *would not*
instead of *wouldn't* and even *am not* instead of *ain't*, offers a
comprehensive and highly instructive panorama of popular
speech habits. To him the forms of the subjunctive mood have
no existence, and *will* and *shall* are identical, and adjectives and
adverbs are indistinguishable, and the objective case is merely a
variorum form of the nominative. His past tense is, more often
than not, the orthodox present tense. All fine distinctions are
obliterated in his speech. He uses invariably the word that is
simplest, the grammatical form that is handiest. And so he
moves toward the philological millennium dreamed of by George
T. Lanigan, when "the singular verb shall lie down with the
plural noun, and a little conjugation shall lead them."

§ 3

The Verb—A study of the materials amassed by Charters and
Lardner, if it be reinforced by observation of what is heard on
the streets every day, will show that the chief grammatical peculiarities of spoken American lie among the verbs and pronouns.
The nouns in common use, in the overwhelming main, are quite
sound in form. Very often, of course, they do not belong to
the vocabulary of English, but they at least belong to the vocabulary of American: the proletariat, setting aside transient slang,
calls things by their proper names, and pronounces those names
more or less correctly. The adjectives, too, are treated rather
politely, and the adverbs, though commonly transformed into
adjectives, are not further mutilated. But the verbs and pronouns undergo changes which set off the common speech very

sharply from both correct English and correct American. Their grammatical relationships are thoroughly overhauled and sometimes they are radically modified in form.

This process is natural and inevitable, for it is among the verbs and pronouns, as we have seen, that the only remaining grammatical inflections in English, at least of any force or consequence, are to be found, and so they must bear the chief pressure of the influences that have been warring upon all inflections since the earliest days. The primitive Indo-European language, it is probable, had eight cases of the noun; the oldest known Teutonic dialect reduced them to six; in Anglo-Saxon they fell to four, with a weak and moribund instrumental hanging in the air; in Middle English the dative and accusative began to decay; in Modern English they have disappeared altogether, save as ghosts to haunt grammarians. But we still have two plainly defined conjugations of the verb, and we still inflect it for number, and, in part, at least, for person. And we yet retain an objective case of the pronoun, and inflect it for person, number and gender.

Some of the more familiar conjugations of verbs in the American common speech, as recorded by Charters or Lardner or derived from my own collectanea, are here set down:

Present	Preterite	Perfect Participle
Am	was	bin (or ben) [20]
Attack	attackted	attackted
(Be) [21]	was	bin (or ben) [20]
Beat	beaten	beat
Become [22]	become	became
Begin	begun	began
Bend	bent	bent
Bet	bet	bet
Bind	bound	bound
Bite	bitten	bit

[20] *Bin* is the correct American pronunciation. *Bean*, as we have seen, is the English. But I have often found *ben*, rhyming with *pen*, in such phrases as "I *ben* there."

[21] See p. 209.

[22] Seldom used. *Get* is used in the place of it, as in "I am *getting* old" and "he *got* sick."

Present	Preterite	Perfect Participle
Bleed	bled	bled
Blow	blowed (or blew)	blowed (or blew)
Break	broken	broke
Bring	brought (or brung, or brang)	brung
Broke (passive)	broke	broke
Build	built	built
Burn	burnt [23]	burnt
Burst [24]	———	———
Bust	busted	busted
Buy	bought (or boughten)	bought (or boughten)
Can	could	could'a
Catch	caught [25]	caught
Choose	chose	choose
Climb	clum	clum
Cling (to hold fast)	clung	clung
Cling (to ring)	clang	clang
Come	come	came
Creep	crep (or crope)	crep
Crow	crew	crew
Cut	cut	cut
Dare	dared	dared
Deal	dole	dealt
Dig	dug	dug
Dive	dove	dived
Do	done	done (or did)
Drag	drug	dragged
Draw	drawed [26]	drawed (or drew)
Dream	dreampt	dreampt
Drink	drank (or drunk)	drank
Drive	drove	drove
Drown	drownded	drownded
Eat	et (or eat)	ate
Fall	fell (or fallen)	fell
Feed	fed	fed
Feel	felt	felt

[23] *Burned*, with a distinct *d*-sound, is almost unknown in American. See p. 201.

[24] Not used.

[25] *Cotched* is heard only in the South, and mainly among the negroes. *Catch*, of course, is always pronounced *ketch*.

[26] But "I *drew* three jacks," in poker.

Present	Preterite	Perfect Participle
Fetch .	fetched [27]	fetch
Fight	fought [28]	fought
Find	found	found
Fine	found	found
Fling	flang	flung
Flow	flew	flowed
Fly	flew	flew
Forget	forgotten	forgotten
Forsake	forsaken	forsook
Freeze	frozen (or friz)	frozen
Get	got (or gotten)	gotten
Give	give	give
Glide	glode [29]	glode
Go	went	went
Grow	growed	growed
Hang	hung [30]	hung
Have	had	had (or hadden)
Hear	heerd	heerd (or heern)
Heat	het [31]	het
Heave	hove	hove
Hide	hidden	hid
H'ist [32]	h'isted	h'isted
Hit	hit	hit
Hold	helt	held (or helt)
Holler	hollered	hollered
Hurt	hurt	hurt
Keep	kep	kep
Kneel	knelt	knelt
Know	knowed	knew
Lay	laid (or lain)	laid
Lead	led	led
Lean	lent	lent
Leap	lep	lep

[27] *Fotch* is also heard, but it is not general.

[28] *Fit* and *fitten*, unless my observation errs, are heard only in dialect. *Fit* is archaic English. *Cf.* Thornton, vol. i, p. 322.

[29] *Glode* once enjoyed a certain respectability in America. It occurs in the *Knickerbocker Magazine* for April, 1856.

[30] *Hanged* is never heard.

[31] *Het* is incomplete without the addition of *up*. "He was *het up*" is always heard, not "he was *het*."

[32] Always so pronounced. See p. 236.

Present	Preterite	Perfect Participle
Learn	learnt	learnt
Lend	loaned [33]	loaned
Lie (to falsify)	lied	lied
Lie (to recline)	laid (or lain)	laid
Light	lit	lit
Lose	lost	lost
Make	made	made
May	———	might'a
Mean	meant	meant
Meet	met	met
Mow	mown	mowed
Pay	paid	paid
Plead	pled	pled
Prove	proved (or proven)	proven
Put	put	put
Quit	quit	quit
Raise	raised	raised
Read	read	read
Rench [34]	renched	renched
Rid	rid	rid
Ride	ridden	rode
Rile [35]	riled	riled
Ring	rung	rang
Rise	riz (or rose)	riz
Run	run	ran
Say	sez	said
See	seen	saw
Sell	sold	sold
Send	sent	sent
Set	set [36]	sat
Shake	shaken (or shuck)	shook
Shave	shaved	shaved
Shed	shed	shed
Shine (to polish)	shined	shined
Shoe	shoed	shoed
Shoot	shot	shot
Show	shown	showed
Sing	sung	sang
Sink	sunk	sank

[33] See pp. 57 and 202.
[34] Always used in place of *rinse*.
[35] Always used in place of *roil*.
[36] *Sot* is heard as a localism only.

Present	Preterite	Perfect Participle
Sit [37]	—	—
Skin	skun	skun
Sleep	slep	slep
Slide	slid	slid
Sling	slang	slung
Slit	slitted	slitted
Smell	smelt	smelt
Sneak	snuck	snuck
Speed	speeded	speeded
Spell	spelt	spelt
Spill	spilt	spilt
Spin	span	span
Spit	spit	spit
Spoil	spoilt	spoilt
Spring	sprung	sprang
Steal	stole	stole
Sting	stang	stang
Stink	stank	stank
Strike	struck	struck
Swear	swore	swore
Sweep	swep	swep
Swell	swole	swollen
Swim	swum	swam
Swing	swang	swung
Take	taken	took
Teach	taught	taught
Tear	tore	torn
Tell	tole	tole
Think	thought [38]	thought
Thrive	throve	throve
Throw	throwed	threw
Tread	tread	tread
Wake	woke	woken
Wear	wore	wore
Weep	wep	wep
Wet	wet	wet
Win	won (or wan) [39]	won (or wan)
Wind	wound	wound
Wish (wisht)	wisht	wisht
Wring	wrung	wrang
Write	written	wrote

[37] See *set*, which is used almost invariably in place of *sit*.
[38] *Thunk* is never used seriously; it always shows humorous intent.
[39] See pp. 201 and 211.

A glance at these conjugations is sufficient to show several general tendencies, some of them going back, in their essence, to the earliest days of the English language. The most obvious is that leading to the transfer of verbs from the so-called strong conjugation to the weak—a change already in operation before the Norman Conquest, and very marked during the Middle English period. Chaucer used *growed* for *grew* in the prologue to "The Wife of Bath's Tale," and *rised* for *rose* and *smited* for *smote* are in John Purvey's edition of the Bible, *circa* 1385.[40] Many of these transformations were afterward abandoned, but a large number survived, for example, *climbed* for *clomb* as the preterite of *to climb*, and *melted* for *molt* as the preterite of *to melt*. Others showed themselves during the early part of the Modern English period. *Comed* as the perfect participle of *to come* and *digged* as the preterite of *to dig* are both in Shakespeare, and the latter is also in Milton and in the Authorized Version of the Bible. This tendency went furthest, of course, in the vulgar speech, and it has been embalmed in the English dialects. *I seen* and *I knowed,* for example, are common to many of them. But during the seventeenth century it seems to have been arrested, and even to have given way to a contrary tendency—that is, toward strong conjugations. The English of Ireland, which preserves many seventeenth century forms, shows this plainly. *Ped* for *paid, gother* for *gathered,* and *ruz* for *raised* are still in use there, and Joyce says flatly that the Irish, "retaining the old English custom [*i. e.,* the custom of the period of Cromwell's invasion, *circa* 1650], have a leaning toward the strong inflection." [41] Certain verb forms of the American colonial period, now reduced to the estate of localisms, are also probably survivors of the seventeenth century.

"The three great causes of change in language," says Sayce, "may be briefly described as (1) imitation or analogy, (2) a wish to be clear and emphatic, and (3) laziness. Indeed, if we choose to go deep enough we might reduce all three causes to the general one of laziness, since it is easier to imitate than to say

40 *Cf.* Lounsbury: History of the English Language, pp. 309–10.
41 English As We Speak It In Ireland, p. 77.

something new.'' [42] This tendency to take well-worn paths, paradoxically enough, is responsible both for the transfer of verbs from the strong to the weak declension, and for the transfer of certain others from the weak to the strong. A verb in everyday use tends almost inevitably to pull less familiar verbs with it, whether it be strong or weak. Thus *fed* as the preterite of *to feed* and *led* as the preterite of *to lead* paved the way for *pled* as the preterite of *to plead,* and *rode* as plainly performed the same office for *glode,* and *rung* for *brung,* and *drove* for *dove* and *hove,* and *stole* for *dole,* and *won* for *skun.* Moreover, a familiar verb, itself acquiring a faulty inflection, may fasten a similar inflection upon another verb of like sound. Thus *het,* as the preterite of *to heat,* no doubt owes its existence to the example of *et,* the vulgar preterite of *to eat.* So far the irregular verbs. The same combination of laziness and imitativeness works toward the regularization of certain verbs that are historically irregular. In addition, of course, there is the fact that regularization is itself intrinsically simplification—that it makes the language easier. One sees the antagonistic pull of the two influences in the case of verbs ending in *-ow.* The analogy of *knew* suggests *snew* as the preterite of *to snow,* and it is sometimes encountered in the American vulgate. But the analogy of *snowed* also suggests *knowed,* and the superior regularity of the form is enough to overcome the greater influence of *knew* as a more familiar word than *snowed.* Thus *snew* grows rare and is in decay, but *knowed* shows vigor, and so do *growed* and *throwed.* The substitution of *heerd* for *heard* also presents a case of logic and convenience supporting analogy. The form is suggested by *steered, feared* and *cheered,* but its main advantage lies in the fact that it gets rid of a vowel change, always an impediment to easy speech. Here, as in the contrary direction, one barbarism breeds another. Thus *taken,* as the preterite of *to take,* has undoubtedly helped to make preterites of two other perfects, *shaken* and *forsaken.*

But in the presence of two exactly contrary tendencies, the one in accordance with the general movement of the language

[42] The Science of Language, vol. i, p. 166.

since the Norman Conquest and the other opposed to it, it is unsafe, of course, to attempt any very positive generalizations. All one may exhibit with safety is a general habit of treating the verb conveniently. Now and then, disregarding grammatical tendencies, it is possible to discern what appear to be logical causes for verb phenomena. That *lit* is preferred to *lighted* and *hung* to *hanged* is probably the result of an aversion to fine distinctions, and perhaps, more fundamentally, to the passive. Again, the use of *found* as the preterite of *to fine* is obviously due to an ignorant confusion of *fine* and *find*, due to the wearing off of *-d* in *find*, and that of *lit* as the preterite of *to alight* to a confusion of *alight* and *light*. Yet again, the use of *tread* as its own preterite in place of *trod* is probably the consequence of a vague feeling that a verb ending with *d* is already of preterite form. *Shed* exhibits the same process. Both are given a logical standing by such preterites as *bled, fed, fled, led, read, dead* and *spread*. But here, once more, it is hazardous to lay down laws, for *shredded, headed, dreaded, threaded* and *breaded* at once come to mind. In other cases it is still more difficult to account for preterites in common use. *Drug* is wholly illogical, and so are *clum* and *friz*. Neither, fortunately, has yet supplanted the more intelligible form of its verb, and so it is not necessary to speculate about them. As for *crew*, it is archaic English surviving in American, and it was formed, perhaps, by analogy with *knew*, which has succumbed in American to *knowed*.

Some of the verbs of the vulgate show the end products of language movements that go back to the Anglo-Saxon period, and even beyond. There is, for example, the disappearance of the final *t* in such words as *crep, slep, lep, swep* and *wep*. Most of these, in Anglo-Saxon, were strong verbs. The preterite of *to sleep* (*slâepan*), for example, was *slêp*, and that of *to weep* was *weop*. But in the course of time both *to sleep* and *to weep* acquired weak preterite endings, the first becoming *slâepte* and the second *wepte*. This weak conjugation was itself degenerated. Originally, the inflectional suffix had been *-de* or *-ede* and in some cases *-ode*, and the vowels were always pronounced. The wearing down process that set in in the twelfth century disposed of the final *e*, but in certain words the other vowel survived for a good while, and we still observe it in such archaisms as *belovéd*. Finally, however, it became silent in other preterites, and *loved*, for example, began to be pronounced (and often written) as a word of one syllable: *lov'd*.[43] This final *d*-sound now fell upon difficulties of its own. After certain consonants it was hard to pronounce clearly, and so the sonant was changed into the easier surd, and such words as *pushed* and *clipped* became, in ordinary conversation, *pusht* and *clipt*. In other verbs the *t*-sound had come in long before, with the degenerated weak ending, and when the final *e* was dropped their stem vowels tended to change. Thus arose such forms as *slept*. In vulgar American another step is taken, and the suffix is dropped altogether. Thus, by a circuitous route, verbs originally strong, and for many centuries hovering between the two conjugations, have eventually become strong again.

The case of *helt* is probably an example of change by false analogy. During the thirteenth century, according to Sweet,[44] "*d* was changed to *t* in the weak preterites of verbs [ending] in *rd*, *ld* and *nd*." Before that time the preterite of *sende* (*send*) had been *sende*; now it became *sente*. It survives in our modern *sent*, and the same process is also revealed in *built*, *girt*, *lent*, *rent* and *bent*. The popular speech, disregarding the fact that *to hold* is a strong verb, arrives at *helt* by imitation. In the case of *tole*, which I almost always hear in place of *told*, there is a leaping of steps. The *d* is got rid of without any transitional use of *t*. So also, perhaps, in *swole*, which is fast displacing *swelled*. *Attackted* and *drownded* seem to be examples of an effort to dispose of harsh combinations by a contrary process. Both are very old in English. *Boughten* and *dreampt* pre-

---

[43] The last stand of the distinct *-ed* was made in Addison's day. He was in favor of retaining it, and in the *Spectator* for Aug. 4, 1711, he protested against obliterating the syllable in the termination "of our praeter perfect tense, as in these words, *drown'd*, *walk'd*, *arriv'd*, for *drowned*, *walked*, *arrived*, which has very much disfigured the tongue, and turned a tenth part of our smoothest words into so many clusters of consonants."

[44] A New English Grammar, pt. i, p. 380.

sent greater difficulties. Lounsbury says that *boughten* probably originated in the Northern [*i. e.*, Lowland Scotch] dialect
of English, "which . . . inclined to retain the full form of the
past participle," and even to add its termination "to words to
which it did not properly belong."[45] I record *dreampt* without
attempting to account for it. I have repeatedly heard a distinct
p-sound in the word.

The general tendency toward regularization is well exhibited
by the new verbs that come into the language constantly. Practically all of them show the weak conjugation, for example, *to
phone, to bluff, to rubber-neck, to ante, to bunt, to wireless, to
insurge* and *to loop-the-loop.* Even when a compound has as
its last member a verb ordinarily strong, it remains weak itself.
Thus the preterite of *to joy-ride* is not *joy-rode,* nor even *joy-
ridden,* but *joy-rided.* And thus *bust,* from *burst,* is regular
and its preterite is *busted,* though *burst* is irregular and its preterite is the verb itself unchanged. The same tendency toward
regularity is shown by the verbs of the *kneel*-class. They are
strong in English, but tend to become weak in colloquial American. Thus the preterite of *to kneel,* despite the example of *to
sleep* and its analogues, is not *knel',* nor even *knelt,* but *kneeled.*
I have even heard *feeled* as the preterite of *to feel,* as in "I
feeled my way," though here *felt* still persists. *To spread* also
tends to become weak, as in "he *spreaded* a piece of bread."
And *to peep* remains so, despite the example of *to leap.* The
confusion between the inflections of *to lie* and those of *to lay*
extends to the higher reaches of spoken American, and so does
that between *lend* and *loan.* The proper inflections of *to lend*
are often given to *to loan,* and so *leaned* becomes *lent,* as in "I
lent on the counter." In the same way *to set* has almost completely superseded *to sit,* and the preterite of the former, *set,* is
used in place of *sat.* But the perfect participle (which is also
the disused preterite) of *to sit* has survived, as in "I have
sat there." *To speed* and *to shoe* have become regular, not only
because of the general tendency toward the weak conjugation,
but also for logical reasons. The prevalence of speed contests

[45] History of the English Language, p. 398.

of various sorts, always to the intense interest of the proletariat, has brought such words as *speeder, speeding, speed-mania, speed-maniac* and *speed-limit* into daily use, and *speeded* harmonizes with them better than the stronger *sped*. As for *shoed*, it merely reveals the virtual disappearance of the verb in its passive form. An American would never say that his wife was well *shod;* he would say that she wore good shoes. *To shoe* suggests to him only the shoeing of animals, and so, by way of *shoeing* and *horse-shoer,* he comes to *shoed*. His misuse of *to learn* for *to teach* is common to most of the English dialects. More peculiar to his speech is the use of *to leave* for *to let*. Charters records it in "Washington *left* them have it," and there are many examples of it in Lardner. *Spit,* in American, has become invariable; the old preterite, *spat,* has completely disappeared. But *slit,* which is now invariable in English (though it was strong in Old English and had both strong and weak preterites in Middle English), has become regular in American, as in "she *slitted* her skirt."

In studying the American verb, of course, it is necessary to remember always that it is in a state of transition, and that in many cases the manner of using it is not yet fixed. "The history of language," says Lounsbury, "when looked at from the purely grammatical point of view, is little else than the history of corruptions." What we have before us is a series of corruptions in active process, and while some of them have gone very far, others are just beginning. Thus it is not uncommon to find corrupt forms side by side with orthodox forms, or even two corrupt forms battling with each other. Lardner, in the case of *to throw,* hears "if he had *throwed*"; my own observation is that *threw* is more often used in that situation. Again, he uses "the rottenest I ever seen *gave*"; my own belief is that *give* is far more commonly used. The conjugation of *to give,* however, is yet very uncertain, and so Lardner may report accurately. I have heard "I *given*" and "I would of *gave*," but "I *give*" seems to be prevailing, and "I would of *give*" with it, thus reducing *to give* to one invariable form, like those of *to cut, to hit, to put, to cost, to hurt* and *to spit*. My table of verbs shows various other uncertainties and confusions. The preterite of *to hear* is *heerd;* the perfect may be either *heerd* or *heern.* That of *to do* may be either *done* or *did,* with the latter apparently prevailing; that of *to draw* is *drew* if the verb indicates to attract or to abstract and *drawed* if it indicates to draw with a pencil. Similarly, the preterite of *to blow* may be either *blowed* or *blew,* and that of *to drink* oscillates between *drank* and *drunk,* and that of *to fall* is still usually *fell,* though *fallen* has appeared, and that of *to shake* may be either *shaken* or *shuck.* The conjugation of *to win* is yet far from fixed. The correct English preterite, *won,* is still in use, but against it are arrayed *wan* and *winned.* *Wan* seems to show some kinship, by ignorant analogy, with *ran* and *began.* It is often used as the perfect participle, as in "I have *wan* $4."

The misuse of the perfect participle for the preterite, now almost the invariable rule in vulgar American, is common to many other dialects of English, and seems to be a symptom of a general decay of the perfect tenses. That decay has been going on for a long time, and in American, the most vigorous and advanced of all the dialects of the language, it is particularly well marked. Even in the most pretentious written American it shows itself. The English, in their writing, still use the future perfect, albeit somewhat laboriously and self-consciously, but in America it has virtually disappeared: one often reads whole books without encountering a single example of it. Even the present perfect and the past perfect seem to be instinctively avoided. The Englishman says "I *have* dined," but the American says "I *am through* dinner"; the Englishman says "I *had* slept," but the American often says "I *was done* sleeping." Thus the perfect tenses are forsaken for the simple present and the past. In the vulgate a further step is taken, and "I *have been* there" becomes "I *been* there." Even in such phrases as "he *hasn't* been here," *ain't* ($=am$ *not*) is commonly substituted for *have not,* thus giving the present perfect a flavor of the simple present. The step from "I *have taken*" to "*I taken*" was therefore neither difficult nor unnatural, and once it had been made the resulting locution was supported by the greater

apparent regularity of its verb. Moreover, this perfect participle, thus put in place of the preterite, was further reinforced
by the fact that it was the adjectival form of the verb, and
hence collaterally familiar. Finally, it was also the authentic
preterite in the passive voice, and although this influence, in
view of the decay of the passive, may not have been of much
consequence, nevertheless it is not to be dismissed as of no consequence at all.

The contrary substitution of the preterite for the perfect participle, as in "I have *went*" and "he has *did*," apparently has
a double influence behind it. In the first place, there is the
effect of the confused and blundering effort, by an ignorant and
unanalytical speaker, to give the perfect some grammatical differentiation when he finds himself getting into it—an excursion
not infrequently made necessary by logical exigencies, despite
his inclination to keep out. The nearest indicator at hand is the
disused preterite, and so it is put to use. Sometimes a sense of
its uncouthness seems to linger, and there is a tendency to give
it an *en*-suffix, thus bringing it into greater harmony with its
tense. I find that *boughten*, just discussed, is used much oftener
in the perfect than in the simple past tense;[46] for the latter
bought usually suffices. The quick ear of Lardner detects various other coinages of the same sort, among them *tooken*, as in
"little Al might of *tooken* sick."[47] *Hadden* is also met with,
as in "I would of *hadden*." But the majority of preterites remain unchanged. Lardner's baseball player never writes "I
have *written*" or "I have *wroten*," but always "I have *wrote*."
And in the same way he always writes, "I have *did, ate, went,
drank, rode, ran, saw, sang, woke* and *stole*." Sometimes the
simple form of the verb persists through all tenses. This is
usually the case, for example, with *to give*. I have noted "I
give" both as present and as preterite, and "I have *give*," and
even "I had *give*." But even here "I have *gave*" offers rivalry
to "I have *give*," and usage is not settled. So, too, with *to come*.
"I have *come*" and "I have *came*" seem to be almost equally

---

[46] And still more often as an adjective, as in "it was a *boughten* dress."
[47] You Know Me Al, p. 180; see also p. 122.

favored, with the former supported by pedagogical admonition and the latter by the spirit of the language.

Whatever the true cause of the substitution of the preterite for the perfect participle, it seems to be a tendency inherent in English, and during the age of Elizabeth it showed itself even in the most formal speech. An examination of any play of Shakespeare's will show many such forms as "I have *wrote*," "I am *mistook*" and "he has *rode*." In several cases this transfer of the preterite has survived. "I have *stood*," for example, is now perfectly correct English, but before 1550 the form was "I have *stonden*." *To hold* and *to sit* belong to the same class; their original perfect participles were not *held* and *sat*, but *holden* and *sitten*. These survived the movement toward the formalization of the language which began with the eighteenth century, but scores of other such misplaced preterites were driven out. One of the last to go was *wrote*, which persisted until near the end of the century.[48] Paradoxically enough, the very purists who performed the purging showed a preference for *got* (though not for *forgot*), and it survives in correct English today in the preterite-present form, as in "I have *got*," whereas in American, both vulgar and polite, the elder and more regular *gotten* is often used. In the polite speech *gotten* indicates a distinction between a completed action and a continuing action,—between obtaining and possessing. "I have *gotten* what I came for" is correct, and so is "I have *got* the measles." In the vulgar speech, much the same distinction exists, but the perfect becomes a sort of simple tense by the elision of *have*. Thus the two sentences change to "I *gotten* what I come for" and "I *got* the measles," the latter being understood, not as past, but as present.

In "I have *got* the measles" *got* is historically a sort of auxiliary of *have*, and in colloquial American, as we have seen in the examples just given, the auxiliary has obliterated the verb. *To have*, as an auxiliary, probably because of its intimate relationship with the perfect tenses, is under heavy pressure, and

[48] *Cf.* Lounsbury: History of the English Language, pp. 393 *et seq.*

promises to disappear from the situations in which it is still used. I have heard *was* used in place of it, as in "before the Elks *was* come here."[49] Sometimes it is confused ignorantly with a distinct *of*, as in "she would *of* drove," and "I would *of* gave." More often it is shaded to a sort of particle, attached to the verb as an inflection, as in "he would *'a* tole you," and "who could *'a* took it?" But this is not all. Having degenerated to such forms, it is now employed as a sort of auxiliary to itself, in the subjunctive, as in "if you had *of* went," "if it had *of* been hard," and "if I had *of* had."[50] I have encountered some rather astonishing examples of this doubling of the auxiliary: one appears in "I wouldn't had *'a* went." Here, however, the *a* may belong partly to *had* and partly to *went;* such forms as *a-going* are very common in American. But in the other cases, and in such forms as "I had *'a* wanted," it clearly belongs to *had.* Sometimes for syntactical reasons, the degenerated form of *have* is put before *had* instead of after it, as in "I could *of* had her if I had *of* wanted to."[51] Meanwhile, *to have*, ceasing to be an auxiliary, becomes a general verb indicating compulsion. Here it promises to displace *must.* The American seldom says "I *must* go"; he almost invariably says "I *have* to go," or "I *have got* to go," in which last case, as we have seen, *got* is the auxiliary.

The most common inflections of the verb for mode and voice are shown in the following paradigm of *to bite:*

ACTIVE VOICE

Indicative Mode

Present	I bite	*Past Perfect*	I had of bit
Present Perfect	I have bit	*Future*	I will bite
Past	I bitten	*Future Perfect*	(wanting)

[49] Remark of a policeman talking to another. What he actually said was "before the Elks was *c'm 'ere.*" *Come* and *here* were one word, approximately *cmear.* The context showed that he meant to use the past perfect tense.

[50] These examples are from Lardner's story, A New Busher Breaks In, in You Know Me Al, pp. 122 *et seq.*

[51] You Know Me Al, *op. cit.*, p. 124.

Subjunctive Mode

Present	If I bite	*Past Perfect*	If I had of bit
Past	If I bitten		

Potential Mode

Present	I can bite	*Past*	I could bite
Present Perfect	(wanting)	*Past Perfect*	I could of bit

Imperative (or Optative) Mode

Future	I shall (or will) bite

Infinitive Mode

(wanting)

PASSIVE VOICE

Indicative Mode

Present	I am bit	*Past Perfect*	I had been bit
Present Perfect	I been bit	*Future*	I will be bit
Past	I was bit	*Future Perfect*	(wanting)

Subjunctive Mode

Present	If I am bit	*Past Perfect*	If I had of been bit
Past	If I was bit		

Potential Mode

Present	I can be bit	*Past*	I could be bit
Present Perfect	(wanting)	*Past Perfect*	I could of been bit

Imperative Mode

(wanting)

Infinitive Mode

(wanting)

A study of this paradigm reveals several plain tendencies. One has just been discussed: the addition of a degenerated form of *have* to the preterite of the auxiliary, and its use in place of the auxiliary itself. Another is the use of *will* instead of *shall* in the first person future. *Shall* is confined to a sort of optative, indicating much more than mere intention, and even here it is yielding to *will*. Yet another is the consistent use of the transferred preterite in the passive. Here the rule in correct English is followed faithfully, though the perfect participle employed is not the English participle. "I am *broke*" is a good example. Finally, there is the substitution of *was* for *were* and of *am* for *be* in the past and present of the subjunctive. In this last case American is in accord with the general movement of English, though somewhat more advanced. *Be*, in the Shakespearean form of "where *be* thy brothers?" was expelled from the present indicative two hundred years ago, and survives to-day only in dialect. And as it thus yielded to *are* in the indicative, it now seems destined to yield to *am* and *is* in the subjunctive. It remains, of course, in the future indicative: "I will *be*." In American its conjugation coalesces with that of *am* in the following manner:

Present	I am	*Past Perfect*	I had of ben
Present Perfect	I bin (or ben)	*Future*	I will be
Past	I was	*Future Perfect*	(wanting)

And in the subjunction:

Present	If I am	*Past Perfect*	If I had of ben
Past	If I was		

All signs of the subjunctive, indeed, seem to be disappearing from vulgar American. One never hears "if I *were* you," but always "if I *was* you." In the third person the *-s* is not dropped from the verb. One hears, not "if she *go*," but "if she *goes*." "If he *be* the man" is never heard; it is always "if he *is*." This war upon the forms of the subjunctive, of course, extends to the most formal English. "In Old English," says Bradley,[52] "the subjunctive played as important a part as in modern German, and was used in much the same way. Its inflection differed in several respects from that of the indicative. But the only formal trace of the old subjunctive still remaining, except the use of *be* and *were*, is the omission of the final *s* in the third person singular. And even this is rapidly dropping out of use. . . . Perhaps in another generation the subjunctive forms will have ceased to exist except in the single instance of *were*, which serves a useful function, although we manage to

[52] The Making of English, p. 53.

dispense with a corresponding form in other verbs." Here, as elsewhere, unlettered American usage simply proceeds in advance of the general movement. *Be* and the omitted *s* are already dispensed with, and even *were* has been discarded.

In the same way the distinction between *will* and *shall*, preserved in correct English but already breaking down in the most correct American, has been lost entirely in the American common speech. *Will* has displaced *shall* completely, save in the imperative. This preference extends to the inflections of both. *Sha'n't* is very seldom heard; almost always *won't* is used instead. As for *should*, it is displaced by *ought to* (degenerated to *oughter* or *ought'a*), and in its negative form by *hadn't ought'a*, as in "he *hadn't oughter* said that," reported by Charters. Lardner gives various redundant combinations of *should* and *ought*, as in "I don't feel as if I *should ought to* leave" and "they *should not ought to* of had." I have encountered the same form, but I don't think it is as common as the simple *ought'a*-forms. In the main, *should* is avoided, sometimes at considerable pains. Often its place is taken by the more positive *don't*. Thus "I *don't* mind" is used instead of "I *shouldn't* mind." *Don't* has also completely displaced *doesn't*, which is very seldom heard. "He *don't*" and "they *don't*" are practically universal. In the same way *ain't* has displaced *is not, am not, isn't* and *aren't*, and even *have not* and *haven't*. One recalls a famous speech in a naval melodrama of twenty years ago: "We *ain't* got no manners, but we can fight like hell." Such forms as "he *ain't* here," "I *ain't* the man," "them *ain't* what I want" and "I *ain't* heerd of it" are common.

This extensive use of *ain't*, of course, is merely a single symptom of a general disregard of number, obvious throughout the verbs, and also among the pronouns, as we shall see. Charters gives many examples, among them, "how *is* Uncle Wallace and Aunt Clara?" "you *was*," "there *is* six" and the incomparable "it *ain't* right to say, 'He *ain't* here today.'" In Lardner there are many more, for instance, "them Giants is not such rotten hitters, *is* they?" "the people *has* all wanted to shake hands with Matthewson and I" and "some of the men *has* brung their wife along.'' *Sez* (= *says*), used as the preterite of *to say*, shows the same confusion. One observes it again in such forms as "then I *goes* up to him." Here the decay of number helps in what threatens to become a decay of tense. Examples of it are not hard to find. The average race-track follower of the humbler sort seldom says "I *won* $2,'' or even "I *wan* $2,'' but almost always "I *win* $2.'' And in the same way he says "I *see* him come in," not "I *saw* him" or "*seen* him.'' Charters' materials offers other specimens, among them "we *help* distributed the fruit," "she *recognize,* hug, and *kiss* him" and "her father *ask* her if she intended doing what he *ask*.'' Perhaps the occasional use of *eat* as the preterite of *to eat,* as in "I *eat* breakfast as soon as I got up," is an example of the same flattening out of distinctions. Lardner has many specimens, among them "if Weaver and them had not of *begin* kicking" and "they would of *knock* down the fence.'' I notice that *used,* in *used to be,* is almost always reduced to simple *use,* as in "it *use* to be the rule.'' One seldom, if ever, hears a clear *d* at the end. Here, of course, the elision of the *d* is due primarily to assimilation with the *t* of *to*—a second example of one form of decay aiding another form. But the tenses apparently tend to crumble without help. I frequently hear whole narratives in a sort of debased present: "I *says* to him. . . . Then he *ups* and *says.* . . . I *land* him one on the ear. . . . He *goes* down and out, . . .'' and so on.[53] Still under the spell of our disintegrating inflections, we are prone to regard the tense inflections of the verb as absolutely essential, but there are plenty of languages that get on without them, and even in our own language children and foreigners often reduce them to a few simple forms. Some time ago an Italian contractor said to me "I have *go* there often." Here one of our few surviving inflections was displaced by an analytical devise, and yet the man's meaning was quite clear, and it would be absurd to say that his sentence violated the inner spirit of English. That inner spirit, in fact, has inclined steadily toward "I have *go*" for a thousand years.

[53] *Cf. Dialect Notes,* vol. iii, pt. i, p. 59; *ibid.,* vol. III, pt. iv, p. 283.

§ 4

The Pronoun—The following paradigm shows the inflections of the personal pronoun in the American common speech:

FIRST PERSON
Common Gender

Nominative		Singular	Plural
Nominative		I	we
Possessive	Conjoint	my	our
	Absolute	mine	ourn
Objective		me	us

SECOND PERSON
Common Gender

		Singular	
Nominative		you	yous
Possessive	Conjoint	your	your
	Absolute	yourn	yourn
Objective		you	yous

THIRD PERSON
Masculine Gender

Nominative		he	they
Possessive	Conjoint	his	their
	Absolute	hisn	theirn
Objective		him	them

Feminine Gender

Nominative		she	they
Possessive	Conjoint	her	their
	Absolute	hern	theirn
Objective		her	them

Neuter Gender

Nominative		it	they
Possessive	Conjoint	its	theirn
	Absolute	its	their
Objective		it	them

These inflections, as we shall see, are often disregarded in use, but nevertheless it is profitable to glance at them as they stand. The only variations that they show from standard English are the substitution of *n* for *s* as the distinguishing mark of the absolute form of the possessive, and the attempt to differentiate between the logical and the merely polite plurals in the second person by adding the usual sign of the plural to the former. The use of *n* in place of *s* is not an American innovation. It is found in many of the dialects of English, and is, in fact, historically quite as sound as the use of *s*. In John Wiclif's translation of the Bible (*circa* 1380) the first sentence of the Sermon on the Mount (Mark v, 3) is made: "Blessed be the pore in spirit, for the kyngdam in hevenes is *heren*." And in his version of Luke xxiv, 24, is this: "And some of *ouren* wentin to the grave." Here *heren* (or *herun*) represents, of course, not the modern *hers*, but *theirs*. In Anglo-Saxon the word was *heora*, and down to Chaucer's day a modified form of it, *here*, was still used in the possessive plural in place of the modern *their*, though *they* had already displaced *hie* in the nominative.[54] But in John Purvey's revision of the Wiclif Bible, made a few years later, *hern* actually occurs in II Kings viii, 6, thus: "Restore thou to hir alle things that ben *hern*." In Anglo-Saxon there had been no distinction between the conjoint and absolute forms of the possessive pronouns; the simple genitive sufficed for both uses. But with the decay of that language the surviving remnants of its grammar began to be put to service somewhat recklessly, and so there arose a genitive inflection of this genitive—a true double inflection. In the Northern dialects of English that inflection was made by simply adding *s*, the sign of the possessive. In the Southern dialects the old *n*-declension was applied, and so there arose such forms as *minum* and *eowrum* (= *mine* and *yours*), from *min* and *eower* (= *my* and *your*).[55] Meanwhile, the original simple genitive, now become *youre*, also survived, and so the literature of

---

[54] Henry Bradley, in The Making of English, pp. 54–5: "In the parts of England which were largely inhabited by Danes the native pronouns (*i. e.,* *heo, hie, heom* and *heora*) were supplanted by the Scandinavian pronouns which are represented by the modern *she, they, them* and *their*." This substitution, at first dialectical, gradually spread to the whole language.

[55] *Cf.* Sweet: A New English Grammar, pt. i, p. 344, par. 1096.

the fourteenth century shows the three forms flourishing side by side: *youre, youres* and *youren.* All of them are in Chaucer.

Thus, *yourn, hern, hisn, ourn* and *theirn,* whatever their present offense to grammarians, are of a genealogy quite as respectable as that of *yours, hers, his, ours* and *theirs.* Both forms represent a doubling of inflections, and hence grammatical debasement. On the side of the *yours*-form is the standard usage of the past five hundred years, but on the side of the *yourn*-form there is no little force of analogy and logic, as appears on turning to *mine* and *thine.* In Anglo-Saxon, as we have seen, *my* was *min;* in the same way *thy* was *thin.* During the decadence of the language the final *n* was dropped in both cases before nouns—that is, in the conjoint form—but it was retained in the absolute form. This usage survives to our own day. One says *"my* book," but "the book is *mine"; "thy* faith," but "I am *thine."* [56] Also, one says *"no* matter," but "I have *none."* Without question this retention of the *n* in these pronouns had something to do with the appearance of the *n*-declension in the treatment of *your, her, his* and *our,* and, after *their* had displaced *here* in the third person plural, in *their.* And equally without question it supports the vulgar American usage today. What that usage shows is simply the strong popular tendency to make language as simple and as regular as possible—to abolish subtleties and exceptions. The difference between *"his* book" and "the book is *his'n"* is exactly that between *my* and *mine, they* and *thine,* in the examples just given. "Perhaps it would have been better," says Bradley, "if the literary language had accepted *hisn,* but from some cause it did not do so." [57]

As for the addition of *s* to *you* in the nominative and objective of the second person plural, it exhibits no more than an effort to give clarity to the logical difference between the true plural and the mere polite plural. In several other dialects of

---

[56] Before a noun beginning with a vowel *thine* and *mine* are commonly substituted for *thy* and *my,* as in *"thine* eyes" and *"mine* infirmity." But this is solely for the sake of euphony. There is no compensatory use of *my* and *thy* in the absolute.

[57] The Making of English, p. 58.

English the same desire has given rise to cognate forms, and there are even secondary devices in American. In the South, for example, the true plural is commonly indicated by *you-all*, which, despite a Northern belief to the contrary, is never used in the singular by any save the most ignorant.[58] *You-all*, like *yous*, simply means *you-jointly* as opposed to the *you* that means *thou*. Again, there is the form observed in "you can *all of you* go to hell"—another plain effort to differentiate between singular and plural. The substitution of *you* for *thou* goes back to the end of the thirteenth century. It appeared in late Latin and in the other continental languages as well as in English, and at about the same time. In these languages the true singular survives alongside the transplanted plural, but English has dropped it entirely, save in its poetical and liturgical forms and in a few dialects. It passed out of ordinary polite speech before Elizabeth's day. By that time, indeed, its use had acquired an air of the offensive, such as it has today, save between intimates or to children, in Germany. Thus, at the trial of Sir Walter Raleigh in 1603, Sir Edward Coke, then attorney-general, displayed his animosity to Raleigh by addressing him as *thou*, and finally burst into the contemptuous "I *thou* thee, *thou* traitor!" And in "Twelfth Night" Sir Toby Belch urges Sir Andrew Aguecheek to provoke the disguised Viola to combat by *thouing* her. In our own time, with *thou* passed out entirely, even as a pronoun of contempt, the confusion between *you* in the plural and *you* in the singular presents plain difficulties to a man of limited linguistic resources. He gets around them by setting up a distinction that is well supported by logic and analogy. "I seen *yous*" is clearly separated from "I seen *you*." And in the conjoint position "*yous* guys" is separated from "*you* liar."

So much for the personal pronouns. As we shall see, they are used in such a manner that the distinction between the nominative and the objective forms, though still existing grammatically, has begun to break down. But first it may be well to glance at the demonstrative and relative pronouns. Of the former there

<hr>

[58] *Cf.* The Dialect of Southeastern Missouri, by D. S. Crumb, *Dialect Notes*, vol. ii, pt. iv, 1903, p. 337.

are but two in English, *this* and *that*, with their plural forms, *these* and *those*. To them, American adds a third, *them*, which is also the personal pronoun of the third person, objective case.[59] In addition it has adopted certain adverbial pronouns, *this-here*, *these-here*, *that-there*, *those-there* and *them-there*, and set up inflections of the original demonstratives by analogy with *mine*, *hisn* and *yourn*, to wit, *thisn*, *thesen*, *thatn* and *thosen*. I present some examples of everyday use:

> *Them* are the kind I like.
> *Them* men all work here.
> Who is *this-here* Smith I hear about?
> *These-here* are mine.
> *That-there* medicine ain't no good.
> *Those-there* wops has all took to the woods.
> I wisht I had one of *them-there* Fords.
> *Thisn* is better'n *thatn*.
> I like *thesen* better'n *thosen*.

The origin of the demonstratives of the *thisn*-group is plain: they are degenerate forms of *this-one*, *that-one*, etc., just as *none* is a degenerate composition form of *no(t)-one*. In every case of their use that I have observed the simple demonstratives might have been set free and *one* actually substituted for the terminal *n*. But it must be equally obvious that they have been reinforced very greatly by the absolutes of the *hisn*-group, for in their relation to the original demonstratives they play the part of just such absolutes and are never used conjointly. Thus, one says, in American, "I take *thisn*" or "*thisn* is mine," but one never says "I take *thisn* hat" or "*thisn* dog is mine." In this conjoint situation plain *this* is always used, and the same rule

---

[59] It occurs, too, of course, in other dialects of English, though by no means in all. The Irish influence probably had something to do with its prosperity in vulgar American. At all events, the Irish use it in the American manner. Joyce, in English As We Speak It in Ireland, pp. 34–5, argues that this usage was suggested by Gaelic. In Gaelic the accusative pronouns, *e*, *i* and *iad* (= *him*, *her* and *them*) are often used in place of the nominatives, *sé*, *si* and *siad* (= *he*, *she* and *they*), as in "is *iad* sin na buachaillidhe" (= *them* are the boys). This is "good grammar" in Gaelic, and the Irish, when they began to learn English, translated the locution literally. The familiar Irish "John is dead and *him* always so hearty" shows the same influence.

applies to *these, those* and *that*. *Them*, being a newcomer among
the demonstratives, has not yet acquired an inflection in the
absolute. I have never heard *them'n*, and it will probably never
come in, for it is forbiddingly clumsy. One says, in American,
both "*them* are mine" and "*them* collars are mine."

This-here, these-here, that-there, those-there and *them-there*
are plainly combinations of pronouns and adverbs, and their
function is to support the distinction between proximity, as embodied in *this* and *these*, and remoteness, as embodied in *that,
those* and *them*. "*This-here* coat is mine" simply means "this
coat, *here*, or this *present* coat, is mine." But the adverb promises to coalesce with the pronoun so completely as to obliterate all
sense of its distinct existence, even as a false noun or adjective.
As commonly pronounced, *this-here* becomes a single word, somewhat like *thish-yur*, and *these-here* becomes *these-yur*, and *that-
there* and *them-there* become *that-ere* and *them-ere*. *Those-there*,
if I observed accurately, is still pronounced more distinctly, but
it, too, may succumb to composition in time. The adverb will
then sink to the estate of a mere inflectional particle, as *one* has
done in the absolutes of the *thisn*-group. *Them*, as a personal
pronoun in the absolute, of course, is commonly pronounced *em*,
as in "I seen *em*," and sometimes its vowel is almost lost, but
this is also the case in all save the most exact spoken English.
Sweet and Lounsbury, following the German grammarians, argue
that this *em* is not really a debased form of *them*, but the offspring of *hem*, which survived as the regular plural of the third
person in the objective case down to the beginning of the fifteenth century. But in American *them* is clearly pronounced
as a demonstrative. I have never heard "*em* men" or "*em* are
the kind I like," but always "*them* men" and "*them* are the
kind I like."

The relative pronouns, so far as I have been able to make out,
are declined as follows:

Nominative		who	which	what	that
Possessive	{ *Conjoint*	whose	whose		
	{ *Absolute*	whosen	whosen		
Objective		who	which	what	that

Two things will be noted in this paradigm. First there is the disappearance of *whom* as the objective form of *who*, and secondly there is the appearance of an inflected form of *whose* in the absolute, by analogy with *mine, hisn* and *thesen*. *Whom*, as we have seen, is fast disappearing from standard spoken American; [60] in the vulgar language it is already virtually extinct. Not only is *who* used in such constructions as *"who* did you find there?"* where even standard spoken English would tolerate it, but also in such constructions as "the man *who* I saw," "them *who* I trust in" and "to *who?*" Krapp explains this use of *who* on the ground that there is a "general feeling," due to the normal word-order in English, that "the word which precedes the verb is the subject word, or at least the subject form." [61] But this explanation is probably fanciful. Among the plain people no such "general feeling" for case exists. Their only "general feeling" is a prejudice against case inflections in any form whatsoever. They use *who* in place of *whom* simply because they can discern no logical difference between the significance of the one and the significance of the other.

Whosen is obviously the offspring of the other absolutes in *n*. In the conjoint relation plain *whose* is always used, as in *"whose* hat is that?"* and "the man *whose* dog bit me." But in the absolute *whosen* is often substituted, as in "if it ain't *hisn*, then *whosen* is it?" The imitation is obvious. There is an analogous form of *which*, to wit, *whichn*, resting heavily on *which one*. Thus, *"whichn* do you like?"* and "I didn't say *whichn*" are plainly variations of *"which one* do you like?"* and "I didn't say *which one*." *That*, as we have seen, has a like form, *thatn*, but never, of course, in the relative situation. "I like *thatn*," is familiar, but "the one *thatn* I like" is never heard. If *that*, as a relative, could be used absolutely, I have no doubt that it would change to *thatn*, as it does as a demonstrative. So with *what*. As things stand, it is sometimes substituted for *that*, as in "them's the kind *what* I like." Joined to *but* it can also take the place of *that* in other situations, as in "I don't know *but what*."

60 Pp. 144–50.   61 Modern English, p. 300.

The substitution of *who* for *whom* in the objective case, just noticed, is typical of a general movement toward breaking down all case distinctions among the pronouns, where they make their last stand in English and its dialects. This movement, of course, is not peculiar to vulgar American; nor is it of recent beginning. So long ago as the fifteenth century the old clear distinction between *ye*, nominative, and *you*, objective, disappeared, and today the latter is used in both cases. Sweet says that the phonetic similarity between *ye* and *thee*, the objective form of the true second singular, was responsible for this confusion.[62] At the start *ye* actually went over to the objective case, and the usage thus established shows itself in such survivors of the period as *harkee* (*hark ye*) and *look ye*. In modern spoken English, indeed, *you* in the objective often has a sound far more like that of *ye* than like that of *you*, as, for example, in "how do y' do?" and in American its vowel takes the neutral form of the *e* in the definite article, and the word becomes a sort of shortened *yuh*. But whenever emphasis is laid upon it, *you* becomes quite distinct, even in American. In "I mean *you*," for example, there is never any chance of mistaking it for *ye*.

In Shakespeare's time the other personal pronouns of the objective case threatened to follow *you* into the nominative, and there was a compensatory movement of the nominative pronouns toward the objective. Lounsbury has collected many examples.[63] Marlowe used "is it *him* you seek?" " 'tis *her* I esteem" and "nor *thee* nor *them* shall want"; Fletcher used " 'tis *her* I admire"; Shakespeare himself used "that's *me*." Contrariwise, Webster used "what difference is between the duke and *I?*" and Greene used "nor earth nor heaven shall part my love and *I*." Krapp has unearthed many similar examples from the Restoration dramatists.[64] Etheredge used " 'tis *them*," "it may be *him*," "let you and *I*" and "nor is it *me*"; Matthew Prior, in a famous couplet, achieved this:

[62] A New English Grammar, pt. i, p. 339.
[63] History of the English Language, pp. 274–5.
[64] Modern English, p. 288–9.

> For thou art a girl as much brighter than *her.*
> As he was a poet sublimer than *me.*

The free exchange continued, in fact, until the eighteenth century was well advanced; there are examples of it in Addison. Moreover, it survived, at least in part, even the attack that was then made upon it by the professors of the new-born science of English grammar, and to this day "it is *me*" is still in more or less good colloquial use. Sweet thinks that it is supported in such use, though not, of course, grammatically, by the analogy of the correct "it is *he*" and "it is *she.*" Lounsbury, following Dean Alford, says it came into English in imitation of the French *c'est moi,* and defends it as at least as good as "it is *I.*" [65] The contrary form, "between you and *I,*" has no defenders, and is apparently going out. But in the shape of "between my wife and *I*" it is seldom challenged, at least in spoken English.

All these liberties with the personal pronouns, however, fade to insignificance when put beside the thoroughgoing confusion of the case forms in vulgar American. "*Us* fellers" is so far established in the language that "*we* fellers," from the mouth of a car conductor, would seem almost an affectation. So, too, is "*me* and *her* are friends." So, again, are "I seen you and *her,*" "*her* and I set down together," "*him* and his wife," and "I knowed it was *her.*" Here are some other characteristic examples of the use of the objective forms in the nominative from Charters and Lardner:

Me and *her* was both late.
His brother is taller than *him.*
That little boy was *me.*
Us girls went home.
They were John and *him.*
Her and little Al is to stay here.
She says she thinks *us* and the Allens.
If Weaver and *them* had not of begin kicking.
But not *me.*
Him and I are friends.
Me and *them* are friends.

[65] *Cf.* p. 145n.

Less numerous, but still varied and plentiful, are the substitutions of nominative forms for objective forms:

She gave it to mother and *I*.
She took all of *we* children.
I want you to meet *he* and I at 20th street.
He gave *he* and I both some.
It is going to cost me $6 a week for a room for *she* and the baby.
Anything she has is O. K. for *I* and Florrie.

Here are some grotesque confusions, indeed. Perhaps the best way to get at the principles underlying them is to examine first, not the cases of their occurrence, but the cases of their non-occurrence. Let us begin with the transfer of the objective form to the nominative in the subject relation. "*Me* and *her* was both late" is obviously sound American; one hears it, or something like it, on the streets every day. But one never hears "*me* was late" or "*her* was late" or "*us* was late" or "*him* was late" or "*them* was late." Again, one hears "*us* girls was there" but never "*us* was there." Yet again, one hears "*her* and John was married," but never "*her* was married." The distinction here set up should be immediately plain. It exactly parallels that between *her* and *hern*, *our* and *ourn*, *their* and *theirn*: the tendency, as Sweet says, is "to merge the distinction of nominative and objective in that of conjoint and absolute." [66] The nominative, in the subject relation, takes the usual nominative form only when it is in immediate contact with its verb. If it be separated from its verb by a conjunction or any other part of speech, even including another pronoun, it takes the objective form. Thus "*me* went home" would strike even the most ignorant shopgirl as "bad grammar," but she would use "*me* and my friend went," or "*me* and *him*," or "*he* and *her*," or "*me* and *them*" without the slightest hesitation. What is more, if the separation be effected by a conjunction and another pronoun, the other pronoun also changes to the objective form, even though its contact with the verb may be immediate. Thus one hears "*me* and *her* was there," not "*me* and *she*"; *her* and *him* kissed," not "*her* and *he*." Still more, this second pro-

[66] A New English Grammar, pt. i, p. 341.

noun commonly undergoes the same inflection even when the first member of the group is not another pronoun, but a noun. Thus one hears "John and *her* were married," not "John and *she*." To this rule there is but one exception, and that is in the case of the first person pronoun, especially in the singular. "*Him* and *me* are friends" is heard often, but "*him* and *I* are friends" is also heard. *I* seems to suggest the subject very powerfully; it is actually the subject of perhaps a majority of the sentences uttered by an ignorant man. At all events, it resists the rule, at least partially, and may even do so when actually separated from the verb by another pronoun, itself in the objective form, as for example, in "*I* and *him* were there."

In the predicate relation the pronouns respond to a more complex regulation. When they follow any form of the simple verb of being they take the objective form, as in "it's *me*," "it ain't *him*," and "I am *him*," probably because the transitiveness of this verb exerts a greater pull than its function as a mere copula, and perhaps, too, because the passive naturally tends to put the speaker in the place of the object. "I seen *he*" or "he kissed *she*" or "he struck *I*" would seem as ridiculous to an ignorant American as to the Archbishop of Canterbury, and his instinct for simplicity and regularity naturally tends to make him reduce all similar expressions, or what seem to him to be similar expressions, to coincidence with the more seemly "I seen *him*." After all, the verb of being is fundamentally transitive, and, in some ways, the most transitive of all verbs, and so it is not illogical to bring its powers over the pronoun into accord with the powers exerted by the others. I incline to think that it is some such subconscious logic, and not the analogy of "it is *he*," as Sweet argues, that has brought "it is *me*" to conversational respectability, even among rather careful speakers of English.[67]

But against this use of the objective form in the nominative

[67] It may be worth noting here that the misuse of *me* for *my*, as in "I lit *me* pipe" is quite unknown in American, either standard or vulgar. Even "*me* own" is seldom heard. This boggling of the cases is very common in spoken English.

position after the verb of being there also occurs in American a use of the nominative form in the objective position, as in "she gave it to mother and *I*" and "she took all of *we* children." What lies at the bottom of it seems to be a feeling somewhat resembling that which causes the use of the objective form before the verb, but exactly contrary in its effects. That is to say, the nominative form is used when the pronoun is separated from its governing verb, whether by a noun, a noun-phrase or another pronoun, as in "she gave it to mother and *I*," "she took all of *we* children" and "he paid her and *I*" respectively. But here usage is far from fixed, and one observes variations in both directions—that is, toward using the correct objective when the pronoun is detached from the verb, and toward using the nominative even when it directly follows the verb. "She gave it to mother and *me*," "she took all of *us* children" and "he paid her and *me*" would probably sound quite as correct, to a Knight of Pythias, as the forms just given. And at the other end Charters and Lardner report such forms as "I want you to meet *he* and *I*" and "it is going to cost me $6 a week for a room for *she* and the baby." I have noticed, however, that, in the overwhelming main, the use of the nominative is confined to the pronoun of the first person, and particularly to its singular. Here again we have an example of the powerful way in which *I* asserts itself. And superimposed upon that influence is a cause mentioned by Sweet in discussing "between you and *I*."[68] It is a sort of by-product of the pedagogical war upon "it is *me*." "As such expressions," he says, "are still denounced by the grammars, many people try to avoid them in speech as well as in writing. The result of this reaction is that the *me* in such constructions as 'between John and *me*' and 'he saw John and *me*' sounds vulgar and ungrammatical, and is consequently corrected into *I*." Here the pedagogues, seeking to impose an inelastic and illogical grammar upon a living speech, succeed only in corrupting it still more.

Following *than* and *as* the American uses the objective form of the pronoun, as in "he is taller than *me*" and "such as *her*."

[68] A New English Grammar, pt. i, p. 341.

He also uses it following *like*, but not when, as often happens, he uses the word in place of *as* or *as if*. Thus he says "do it like *him*," but "do it like *he* does" and "she looks like *she* was sick." What appears here is an instinctive feeling that these words, followed by a pronoun only, are not adverbs, but prepositions, and that they should have the same power to put the pronoun into an oblique case that other prepositions have. Just as "the taller of *we*" would sound absurd to all of us, so "taller than *he*," to the unschooled American, sounds absurd. This feeling has a good deal of respectable support. "As *her*" was used by Swift, "than *me*" by Burke, and "than *whom*" by Milton. The brothers Fowler show that, in some cases, "than *him*," is grammatically correct and logically necessary.[69] For example, compare "I love you more than *him*" and "I love you more than *he*." The first means "I love you more than (I love) *him*"; the second, "I love you more than *he* (loves you)." In the first *him* does not refer to *I*, which is nominative, but to *you*, which is objective, and so it is properly objective also. But the American, of course, uses *him* even when the preceding noun is in the nominative, save only when another verb follows the pronoun. Thus, he says, "I love you better than *him*," but "I love you better than *he* does."

In the matter of the reflexive pronouns the American vulgate exhibits forms which plainly show that it is the spirit of the language to regard *self*, not as an adjective, which it is historically, but as a noun. This confusion goes back to Anglo-Saxon days; it originated at a time when both the adjectives and the nouns were losing their old inflections. Such forms as *Petrussylf* (= *Peter's self*), *Cristsylf* (= *Christ's self*) and *Icsylf* (= *I, self*) then came into use, and along with them came combinations of *self* and the genitive, still surviving in *hisself* and *theirselves* (or *theirself*). Down to the sixteenth century these forms remained in perfectly good usage. "Each for *hisself*," for example, was written by Sir Philip Sidney, and is to be found in the dramatists of the time, though modern editors always change it to *himself*. How the dative pronoun got itself

[69] The King's English, p. 63.

fastened upon *self* in the third person masculine and neuter is one of the mysteries of language, but there it is, and so, against all logic, history and grammatical regularity, *himself, themselves* and *itself* (not *its-self*) are in favor today. But the American, as usual, inclines against these illogical exceptions to the rule set by *myself*. I constantly hear *hisself* and *theirselves,* as in "he done it *hisself*" and "they don't know *theirselves.*" Sometimes *theirself* is substituted for theirselves, as in "they all seen it *theirself.*" Also, the emphatic *own* is often inserted between the pronoun and the noun, as in "let every man save his *own* self."

The American pronoun does not necessarily agree with its noun in number. I find "I can tell each one what *they* make," "each fellow put *their* foot on the line," "nobody can do what *they* like" and "she was one of *these* kind of people" in Charters, and "I am not the kind of man that is always thinking about *their* record," "if he was to hit a man in the head . . . *they* would think *their* nose tickled" in Lardner. At the bottom of this error there is a real difficulty: the lack of a pronoun of the true common gender in English, corresponding to the French *soi* and *son*. *His*, after a noun or pronoun connoting both sexes, often sounds inept, and *his-or-her* is intolerably clumsy. Thus the inaccurate plural is often substituted. The brothers Fowler have discovered "anybody else who have only *themselves* in view" in Richardson and "everybody is discontented with *their* lot" in Disraeli, and Ruskin once wrote "if a customer wishes you to injure *their* foot." In spoken American, even the most careful, *they* and *their* often appear; I turn to the *Congressional Record* at random and in two minutes find "if anyone will look at the bank statements *they* will see." [70] In the lower reaches of the language the plural seems to get into every sentence of any complexity, even when the preceding noun or pronoun is plainly singular.

---

[70] "Hon." Edward E. Browne, of Wisconsin, in the House of Representatives, July 18, 1918, p. 9965.

§ 5

The Adverb—All the adverbial endings in English, save *-ly*, have gradually fallen into decay; it is the only one that is ever used to form new adverbs. At earlier stages of the language various other endings were used, and some of them survive in a few old words, though they are no longer employed in making new words. The Anglo-Saxon endings were *-e* and *-lice*. The latter was, at first, merely an *-e*-ending to adjectives in *-lic*, but after a time it attained to independence and was attached to adjectives not ending in *-lic*. In early Middle English this *-lice* changes to *-like*, and later on to *-li* and *-ly*. Meanwhile, the *-e*-ending, following the *-e*-endings of the nouns, adjectives and verbs, ceased to be pronounced, and so it gradually fell away. Thus a good many adverbs came to be indistinguishable from their ancestral adjectives, for example, *hard* in to *pull hard*, *loud* in *to speak loud*, and *deep* in *to bury deep* (= Anglo-Saxon, *dĕop-e*). Worse, not a few adverbs actually became adjectives, for example, *wide*, which was originally the Anglo-Saxon adjective *wid* (= wide) with the adverbial *-e*-ending, and *late*, which was originally the Anglo-Saxon adjective *laet* (= *slow*) with the same ending.

The result of this movement toward identity in form was a confusion between the two classes of words, and from the time of Chaucer down to the eighteenth century one finds innumerable instances of the use of the simple adjective as an adverb. "He will answer *trewe*" is in Sir Thomas More; "and *soft* unto himself he sayd" in Chaucer; "the singers sang *loud*" in the Revised Version of the Bible (Nehemiah xii, 42), and *"indifferent* well" in Shakespeare. Even after the purists of the eighteenth century began their corrective work this confusion continued. Thus, one finds, "the people are *miserable* poor" in Hume, "how *unworthy* you treated mankind" in *The Spectator*, and *"wonderful* silly" in Joseph Butler. To this day the grammarians battle with the barbarism, still without complete success; every new volume of rules and regulations for those who would speak by the book is full of warnings against it. Among the great masses of the plain people, it goes without saying, it flourishes unimpeded. The cautions of the school-marm, in a matter so subtle and so plainly lacking in logic or necessity, are forgotten as quickly as her prohibition of the double negative, and thereafter the adjective and the adverb tend more and more to coalesce in a part of speech which serves the purposes of both, and is simple and intelligible and satisfying.

Charters gives a number of characteristic examples of its use: "wounded very *bad,*" "I *sure* was stiff," "drank out of a cup *easy,*" "he looked up *quick.*" Many more are in Lardner: "a chance to see me work *regular,*" "I am glad I was lucky enough to marry *happy,*" "I beat them *easy,*" and so on. And others fall upon the ear every day: "he done it *proper,*" "he done himself *proud,*" "she was dressed *neat,*" "she was *awful* ugly," "the horse ran *O. K.,*" "it *near* finished him," "it sells *quick,*" "I like it *fine,*" "he et *hoggish,*" "she acted *mean,*" "they keep company *steady.*" The bob-tailed adverb, indeed, enters into a large number of the commonest coins of vulgar speech. *Near-silk,* I daresay, is properly *nearly-silk.* The grammarians protest that "run *slow*" should be "run *slowly.*" But *near-silk* and "run *slow*" remain, and so do "to be in *bad,*" "to play it up *strong*" and their brothers. What we have here is simply an incapacity to distinguish any ponderable difference between adverb and adjective, and beneath it, perhaps, is the incapacity, already noticed in dealing with "it is *me,*" to distinguish between the common verb of being and any other verb. If "it *is* bad" is correct, then why should "it *leaks* bad" be incorrect? It is just this disdain of purely grammatical reasons that is at the bottom of most of the phenomena visible in vulgar American, and the same impulse is observable in all other languages during periods of inflectional decay. During the highly inflected stage of a language the parts of speech are sharply distinct, but when inflections fall off they tend to disappear. The adverb, being at best the step-child of grammar— as the old Latin grammarians used to say, "*Omnis pars orationis migrat in adverbium*"—is one of the chief victims of this anarchy. John Horne Tooke, despairing of bringing it to any order, even in the most careful English, called it, in his "Epea Ptercenta," "the common sink and repository of all heterogeneous and unknown corruptions."

Where an obvious logical or lexical distinction has grown up between an adverb and its primary adjective the unschooled American is very careful to give it its terminal -*ly*. For example, he seldom confuses *hard* and *hardly*, *scarce* and *scarcely*, *real* and *really*. These words convey different ideas. *Hard* means unyielding; *hardly* means barely. *Scarce* means present only in small numbers; *scarcely* is substantially synonymous with *hardly*. *Real* means genuine; *really* is an assurance of veracity. So, again, with *late* and *lately*. Thus, an American says "I don't know, *scarcely*," not "I don't know, *scarce*"; "he died *lately*, "not "he died *late*." But in nearly all such cases syntax is the preservative, not grammar. These adverbs seem to keep their tails largely because they are commonly put before and not after verbs, as in, for example, "I *hardly* (or *scarcely*) know," and "I *really* mean it." Many other adverbs that take that position habitually are saved as well, for example, *generally, usually, surely, certainly.* But when they follow verbs they often succumb, as in "I'll do it *sure*" and "I seen him *recent*." And when they modify adjectives they sometimes succumb, too, as in "it was *sure* hot." Practically all the adverbs made of adjectives in -*y* lose the terminal -*ly* and thus become identical with their adjectives. I have never heard *mightily* used; it is always *mighty*, as in "he hit him *mighty* hard." So with *filthy, dirty, nasty, lowly, naughty* and their cognates. One hears "he acted *dirty*," "he spoke *nasty*," "the child behaved *naughty*," and so on. Here even standard English has had to make concessions to euphony. *Cleanlily* is seldom used; *cleanly* nearly always takes its place. And the use of *illy* is confined to pedants.

Vulgar American, like all the higher forms of American and all save the most precise form of written English, has abandoned the old inflections of *here, there* and *where*, to wit, *hither* and *hence, thither* and *thence, whither* and *whence*. These fossil remains of dead cases are fast disappearing from the language.

In the case of *hither* (= *to here*) even the preposition has been abandoned. One says, not "I came *to here*," but simply "I came *here*." In the case of *hence*, however, *from here* is still used, and so with *from there* and *from where*. Finally, it goes without saying that the common American tendency to add *-s* to such adverbs as *towards* is carried to full length in the vulgar language. One constantly hears, not only *somewheres* and *forwards*, but even *noways* and *anyways*. Here we have but one more example of the movement toward uniformity and simplicity. *Anyways* is obviously fully supported by *sideways* and *always*.

§ 6

The Noun and Adjective—The only inflections of the noun remaining in English are those for number and for the genitive, and so it is in these two regions that the few variations to be noted in vulgar American occur. The rule that, in forming the plurals of compound nouns or noun-phrases, the *-s* shall be attached to the principal noun is commonly disregarded, and it goes at the end. Thus, "I have two *sons-in-law*" is never heard; one always hears "I have two *son-in-laws*." So with the genitive. I once overheard this: "that umbrella is *the young lady I go with's*." Often a false singular is formed from a singular ending in *s*, the latter being mistaken for a plural. *Chinee*, *Portugee* and *Japanee* are familiar; I have also noted *trapee*, *tactic* and *summon* (from *trapeze*, *tactics* and *summons*). Paradoxically, the word *incidence* is commonly misused for *incident*, as in "he told an *incidence*." Here *incidence* (or *incident*) seems to be regarded as a synonym, not for *happening*, but for *story*. I have never heard "he told *of* an incidence." The *of* is always omitted. The general disregard of number often shows itself when the noun is used as object. I have already quoted Lardner's "some of the men has brung their *wife* along"; in a popular magazine I lately encountered "those book ethnologists . . . can't see what is before their *nose*." Many similar examples might be brought forward.

The adjectives are inflected only for comparison, and the

American commonly uses them correctly, with now and then a double comparative or superlative to ease his soul. *More better* is the commonest of these. It has a good deal of support in logic. A sick man is reported today to be *better*. Tomorrow he is further improved. Is he to be reported *better* again, or *best?* The standard language gets around the difficulty by using *still better*. The American vulgate boldly employs *more better*. In the case of *worse, worser* is used, as Charters shows. He also reports *baddest, more queerer* and *beautifulest. Littler,* which he notes, is still outlawed from standard English, but it has, with *littlest,* a respectable place in American. The late Richard Harding Davis wrote a play called "The *Littlest* Girl." The American freely compares adjectives that are incapable of the inflection logically. Charters reports *most principal,* and I myself have heard *uniquer* and even *more uniquer,* as in "I have never saw nothing *more uniquer.*" I have also heard *more ultra, more worse, idealer, liver* (that is, *more alive*), and *wellest,* as in "he was the *wellest* man you ever seen." In general, the -*er* and -*est* terminations are used instead of the *more* and *most* prefixes, as in *beautiful, beautifuller, beautifullest.* The fact that the comparative relates to two and the superlative to more than two is almost always forgotten. I have never heard "the *better* of the two," but always "the *best* of the two." Charters also reports "the *hardest* of the two" and "my brother and I measured and he was the *tallest.*" I have frequently heard "it ain't so *worse,*" but here a humorous effect seems to have been intended.

Adjectives are made much less rapidly in American than either substantives or verbs. The only suffix that seems to be in general use for that purpose is -*y,* as in *tony, classy, daffy, nutty, dinky, leery,* etc. The use of the adjectival prefix *super-* is confined to the more sophisticated classes; the plain people seem to be unaware of it.[71] This relative paucity of adjectives appears to be common to the more primitive varieties of speech. E. J.

---

[71] *Cf.* Vogue Affixes in Present-Day Word-Coinage, by Louise Pound, *Dialect Notes,* vol. v, pt. i, 1918.

Hills, in his elaborate study of the vocabulary of a child of two,[72] found that it contained but 23 descriptive adjectives, of which six were the names of colors, as against 59 verbs and 173 common nouns. Moreover, most of the 23 minus six were adjectives of all work, such as *nasty, funny* and *nice.* Colloquial American uses the same rubber-stamps of speech. *Funny* connotes the whole range of the unusual; *hard* indicates every shade of difficulty; *nice* is everything satisfactory; *bully* is a superlative of almost limitless scope.

The decay of *one* to a vague *n*-sound, as in *this'n*, is matched by a decay of *than* after comparatives. *Earlier than* is seldom if ever heard; composition reduces the two words to *earlier'n.* So with *better'n, faster'n, hotter'n, deader'n,* etc. Once I overheard the following dialogue: "I like a belt *more looser'n* what this one is." "Well, then, why don't you unloosen it *more'n* you got it unloosened?"

§ 7

The Double Negative—Syntactically, perhaps the chief characteristic of vulgar American is its sturdy fidelity to the double negative. So freely is it used, indeed, that the simple negative appears to be almost abandoned. Such phrases as "I see nobody" or "I know nothing about it" are heard so seldom that they appear to be affectations when encountered; the well-nigh universal forms are "I *don't* see nobody" and "I *don't* know nothing about it." Charters lists some very typical examples, among them, "he ain't *never* coming back *no* more," "you *don't* care for nobody but yourself," "couldn't be *no* more happier" and "I *can't* see nothing." In Lardner there are innumerable examples: "they was *not* no team," "I have *not* never thought of that," "I can't write *no* more," "no chance to get *no* money from *nowhere*," "we *can't* have nothing to do," and so on. Some of his specimens show a considerable complexity, for ex-

[72] The Speech of a Child Two Years of Age, *Dialect Notes*, vol. iv, pt. ii, 1914.

ample, "Matthewson was *not* only going as far as the coast," meaning, as the context shows, that he was going as far as the coast and no further. *Only* gets into many other examples, *e. g.*, "he hadn't *only* the one pass" and "I don't work nights no more, *only* except Sunday nights." This latter I got from a car conductor. Many other curious specimens are in my collectanea, among them: "one swaller don't make *no* summer," "I *never* seen nothing I would of rather saw," and "once a child gets burnt once it *won't* never stick its hand in *no* fire *no* more," and so on. The last embodies a triple negative. In "the more faster you go, the sooner you *don't* get there" there is an elaborate muddling of negatives that is very characteristic.

Like most other examples of "bad grammar" encountered in American the compound negative is of great antiquity and was once quite respectable. The student of Anglo-Saxon encounters it constantly. In that language the negative of the verb was formed by prefixing a particle, *ne*. Thus, *singan* (= *to sing*) became *ne singan* (= *not to sing*). In case the verb began with a vowel the *ne* dropped its *e* and was combined with the verb, as in *naefre* (never), from *ne-aefre* (= *not ever*). In case the verb began with an *h* or a *w* followed by a vowel, the *h* or *w* of the verb and the *e* of *ne* were both dropped, as in *naefth* (= *has not*), from *ne-haefth* (= *not has*), and *nolde* (= *would not*), from *ne-wolde*. Finally, in case the vowel following a *w* was an *i*, it changed to *y*, as in *nyste* (= *knew not*), from *ne-wiste*. But inasmuch as Anglo-Saxon was a fully inflected language the inflections for the negative did not stop with the verbs; the indefinite article, the indefinite pronoun and even some of the nouns were also inflected, and survivors of those forms appear to this day in such words as *none* and *nothing*. Moreover, when an actual inflection was impossible it was the practise to insert this *ne* before a word, in the sense of our *no* or *not*. Still more, it came to be the practise to reinforce *ne*, before a vowel, with *nā* (= *not*) or *naht* (= *nothing*), which later degenerated to *nat* and *not*. As a result, there were fearful and wonderful combinations of negatives, some of them fully matching the best efforts of Lardner's baseball player. Sweet gives several curious examples.[73] "Nān ne dorste nān thing āscian," translated literally, becomes "*no* one dares *not* ask *nothing.*" "Thaet hus nā ne feoll" becomes "the house did *not* fall *not.*" As for the Middle English "he *never* nadde *nothing,*" it has too modern and familiar a ring to need translating at all. Chaucer, at the beginning of the period of transition to Modern English, used the double negative with the utmost freedom. In "The Knight's Tale" is this:

> He *nevere* yet *no* vileynye *ne* sayde
> In al his lyf unto *no* maner wight.

By the time of Shakespeare this license was already much restricted, but a good many double negatives are nevertheless to be found in his plays, and he was particularly shaky in the use of *nor*. In "Richard III" one finds "I never was *nor never* will be"; in "Measure for Measure," "harp not on that *nor* do *not* banish treason," and in "Romeo and Juliet," "thou expectedst not, *nor* I looked not for." This misuse of *nor* is still very frequent. In other directions, too, the older forms show a tendency to survive all the assaults of grammarians. *"No* it *doesn't,"* heard every day and by no means from the ignorant only, is a sort of double negative. The insertion of *but* before that, as in "I doubt *but* that" and "there is no question *but* that," makes a double negative that is probably full-blown. Nevertheless, as we have seen, it is heard on the floor of Congress every day, and the Fowlers show that it is also common in England.[74] Even worse forms get into the *Congressional Record.* Not long ago, for example, I encountered "without *hardly* an exception" in a public paper of the utmost importance.[75] There are, indeed, situations in which the double negative leaps to the lips or from the pen almost irresistibly; even such careful writers as Huxley, Robert Louis Stevenson and Leslie Stephen have

[73] A New English Grammar, pt. i, pp. 437-8.
[74] The King's English, p. 322. See especially the quotation from Frederick Greenwood, the distinguished English journalist.
[75] Report of Edward J. Brundage, attorney-general of Illinois, on the East St. Louis massacre, *Congressional Record,* Jan. 7, 1918, p. 661.

occasionally dallied with it.[76] It is perfectly allowable in the
Romance languages, and, as we have seen, is almost the rule in
the American vulgate. Now and then some anarchistic student
of the language boldly defends and even advocates it. "The
double negative," said a writer in the *London Review* a long
time ago,[77] "has been abandoned to the great injury of strength
of expression." Surely "I won't take nothing" is stronger
than either "I will take nothing" or "I won't take anything."

"Language begins," says Sayce, "with sentences, not with
single words." In a speech in process of rapid development,
unrestrained by critical analysis, the tendency to sacrifice the
integrity of words to the needs of the complete sentence is especially marked. One finds it clearly in American. Already we
have examined various assimilation and composition forms:
that'n, use' to, would'a, them 'ere and so on. Many others are observable. *Off'n* is a good example; it comes from *off of* and shows
a preposition decaying to the form of a mere inflectional particle.
One constantly hears "I bought it *off'n* John." *Sort'a, kind'a*
and their like follow in the footsteps of *would'a*. *Usen't* follows
the analogy of *don't* and *wouldn't*. *Would 've* and *should 've*
are widely used; Lardner commonly hears them as *would of* and
should of. The neutral *a*-particle also appears in other situations, especially before *way*, as in *that'a way* and *this'a way*.
It is found again in *a tall*, a liaison form of *at all*.[78]

§ 8

Pronunciation—Before anything approaching a thorough and
profitable study of the sounds of the American common speech
is possible, there must be a careful assembling of the materials,
and this, unfortunately, still awaits a philologist of sufficient enterprise and equipment. Dr. William A. Read, of the State
University of Louisiana, has made some excellent examinations

[76] The King's English, *op. cit.*
[77] Oct. 1, 1864.
[78] *At all*, by the way, is often displaced by *any* or *none*, as in "he don't
lover her *any*" and "it didn't hurt me *none*."

of vowel and consonant sounds in the South, Dr. Louise Pound has done capital work of the same sort in the Middle West,[79] and there have been other regional studies of merit. But most of these become misleading by reason of their lack of scope; forms practically universal in the nation are discussed as dialectical variations. This is the central defect in the work of the American Dialect Society, otherwise very industrious and meritorious. It is essaying to study localisms before having first platted the characteristics of the general speech. The dictionaries of Americanisms deal with pronunciation only casually, and often very inaccurately; the remaining literature is meagre and unsatisfactory.[80] Until the matter is gone into at length it will be impossible to discuss any phase of it with exactness. No single investigator can examine the speech of the whole country; for that business a pooling of forces is necessary. But meanwhile it may be of interest to set forth a few provisional ideas.

At the start two streams of influence upon American pronunciation may be noted, the one an inheritance from the English of the colonists and the other arising spontaneously within the country, and apparently much colored by immigration. The first influence, it goes without saying, is gradually dying out. Consider, for example, the pronunciation of the diphthong *oi*. In Middle English it was as in *boy*, but during the early Modern English period it was assimilated with that of the *i* in *wine*, and this usage prevailed at the time of the settlement of America. The colonists thus brought it with them, and at the same time it lodged in Ireland, where it still prevails. But in England, during the pedantic eighteenth century, this *i*-sound was displaced by the original *oi*-sound, not by historical research but by mere deduction from the spelling, and the new pronunciation soon extended to the polite speech of America. In the common speech, however, the *i*-sound persisted, and down to the time of

---

[79] See the bibliography for the publication of Drs. Read and Pound.

[80] The only book that I can find definitely devoted to American sounds is A Handbook of American Speech, by Calvin L. Lewis; Chicago, 1916. It has many demerits. For example, the author gives a *z*-sound to the *s* in *venison* (p. 52). This is surely not American.

the Civil War it was constantly heard in such words as *boil*, *hoist*, *oil*, *join*, *poison* and *roil*, which thus became *bile*, *hist*, *ile*, *jine*, *pisen* and *rile*. Since then the school-marm has combatted it with such vigor that it has begun to disappear, and such forms as *pisen*, *jine*, *bile* and *ile* are now very seldom heard, save as dialectic variations. But in certain other words, perhaps supported by Irish influence, the *i*-sound still persists. Chief among them are *hoist* and *roil*. An unlearned American, wishing to say that he was enraged, never says that he was *roiled*, but always that he was *riled*. Desiring to examine the hoof of his horse, he never orders the animal to *hoist* but always to *hist*. In the form of *booze-hister*, the latter is almost in good usage. I have seen *booze-hister* thus spelled and obviously to be thus pronounced, in an editorial article in the *American Issue*, organ of the Anti-Saloon League of America.[81]

Various similar misplaced vowels were brought from England by the colonists and have persisted in America, while dying out of good England usage. There is, for example, short *i* in place of long *e*, as in *critter* for *creature*. *Critter* is common to almost all the dialects of English, but American has embedded the vowel in a word that is met with nowhere else and has thus become characteristic, to wit, *crick* for *creek*. Nor does any other dialect make such extensive use of *slick* for *sleek*. Again, there is the substitution of the flat *a* for the broad *a* in *sauce*. England has gone back to the broad *a*, but in America the flat *a* persists, and many Americans who use *sassy* every day would scarcely recognize *saucy* if they heard it. Yet again, there is *quoit*. Originally, the English pronounced it *quate*, but now they pronounce the diphthong as in *doily*. In the United States the *quate* pronunciation remains. Finally, there is *deaf*. Its proper pronunciation, in the England that the colonists left, was *deef*, but it now rhymes with *Jeff*. That new pronunciation has been adopted by polite American, despite the protests of Noah Webster, but in the common speech the word is still always *deef*.

However, a good many of the vowels of the early days have

[81] Maryland edition, July 18, 1914, p. 1.

succumbed to pedagogy. The American proletarian may still use *skeer* for *scare*, but in most of the other words of that class he now uses the vowel approved by correct English usage. Thus he seldom permits himself such old forms as *dreen* for *drain*, *keer* for *care*, *skeerce* for *scarce* or even *cheer* for *chair*. The Irish influence supported them for a while, but now they are fast going out. So, too, are *kivver* for *cover*, *crap* for *crop*, and *chist* for *chest*. But *kittle* for *kettle* still shows a certain vitality, *rench* is still used in place of *rinse*, and *squinch* in place of *squint*, and a flat *a* continues to displace various *e*-sounds in such words as *rare* for *rear* (e. g., as a horse) and *wrassle* for *wrestle*. Contrariwise, *e* displaces *a* in *catch* and *radish*, which are commonly pronounced *ketch* and *reddish*. This *e*-sound was once accepted in standard English; when it got into spoken American it was perfectly sound; one still hears it from the most pedantic lips in *any*.[52] There are also certain other ancients that show equally unbroken vitality among us, for example, *stomp* for *stamp*,[53] *snoot* for *snout*, *guardeen* for *guardian*, and *champeen* for *champion*.

But all these vowels, whether approved or disapproved, have been under the pressure, for the past century, of a movement toward a general vowel neutralization, and in the long run it promises to dispose of many of them. The same movement also affects standard English, as appears by Robert Bridges' "Tract on the Present State of English Pronunciation," but I believe that it is stronger in America, and will go farther, at least with the common speech, if only because of our unparalleled immigration. Standard English has 19 separate vowel sounds. No other living tongue of Europe, save Portuguese, has so many; most of the others have a good many less; Modern Greek has but five. The immigrant, facing all these vowels, finds some of them quite impossible; the Russian Jew, as we have seen, cannot manage *ur*. As a result, he tends to employ a neutralized

[52] *Cf.* Lounsbury: The Standard of Pronunciation in English, p. 172 *et seq.*

[53] *Stomp* is used only in the sense of to stamp with the foot. One always *stamps* a letter. An analogue of *stomp*, accepted in correct English, is *strop* (e. g., *razor-strop*), from *strap*.

vowel in all the situations which present difficulties, and this neutralized vowel, supported by the slip-shod speech-habits of the native proletariat, makes steady progress. It appears in many of the forms that we have been examining—in the final *a* of *would'a*, vaguely before the *n* in *this'n* and *off'n*, in place of the original *d* in *use' to*, and in the common pronunciation of such words as *been, come* and *have*, particularly when they are sacrificed to sentence exigencies, as in "I *b'n* thinking," "*c'm 'ere*," and "he would *'ve* saw you."

Here we are upon a wearing down process that shows many other symptoms. One finds, not only vowels disorganized, but also consonants. Some are displaced by other consonants, measurably more facile; others are dropped altogether. *D* becomes *t*, as in *holt*, or is dropped, as in *tole, han'kerchief, bran-new* and *fine* (for *find*). In *ast* (for *ask*) *t* replaces *k*: when the same word is used in place of *asked*, as often happens, *e. g.*, in "I *ast* him his name," it shoulders out *ked*. It is itself lopped off in *bankrup, quan'ity, crep, slep, wep, kep, gris'-mill* and *les* (= *let's* = *let us*), and is replaced by *d* in *kindergarden* and *pardner*. *L* disappears, as in *a'ready* and *gent'man*. *S* becomes *tsh*, as in *pincers*. The same *tsh* replaces *c*, as in *pitcher* for *picture*, and *t*, as in *amachoor*. *G* disappears from the ends of words, and sometimes, too, in the middle, as in *stren'th* and *reco'nize*. *R*, though it is better preserved in American than in English, is also under pressure, as appears by *bust, stuck on* (for *struck on*), *cuss* (for *curse*), *yestiddy, sa's'parella, pa'-tridge, ca'tridge, they is* (for *there is*) and *Sadd'y* (for *Saturday*). An excrescent *t* survives in a number of words, *e. g.*, *onc't, twic't, clos't, wisht* (for *wish*) and *chanc't*; it is an heir-loom from the English of two centuries ago. So is the final *h* in *heighth*. An excrescent *b*, as in *chimbley* and *fambly*, seems to be native. Whole syllables are dropped out of words, paralleling the English butchery of *extraordinary*; for example, in *bound'ry, hist'ry, lib'ry* and *prob'ly*. *Ordinary*, like *extraordinary*, is commonly enunciated clearly, but it has bred a degenerated form, *onry* or *onery*, differentiated in meaning. Consonants are misplaced by metathesis, as in *prespiration, hunderd*, *brethern, childern, interduce, apern, calvary, govrenment, modren* and *wosterd* (for *worsted*). *Ow* is changed to *er*, as in *feller, swaller, yeller, beller, umbreller* and *holler; ice* is changed to *ers* in *jaunders*. Words are given new syllables, as in *ellum, mischievious* and *municipial*.

In the complete sentence, assimilation makes this disorganization much more obvious. Mearns, in a brief article [84] gives many examples of the extent to which it is carried. He hears "wah zee say?" for "what does he say?" "ware zee?" for "where is he?" "ast 'er in" for "ask her in," "itt'm owd" for "hit them out," "sry" for "that is right," and "c'meer" for "come here." He believes that *t* is gradually succumbing to *d*, and cites "ass bedder" (for "that's better"), "wen juh ged din?" (for "when did you get in?"), and "siddup" (for "sit up"). One hears countless other such decayed forms on the street every day. *Have to* is almost invariably made *hafta*, with the neutral vowel where I have put the second *a*. *Let's*, already noticed, is *le' 's*. The neutral vowel replaces the *oo* of *good* in *g'by*. "What did you say" reduces itself to "wuz ay?" *Maybe* is *mebby*, perhaps is *p'raps*, so long is *s'long*, excuse me is *skus me;* the common salutation, "How are you?" is so dismembered that it finally emerges as a word almost indistinguishable from *high*. Here there is room for inquiry, and that inquiry deserves the best effort of American phonologists, for the language is undergoing rapid changes under their very eyes, or, perhaps more accurately, under their very ears, and a study of those changes should yield a great deal of interesting matter. How did the word *stint*, on American lips, first convert itself into *stent* and then into *stunt?* By what process was *baulk* changed into *buck?* Both *stunt* and *buck* are among the commonest words in the everyday American vocabulary, and yet no one, so far, has investigated them scientifically.

A by-way that is yet to be so much as entered is that of naturalized loan-words in the common speech. A very characteristic word of that sort is *sashay*. Its relationship to the French *chassé* seems to be plain, and yet it has acquired meanings in

[84] Our Own, Our Native Speech, *McClure's Magazine*, Oct., 1916.

American that differ very widely from the meaning of *chassé.* How widely it is dispersed may be seen by the fact that it is reported in popular use, as a verb signifying to prance or to walk consciously, in Southeastern Missouri, Nebraska, Northwestern Arkansas, Eastern Alabama and Western Indiana, and, with slightly different meaning, on Cape Cod. The travels of *café* in America would repay investigation; particularly its variations in pronunciation. I believe that it is fast becoming *kaif.* *Plaza, boulevard, vaudeville, menu* and *rathskeller* have entered into the common speech of the land, and are pronounced as American words. Such words, when they come in verbally, by actual contact with immigrants, commonly retain some measure of their correct native pronunciation. *Spiel, kosher, ganof* and *matzoh* are examples; their vowels remain un-American. But words that come in visually, say through street-signs and the newspapers, are immediately overhauled and have thoroughly Americanized vowels and consonants thereafter. School-teachers have been trying to establish various pseudo-French pronunciations of *vase* for fifty years past, but it still rhymes with *face* in the vulgate. *Vaudeville* is *vawd-vill; boulevard* has a hard *d* at the end; *plaza* has two flat *a*'s; the first syllable of *menu* rhymes with *bee;* the first of *rathskeller* with *cats; fiancée* is *fy-ancé-y; née* rhymes with *see; décolleté* is *de-coll-ty; hofbräu* is *huffbrow;* the German *w* has lost its *v*-sound and becomes an American *w.* I have, in my day, heard *proteege* for *protégé,* habichoo for *habitué,* connisoor for *connisseur,* shirtso for *scherzo,* premeer for *première,* eetood for *étude* and prelood for *prelude.* *Divorcée* is *divorcey,* and has all the rakishness of the adjectives in *-y.* The first syllable of *mayonnaise* rhymes with *hay.* *Crème de menthe* is *cream de mint.* *Schweizer* is *swite-ser.* *Rochefort* is *roke-fort.* I have heard *début* with the last syllable rhyming with *nut.* I have heard *minoot* for *minuet.* I have heard tchef doover for *chef d'œuvre.* And who doesn't remember

> As I walked along the *Boys Boo-long*
> With an independent air

and

Say *aw re-vore,*
But not good-by!

Charles James Fox, it is said, called the red wine of France *Bordox* to the end of his days. He had an American heart; his great speeches for the revolting colonies were more than mere oratory.

VII

Differences in Spelling

§ 1

Typical Forms—Some of the salient differences between American and English spelling are shown in the following list of common words:

American	English
Anemia	anaemia
aneurism	aneurysm
annex (noun)	annexe
arbor	arbour
armor	armour
asphalt	asphalte
ataxia	ataxy
ax	axe
balk (verb)	baulk
baritone	barytone
bark (ship)	barque
behavior	behaviour
behoove	behove
buncombe	bunkum
burden (ship's)	burthen
cachexia	cachexy
caliber	calibre
candor	candour
center	centre
check (bank)	cheque
checkered	chequered
cider	cyder
clamor	clamour
clangor	clangour
cloture	closure [1]

[1] Fowler & Fowler, in The King's English, p. 23, say that "when it was proposed to borrow from France what we [*i. e.*, the English] now know

American	English
color	colour
connection	connexion
councilor	councillor
counselor	counsellor
cozy	cosy
curb	kerb
cyclopedia	cyclopaedia
defense	defence
demeanor	demeanour
diarrhea	diarrhoea
draft (ship's)	draught
dreadnaught	dreadnought
dryly	drily
ecology	oecology
ecumenical	oecumenical
edema	oedema
encyclopedia	encyclopaedia
endeavor	endeavour
eon	aeon
epaulet	epaulette
esophagus	oesophagus
fagot	faggot
favor	favour
favorite	favourite
fervor	fervour
flavor	flavour
font (printer's)	fount
foregather	forgather
forego	forgo
form (printer's)	forme
fuse	fuze
gantlet (to run the—)	gauntlet
glamor	glamour
good-by	good-bye
gram	gramme
gray	grey
harbor	harbour
honor	honour

as the *closure*, it seemed certain for some time that with the thing we should borrow the name, *clôture;* a press campaign resulted in *closure.*" But in the *Congressional Record* it is still *cloture*, though with the loss of the circumflex accent, and this form is generally retained by American newspapers.

American	English
hostler	ostler
humor	humour
inclose	enclose
indorse	endorse
inflection	inflexion
inquiry	enquiry
jail	gaol
jewelry	jewellery
jimmy (burglar's)	jemmy
labor	labour
laborer	labourer
liter	litre
maneuver	manoeuvre
medieval	mediaeval
meter	metre
misdemeanor	misdemeanour
mold	mould
mollusk	mollusc
molt	moult
mustache	moustache
neighbor	neighbour
neighborhood	neighbourhood
net (adj.)	nett
odor	odour
offense	offence
pajamas	pyjamas
parlor	parlour
peas (plu. of pea)	pease
picket (military)	piquet
plow	plough
pretense	pretence
program	programme
pudgy	podgy
pygmy	pigmy
rancor	rancour
rigor	rigour
rumor	rumour
savory	savoury
scimitar	scimetar
septicemia	septicaemia
show (verb)	shew
siphon	syphon
siren	syren

American	English
skeptic	sceptic
slug (verb)	slog
slush	slosh
splendor	splendour
stanch	staunch
story (of a house)	storey
succor	succour
taffy	toffy
tire (noun)	tyre
toilet	toilette
traveler	traveller
tumor	tumour
valor	valour
vapor	vapour
veranda	verandah
vial	phial
vigor	vigour
vise (a tool)	vice
wagon	waggon
woolen	woollen

§ 2

General Tendencies—This list is by no means exhaustive. According to a recent writer upon the subject, "there are 812 words in which the prevailing American spelling differs from the English." [2] But enough examples are given to reveal a number of definite tendencies. American, in general, moves toward simplified forms of spelling more rapidly than English, and has got much further along the road. Redundant and unnecessary letters have been dropped from whole groups of words —the *u* from the group of nouns in *-our,* with the sole exception of *Saviour,* and from such words as *mould* and *baulk;* the *e* from *annexe, asphalte, axe, forme, pease, storey,* etc.; the duplicate consonant from *waggon, nett, faggot, woollen, jeweller, councillor,* etc., and the silent foreign suffixes from *toilette, epaulette, programme, verandah,* etc. In addition, simple vowels have been substituted for degenerated diphthongs in such words as *anaemia,*

[2] Richard P. Read: The American Language, *New York Sun,* March 7, 1918.

oesophagus, diarrhoea and *mediaeval,* most of them from the Greek.

Further attempts in the same direction are to be seen in the substitution of simple consonants for compound consonants, as in *plow, bark, check, vial* and *draft;* in the substitution of *i* for *y* to bring words into harmony with analogues, as in *tire, cider* and *baritone* (*cf. wire, rider, merriment*), and in the general tendency to get rid of the somewhat uneuphonious *y,* as in *ataxia* and *pajamas.* Clarity and simplicity are also served by substituting *ct* for *x* in such words as *connection* and *inflection,* and *s* for *c* in words of the *defense* group. The superiority of *jail* to *gaol* is made manifest by the common mispronunciation of the latter, making it rhyme with *coal.* The substitution of *i* for *e* in such words as *indorse, inclose* and *jimmy* is of less patent utility, but even here there is probably a slight gain in euphony. Of more obscure origin is what seems to be a tendency to avoid the *o*-sound, so that the English *slog* becomes *slug, podgy* becomes *pudgy, nought* becomes *naught, slosh* becomes *slush, toffy* becomes *taffy,* and so on. Other changes carry their own justification. *Hostler* is obviously better American than *ostler,* though it may be worse English. *Show* is more logical than *shew.*[3] *Cozy* is more nearly phonetic than *cosy.* *Curb* has analogues in *curtain, curdle, curfew, curl, currant, curry, curve, curtsey, curse, currency, cursory, curtail, cur, curt* and many other common words: *kerb* has very few, and of them only *kerchief* and *kernel* are in general use. Moreover, the English themselves use *curb* as a verb and in all noun senses save that shown in *kerbstone.*

But a number of anomalies remain. The American substitution of *a* for *e* in *gray* is not easily explained, nor is the substitution of *k* for *c* in *skeptic* and *mollusk,* nor the retention of *e* in *forego,* nor the unphonetic substitution of *s* for *z* in *fuse,*

---

[3] *To shew* has completely disappeared from American, but it still survives in English usage. *Cf.* The *Shewing*-Up of Blanco Posnet, by George Bernard Shaw. The word, of course, is pronounced *show,* not *shoe.* *Shrew,* a cognate word, still retains the early pronunciation of *shrow* in English, but is now phonetic in American.

nor the persistence of the first *y* in *pygmy*. Here we have plain vagaries, surviving in spite of attack by orthographers. Webster, in one of his earlier books, denounced the *k* in *skeptic* as "a mere pedantry," but later on he adopted it. In the same way *pygmy*, *gray* and *mollusk* have been attacked, but they still remain sound American. The English themselves have many more such illogical forms to account for. In the midst of the *our*-words they cling to a small number in *or*, among them, *stupor*. Moreover, they drop the *u* in many derivatives, for example, in *arboreal*, *armory*, *clamorously*, *clangorous*, *odoriferous*, *humorist*, *laborious* and *rigorism*. If it were dropped in all derivatives the rule would be easy to remember, but it is retained in some of them, for example, *colourable*, *favourite*, *misdemeanour*, *coloured* and *labourer*. The derivatives of *honour* exhibit the confusion clearly. *Honorary*, *honorarium* and *honorific* drop the *u*, but *honourable* retains it. Furthermore, the English make a distinction between two senses of *rigor*. When used in its pathological sense (not only in the Latin form of *rigor mortis*, but as an English word) it drops the *u;* in all other senses it retains the *u*. The one American anomaly in this field is *Saviour*. In its theological sense it retains the *u;* but in that sense only. A sailor who saves his ship is its *savior*, not its *saviour*.

§ 3

The Influence of Webster—At the time of the first settlement of America the rules of English orthography were beautifully vague, and so we find the early documents full of spellings that would give an English lexicographer much pain today. Now and then a curious foreshadowing of later American usage is encountered. On July 4, 1631, for example, John Winthrop wrote in his journal that "the governour built a *bark* at Mistick, which was launched this day." But during the eighteenth century, and especially after the publication of Johnson's dictionary, there was a general movement in England toward a more inflexible orthography, and many hard and fast rules, still surviving, were then laid down. It was Johnson himself who established the position of the *u* in the *our* words. Bailey, Dyche and the other lexicographers before him were divided and uncertain; Johnson declared for the *u*, and though his reasons were very shaky [4] and he often neglected his own precept, his authority was sufficient to set up a usage which still defies attack in England. Even in America this usage was not often brought into question until the last quarter of the eighteenth century. True enough, *honor* appears in the Declaration of Independence, but it seems to have got there rather by accident than by design. In Jefferson's original draft it is spelled *honour*. So early as 1768 Benjamin Franklin had published his "Scheme for a New Alphabet and a Reformed Mode of Spelling, with Remarks and Examples Concerning the Same, and an Enquiry Into its Uses," and induced a Philadelphia typefounder to cut type for it, but this scheme was too extravagant to be adopted anywhere, or to have any appreciable influence upon spelling. [5]

It was Noah Webster who finally achieved the divorce between English example and American practise. He struck the first blow in his "Grammatical Institute of the English Language," published at Hartford in 1783. Attached to this work was an appendix bearing the formidable title of "An Essay on the Necessity, Advantages and Practicability of Reforming the Mode of Spelling, and of Rendering the Orthography of Words Correspondent to the Pronunciation," and during the same year, at Boston, he set forth his ideas a second time in the first edition of his "American Spelling Book." The influence of this spelling book was immediate and profound. It took the place in the schools of Dilworth's "Aby-sel-pha," the favorite of the generation preceding, and maintained its authority for fully a century. Until Lyman Cobb entered the lists with his "New Spelling Book," in 1842, its innumerable editions scarcely had

[4] *Cf.* Lounsbury; English Spelling and Spelling Reform; p. 209 *et seq.* Johnson even advocated *translatour, emperour, oratour* and *horrour.* But, like most other lexicographers, he was often inconsistent, and the conflict between *interiour* and *exterior,* and *anteriour* and *posterior,* in his dictionary, laid him open to much mocking criticism.

[5] In a letter to Miss Stephenson, Sept. 20, 1768, he exhibited the use of his new alphabet. The letter is to be found in most editions of his writings.

any rivalry, and even then it held its own. I have a New York edition, dated 1848, which contains an advertisement stating that the annual sale at that time was more than a million copies, and that more than 30,000,000 copies had been sold since 1783. In the late 40's the publishers, George F. Cooledge & Bro., devoted the whole capacity of the fastest steam press in the United States to the printing of it. This press turned out 525 copies an hour, or 5,250 a day. It was "constructed expressly for printing Webster's Elementary Spelling Book [the name had been changed in 1829] at an expense of $5,000." Down to 1889, 62,000,000 copies of the book had been sold.

The appearance of Webster's first dictionary, in 1806, greatly strengthened his influence. The best dictionary available to Americans before this was Johnson's in its various incarnations, but against Johnson's stood a good deal of animosity to its compiler, whose implacable hatred of all things American was well known to the citizens of the new republic. John Walker's dictionary, issued in London in 1791, was also in use, but not extensively. A home-made school dictionary, issued at New Haven in 1798 or 1799 by one Samuel Johnson, Jr.—apparently no relative of the great Sam—and a larger work published a year later by Johnson and the Rev. John Elliott, pastor in East Guilford, Conn., seem to have made no impression, despite the fact that the latter was commended by Simeon Baldwin, Chauncey Goodrich and other magnificoes of the time and place, and even by Webster himself. The field was thus open to the laborious and truculent Noah. He was already the acknowledged magister of lexicography in America, and there was an active public demand for a dictionary that should be wholly American. The appearance of his first duodecimo, according to Williams,[6] thereby took on something of the character of a national event. It was received, not critically, but patriotically, and its imperfections were swallowed as eagerly as its merits. Later on Webster had to meet formidable critics, at home as well as abroad, but for nearly a quarter of a century he reigned almost unchallenged. Edition after edition of his dictionary was published,

6 R. C. Williams: Our Dictionaries; New York, 1890, p. 30.

each new one showing additions and improvements. Finally, in 1828, he printed his great *"American* Dictionary of the English Language,'' in two large octavo volumes. It held the field for half a century, not only against Worcester and the other American lexicographers who followed him, but also against the best dictionaries produced in England. Until very lately, indeed, America remained ahead of England in practical dictionary making.

Webster had declared boldly for simpler spellings in his early spelling books; in his dictionary of 1806 he made an assault at all arms upon some of the dearest prejudices of English lexicographers. Grounding his wholesale reforms upon a saying by Franklin, that ''those people spell best who do not know how to spell''—*i. e.*, who spell phonetically and logically—he made an almost complete sweep of whole classes of silent letters—the *u* in the *-our* words, the final *e* in *determine* and *requisite,* the silent *a* in *thread, feather* and *steady,* the silent *b* in *thumb,* the *s* in *island,* the *o* in *leopard,* and the redundant consonants in *traveler, wagon, jeweler,* etc. (English: *traveller, waggon, jeweller).* More, he lopped the final *k* from *frolick, physick* and their analogues. Yet more, he transposed the *e* and the *r* in all words ending in *re,* such as *theatre, lustre, centre* and *calibre.* Yet more, he changed the *c* in all words of the *defence* class to *s.* Yet more, he changed *ph* to *f* in words of the *phantom* class, *ou* to *oo* in words of the *group* class, *ow* to *ou* in *crowd, porpoise* to *porpess, acre* to *aker, sew* to *soe, woe* to *wo, soot* to *sut, gaol* to *jail,* and *plough* to *plow.* Finally, he antedated the simplified spellers by inventing a long list of boldly phonetic spellings, ranging from *tung* for *tongue* to *wimmen* for *women,* and from *hainous* for *heinous* to *cag* for *keg.*

A good many of these new spellings, of course, were not actually Webster's inventions. For example, the change from *-our* to *-or* in words of the *honor* class was a mere echo of an earlier English usage, or, more accurately, of an earlier English uncertainty. In the first three folios of Shakespeare, 1623, 1632 and 1663-6, *honor* and *honour* were used indiscriminately and in almost equal proportions; English spelling was still fluid, and the -*our*-form was not consistently adopted until the fourth folio of 1685. Moreover, John Wesley, the founder of Methodism, is authority for the statement that the -*or*-form was "a fashionable impropriety" in England in 1791. But the great authority of Johnson stood against it, and Webster was surely not one to imitate fashionable improprieties. He deleted the *u* for purely etymological reasons, going back to the Latin *honor, favor* and *odor* without taking account of the intermediate French *honneur, faveur* and *odeur*. And where no etymological reasons presented themselves, he made his changes by analogy and for the sake of uniformity, or for euphony or simplicity, or because it pleased him, one guesses, to stir up the academic animals. Webster, in fact, delighted in controversy, and was anything but free from the national yearning to make a sensation.

A great many of his innovations, of course, failed to take root, and in the course of time he abandoned some of them himself. In his early "Essay on the Necessity, Advantage and Practicability of Reforming the Mode of Spelling" he advocated reforms which were already discarded by the time he published the first edition of his dictionary. Among them were the dropping of the silent letter in such words as *head, give, built* and *realm,* making them *hed, giv, bilt* and *relm;* the substitution of doubled vowels for decayed diphthongs in such words as *mean, zeal* and *near,* making them *meen, zeel* and *neer;* and the substitution of *sh* for *ch* in such French loan-words as *machine* and *chevalier,* making them *macheen* and *shevaleer.* He also declared for *stile* in place of *style,* and for many other such changes, and then quietly abandoned them. The successive editions of his dictionary show still further concessions. *Croud, fether, groop, gillotin, iland, insted, leperd, soe, sut, steddy, thret, thred, thum* and *wimmen* appear only in the 1806 edition. In 1828 he went back to *crowd, feather, group, island, instead, leopard, sew, soot, steady, thread, threat, thumb* and *women,* and changed *gillotin* to *guillotin.* In addition, he restored the final *e* in *determine, discipline, requisite, imagine,* etc. In 1838, revising his dictionary, he abandoned a good many spellings that had appeared in either the 1806 or the 1828 edition, notably *maiz* for *maize, suveran* for *sovereign* and *guillotin* for *guillotine*. But he stuck manfully to a number that were quite as revolutionary—for example, *aker* for *acre*, *cag* for *keg*, *grotesk* for *grotesque*, *hainous* for *heinous*, *porpess* for *porpoise* and *tung* for *tongue*—and they did not begin to disappear until the edition of 1854, issued by other hands and eleven years after his death. Three of his favorites, *chimist* for *chemist*, *neger* for *negro* and *zeber* for *zebra*, are incidentally interesting as showing changes in American pronunciation. He abandoned *zeber* in 1828, but remained faithful to *chimist* and *neger* to the last.

But though he was thus forced to give occasional ground, and in more than one case held out in vain, Webster lived to see the majority of his reforms adopted by his countrymen. He left the ending in *-or* triumphant over the ending in *-our*, he shook the security of the ending in *-re*, he rid American spelling of a great many doubled consonants, he established the *s* in words of the *defense* group, and he gave currency to many characteristic American spellings, notably *jail*, *wagon*, *plow*, *mold* and *ax*. These spellings still survive, and are practically universal in the United States today; their use constitutes one of the most obvious differences between written English and written American. Moreover, they have founded a general tendency, the effects of which reach far beyond the field actually traversed by Webster himself. New words, and particularly loan-words, are simplified, and hence naturalized in American much more quickly than in English. *Employé* has long since become *employee* in our newspapers, and *asphalte* has lost its final *e*, and *manoeuvre* has become *maneuver*, and *pyjamas* has become *pajamas*. Even the terminology of science is simplified and Americanized. In medicine, for example, the highest American usage countenances many forms which would seem barbarisms to an English medical man if he encountered them in the *Lancet*. In derivatives of the Greek *haima* it is the almost invariable American custom to spell the root syllable *hem*, but the more conservative English make it *haem*—e. g., in *haemorrhage* and *haemiplegia*. In an exhaustive list of diseases issued by the United States Public Health Service [7] the *haem*-form does not appear once. In the same way American usage prefers *esophagus, diarrhea* and *gonorrhea* to the English *oesophagus, diarrhoea* and *gonorrhoea*. In the style-book of the *Journal* of the American Medical Association [8] I find many other spellings that would shock an English medical author, among them *curet* for *curette, cocain* for *cocaine, gage* for *gauge, intern* for *interne, lacrimal* for *lachrymal,* and a whole group of words ending in *-er* instead of in *-re.*

Webster's reforms, it goes without saying, have not passed unchallenged by the guardians of tradition. A glance at the literature of the first years of the nineteenth century shows that most of the serious authors of the time ignored his new spellings, though they were quickly adopted by the newspapers. Bancroft's "Life of Washington" contains *-our* endings in all such words as *honor, ardor* and *favor.* Washington Irving also threw his influence against the *-or* ending, and so did Bryant and most of the other literary big-wigs of that day. After the appearance of "An American Dictionary of the English Language," in 1828, a formal battle was joined, with Lyman Cobb and Joseph E. Worcester as the chief opponents of the reformer. Cobb and Worcester, in the end, accepted the *-or* ending and so surrendered on the main issue, but various other champions arose to carry on the war. Edward S. Gould, in a once famous essay,[9] denounced the whole Websterian orthography with the utmost fury, and Bryant, reprinting this philippic in the *Evening Post,* said that on account of Webster "the English language has been undergoing a process of corruption for the last quarter of a century," and offered to contribute to a fund to have Gould's denunciation "read twice a year in every school-house in the United States, until every trace of Websterian spelling disappears from the land." But Bryant was forced to admit that, even in 1856, the chief novelties of the Connecticut school-master "who taught millions to read but not one to sin" were "adopted

---

[7] Nomenclature of Diseases and Condition, prepared by direction of the Surgeon General; Washington, 1916.

[8] American Medical Association Style Book; Chicago, 1915.

[9] *Democratic Review,* March, 1856.

and propagated by the largest publishing house, through the columns of the most widely circulated monthly magazine, and through one of the ablest and most widely circulated newspapers in the United States''—which is to say, the *Tribune* under Greeley. The last academic attack was delivered by Bishop Coxe in 1886, and he contented himself with the resigned statement that ''Webster has corrupted our spelling sadly.'' Lounsbury, with his active interest in spelling reform, ranged himself on the side of Webster, and effectively disposed of the controversy by showing that the great majority of his spellings were supported by precedents quite as respectable as those behind the fashionable English spellings. In Lounsbury's opinion, a good deal of the opposition to them was no more than a symptom of antipathy to all things American among certain Englishmen and of subservience to all things English among certain Americans.[10]

Webster's inconsistency gave his opponents a formidable weapon for use against him—until it began to be noticed that the orthodox English spelling was quite as inconsistent. He sought to change *acre* to *aker*, but left *lucre* unchanged. He removed the final *f* from *bailiff*, *mastiff*, *plaintiff* and *pontiff*, but left it in *distaff*. He changed *c* to *s* in words of the *offense* class, but left the *c* in *fence*. He changed the *ck* in *frolick*, *physick*, etc., into a simple *c*, but restored it in such derivatives as *frolicksome*. He deleted the silent *u* in *mould*, but left it in *court*. These slips were made the most of by Cobb in a pamphlet printed in 1831.[11] He also detected Webster in the frequent *faux pas* of using spellings in his definitions and explanations that conflicted with the spellings he advocated. Various other purists joined in the attack, and it was renewed with great fury after the appearance of Worcester's dictionary, in 1846. Worcester, who had begun his lexicographical labors by editing Johnson's dictionary, was a good deal more conservative than Webster, and so the partisans of conformity rallied around him, and for

---

[10] *Vide* English Spelling and Spelling Reform, p. 229.
[11] A Critical Review of the Orthography of Dr. Webster's Series of Books . . .; New York, 1831.

a while the controversy took on all the rancor of a personal quarrel. Even the editions of Webster printed after his death, though they gave way on many points, were violently arraigned. Gould, in 1867, belabored the editions of 1854 and 1866,[12] and complained that "for the past twenty-five years the Websterian replies have uniformly been bitter in tone, and very free in the imputation of personal motives, or interested or improper motives, on the part of opposing critics." At this time Webster himself had been dead for twenty-two years. Schele de Vere, during the same year, denounced the publishers of the Webster dictionaries for applying "immense capital and a large stock of energy and perseverance" to the propagation of his "new and arbitrarily imposed orthography."[13]

§ 4

Exchanges—As in vocabulary and in idiom, there are constant exchanges between English and American in the department of orthography. Here the influence of English usage is almost uniformly toward conservatism, and that of American usage is as steadily in the other direction. The logical superiority of American spelling is well exhibited by its persistent advance in the face of the utmost hostility. The English objection to our simplifications, as Brander Matthews points out, is not wholly or even chiefly etymological; its roots lie, to borrow James Russell Lowell's phrase, in an esthetic hatred burning "with as fierce a flame as ever did theological hatred." There is something inordinately offensive to English purists in the very thought of taking lessons from this side of the water, particularly in the mother tongue. The opposition, transcending the academic, takes on the character of the patriotic. "Any American," continues Matthews, "who chances to note the force and the fervor and the frequency of the objurgations against American spelling in the columns of the *Saturday Review*, for example, and of the *Athenaeum,* may find himself wondering as to the date of the

[12] Good English; p. 137 *et seq.*
[13] Studies in English; pp. 64–5.

papal bull which declared the infallibility of contemporary British orthography, and as to the place where the council of the Church was held at which it was made an article of faith."[14] This was written more than a quarter of a century ago. Since then there has been a lessening of violence, but the opposition still continues. No self-respecting English author would yield up the -our ending for an instant, or write *check* for *cheque*, or transpose the last letters in the -re words.

Nevertheless, American spelling makes constant gains across the water, and they more than offset the occasional fashions for English spellings on this side. Schele de Vere, in 1867, consoled himself for Webster's "arbitrarily imposed orthography" by predicting that it could be "only temporary"—that, in the long run, "North America depends exclusively on the mother-country for its models of literature." But the event has blasted this prophecy and confidence, for the English, despite their furious reluctance, have succumbed to Webster more than once. The New English Dictionary, a monumental work, shows many silent concessions, and quite as many open yieldings—for example, in the case of *ax*, which is admitted to be "better than *axe* on every ground." Moreover, English usage tends to march ahead of it, outstripping the liberalism of its editor, Sir James A. H. Murray. In 1914, for example, Sir James was still protesting against dropping the first *e* from *judgement*, a characteristic Americanism, but during the same year the Fowlers, in their Concise Oxford Dictionary, put *judgment* ahead of *judgement;* and two years earlier the Authors' and Printers' Dictionary, edited by Horace Hart,[15] had dropped *judgement* altogether. Hart is Controller of the Oxford University Press, and the Authors' and Printers' Dictionary is an authority accepted by nearly all of the great English book publishers and newspapers. Its last edition shows a great many American spellings. For example, it recommends the use of *jail* and *jailer* in place

[14] Americanisms and Briticisms; New York, 1892, p. 37.

[15] Authors' & Printers' Dictionary . . . an attempt to codify the best typographical practices of the present day, by F. Howard Collins; 4th ed., revised by Horace Hart; London, 1912.

of the English *gaol* and *gaoler,* says that *ax* is better than *axe,* drops the final *e* from *asphalte* and *forme,* changes the *y* to *i* in *cyder, cypher* and *syren* and advocates the same change in *tyre,* drops the redundant *t* from *nett,* changes *burthen* to *burden,* spells *wagon* with one *g,* prefers *fuse* to *fuze,* and takes the *e* out of *storey.* "Rules for Compositors and Readers at the University Press, Oxford," also edited by Hart (with the advice of Sir James Murray and Dr. Henry Bradley), is another very influential English authority.[16] It gives its imprimatur to *bark* (a ship), *cipher, siren, jail, story, tire* and *wagon,* and even advocates *kilogram* and *omelet.* Finally, there is Cassell's English Dictionary.[17] It clings to the *-our* and *-re* endings and to *annexe, waggon* and *cheque,* but it prefers *jail* to *gaol, net* to *nett, asphalt* to *asphalte* and *story* to *storey,* and comes out flatly for *judgment, fuse* and *siren.*

Current English spelling, like our own, shows a number of uncertainties and inconsistencies, and some of them are undoubtedly the result of American influences that have not yet become fully effective. The lack of harmony in the *-our* words, leading to such discrepancies as *honorary* and *honourable,* I have already mentioned. The British Board of Trade, in attempting to fix the spelling of various scientific terms, has often come to grief. Thus it detaches the final *-me* from *gramme* in such compounds as *kilogram* and *milligram,* but insists upon *gramme* when the word stands alone. In American usage *gram* is now common, and scarcely challenged. All the English authorities that I have consulted prefer *metre* and *calibre* to the American *meter* and *caliber.*[18] They also support the *ae* in such words as *aetiology, aesthetics, mediaeval* and *anaemia,* and the *oe* in *oesophagus,*

---

[16] Horace Hart: Rules for Compositors and Readers at the University Press, Oxford: 23rd ed.; London, 1914. I am informed by Mr. Humphrey Davy, of the *London Times,* that, with one or two minor exceptions, the *Times* observes the rules laid down in this book.

[17] Cassell's English Dictionary, ed. by John Williams, 37th thousand: London, 1908. This work is based upon the larger Encyclopaedic Dictionary, also edited by Williams.

[18] *Caliber* is now the official spelling of the United States Army. *Cf.* Description and Rules for the Management of the U. S. Rifle, *Caliber* .30 Model of 1903; Washington, 1915. But *calibre* is still official in England

manoeuvre and *diarrhoea*. They also cling to such forms as
mollusc, kerb, pyjamas and *ostler*, and to the use of *x* instead
of *ct* in *connexion* and *inflexion*. The Authors' and Printers'
Dictionary admits the American *curb*, but says that the English
kerb is more common. It gives *barque, plough* and *fount*, but
grants that *bark, plow* and *font* are good in America. As between *inquiry* and *enquiry*, it prefers the American *inquiry* to
the English *enquiry*, but it rejects the American *inclose* and
indorse in favor of the English *enclose* and *endorse*.[19] Here
American spelling has driven in a salient, but has yet to take
the whole position. A number of spellings, nearly all American, are trembling on the brink of acceptance in both countries.
Among them is *rime* (for *rhyme*). This spelling was correct in
England until about 1530, but its recent revival was of American
origin. It is accepted by the Oxford Dictionary and by the
editors of the Cambridge History of English Literature, but it
seldom appears in an English journal. The same may be said
of *grewsome*. It has got a footing in both countries, but the
weight of English opinion is still against it. *Develop* (instead
of *develope*) has gone further in both countries. So has *engulf*,
for *engulph*. So has *gipsy* for *gypsy*.

American imitation of English orthography has two impulses
behind it. First, there is the colonial spirit, the desire to pass
as English—in brief, mere affectation. Secondly, there is the
wish among printers, chiefly of books and periodicals, to reach
a compromise spelling acceptable in both countries, thus avoid-
ing expensive revisions in case of republication in England.[20]

as appears by the Field Service Pocket-Book used in the European war
(London, 1914, p. viii.)

[19] Even worse inconsistencies are often encountered. Thus *enquiry*
appears on p. 3 of the Dardanelles Commission's First Report; London,
1917; but *inquiring* is on p. 1.

[20] Mere stupid copying may perhaps be added. An example of it appears
on a map printed with a pamphlet entitled Conquest and Kultur, compiled
by two college professors and issued by the Creel press bureau (Washington, 1918). On this map, borrowed from an English periodical called
New Europe without correction, *annex* is spelled *annexe*. In the same
way English spellings often appear in paragraphs reprinted from the
English newspapers. As compensation in the case of *annexe* I find *annex*

The first influence need not detain us. It is chiefly visible among folk of fashionable pretensions, and is not widespread. At Bar Harbor, in Maine, some of the summer residents are at great pains to put *harbour* instead of *harbor* on their stationery, but the local postmaster still continues to stamp all mail *Bar Harbor*, the legal name of the place. In the same way American haberdashers sometimes advertise *pyjamas* instead of *pajamas*, just as they advertise *braces* instead of *suspenders* and *vests* instead of *undershirts*. But this benign folly does not go very far. Beyond occasionally clinging to the *-re* ending in words of the *theatre* group, all American newspapers and magazines employ the native orthography, and it would be quite as startling to encounter *honour* or *jewellery* in one of them as it would be to encounter *gaol* or *waggon*. Even the most fashionable jewelers in Fifth avenue still deal in *jewelry*, not in *jewellery*.

The second influence is of more effect and importance. In the days before the copyright treaty between England and the United States, one of the standing arguments against it among the English was based upon the fear that it would flood England with books set up in America, and so work a corruption of English spelling.[21] This fear, as we have seen, had a certain plausibility; there is not the slightest doubt that American books and American magazines have done valiant missionary service for American orthography. But English conservatism still holds out stoutly enough to force American printers to certain compromises. When a book is designed for circulation in both countries it is common for the publisher to instruct the printer to employ ''English spelling.'' This English spelling, at the Riverside Press,[22] embraces all the *-our* endings and the following further forms:

on pages 11 and 23 of A Report on the Treatment by the Enemy of British Prisoners of War Behind the Firing Lines in France and Belgium; Miscellaneous No. 7 (1918). When used as a verb the English always spell the word *annex*. *Annexe* is only the noun form.

[21] *Vide* Matthews: Americanisms and Briticisms, pp. 33–34.

[22] Handbook of Style in Use at the Riverside Press, Cambridge, Mass.; Boston, 1913.

cheque	grey
chequered	inflexion
connexion	jewellery
dreamt	leapt
faggot	premises (in logic)
forgather	waggon
forgo	

It will be noted that *gaol, tyre, storey, kerb, asphalte, annexe, ostler, mollusc* and *pyjamas* are not listed, nor are the words ending in -*re*. These and their like constitute the English contribution to the compromise. Two other great American book presses, that of the Macmillan Company [23] and that of the J. S. Cushing Company,[24] add *gaol* and *storey* to the list, and also *behove, briar, drily, enquire, gaiety, gipsy, instal, judgement, lacquey, moustache, nought, pigmy, postillion, reflexion, shily, slily, staunch* and *verandah*. Here they go too far, for, as we have seen, the English themselves have begun to abandon *briar, enquire* and *judgement*. Moreover, *lacquey* is going out over there, and *gipsy* is not English, but American. The Riverside Press, even in books intended only for America, prefers certain English forms, among them, *anaemia, axe, mediaeval, mould, plough, programme* and *quartette*, but in compensation it stands by such typical Americanisms as *caliber, calk, center, cozy, defense, foregather, gray, hemorrhage, luster, maneuver, mustache, theater* and *woolen*. The Government Printing Office at Washington follows Webster's New International Dictionary,[25] which supports most of the innovations of Webster himself. This dictionary is the authority in perhaps a majority of American printing offices, with the Standard and the Century supporting it. The latter two also follow Webster, notably in his -*er* end-

---

[23] Notes for the Guidance of Authors; New York, 1918.

[24] Preparation of Manuscript, Proof Reading, and Office Style at J. S. Cushing Company's; Norwood, Mass., n. d.

[25] Style Book, a Compilation of Rules Governing Executive, Congressional and Departmental Printing, Including the *Congressional Record*, ed. of Feb., 1917; Washington, 1917. A copy of this style book is in the proof-room of nearly every American daily newspaper and its rules are generally observed.

ings and in his substitution of *s* for *c* in words of the *defense* class. The Worcester Dictionary is the sole exponent of English spelling in general circulation in the United States. It remains faithful to most of the *-re* endings, and to *manoeuvre, gramme, plough, sceptic, woollen, axe* and many other English forms. But even Worcester favors such characteristic American spellings as *behoove, brier, caliber, checkered, dryly, jail* and *wagon.*

§ 5.

Simplified Spelling—The current movement toward a general reform of English-American spelling is of American origin, and its chief supporters are Americans today. Its actual father was Webster, for it was the long controversy over his simplified spellings that brought the dons of the American Philological Association to a serious investigation of the subject. In 1875 they appointed a committee to inquire into the possibility of reform, and in 1876 this committee reported favorably. During the same year there was an International Convention for the Amendment of English Orthography at Philadelphia, with several delegates from England present, and out of it grew the Spelling Reform Association.[28] In 1878 a committee of American philologists began preparing a list of proposed new spellings, and two years later the Philological Society of England joined in the work. In 1883 a joint manifesto was issued, recommending various general simplifications. In 1886 the American Philological Association issued independently a list of recommendations affecting about 3,500 words, and falling under ten headings. Practically all of the changes proposed had been put forward 80 years before by Webster, and some of them had entered into unquestioned American usage in the meantime, *e. g.,* the deletion of the *u* from the *-our* words, the substitution of

[28] Accounts of earlier proposals of reform in English spelling are to be found in Sayce's Introduction to the Science of Language, vol. i, p. 330 *et seq.,* and White's Everyday English, p. 152 *et seq.* The best general treatment of the subject is in Lounsbury's English Spelling and Spelling Reform; New York, 1909.

er for *re* at the end of words, the reduction of *traveller* to *traveler*, and the substitution of *z* for *s* wherever phonetically demanded, as in *advertize* and *cozy*.

The trouble with the others was that they were either too uncouth to be adopted without a struggle or likely to cause errors in pronunciation. To the first class belonged *tung* for *tongue*, *ruf* for *rough*, *batl* for *battle* and *abuv* for *above*, and to the second such forms as *cach* for *catch* and *troble* for *trouble*. The result was that the whole reform received a set-back: the public dismissed the industrious professors as a pack of dreamers. Twelve years later the National Education Association revived the movement with a proposal that a beginning be made with a very short list of reformed spellings, and nominated the following by way of experiment: *tho, altho, thru, thruout, thoro, thoroly, thorofare, program, prolog, catalog, pedagog* and *decalog*. This scheme of gradual changes was sound in principle, and in a short time at least two of the recommended spellings, *program* and *catalog*, were in general use. Then, in 1906, came the organization of the Simplified Spelling Board, with an endowment of $15,000 a year from Andrew Carnegie, and a formidable membership of pundits. The board at once issued a list of 300 revised spellings, new and old, and in August, 1906, President Roosevelt ordered their adoption by the Government Printing Office. But this unwise effort to hasten matters, combined with the buffoonery characteristically thrown about the matter by Roosevelt, served only to raise up enemies, and since then, though it has prudently gone back to more discreet endeavors and now lays main stress upon the original 12 words of the National Education Association, the Board has not made a great deal of progress.[27] From time to time it issues impressive lists of newspapers and periodicals that are using some, at least, of its revised spellings and of colleges that have made them optional, but an inspection of these lists shows that very few

[27] Its second list was published on January 28, 1908, its third on January 25, 1909, and its fourth on March 24, 1913, and since then there have been several others. But most of its literature is devoted to the 12 words and to certain reformed spellings of Webster, already in general use.

publications of any importance have been converted [28] and that most of the great universities still hesitate. It has, however, greatly reinforced the authority behind many of Webster's spellings, and it has done much to reform scientific orthography. Such forms as *gram, cocain, chlorid, anemia* and *anilin* are the products of its influence.

Despite the large admixture of failure in this success there is good reason to believe that at least two of the spellings on the National Education Association list, *tho* and *thru*, are making not a little quiet progress. I read a great many manuscripts by American authors, and find in them an increasing use of both forms, with the occasional addition of *altho, thoro* and *thoroly*. The spirit of American spelling is on their side. They promise to come in as *honor, bark, check, wagon* and *story* came in many years ago, as *tire*,[29] *esophagus* and *theater* came in later on, as *program, catalog* and *cyclopedia* came in only yesterday, and as *airplane* (for *aëroplane*) [30] is coming in today. A constant tendency toward logic and simplicity is visible; if the spelling of English and American does not grow farther and farther apart it is only because American drags English along. There is incessant experimentalization. New forms appear, are tested, and then either gain general acceptance or disappear. One such, now struggling for recognition, is *alright*, a compound of *all* and *right*, made by analogy with *already* and *almost*. I find it in American manuscripts every day, and it not infrequently gets into print.[31] So far no dictionary supports it, but

[28] The *Literary Digest* is perhaps the most important. Its usage is shown by the Funk & Wagnalls Company Style Card; New York, 1914.

[29] *Tyre* was still in use in America in the 70's. It will be found on p. 150 of Mark Twain's Roughing It; Hartford, 1872.

[30] *Vide* the *Congressional Record* for March 26, 1918, p. 4374. It is curious to note that the French themselves are having difficulties with this and the cognate words. The final e has been dropped from *biplan, monoplan* and *hydroplan*, but they seem to be unable to dispense with it in *aéroplane*.

[31] For example, in Teepee Neighbors, by Grace Coolidge; Boston, 1917, p. 220; Duty and Other Irish Comedies, by Seumas O'Brien; New York, 1916, p. 52; Salt, by Charles G. Norris; New York, 1918, p. 135, and The Ideal Guest, by Wyndham Lewis, *Little Review*, May, 1918, p. 3. O'Brien is an Irishman and Lewis an Englishman, but the printer in each case was American. I find *allright*, as one word but with two *ll's*, in

it has already migrated to England.[32] Meanwhile, one often encounters, in American advertising matter, such experimental forms as *burlesk, foto, fonograph, kandy, kar, holsum, kumfort* and *Q-room*, not to mention *sulfur*. *Segar* has been more or less in use for half a century, and at one time it threatened to displace *cigar*. At least one American professor of English predicts that such forms will eventually prevail. Even *fosfate* and *fotograph*, he says, "are bound to be the spellings of the future." [33]

§ 6

Minor Differences—Various minor differences remain to be noticed. One is a divergence in orthography due to differences in pronunciation. *Specialty, aluminum* and *alarm* offer examples. In English they are *speciality, aluminium* and *alarum*, though *alarm* is also an alternative form. *Specialty*, in America, is always accented on the first syllable; *speciality*, in England, on the third. The result is two distinct words, though their meaning is identical. How *aluminium*, in America, lost its fourth syllable I have been unable to determine, but all American authorities now make it *aluminum* and all English authorities stick to *aluminium*.

Another difference in usage is revealed in the spelling and pluralization of foreign words. Such words, when they appear in an English publication, even a newspaper, almost invariably bear the correct accents, but in the United States it is almost as invariably the rule to omit these accents, save in publications of considerable pretensions. This is notably the case with *café crêpe, début, débutante, portière, levée, éclat, fête, régime, rôle, soirée, protégé, élite, mêlée, tête-à-tête* and *répertoire*. It is rare to encounter any of them with its proper accents in an American newspaper; it is rare to encounter them unaccented in an Eng-

Diplomatic Correspondence With Belligerent Governments, etc., European War, No. 4; Washington, 1918, p. 214.

[32] *Vide* How to Lengthen Our Ears, by Viscount Harberton; London, 1917, p. 28.

[33] Krapp: Modern English, p. 181.

lish newspaper. This slaughter of the accents, it must be obvious, greatly aids the rapid naturalization of a newcomer. It loses much of its foreignness at once, and is thus easier to absorb. *Dépôt* would have been a long time working its way into American had it remained *dépôt*, but immediately it became plain *depot* it got in. The process is constantly going on. I often encounter *naïveté* without its accents, and even *déshabille, hofbräu, señor* and *résumé*. *Cañon* was changed to *canyon* years ago, and the cases of *exposé, divorcée, schmierkäse, employé* and *matinée* are familiar. At least one American dignitary of learning, Brander Matthews, has openly defended and even advocated this clipping of accents. In speaking of *naïf* and *naïveté*, which he welcomes because "we have no exact equivalent for either word," he says: "But they will need to shed their accents and to adapt themselves somehow to the traditions of our orthography."[34] He goes on: "After we have decided that the foreign word we find knocking at the doors of English [he really means American, as the context shows] is likely to be useful, we must fit it for naturalization by insisting that it shall shed its accents, if it has any; that it shall change its spelling, if this is necessary; that it shall modify its pronunciation, if this is not easy for us to compass; and that it shall conform to all our speech-habits, especially in the formation of the plural."[35]

In this formation of the plural, as elsewhere, English regards the precedents and American makes new ones. All the English authorities that I have had access to advocate retaining the foreign plurals of most of the foreign words in daily use, *e. g.*, *sanatoria, appendices, virtuosi, formulae* and *libretti*. But American usage favors plurals of native cut, and the *Journal* of the American Medical Association goes so far as to approve *curriculums* and *septums*. *Banditti*, in place of *bandits*, would seem an affectation in America, and so would *soprani* for *sopranos*

[34] Why Not Speak Your Own Language? in *Delineator*, Nov., 1917, p. 12.

[35] I once noted an extreme form of this naturalization in a leading Southern newspaper, the *Baltimore Sun*. In an announcement of the death of an American artist it reported that he had studied at the *Bozart* in Paris. In New York I have also encountered *chaufer*.

and *soli* for *solos*.[36] The last two are common in England. Both English and American labor under the lack of native plurals for the two everyday titles, *Mister* and *Missus*. In the written speech, and in the more exact forms of the spoken speech, the French plurals, *Messieurs* and *Mesdames,* are used, but in the ordinary spoken speech, at least in America, they are avoided by circumlocution. When *Messieurs* has to be spoken it is almost invariably pronounced *messers*, and in the same way *Mesdames* becomes *mez-dames*, with the first syllable rhyming with *sez* and the second, which bears the accent, with *games*. In place of *Mesdames* a more natural form, *Madames*, seems to be gaining ground in America. Thus, I lately found *Dames du Sacré Coeur* translated as *Madames of the Sacred Heart* in a Catholic paper of wide circulation,[37] and the form is apparently used by American members of the community.

In capitalization the English are a good deal more conservative than we are. They invariably capitalize such terms as *Government, Prime Minister* and *Society*, when used as proper nouns; they capitalize *Press, Pulpit, Bar*, etc., almost as often. In America a movement against this use of capitals appeared during the latter part of the eighteenth century. In Jefferson's first draft of the Declaration of Independence *nature* and *creator,* and even *god* are in lower case.[38] During the 20's and 30's of the succeeding century, probably as a result of French influence, the disdain of capitals went so far that the days of the week were often spelled with small initial letters, and even *Mr.* became *mr*. Curiously enough, the most striking exhibition of this tendency of late years is offered by an English work of the highest scholarship, the Cambridge History of English Literature. It uses the lower case for all titles, even *baron* and *colonel* before proper names, and also avoids capitals in such

---

[36] Now and then, of course, a contrary tendency asserts itself. For example, the plural of *medium*, in the sense of advertising medium, is sometimes made *media* by advertising men. *Vide* the *Editor and Publisher,* May 11, 1918.

[37] *Irish World*, June 26, 1918.

[38] *Vide* The Declaration of Independence, by Herbert Friedenwald, New York, 1904, p. 262 *et seq.*

words as *presbyterian, catholic* and *christian,* and in the second parts of such terms as Westminster *abbey* and Atlantic *ocean.*

Finally, there are certain differences in punctuation. The English, as everyone knows, put a comma after the street number of a house, making it, for example, *34, St. James street.* They usually insert a comma instead of a period after the hour when giving the time in figures, *e. g., 9,27,* and omit the *0* when indicating less than 10 minutes, *e. g., 8,7* instead of *8.07.* They do not use the period as the mark of the decimal, but employ a dot at the level of the upper dot of a colon, as in *3·1416.* They cling to the hyphen in such words as *to-day* and *to-night;* it begins to disappear in America. They use *an* before *hotel* and *historical;* [39] Kipling has even used it before *hydraulic;* [39] American usage prefers *a.* But these small differences need not be pursued further.

[39] Now and then the English flirt with the American usage. Hart says, for example, that "originally the cover of the large Oxford Dictionary had '*a* historical.'" But "*an* historical" now appears there.

VIII

Proper Names in America

§ 1

Surnames—A glance at any American city directory is sufficient to show that, despite the continued political and cultural
preponderance of the original English strain, the American people have quite ceased to be authentically English in race, or even
authentically British. The blood in their arteries is inordinately
various and inextricably mixed, but yet not mixed enough to run
a clear stream. A touch of foreignness still lingers about millions of them, even in the country of their birth. They show
their alien origin in their speech, in their domestic customs, in
their habits of mind, and in their very names. Just as the
Scotch and the Welsh have invaded England, elbowing out the
actual English to make room for themselves, so the Irish, the
Germans, the Italians, the Scandinavians and the Jews of Eastern Europe, and in some areas, the French, the Slavs and the
hybrid-Spaniards have elbowed out the descendants of the first
colonists. It is not exaggerating, indeed, to say that wherever
the old stock comes into direct and unrestrained conflict with
one of these new stocks, it tends to succumb, or, at all events, to
give up the battle. The Irish, in the big cities of the East, attained to a truly impressive political power long before the first
native-born generation of them had grown up.[1] The Germans,
following the limestone belt of the Alleghany foothills, pre-
empted the best lands East of the mountains before the new

[1] The great Irish famine, which launched the chief emigration to
America, extended from 1845 to 1847. The Know Nothing movement, which
was chiefly aimed at the Irish, extended from 1852 to 1860.

republic was born.[2] And so, in our own time, we have seen the Swedes and Norwegians shouldering the native from the wheat lands of the Northwest, and the Italians driving the decadent New Englanders from their farms, and the Jews gobbling New York, and the Slavs getting a firm foothold in the mining regions, and the French Canadians penetrating New Hampshire and Vermont, and the Japanese and Portuguese menacing Hawaii, and the awakened negroes gradually ousting the whites from the farms of the South.[3] The birth-rate among all these foreign stocks is enormously greater than among the older stock, and though the death-rate is also high, the net increase remains relatively formidable. Even without the aid of immigration it is probable that they would continue to rise in numbers faster than the original English and so-called Scotch-Irish.[4]

Turn to the letter z in the New York telephone directory and you will find a truly astonishing array of foreign names, some of them in process of anglicization, but many of them still arrestingly outlandish. The only Anglo-Saxon surname beginning with z is *Zacharias*,[5] and even that was originally borrowed from the Greek. To this the Norman invasion seems to have added only *Zouchy*. But in Manhattan and the Bronx, even among the necessarily limited class of telephone subscribers, there are nearly 1500 persons whose names begin with the letter, and among them one finds fully 150 different surnames. The German *Zimmermann*, with either one n or two, is naturally the most numerous single name, and following close upon it are its derivatives, *Zimmer* and *Zimmern*. With them are many more German names: *Zahn, Zechendorf, Zeffert, Zeitler, Zeller, Zellner, Zeltmacher, Zepp, Ziegfeld, Zabel, Zucker, Zuckermann, Ziegler, Zillman, Zinser* and so on. They are all represented heavily, but they indicate neither the earliest nor the most formidable accretion, for underlying them are many Dutch

[2] A. B. Faust: The German Element in the United States, 2 vols.; Boston, 1909, vol. ii, pp. 34 *et seq.*

[3] Richard T. Ely: Outlines of Economics, 3rd rev. ed.; New York, 1916, p. 68.

[4] *Cf.* Seth K. Humphrey: Mankind; New York, 1917, p. 45.

[5] *Cf.* William G. Searle: Onomasticon Anglo-Saxonicum; Cambridge, 1897.

names, *e. g., Zeeman* and *Zuurmond,* and over them are a large
number of Slavic, Italian and Jewish names. Among the first I
note *Zabludosky, Zabriskie, Zachczynski, Zapinkow, Zaretsky,
Zechnowitz, Zenzalsky* and *Zywachevsky;* among the second,
Zaccardi, Zaccarini, Zaccaro, Zapparano, Zanelli, Zicarelli and
Zucca; among the third, *Zukor, Zipkin* and *Ziskind.* There
are, too, various Spanish names: *Zelaya, Zingaro,* etc. And
Greek: *Zapeion, Zervakos* and *Zouvelekis.* And Armenian:
Zaloom, Zaron and *Zatmajian.* And Hungarian: *Zadek,
Zagor* and *Zichy.* And Swedish: *Zetterholm* and *Zetterlund.*
And a number that defy placing: *Zrike, Zvan, Zwipf, Zula,
Zur* and *Zeve.*

Any other American telephone directory will show the same
extraordinary multiplication of exotic patronymics. I choose, at
random, that of Pittsburgh, and confine myself to the saloon-
keepers and clergymen. Among the former I find a great many
German names: *Artz, Bartels, Blum, Gaertner, Dittmer, Hahn,
Pfeil, Schuman, Schlegel, von Hedemann, Weiss* and so on. And
Slavic names: *Blaszkiewicz, Bukosky, Puwalowski, Krzykolski,
Tuladziecke* and *Stratkiewicz.* And Greek and Italian names:
Markopoulos, Martinelli, Foglia, Gigliotti and *Karabinos.* And
names beyond my determination: *Tyburski, Volongiatica, He-
risko* and *Hajduk.* Very few Anglo-Saxon names are on the
list; the continental foreigner seems to be driving out the native, and even the Irishman, from the saloon business. Among
the clerics, naturally enough, there are more men of English
surname, but even here I find such strange names as *Auroroff,
Ashinsky, Bourajanis, Duic, Cillo, Mazure, Przvblski, Pniak,
Bazilevich, Smelsz* and *Vrhunec.* But Pittsburgh and New York,
it may be argued, are scarcely American; unrestricted immigration has swamped them; the newcomers crowd into the cities.
Well, examine the roster of the national House of Representatives, which surely represents the whole country. On it I find
*Bacharach, Dupré, Esch, Estopinal, Focht, Heintz, Kahn, Kiess,
Kreider, La Guardia, Kraus, Lazaro, Lehbach, Romjue, Siegel*
and *Zihlman,* not to mention the insular delegates, *Kalanianole,*

de Veyra, Davila and *Yangko,* and enough Irishmen to organize a parliament at Dublin.

In the New York city directory the fourth most common name is now *Murphy,* an Irish name, and the fifth most common is *Meyer,* which is German and chiefly Jewish. The *Meyers* are the *Smiths* of Austria, and of most of Germany. They outnumber all other clans. After them come the *Schultzes* and *Krauses,* just as the *Joneses* and *Williamses* follow the *Smiths* in Great Britain. *Schultze* and *Kraus* do not seem to be very common names in New York, but *Schmidt, Muller, Schneider* and *Klein* appear among the fifty commonest.[6] *Cohen* and *Levy* rank eighth and ninth, and are both ahead of *Jones,* which is second in England, and *Williams,* which is third. *Taylor,* a highly typical British name, ranking fourth in England and Wales, is twenty-third in New York. Ahead of it, beside *Murphy, Meyer, Cohen* and *Levy,* are *Schmidt, Ryan, O'Brien, Kelly* and *Sullivan.* *Robinson,* which is twelfth in England, is thirty-ninth in New York; even *Schneider* and *Muller* are ahead of it. In Chicago *Olson, Schmidt, Meyer, Hansen* and *Larsen* are ahead of *Taylor,* and *Hoffman* and *Becker* are ahead of *Ward;* in Boston *Sullivan* and *Murphy* are ahead of any English name save *Smith;* in Philadelphia *Myers* is just below *Robinson.* Nor, as I have said, is this large proliferation of foreign surnames confined to the large cities. There are whole regions in the Southwest in which *López* and *Gonzales* are far commoner names than *Smith, Brown* or *Jones,* and whole regions in the Middle West wherein *Olson* is commoner than either *Taylor* or *Williams,* and places both North and South where *Duval* is at least as common as *Brown.*

Moreover, the true proportions of this admixture of foreign blood are partly concealed by a wholesale anglicization of surnames, sometimes deliberate and sometimes the fruit of mere confusion. That *Smith, Brown* and *Miller* remain in first, second and third places among the surnames of New York is surely no sound evidence of Anglo-Saxon survival. The German and

6 *New York World* Almanac, 1914, p. 668.

Scandinavian *Schmidt* has undoubtedly contributed many a *Smith*, and *Braun* many a *Brown*, and *Müller* many a *Miller*. In the same way *Johnson*, which holds first place among Chicago surnames, and *Anderson*, which holds third, are plainly reinforced from Scandinavian sources, and the former may also owe something to the Russian *Ivanof*. *Miller* is a relatively rare name in England; it is not among the fifty most common. But it stands thirtieth in Boston, fourth in New York and Baltimore, and second in Philadelphia.[7] In the last-named city the influence of *Müller*, probably borrowed from the Pennsylvania Dutch, is plainly indicated, and in Chicago it is likely that there are also contributions from the Scandinavian *Möller*, the Polish *Jannszewski* and the Bohemian *Mlinár*. *Myers*, as we have seen, is a common surname in Philadelphia. So are *Fox* and *Snyder*. In some part, at least, they have been reinforced by the Pennsylvania Dutch *Meyer*, *Fuchs* and *Schneider*. Sometimes *Müller* changes to *Miller*, sometimes to *Muller*, and sometimes it remains unchanged, but with the spelling made *Mueller*. *Muller* and *Mueller* do not appear among the commoner names in Philadelphia; all the *Müllers* seem to have become *Millers*, thus putting *Miller* in second place. But in Chicago, with *Miller* in fourth place, there is also *Mueller* in thirty-first place, and in New York, with *Miller* in third place, there is also *Muller* in twenty-fourth place.

Such changes, chiefly based upon transliterations, are met with in all countries. The name of *Taaffe*, familiar in Austrian history, had an Irish prototype, probably *Taft*. General *Demikof*, one of the Russian commanders at the battle of Zorndorf, in 1758, was a Swede born *Themicoud*. Franz Maria von *Thugut*, the Austrian diplomatist, was a member of an Italian Tyrolese family named *Tunicotto*. This became *Thunichgut* (= *do no good*) in Austria, and was changed to *Thugut* (= *do good*) to bring it into greater accord with its possessor's deserts.[8] In

---

[7] It was announced by the Bureau of War Risk Insurance on March 30, 1918, that there were then 15,000 *Millers* in the United States Army. On the same day there were 262 *John J. O'Briens*, of whom 50 had wives named *Mary*.

[8] *Cf.* Carlyle's Frederick the Great, bk. xxi, ch. vi.

Bonaparte the Italian *buon*(*o*) became the French *bon*. Many English surnames are decayed forms of Norman-French names, for example, *Sidney* from *St. Denis, Divver* from *De Vere, Bridgewater* from *Burgh de Walter, Montgomery* from *de Mungumeri, Garnett* from *Guarinot*, and *Seymour* from *Saint-Maure.* A large number of so-called Irish names are the products of rough-and-ready transliterations of Gaelic patronymics, for example, *Findlay* from *Fionnlagh, Dermott* from *Diarmuid*, and *McLane* from *Mac Illeathiain.* In the same way the name of *Phoenix* Park, in Dublin, came from *Fion Uisg* (= *fine water*). Of late some of the more ardent Irish authors and politicians have sought to return to the originals. Thus, *O'Sullivan* has become *O Suilleabháin, Pearse* has become *Piarais, Mac Sweeney* has become *Mac Suibhne*, and *Patrick* has suffered a widespread transformation to *Padraic*. But in America, with a language of peculiar vowel-sounds and even consonant-sounds struggling against a foreign invasion unmatched for strength and variety, such changes have been far more numerous than across the ocean, and the legal rule of *idem sonans* is of much wider utility than anywhere else in the world. If it were not for that rule there would be endless difficulties for the *Wises* whose grandfathers were *Weisses*, and the *Leonards* born *Leonhards, Leonhardts* or *Lehnerts*, and the *Manneys* who descend and inherit from *Le Maines.*

"A crude popular etymology," says a leading authority on surnames,[9] "often begins to play upon a name that is no longer significant to the many. So the *Thurgods* have become *Thoroughgoods*, and the *Todenackers* have become the Pennsylvania Dutch *Toothakers*, much as *asparagus* has become *sparrowgrass*." So, too, the *Wittnachts* of Boyle county, Kentucky, descendants of a Hollander, have become *Whitenecks*, and the *Lehns* of lower Pennsylvania, descendants of some far-off German, have become *Lanes.*[10] Edgar Allan *Poe* was a member of a family long settled in Western Maryland, the founder being one *Poh* or *Pfau*, a native of the Palatinate. Major George

---

[9] S. Grant Oliphant, in the *Baltimore Sun*, Dec. 2, 1906.
[10] Harriet *Lane* Johnston was of this family.

Armistead, who defended Fort McHenry in 1814, when Francis Scott Key wrote "The Star-Spangled Banner," was the descendant of an *Armstädt* who came to Virginia from Hesse-Darmstadt. General George A. *Custer,* the Indian fighter, was the great-grandson of one *Küster,* a Hessian soldier paroled after Burgoyne's surrender. William *Wirt,* anti-Masonic candidate for the presidency in 1832, was the son of one *Wörth.* William *Paca,* a signer of the Declaration of Independence, was the great-grandson of a Bohemian named *Paka.* General W. S. *Rosecrans* was really a *Rosenkrantz.* Even the surname of Abraham *Lincoln,* according to some authorities, was an anglicized form of *Linkhorn.*[11]

Such changes, in fact, are almost innumerable; every work upon American genealogy is full of examples. The first foreign names to undergo the process were Dutch and French. Among the former, *Reiger* was debased to *Riker, Van de Veer* to *Vandiver, Van Huys* to *Vannice, Van Siegel* to *Van Sickle, Van Arsdale* to *Vannersdale,* and *Haerlen* (or *Haerlem*) to *Harlan;*[12] among the latter, *Petit* became *Poteet, Caillé* changed to *Kyle, De la Haye* to *Dillehay, Dejean* to *Deshong, Guizot* to *Gossett, Guereant* to *Caron, Soule* to *Sewell, Gervaise* to *Jarvis, Bayle* to *Bailey, Fontaine* to *Fountain, Denis* to *Denny, Pebaudière* to *Peabody, Bon Pas* to *Bumpus* and *de l'Hôtel* to *Doolittle.* "Frenchmen and French Canadians who came to New England," says Schele de Vere, "had to pay for such hospitality as they there received by the sacrifice of their names. The brave *Bon Coeur,* Captain Marryatt tells us in his Diary, became Mr. *Bunker,* and gave his name to Bunker's Hill."[13] But it was the German immigration that provoked the first really wholesale slaughter. A number of characteristic German sounds—for example, that of *ü* and the guttural in *ch* and *g* —are almost impossible to the Anglo-Saxon pharynx, and so they had to go. Thus, *Bloch* was changed to *Block* or *Black, Ochs* to

[11] *Cf.* Faust, *op. cit.,* vol. ii, pp. 183–4.

[12] A Tragedy of Surnames, by Fayette Dunlap, *Dialect Notes,* vol. iv, pt. 1, 1913, p. 7–8.

[13] Americanisms, p. 112.

Oakes, Hoch to *Hoke, Fischbach* to *Fishback, Albrecht* to *Albert* or *Albright,* and *Steinweg* to *Steinway,* and the *Grundwort, bach,* was almost universally changed to *baugh,* as in *Brumbaugh.* The *ü* met the same fate: *Grün* was changed to *Green, Führ* to *Fear* or *Fuhr, Wärner* to *Warner, Düring* to *Deering,* and *Schnäbele* to *Snavely, Snabely* or *Snively.* In many other cases there were changes in spelling to preserve vowel sounds differently represented in German and English. Thus, *Blum* was changed to *Bloom,*[14] *Reuss* to *Royce, Koester* to *Kester, Kuehle* to *Keeley, Schroeder* to *Schrader, Stehli* to *Staley, Weymann* to *Wayman, Friedmann* to *Freedman, Bauman* to *Bowman,* and *Lang* (as the best compromise possible) to *Long.* The change of *Oehm* to *Ames* belongs to the same category; the addition of the final *s* represents a typical effort to substitute the nearest related Anglo-Saxon name. Other examples of that effort are to be found in *Michaels* for *Michaelis, Bowers* for *Bauer, Johnson* for *Johannsen, Ford* for *Furth, Hines* for *Heintz, Kemp* for *Kempf, Foreman* for *Fuhrmann, Kuhns* or *Coons* for *Kuntz, Hoover* for *Huber, Levering* for *Liebering, Jones* for *Jonas, Swope* for *Schwab, Hite* or *Hyde* for *Heid, Andrews* for *André, Young* for *Jung,* and *Pence* for *Pentz.*[15]

The American antipathy to accented letters, mentioned in the chapter on spelling, is particularly noticeable among surnames. An immigrant named *Fürst* inevitably becomes plain *Furst* in the United States, and if not the man, then surely his son. *Löwe,* in the same way, is transformed into *Lowe* (pro. *low*),[16]

---

[14] Henry Harrison, in his Dictionary of the Surnames of the United Kingdom; London, 1912, shows that such names as *Bloom, Cline,* etc., always represent transliterations of German names. They are unknown to genuinely British nomenclature.

[15] A great many more such transliterations and modifications are listed by Faust, *op. cit.,* particularly in his first volume. Others are in Pennsylvania Dutch, by S. S. Haldemann; London, 1872, p. 60 *et seq.,* and in The Origin of Pennsylvania Surnames, by L. Oscar Kuhns, *Lippincott's Magazine, March,* 1897, p. 395.

[16] I lately encountered the following sign in front of an automobile repair shop:

> For puncture or blow
> Bring it to *Lowe.*

Lürmann into *Lurman*, *Schön* into *Schon*, *Suplée* into *Suplee* or *Supplee*, *Lüders* into *Luders* and *Brühl* into *Brill*. Even when no accent betrays it, the foreign diphthong is under hard pressure. Thus the German *oe* disappears, and *Loeb* is changed to *Lobe* or *Laib*, *Oehler* to *Ohler*, *Loeser* to *Leser*, and *Schoen* to *Schon* or *Shane*. In the same way the *au* in such names as *Rosenau* changes to *aw*. So too, the French *oi*-sound is disposed of, and *Dubois* is pronounced *Doo-bóys*, and *Boileau* acquires a first syllable rhyming with *toil*. So with the *kn* in the German names of the *Knapp* class; they are all pronounced, probably by analogy with *Knight*, as if they began with *n*. So with *sch*; *Schneider* becomes *Snyder*, *Schlegel* becomes *Slagel*, and *Schluter* becomes *Sluter*. If a foreigner clings to the original spelling of his name he must usually expect to hear it mispronounced. *Roth*, in American, quickly becomes *Rawth*; *Frémont*, losing both accent and the French *e*, become *Freemont*; *Blum* begins to rhyme with *dumb*; *Mann* rhymes with *van*, and *Lang* with *hang*; *Krantz*, *Lantz* and their cognates with *chance*; *Kurtz* with *shirts*; the first syllable of *Gutmann* with *but*; the first of *Kahler* with *bay*; the first of *Werner* with *turn*; the first of *Wagner* with *nag*. *Uhler*, in America, is always *Youler*. *Berg* loses its German *e*-sound for an English *u*-sound, and its German hard *g* for an English *g*; it becomes identical with the *berg* of *iceberg*. The same change in the vowel occurs in *Erdmann*. In *König* the German diphthong succumbs to a long *o*, and the hard *g* becomes *k*; the common pronunciation is *Cone-ik*. Often, in *Berger*, the *g* becomes soft, and the name rhymes with *verger*. It becomes soft, too, in *Bittinger*. In *Wilstach* and *Welsbach* the *ch* becomes a *k*. In *Anheuser* the *eu* changes to a long *i*. The final *e*, important in German, is nearly always silenced; *Dohme* rhymes with *foam*; *Kühne* becomes *Keen*.

In addition to these transliterations, there are constant translations of foreign proper names. "Many a Pennsylvania *Carpenter*," says Dr. Oliphant,[17] "bearing a surname that is English, from the French, from the Latin, and there a Celtic loan-

17 *Baltimore Sun*, March 17, 1907.

word in origin, is neither English, nor French, nor Latin, nor Celt, but an original German ̃Zimmermann." [18] A great many other such translations are under everyday observation. Pfund becomes Pound; Becker, Baker; Schumacher, Shoemaker; König, King; Weisberg, Whitehill; Koch, Cook; [19] Neuman, Newman; Schaefer, Shepherd or Sheppard; Gutmann, Goodman; Goldschmidt, Goldsmith; Edelstein, Noblestone; Steiner, Stoner; Meister, Master(s); Schwartz, Black; Weiss, White; Weber, Weaver; Bucher, Booker; Vogelgesang, Birdsong; Sontag, Sunday, and so on. Partial translations are also encountered, e. g., Studebaker from Studebecker, and Reindollar from Rheinthaler. By the same process, among the newer immigrants, the Polish Wilkiewicz becomes Wilson, the Bohemian Bohumil becomes Godfrey, and the Bohemian Kovár and the Russian Kuznetzov become Smith. Some curious examples are occasionally encountered. Thus Henry Woodhouse, a gentleman prominent in aeronautical affairs, came to the United States from Italy as Mario Terenzio Enrico Casalegno; his new surname is simply a translation of his old one. And the Belmonts, the bankers, unable to find a euphonious English equivalent for their German-Jewish patronymic of Schönberg, chose a French one that Americans could pronounce.

In part, as I say, these changes in surname are enforced by the sheer inability of Americans to pronounce certain Continental consonants, and their disinclination to remember the Continental vowel sounds. Many an immigrant, finding his name constantly mispronounced, changes its vowels or drops some of its consonants; many another shortens it, or translates it, or changes it entirely for the same reason. Just as a well-known Graeco-French poet changed his Greek name of Papadiamantopoulos to Moréas because Papadiamantopoulos was too much for Frenchmen, and as an eminent Polish-English novelist

[18] Cf. The Origin of Pennsylvania Surnames, op. cit.
[19] Koch, a common German name, has very hard sledding in America. Its correct pronunciation is almost impossible to Americans; at best it becomes Coke. Hence it is often changed, not only to Cook, but to Cox, Koke or even Cockey.

changed his Polish name of *Karzeniowski* to *Conrad* because few Englishmen could pronounce *owski* correctly, so the Italian or Greek or Slav immigrant, coming up for naturalization, very often sheds his family name with his old allegiance, and emerges as *Taylor, Jackson* or *Wilson.* I once encountered a firm of Polish Jews, showing the name of *Robinson & Jones* on its signboard, whose partners were born *Rubinowitz* and *Jonas.* I lately heard of a German named *Knoche*—a name doubly difficult to Americans, what with the *kn* and the *ch*—who changed it boldly to *Knox* to avoid being called *Nokky.* A Greek named *Zoyiopoulous, Kolokotronis, Mavrokerdatos* or *Constantinopolous* would find it practically impossible to carry on amicable business with Americans; his name would arouse their mirth, if not their downright ire. And the same burden would lie upon a Hungarian named *Beniczkyné* or *Gyalui*, or *Szilagyi*, or *Vezercsil-lagok.* Or a Finn named *Kyyhkysen*, or *Jääskelainen, or Tuulensuu*, or *Uotinen,*—all honorable Finnish patronymics. Or a Swede named *Sjogren*, or *Schjtt*, or *Leijonhufvud.* Or a Bohemian named *Srb*, or *Hrubka.* Or, for that matter, a German named *Kannengiesser*, or *Schnapaupf*, or *Pfannenbecker.*

But more important than this purely linguistic hostility, there is a deeper social enmity, and it urges the immigrant to change his name with even greater force. For a hundred years past all the heaviest and most degrading labor of the United States has been done by successive armies of foreigners, and so a concept of inferiority has come to be attached to mere foreignness. In addition, these newcomers, pressing upward steadily in the manner already described, have offered the native a formidable, and considering their lower standards of living, what has appeared to him to be an unfair competition on his own plane, and as a result a hatred born of disastrous rivalry has been added to his disdain. Our unmatchable vocabulary of derisive names for foreigners reveals the national attitude. The French *boche*, the German *hunyadi* (for Hungarian),[20] and the old English *froggy* (for Frenchman) seem lone and feeble beside our great reper-

[20] This is army slang, but promises to survive. The Germans, during the war, had no opprobrious nicknames for their foes. The French were always

toire: *dago, wop, guinea, kike, goose, mick, harp,*[21] *bohick, bohunk, square-head, greaser, canuck, spiggoty,*[22] *chink, polack, dutchie, scowegian, hunkie* and *yellow-belly.* This disdain tends to pursue an immigrant with extraordinary rancor when he bears a name that is unmistakably foreign and hence difficult to the native, and open to his crude burlesque. Moreover, the general feeling penetrates the man himself, particularly if he be ignorant, and he comes to believe that his name is not only a handicap, but also intrinsically discreditable—that it wars subtly upon his worth and integrity.[23] This feeling, perhaps, accounted for a good many changes of surnames among Germans upon the entrance of the United States into the war. But in the majority of cases, of course, the changes so copiously reported—*e. g.,* from *Bielefelder* to *Benson,* and from *Pulvermacher* to *Pullman*— were merely efforts at protective coloration. The immigrant, in a time of extraordinary suspicion and difficulty, tried to get rid of at least one handicap.[24]

die Franzosen, the English were *die Engländer,* and so on, even when most violently abused. Even *der Yankee* was rare.

[21] *Cf.* Some Current Substitutes for Irish, by W. A. McLaughlin, *Dialect Notes,* vol. iv, pt. ii.

[22] *Spiggoty,* originating at Panama, now means a native of any Latin-American region under American protection, and in general any Latin-American. It is navy slang, but has come into extensive civilian use. It is a derisive daughter of "No *spik* Inglese."

[23] *Cf.* Reaction to Personal Names, by Dr. C. P. Oberndorf, *Psychoanalytic Review,* vol. v, no. 1, January, 1918, p. 47 *et seq.* This, so far as I know, is the only article in English which deals with the psychological effects of surnames upon their bearers. Abraham, Silberer and other German psychoanalysts have made contributions to the subject. Dr. Oberndorf alludes, incidentally, to the positive social prestige which goes with an English air, and, to a smaller extent, with a French air in America. He tells of an Italian who changed his patronymic of *Dipucci* into *de Pucci* to make it more "aristocratic." And of a German bearing the genuinely aristocratic name of *von Landsschaffshausen* who changed it to "a typically English name" because the latter seemed more distinguished to his neighbors.

[24] The effects of race antagonism upon language are still to be investigated. The etymology of *slave* indicates that the inquiry might yield interesting results. The word *French,* in English, is largely used to suggest sexual perversion. In German anything *Russian* is barbarous, and *English* education hints at flaggelation. The French, for many years, called a certain contraband appliance a *capote Anglaise,* but after the *entente cordiale* they changed the name to *capote Allemande.* The com-

This motive constantly appears among the Jews, who face an anti-Semitism that is imperfectly concealed and may be expected to grow stronger hereafter. Once they have lost the faith of their fathers, a phenomenon almost inevitable in the first native-born generation, they shrink from all the disadvantages that go with Jewishness, and seek to conceal their origin, or, at all events, to avoid making it unnecessarily noticeable.[25] To this end they modify the spelling of the more familiar Jewish surnames, turning *Levy* into *Lewy, Lewyt, Levitt, Levin, Levine, Levey, Levie*[26] and even *Lever, Cohen* into *Cohn, Cahn, Kahn, Kann, Coyne* and *Conn, Aarons* into *Arens* and *Ahrens* and *Solomon* into *Salmon, Salomon* and *Solmson.* In the same way they shorten their long names, changing *Wolfsheimer* to *Wolf, Goldschmidt* to *Gold,* and *Rosenblatt, Rosenthal, Rosenbaum, Rosenau, Rosenberg, Rosenbusch, Rosenblum, Rosenstein, Rosenheim* and *Rosenfeldt* to *Rose.* Like the Germans, they also seek refuge in translations more or less literal. Thus, on the East Side of New York, *Blumenthal* is often changed to *Bloomingdâle, Schneider* to *Taylor, Reichman* to *Richman,* and *Schlachtfeld* to *Warfield. Fiddler,* a common Jewish name, becomes *Harper;* so does *Pikler,* which is Yiddish for *drummer. Stolar,* which is a Yiddish word borrowed from the Russian, signifying *carpenter,* is often changed to *Carpenter. Lichtman* and *Lichtenstein* become *Chandler. Meilach,* which is Hebrew for *king,* becomes *King,* and so does *Meilachson.* The strong tendency to seek English-sounding equivalents for names of noticeably foreign origin changes *Sher* into *Sherman, Michel* into *Mitchell, Rogowsky* into *Rogers, Kolinsky* into *Collins, Rabinovitch* into *Robbins, Davidovitch* into *Davis, Moiseyev* into *Macy* or *Mason,* and *Jacobson, Jacobovitch* and *Jacobovsky* into *Jackson.* This last

mon English name to this day is *French letter. Cf.* The Criminal, by Havelock Ellis; London, 1910, p. 208.

[25] *Cf.* The Jews, by Maurice Fishberg; New York, 1911, ch. xxii, and especially p. 485 *et seq.*

[26] The English Jews usually change *Levy* to *Lewis,* a substitution almost unknown in America. They also change *Abraham* to *Braham* and *Moses* to *Moss. Vide* Surnames, Their Origin and Nationality, by L. B. McKenna; Quincy (Ill.), 1913, pp. 13–14.

change proceeds by way of a transient change to *Jake* or *Jack* as a nickname. *Jacob* is always abbreviated to one or the other on the East Side. *Yankelevitch* also becomes *Jackson,* for *Yankel* is Yiddish for *Jacob.*[27]

Among the immigrants of other stocks some extraordinarily radical changes in name are to be observed. Greek names of five, and even eight syllables shrink to *Smith;* Hungarian names that seem to be all consonants are reborn in such euphonious forms as *Martin* and *Lacy.* I have encountered a *Gregory* who was born *Grgurevich* in Serbia; a *Uhler* who was born *Uhlyarik;* a *Graves* who descends from the fine old Dutch family of *'sGrav-enhage.* I once knew a man named *Lawton* whose grandfather had been a *Lautenberger.* First he shed the *berger* and then he changed the spelling of *Lauten* to make it fit the inevitable American mispronunciation. There is, again, a family of *Dicks* in the South whose ancestor was a *Schwettendieck*—apparently a Dutch or Low German name. There is, yet again, a celebrated American artist, of the Bohemian patronymic of *Hrubka,* who has abandoned it for a surname which is common to all the Teutonic languages, and is hence easy for Americans. The Italians, probably because of the relations established by the Catholic church, often take Irish names, as they marry Irish girls; it is common to hear of an Italian pugilist or politician named *Kelly* or *O'Brien.* The process of change is often informal, but even legally it is quite facile. The Naturalization Act of June 29, 1906, authorizes the court, as a part of the naturalization of any alien, to make an order changing his name. This is frequently done when he receives his last papers; sometimes, if the newspapers are to be believed, without his solicitation, and even against his protest. If the matter is overlooked at the time, he may change his name later on, like any other citizen, by simple application to a court of record.

Among names of Anglo-Saxon origin and names naturalized long before the earliest colonization, one notes certain American peculiarities, setting off the nomenclature of the United States

[27] For these observations of name changes among the Jews I am indebted to Abraham Cahan.

from that of the mother country. The relative infrequency of hyphenated names in America is familiar; when they appear at all it is almost always in response to direct English influences.[28] Again, a number of English family names have undergone modification in the New World. *Venable* may serve as a specimen. The form in England is almost invariably *Venables,* but in America the final *s* has been lost, and every example of the name that I have been able to find in the leading American reference-books is without it. And where spellings have remained unchanged, pronunciations have been frequently modified. This is particularly noticeable in the South. *Callowhill,* down there, is commonly pronounced *Carrol; Crenshawe* is *Granger; Hawthorne, Horton; Heyward, Howard; Norsworthy, Nazary; Ironmonger, Munger; Farinholt, Fernall; Camp, Kemp; Buchanan, Bohannan; Drewry, Droit, Enroughty, Darby;* and *Taliaferro, Tolliver.*[29] The English *Crowninshields* pronounce every syllable of their name; the American *Crowninshields* commonly make it *Crunshel. Van Schaick,* an old New York name, is pronounced *Von Scoik.* A good many American Jews, aiming at a somewhat laborious refinement, change the pronunciation of the terminal *stein* in their names so that it rhymes, not with *line,* but with *bean.* Thus, in fashionable Jewish circles, there are no longer any *Epsteins, Goldsteins* and *Hammersteins* but only *Epsteens, Goldsteens* and *Hammersteens.* The American Jews differ further from the English in pronouncing *Levy* to make the first syllable rhyme with *tea;* the English Jews always make the name *Lev-vy.* To match such

[28] They arose in England through the custom of requiring an heir by the female line to adopt the family name on inheriting the family property. Formerly the heir dropped his own surname. Thus the ancestor of the present Duke of Northumberland, born *Smithson,* took the ancient name of *Percy* on succeeding to the underlying earldom in the eighteenth century. But about a hundred years ago, heirs in like case began to join the two names by hyphenation, and such names are now very common in the British peerage. Thus the surname of Lord Barrymore is *Smith-Barry,* that of Lord Vernon is *Venables-Vernon,* and that of the Earl of Wharncliffe is *Montagu-Stuart-Wortley-Mackenzie.*

[29] B. W. Green: Word-Book of Virginia Folk-Speech; Richmond, 1899, pp. 13–16.

American prodigies as *Darby* for *Enroughty,* the English themselves have *Hools* for *Howells, Sillinger* for *St. Leger, Sinjin* for *St. John, Pool* for *Powell, Weems* for *Wemyss, Kerduggen* for *Cadogen, Mobrer* for *Marlborough, Key* for *Cains, Marchbanks* for *Marjoribanks, Beecham* for *Beauchamp, Chumley* for *Cholmondeley, Trosley* for *Trotterscliffe,* and *Darby* for *Derby,* not to mention *Maudlin* for *Magdalen.*

§ 2

Given Names—The non-Anglo Saxon American's willingness to anglicize his patronymic is far exceeded by his eagerness to give "American" baptismal names to his children. The favorite given names of the old country almost disappear in the first native-born generation. The Irish immigrants quickly dropped such names as *Terence, Dennis* and *Patrick,* and adopted in their places the less conspicuous *John, George* and *William.* The Germans, in the same way, abandoned *Otto, August, Hermann, Ludwig, Heinrich, Wolfgang, Albrecht, Wilhelm, Kurt, Hans, Rudolf, Gottlieb, Johann* and *Franz.* For some of these they substituted the English equivalents: *Charles, Lewis, Henry, William, John, Frank* and so on. In the room of others they began afflicting their offspring with more fanciful native names: *Milton* and *Raymond* were their chief favorites thirty or forty years ago.[30] The Jews carry the thing to great lengths. At present they seem to take most delight in *Sidney, Irving, Milton, Roy, Stanley* and *Monroe,* but they also call their sons *John, Charles, Henry, Harold, William, Richard, James, Albert, Edward, Alfred, Frederick, Thomas,* and even *Mark, Luke* and *Matthew,* and their daughters *Mary, Gertrude, Estelle, Pauline, Alice* and *Edith.* As a boy I went to school with many Jewish boys. The commonest given names among them were *Isadore, Samuel, Jonas, Isaac* and *Israel.* These are seldom bestowed by

[30] The one given name that they have clung to is *Karl.* This, in fact, has been adopted by Americans of other stocks, always, however, spelled *Carl.* Such combinations as *Carl* Gray, *Carl* Williams and even *Carl* Murphy are common. Here intermarriage has doubtless had its effect.

the rabbis of today. In the same school were a good many German pupils, boy and girl. Some of the girls bore such fine old German given names as *Katharina, Wilhelmina, Elsa, Lotta, Ermentrude* and *Frankziska*. All these have begun to disappear.

The newer immigrants, indeed, do not wait for the birth of children to demonstrate their naturalization; they change their own given names immediately they land. I am told by Abraham Cahan that this is done almost universally on the East Side of New York. "Even the most old-fashioned Jews immigrating to this country," he says, "change *Yosel* to *Joseph*, *Yankel* to *Jacob*, *Liebel* to *Louis*, *Feivel* to *Philip*, *Itzik* to *Isaac*, *Ruven* to *Robert*, and *Moise* or *Motel* to *Morris*." Moreover, the spelling of *Morris*, as the position of its bearer improves, commonly changes to *Maurice*, though the pronunciation may remain *Mawruss*, as in the case of Mr. Perlmutter. The immigrants of other stocks follow the same habit. Every Bohemian *Vaclav* or *Vojtěch* becomes a *William*, every *Jaroslav* becomes a *Jerry*, every *Bronislav* a *Barney*, and every *Stanislav* a *Stanley*. The Italians run to *Frank* and *Joe;* so do the Hungarians and the Balkan peoples; the Russians quickly drop their national system of nomenclature and give their children names according to the American plan. Even the Chinese laundrymen of the big cities become *John, George, Charlie* and *Frank;* I once encountered one boasting the name of *Emil*.

The Puritan influence, in names as in ideas, has remained a good deal more potent in American than in England. The given name of the celebrated *Praise-God* Barebones marked a fashion which died out in England very quickly, but one still finds traces of it in America, e. g., in such women's names as *Faith, Hope, Prudence, Charity* and *Mercy*, and in such men's names as *Peregrine*.[31] The religious obsession of the New England colonists is also kept in mind by the persistence of Biblical names: *Ezra, Hiram, Ezekial, Zachariah, Elijah, Elihu*, and so on. These

31 *Cf.* Curiosities of Puritan Nomenclature, by Charles W. Bardsley; London, 1880.

names excite the derision of the English; an American comic character, in an English play or novel, always bears one of them. Again, the fashion of using surnames as given names is far more widespread in America than in England. In this country, indeed, it takes on the character of a national habit; fully three out of four eldest sons, in families of any consideration, bear their mothers' surnames as middle names. This fashion arose in England during the seventeenth century, and one of its fruits was the adoption of such well-known surnames as *Stanley, Cecil, Howard, Douglas* and *Duncan* as common given names.[32] It died out over there during the eighteenth century, and today the great majority of Englishmen bear such simple given names as *John, Charles* and *William*—often four or five of them—but in America it has persisted. A glance at a roster of the Presidents of the United States will show how firmly it has taken root. Of the ten that have had middle names at all, six have had middle names that were family surnames, and two of the six have dropped their other given names and used these surnames. This custom, perhaps, has paved the way for another: that of making given names of any proper nouns that happen to strike the fancy. Thus General Sherman was named after an Indian chief, *Tecumseh*, and a Chicago judge was baptized *Kenesaw Mountain* [33] in memory of the battle that General Sherman fought there. A late candidate for governor of New York had the curious given name of *D-Cady*.[34] Various familiar American given names, originally surnames, are almost unknown in England, among them, *Washington, Jefferson, Jackson, Lincoln, Columbus* and *Lee*. *Chauncey* forms a curious addition to the list. It was the surname of the second president of Harvard College, and was bestowed upon their offspring by numbers of his graduates. It then got into

---

[32] *Cf.* Bardsley, *op. cit.,* p. 205 *et seq.*

[33] The Geographic Board has lately decided that *Kenesaw* should be *Kennesaw*, but the learned jurist sticks to one *n*.

[34] Thornton reprints a paragraph from the *Congressional Globe* of June 15, 1854, alleging that in 1846, during the row over the Oregon boundary, when "Fifty-four forty or fight" was a political slogan, many "canal-boats, and even some of the babies, . . . were christened *54° 40'*."

general use and acquired a typically American pronunciation, with the *a* of the first syllable flat. It is never encountered in England.

In the pronunciation of various given names, as in that of many surnames, English and American usages differ. *Evelyn,* in England, is given two syllables instead of three, and the first is made to rhyme with *leave. Irene* is given two syllables, making it *Irene-y. Ralph* is pronounced *Rafe. Jerome* is accented on the first syllable; in America it is always accented on the second.[35]

§ 3

Geographical Names—"There is no part of the world," said Robert Louis Stevenson, "where nomenclature is so rich, poetical, humorous and picturesque as in the United States of America." A glance at the latest United States Official Postal Guide [36] or report of the United States Geographic Board [37] quite bears out this opinion. The map of the country is besprinkled with place names from at least half a hundred languages, living and dead, and among them one finds examples of the most daring and elaborate fancy. There are Spanish, French and Indian names as melodious and charming as running water; there are names out of the histories and mythologies of all the great races of man; there are names grotesque and names almost sublime. No other country can match them for interest and variety. When there arises among us a philologist who will study them as thoroughly and intelligently as the Swiss, Johann Jakob Egli, studied the place names of Central Europe, his work will be an invaluable contribution to the history of the nation, and no less to an understanding of the psychology of its people.

The original English settlers, it would appear, displayed little imagination in naming the new settlements and natural features

[35] The Irish present several curious variations. Thus, they divide *Charles* into two syllables. They also take liberties with various English surnames. *Bermingham,* for example, is pronounced *Brimmingham* in Ireland.

[36] Issued annually in July, with monthly supplements.

[37] The latest report is the fourth, covering the period 1890–1916; Washington, 1916.

of the land that they came to. Their almost invariable tendency, at the start, was to make use of names familiar at home, or to invent banal compounds. *Plymouth Rock* at the North and *Jamestown* at the South are examples of their poverty of fancy; they filled the narrow tract along the coast with new *Bostons, Cambridges, Bristols* and *Londons*, and often used the adjective as a prefix. But this was only in the days of beginning. Once they had begun to move back from the coast and to come into contact with the aborigines and with the widely dispersed settlers of other races, they encountered rivers, mountains, lakes and even towns that bore far more engaging names, and these, after some resistance, they perforce adopted. The native names of such rivers as the *James*, the *York* and the *Charles* succumbed, but those of the *Potomac*, the *Patapsco*, the *Merrimack* and the *Penobscot* survived, and they were gradually reinforced as the country was penetrated. Most of these Indian names, in getting upon the early maps, suffered somewhat severe simplifications. *Potowánmeac* was reduced to *Potomack* and then to *Potomac; Unéaukara* became *Niagara; Reckawackes*, by the law of Hobson-Jobson, was turned into *Rockaway*, and *Pentapang* into *Port Tobacco*.[38] But, despite such elisions and transformations, the charm of thousands of them remained, and today they are responsible for much of the characteristic color of American geographical nomenclature. Such names as *Tallahassee, Susquehanna, Mississippi, Allegheny, Chicago, Kennebec, Patuxent* and *Arkansas* give a barbaric brilliancy to the American map. Only the map of Australia, with its mellifluous Maori names, can match it.

The settlement of the American continent, once the eastern coast ranges were crossed, proceeded with unparalleled speed, and so the naming of the new rivers, lakes, peaks and valleys, and of the new towns and districts no less, strained the inventiveness of the pioneers. The result is the vast duplication of names that shows itself in the Postal Guide. No less than eighteen imi-

---

[38] The authority here is River and Lake Names in the United States, by Edmund T. Ker; New York, 1911. Stephen G. Boyd, in Indian Local Names; York (Pa.), 1885, says that the original Indian name was *Pootuppag*.

tative *Bostons* and *New Bostons* still appear, and there are nineteen *Bristols*, twenty-eight *Newports*, and twenty-two *Londons* and *New Londons*.   Argonauts starting out from an older settlement on the coast would take its name with them, and so we find *Philadelphias* in Illinois, Mississippi, Missouri and Tennessee, *Richmonds* in Iowa, Kansas and nine other western states, and *Princetons* in fifteen.   Even when a new name was hit upon it seems to have been hit upon simultaneously by scores of scattered bands of settlers; thus we find the whole land bespattered with *Washingtons, Lafayettes, Jeffersons* and *Jacksons,* and with names suggested by common and obvious natural objects, *e. g., Bear Creek, Bald Knob* and *Buffalo.*   The Geographic Board, in its last report, made a belated protest against this excessive duplication.   "The names *Elk, Beaver, Cottonwood* and *Bald,*" it said, "are altogether too numerous." [39]   Of postoffices alone there are fully a hundred embodying *Elk;* counting in rivers, lakes, creeks, mountains and valleys, the map of the United States probably shows at least twice as many such names.

A study of American geographical and place names reveals eight general classes, as follows: (*a*) those embodying personal names, chiefly the surnames of pioneers or of national heroes; (*b*) those transferred from other and older places, either in the eastern states or in Europe; (*c*) Indian names; (*d*) Dutch, Spanish and French names; (*e*) Biblical and mythological names; (*f*) names descriptive of localities; (*g*) names suggested by the local flora, fauna or geology; (*h*) purely fanciful names.   The names of the first class are perhaps the most numerous.   Some consist of surnames standing alone, as *Washington, Cleveland, Bismarck, Lafayette, Taylor* and *Randolph;* others consist of surnames in combination with various old and new *Grundwörter,* as *Pittsburgh, Knoxville, Bailey's Switch, Hagerstown, Franklinton, Dodge City, Fort Riley, Wayne Junction* and *McKeesport;* and yet others are contrived of given names, either alone or in combination, as *Louisville, St. Paul, Elizabeth, Johnstown, Charlotte, Williamsburg* and *Marysville.*   The number of towns in the United States bearing women's given names is enormous.

[39] P. 17.

I find, for example, eleven postoffices called *Charlotte,* ten called *Ada* and no less than nineteen called *Alma.* Most of these places are small, but there is an *Elizabeth* with 75,000 population, an *Elmira* with 40,000, and an *Augusta* with nearly 45,000.

The names of the second class we have already briefly observed. They are betrayed in many cases by the prefix *New;* more than 600 such postoffices are recorded, ranging from *New Albany* to *New Windsor.* Others bear such prefixes as *West, North* and *South,* or various distinguishing affixes, *e. g., Bostonia, Pittsburgh Landing, Yorktown* and *Hartford City.* One often finds eastern county names applied to western towns and eastern town names applied to western rivers and mountains. Thus, *Cambria,* which is the name of a county but not of a postoffice in Pennsylvania, is a town name in seven western states; *Baltimore* is the name of a glacier in Alaska, and *Princeton* is the name of a peak in Colorado. In the same way the names of the more easterly states often reappear in the west, *e. g.,* in *Mount Ohio,* Colo., *Delaware,* Okla., and *Virginia City,* Nev. The tendency to name small American towns after the great capitals of antiquity has excited the derision of the English since the earliest days; there is scarcely an English book upon the states without some fling at it. Of late it has fallen into abeyance, though sixteen *Athenses* still remain, and there are yet many *Carthages, Uticas, Syracuses, Romes, Alexandrias, Ninevahs* and *Troys.* The third city of the nation, *Philadelphia,* got its name from the ancient stronghold of Philadelphus of Pergamun. To make up for the falling off of this old and flamboyant custom, the more recent immigrants have brought with them the names of the capitals and other great cities of their fatherlands. Thus the American map bristles with *Berlins, Bremens, Hamburgs, Warsaws* and *Leipzigs,* and is beginning to show *Stockholms, Venices, Belgrades* and *Christianias.*

The influence of Indian names upon American nomenclature is quickly shown by a glance at the map. No less than 26 of the states have names borrowed from the aborigines, and the same thing is true of most of our rivers and mountains. There was an effort, at one time, to get rid of these Indian names. Thus the early Virginians changed the name of the *Powhatan* to the *James*, and the first settlers in New York changed the name of *Horicon* to *Lake George*. In the same way the present name of the *White Mountains* displaced *Agiochook*, and *New Amsterdam*, and later *New York*, displaced *Manhattan*, which has been recently revived. The law of Hobson-Jobson made changes in other Indian names, sometimes complete and sometimes only partial. Thus, *Mauwauwaming* became *Wyoming*, *Maucwachoong* became *Mauch Chunk*, *Ouabache* became *Wabash*, *Asingsing* became *Sing-Sing*, and *Machihiganing* became *Michigan*. But this vandalism did not go far enough to take away the brilliant color of the aboriginal nomenclature. The second city of the United States bears an Indian name, and so do the largest American river, and the greatest American water-fall, and four of the five great Lakes, and the scene of the most important military decision ever reached on American soil.

The Dutch place-names of the United States are chiefly confined to the vicinity of New York, and a good many of them have become greatly corrupted. *Brooklyn*, *Wallabout* and *Gramercy* offer examples. The first-named was originally *Breuckelen*, the second was *Waale Bobht*, and the third was *De Kromme Zee*. *Hell-Gate* is a crude translation of the Dutch *Helle-Gat*. During the early part of the last century the more delicate New Yorkers transformed the term into *Hurlgate*, but the change was vigorously opposed by Washington Irving, and so *Hell-Gate* was revived. The law of Hobson-Jobson early converted the Dutch *hoek* into *hook*, and it survives in various place-names, *e. g.*, *Kinderhook* and *Sandy Hook*. The Dutch *kill* is a *Grundwort* in many other names, *e. g.*, *Catskill*, *Schuylkill*, *Peekskill*, *Fishkill* and *Kill van Kull;* it is the equivalent of the American *creek*. Many other Dutch place-names will come familiarly to mind: *Harlem*, *Staten*, *Flushing*, *Cortlandt*, *Calver Plaat*, *Nassau*, *Coenties*, *Spuyten Duyvel*, *Yonkers*, *Hoboken* and *Bowery* (from *Bouvery*).[40] *Block* Island was originally *Blok*, and Cape *May*, according to Schele de Vere, was *Mey*, both Dutch.

---

40 *Cf.* Dutch Contributions to the Vocabulary of English in America, by W. H. Carpenter, *Modern Philology*, July, 1908.

A large number of New York street and neighborhood names come down from Knickerbocker days, often greatly changed in pronunciation. *Desbrosses* offers an example. The Dutch called it *de Broose*, but in New York today it is commonly spoken of as *Dez-bros-sez*.

French place-names have suffered almost as severely. Few persons would recognize *Smackover*, the name of a small town in Arkansas, as French, and yet in its original form it was *Chemin Couvert*. Schele de Vere, in 1871, recorded the degeneration of the name to *Smack Cover;* the Postoffice, always eager to shorten and simplify names, has since made one word of it and got rid of the redundant *c*. In the same way *Bob Ruly*, a Missouri name, descends from *Bois Brulé*. "The American tongue," says W. W. Crane, "seems to lend itself reluctantly to the words of alien languages." [41] This is shown plainly by the history of French place-names among us. A large number of them, *e. g., Lac Superieur*, were translated into English at an early day, and most of those that remain are now pronounced as if they were English. Thus *Des Moines* is *dee-moyns, Terre Haute* is *terry-hut, Beaufort* is *byu-fort, New Orleans* is *or-leens, Lafayette* has a flat *a, Havre de Grace* has another, and *Versailles* is *ver-sales*. The pronunciation of *sault*, as in *Sault Ste. Marie*, is commonly more or less correct; the Minneapolis, St. Paul and Sault Ste. Marie Railroad is popularly called the *Soo*. This may be due to Canadian example, or to some confusion between *Sault* and *Sioux*. The French *Louis*, in *St. Louis* and *Louisville*, is usually pronounced correctly. So is the *rouge* in *Baton Rouge*, though the *baton* is commonly boggled. It is possible that familiarity with *St. Louis* influenced the local pronunciation of *Illinois*, which is *Illinoy*, but this may be a mere attempt to improve upon the vulgar *Illin-i*.[42]

For a number of years the Geographic Board has been seek-

41 Our Naturalized Names, *Lippincott's Magazine*, April, 1899. It will be recalled how Pinaud, the French perfumer, was compelled to place advertisements in the street-cars, instructing the public in the proper pronunciation of his name.

42 The same compromise is apparent in the pronunciation of *Iroquois*, which is *Iro-quoy* quite as often as it is *Iro-quoys*.

ing vainly to reestablish the correct pronunciation of the name of the *Purgatoire* river in Colorado. Originally named the *Rio de las Animas* by the Spaniards, it was renamed the *Rivière du Purgatoire* by their French successors. The American pioneers changed this to *Picketwire*, and that remains the local name of the stream to this day, despite the effort of the Geographic Board to compromise on *Purgatoire* river. Many other French names are being anglicized with its aid and consent. Already half a dozen *Bellevues* have been changed to *Belleviews* and *Bellviews*, and the spelling of nearly all the *Belvédères* has been changed to *Belvidere*. *Belair*, La., represents the end-product of a process of decay which began with *Belle Aire*, and then proceeded to *Bellaire* and *Bellair*. All these forms are still to be found, together with *Bel Air*. The Geographic Board's antipathy to accented letters and to names of more than one word [43] has converted *Isle Ste. Thérèse*, in the St. Lawrence river, to *Isle Ste. Therese*, a truly abominable barbarism, and *La Cygne*, in Kansas, to *Lacygne*, which is even worse. *Lamoine, Labelle, Lagrange* and *Lamonte* are among its other improvements; *Lafayette*, for *La Fayette*, long antedates the beginning of its labors.

The Spanish names of the Southwest are undergoing a like process of corruption, though without official aid. *San Antonio* has been changed to *San Antone* in popular pronunciation and seems likely to go to *San Tone*; *El Paso* has acquired a flat American *a* and a *z*-sound in place of the Spanish *s*; *Los Angeles* presents such difficulties that no two of its inhabitants agree upon the proper pronunciation, and many compromise on simple *Los*, as the folks of *Jacksonville* commonly call their town *Jax*. Some of the most mellifluous of American place-names are in the areas once held by the Spaniards. It would be hard to match the beauty of *Santa Margarita, San Anselmo, Alamogordo, Terra Amarilla, Sabinoso, Las Palomas, Ensenada, Nogales, San Patricio* and *Bernalillo*. But they are under a severe and double assault. Not only do the present lords of the soil debase them in speaking them; in many cases they are formally displaced by native names of the utmost harshness and banality. Thus,

[43] *Vide* its Fourth Report (1890–1916), p. 15.

one finds in New Mexico such absurdly-named towns as *Sugarite,
Shoemaker, Newhope, Lordsburg, Eastview* and *Central;* in
Arizona such places as *Old Glory, Springerville, Wickenburg*
and *Congress Junction,* and even in California such abomina-
tions as *Oakhurst, Ben Hur, Drytown, Skidoo, Susanville, Uno*
and *Ono.*

The early Spaniards were prodigal with place-names testify-
ing to their piety, but these names, in the overwhelming main,
were those of saints. Add *Salvador, Trinidad* and *Concepcion,*
and their repertoire is almost exhausted. If they ever named
a town *Jesus* the name has been obliterated by Anglo-Saxon
prudery; even their use of the name as a personal appellation
violates American notions of the fitting. The names of the Jewish patriarchs and those of the holy places in Palestine do not
appear among their place-names; their Christianity seems to
have been exclusively of the New Testament. But the Americans
who displaced them were intimately familiar with both books
of the Bible, and one finds copious proofs of it on the map of
the United States. There are no less than seven *Bethlehems*
in the Postal Guide, and the name is also applied to various
mountains, and to one of the reaches of the Ohio river. I find
thirteen *Bethanys,* seventeen *Bethels,* eleven *Beulahs,* nine *Ca-
naans,* eleven *Jordans* and twenty-one *Sharons. Adam* is sponsor
for a town in West Virginia and an island in the Chesapeake, and
Eve for a village in Kentucky. There are five postoffices named
Aaron, two named *Abraham,* two named *Job,* and a town and a
lake named *Moses.* Most of the *St. Pauls* and *St. Josephs* of
the country were inherited from the French, but the two *St.
Patricks* show a later influence. Eight *Wesleys* and *Wesley-
villes,* eight *Asburys* and twelve names embodying *Luther* indicate the general theological trend of the plain people. There
is a village in Maryland, too small to have a postoffice, named
Gott, and I find *Gotts Island* in Maine and *Gottville* in California, but no doubt these were named after German settlers
of that awful name, and not after the Lord God directly. There
are four *Trinities,* to say nothing of the inherited Spanish *Trini-
dads.*

Names wholly or partly descriptive of localities are very numerous throughout the country, and among the *Grundwörter* embodied in them are terms highly characteristic of America and almost unknown to the English vocabulary. *Bald Knob* would puzzle an Englishman, but the name is so common in the United States that the Geographic Board has had to take measures against it. Others of that sort are *Council Bluffs, Patapsco Neck, Delaware Water Gap, Curtis Creek, Walden Pond, Sandy Hook, Key West, Bull Run, Portage, French Lick, Jones Gulch, Watkins Gully, Cedar Bayou, Keams Canyon, Parker Notch, Sucker Branch, Fraziers Bottom* and *Eagle Pass*. *Butte Creek*, in *Montana*, is a name made up of two Americanisms. There are thirty-five postoffices whose names embody the word *prairie*, several of them, *e. g., Prairie du Chien*, Wis., inherited from the French. There are seven *Divides*, eight *Buttes*, eight town-names embodying the word *burnt*, innumerable names embodying *grove, barren, plain, fork, center, cross-roads, courthouse, cove* and *ferry*, and a great swarm of *Cold Springs, Coldwaters, Summits, Middletowns* and *Highlands*. The flora and fauna of the land are enormously represented. There are twenty-two *Buffalos* beside the city in New York, and scores of *Buffalo Creeks, Ridges, Springs* and *Wallows*. The *Elks*, in various forms, are still more numerous, and there are dozens of towns, mountains, lakes, creeks and country districts named after the *beaver, martin, coyote, moose* and *otter*, and as many more named after such characteristic flora as the *paw-paw*, the *sycamore*, the *cottonwood*, the *locust* and the *sunflower*. There is an *Alligator* in Mississippi, a *Crawfish* in Kentucky and a *Rat Lake* on the Canadian border of Minnesota. The endless search for mineral wealth has besprinkled the map with such names as *Bromide, Oil City, Anthracite, Chrome, Chloride, Coal Run, Goldfield, Telluride, Leadville* and *Cement*.

There was a time, particularly during the gold rush to California, when the rough humor of the country showed itself in the invention of extravagant and often highly felicitous place-names, but with the growth of population and the rise of civic spirit they have tended to be replaced with more seemly coinages. *Catfish* creek, in Wisconsin, is now the *Yahara* river; the *Bulldog* mountains, in Arizona, have become the *Harosomas;* the *Picketwire* river, as we have seen, has resumed its old French name of *Purgatoire*. As with natural features of the landscape, so with towns. Nearly all the old *Boozevilles, Jackass Flats, Three Fingers, Hell-For-Sartains, Undershirt Hills, Razzle-Dazzles, Cow-Tails, Yellow Dogs, Jim-Jamses, Jump-Offs, Poker Citys* and *Skunktowns* have yielded to the growth of delicacy, but *Tombstone* still stands in Arizona, *Goose Bill* remains a postoffice in Montana, and the Geographic Board gives its imprimatur to the *Horsethief* trail in Colorado, to *Burning Bear* creek in the same state, and to *Pig Eye* lake in Minnesota. Various other survivors of a more lively and innocent day linger on the map: *Blue Ball*, Ark., *Cowhide*, W. Va., *Dollarville*, Mich., *Oven Fork*, Ky., *Social Circle*, Ga., *Sleepy Eye*, Minn., *Bubble*, Ark., *Shy Beaver*, Pa., *Shin Pond*, Me., *Rough-and-Ready*, Calif., *Non Intervention*, Va., *Noodle*, Tex., *Nursery*, Mo., *Number Four*, N. Y., *Oblong*, Ill., *Stock Yards*, Neb., *Stout*, Iowa, and so on. West Virginia, the wildest of the eastern states, is full of such place-names. Among them I find *Affinity, Annamoriah (Anna Maria?), Bee, Bias, Big Chimney, Billie, Blue Jay, Bulltown, Caress, Cinderella, Cyclone, Czar, Cornstalk, Duck, Halcyon, Jingo, Left Hand, Ravens Eye, Six, Skull Run, Three Churches, Uneeda, Wide Mouth, War Eagle* and *Stumptown*. The Postal Guide shows two *Ben Hurs*, five *St. Elmos* and ten *Ivanhoes*, but only one *Middlemarch*. There are seventeen *Roosevelts*, six *Codys* and six *Barnums*, but no *Shakespeare*. *Washington*, of course, is the most popular of American place-names. But among names of postoffices it is hard pushed by *Clinton, Centerville, Liberty, Canton, Marion* and *Madison*, and even by *Springfield, Warren* and *Bismarck*.

The Geographic Board, in its laudable effort to simplify American nomenclature, has played ducks and drakes with some of the most picturesque names on the national map. Now and then, as in the case of *Purgatoire*, it has temporarily departed from this policy, but in the main its influence has been thrown against the fine old French and Spanish names, and against the more piquant native names no less. Thus, I find it deciding against *Portage des Flacons* and in favor of the hideous *Bottle portage*, against *Cañada del Burro* and in favor of *Burro canyon*, against *Canos y Ylas de la Cruz* and in favor of the barbarous *Cruz island*. In *Bougére landing* and *Cañon City* it has deleted the accents. The name of the *De Grasse river* it has changed to *Grass*. *De Laux* it has changed to the intolerable *Dlo*. And, as we have seen, it has steadily amalgamated French and Spanish articles with their nouns, thus achieving such forms as *Duchesne, Eldorado, Deleon* and *Laharpe*. But here its policy is fortunately inconsistent, and so a number of fine old names has escaped. Thus, it has decided in favor of *Bon Secours* and against *Bonsecours*, and in favor of *De Soto, La Crosse* and *La Moure*, and against *Desoto, Lacrosse* and *Lamoure*. Here its decisions are confused and often unintelligible. Why *Laporte*, Pa., and *La Porte*, Iowa? Why *Lagrange*, Ind., and *La Grange*, Ky.? Here it would seem to be yielding a great deal too much to local usage.

The Board proceeds to the shortening and simplification of native names by various devices. It deletes such suffixes as *town, city* and *courthouse;* it removes the apostrophe and often the genitive *s* from such names as *St. Mary's;* it shortens *burgh* to *burg* and *borough* to *boro;* and it combines separate and often highly discreet words. The last habit often produces grotesque forms, *e. g., Newberlin, Boxelder, Sabbathday lake, Fallentimber, Bluemountain, Westtown, Threepines* and *Missionhill*. It apparently cherishes a hope of eventually regularizing the spelling of *Allegany*. This is now *Allegany* for the Maryland county, the Pennsylvania township and the New York and Oregon towns, *Alleghany* for the mountains, the Colorado town and the Virginia town and springs, and *Allegheny* for the Pittsburgh borough and the Pennsylvania county, college and river. The Board inclines to *Allegheny* for both river and mountains. Other Indian names give it constant concern. Its struggles to set up *Chemquasabamticook* as the name of a Maine lake in place of *Chemquasabamtic* and *Chemquassabamticook*, and *Chatahospee* as the name of an Alabama creek in place of *Chatta-*

hospee, Hoolethlocco, Hoolethloces, Hoolethloco and *Hootethlocco*
are worthy of its learning and authority.[44]

The American tendency to pronounce all the syllables of a
word more distinctly than the English shows itself in geographical names. White, in 1880,[45] recorded the increasing habit of
giving full value to the syllables of such borrowed English names
as *Worcester* and *Warwick*. I have frequently noted the same
thing. In Worcester county, Maryland, the name is usually
pronounced *Wooster,* but on the Western Shore of the state one
hears *Worcest-'r.*[46] *Norwich* is another such name; one hears
Nor-wich quite as often as *Norrich.*[47] Yet another is *Delhi;* one
often hears *Del-high.* White said that in his youth the name
of the *Shawangunk* mountains, in New York, was pronounced
Shongo, but that the custom of pronouncing it as spelled had
arisen during his manhood. So with *Winnipiseogee,* the name
of a lake; once *Winipisaukie,* it gradually came to be pronounced
as spelled. There is frequently a considerable difference between the pronunciation of a name by natives of a place and its
pronunciation by those who are familiar with it only in print.
Baltimore offers an example. The natives always drop the
medial *i* and so reduce the name to two syllables; the habit iden-
tifies them. *Anne Arundel,* the name of a county in Maryland,

---

[44] The Geographic Board is composed of representatives of the Coast and
Geodetic Survey, the Geological Survey, the General Land Office, the Post
Office, the Forest Service, the Smithsonian Institution, the Biological Sur-
vey, the Government Printing Office, the Census and Lighthouse Bureaus,
the General Staff of the Army, the Hydrographic Office, Library and War
Records Office of the Navy, the Treasury and the Department of State.
It was created by executive order Sept. 4, 1890, and its decisions are binding
upon all federal officials. It has made, to date, about 15,000 decisons.
They are recorded in reports issued at irregular intervals and in more
frequent bulletins.

[45] Every-Day English, p. 100.

[46] I have often noted that Americans, in speaking of the familiar *Wor-
cestershire* sauce, commonly pronounce every syllable and enunciated *shire*
distinctly. In England it is always *Woostersh'r.*

[47] The English have a great number of such decayed pronunciations, *e. g.,
Maudlin* for *Magdalen College, Sister* for *Cirencester, Merrybone* for *Maryle-
bone.* Their geographical nomenclature shows many corruptions due to
faulty pronunciation and the law of Hobson-Jobson, *e. g., Leighton Buz-
zard* for the Norman French *Leiton Beau Desart.*

is usually pronounced *Ann 'ran'l* by its people. *Arkansas,* as everyone knows, is pronounced *Arkansaw* by the Arkansans, and the Nevadans give the name of their state a flat *a.* The local pronunciation of *Illinois* I have already noticed. *Iowa,* at home, is often *Ioway.*[48] Many American geographical names offer great difficulty to Englishmen. One of my English acquaintances tells me that he was taught at school to accent *Massachusetts* on the second syllable, to rhyme the second syllable of *Ohio* with *tea,* and to sound the first *c* in *Connecticut.* In Maryland the name of *Calvert* county is given a broad *a,* whereas the name of *Calvert* street, in Baltimore, has a flat *a.* This curious distinction is almost always kept up. A Scotchman, coming to America, would give the *ch* in such names as *Loch Raven* and *Lochvale* the guttural Scotch (and German) sound, but locally it is always pronounced as if it were *k.*

Finally, there is a curious difference between English and American usage in the use of the word *river.* The English invariably put it before the proper name, whereas we almost as invariably put it after. *The Thames river* would seem quite as strange to an Englishman as *the river Chicago* would seem to us. This difference arose more than a century ago and was noticed by Pickering. But in his day the American usage was still somewhat uncertain, and such forms as *the river Mississippi* were yet in use. Today *river* almost always goes after the proper name.

§ 4

Street Names—"Such a locality as 'the *corner* of *Avenue H* and *Twenty-third* street,'" says W. W. Crane, "is about as distinctively American as Algonquin and Iroquois names like *Mississippi* and *Saratoga.*"[49] Kipling, in his "American Notes,"[50] gives testimony to the strangeness with which the

[48] Curiously enough, Americans always use the broad *a* in the first syllable of *Albany,* whereas Englishmen rhyme the syllable with *pal.* The English also pronounce *Pall Mall* as if it were spelled *pal mal.* Americans commonly give it two broad *a's.*

[49] Our Street Names, *Lippincott's Magazine,* Aug., 1897, p. 264.

[50] Ch. i.

number-names, the phrase "the corner of," and the custom of omitting *street* fall upon the ear of a Britisher. He quotes with amazement certain directions given to him on his arrival in San Francisco from India: "Go six blocks north to [the] corner of *Geary* and *Markey* [*Market?*]; then walk around till you strike [the] corner of *Gutter* and *Sixteenth.*" The English always add the word *street* (or *road* or *place* or *avenue*) when speaking of a thoroughfare; such a phrase as "*Oxford* and *New Bond*" would strike them as incongruous. The American custom of numbering and lettering streets is almost always ascribed by English writers who discuss it, not to a desire to make finding them easy, but to sheer poverty of invention. The English apparently have an inexhaustible fund of names for streets; they often give one street more than one name. Thus, *Oxford* street, London, becomes the *Bayswater* road, *High* street, *Holland Park* avenue, *Goldhawke* road and finally the *Oxford* road to the westward, and *High Holborn*, *Holborn* viaduct, *Newgate* street, *Cheapside*, the *Poultry*, *Cornhill* and *Leadenhall* street to the eastward. The Strand, in the same way, becomes *Fleet* street, *Ludgate* hill and *Cannon* street. Nevertheless, there is a *First* avenue in *Queen's Park*, and parallel to it are *Second, Third, Fourth, Fifth* and *Sixth* avenues—all small streets leading northward from the Harrow road, just east of Kensal Green cemetery. I have observed that few Londoners have ever heard of them. There is also a *First* street in Chelsea—a very modest thoroughfare near Lennox gardens and not far from the Brompton Oratory.

Next to the numbering and lettering of streets, a fashion apparently set up by Major Pierre-Charles L'Enfant's plans for Washington, the most noticeable feature of American street nomenclature, as opposed to that of England, is the extensive use of such designations as *avenue, boulevard, drive* and *speedway.* *Avenue* is used in England, but only rather sparingly; it is seldom applied to a mean street, or to one in a warehouse district. In America the word is scarcely distinguished in meaning from *street.*[51] *Boulevard, drive* and *speedway* are almost

[51] There are, of course, local exceptions. In Baltimore, for example,

unknown to the English, but they use *road* for urban thorough-
fares, which is very seldom done in America, and they also make
free use of *place, walk, passage, lane* and *circus*, all of which are
obsolescent on this side of the ocean. Some of the older American cities, such as Boston and Baltimore, have surviving certain
ancient English designations of streets, *e. g., Cheapside* and *Cornhill;* these are unknown in the newer American towns. *Broadway,* which is also English, is more common. Many American
towns now have *plazas,* which are unknown in England. Nearly
all have *City Hall parks, squares* or *places; City Hall* is also
unknown over there. The principal street of a small town, in
America, is almost always *Main* street; in England it is as invariably *High* street, usually with the definite article before
High.

I have mentioned the corruption of old Dutch street and
neighborhood names in New York. Spanish names are corrupted
in the same way in the Southwest and French names in the Great
Lakes region and in Louisiana. In New Orleans the street names,
many of them strikingly beautiful, are pronounced so barba-
rously by the people that a Frenchman would have difficulty
recognizing them. Thus, *Bourbon* has become *Bur-bun, Dau-
phine* is *Daw-fin, Foucher* is *Foosh'r, Enghien* is *En-gine,* and
Felicity (originally *Félicité*) is *Fill-a-city.* The French, in their
days, bestowed the names of the Muses upon certain of the city
streets. They are now pronounced *Cal'-y-ope, Terp'-si-chore,
Mel-po-mean', You-terp',* and so on. *Bon Enfants,* apparently
too difficult for the native, has been translated into *Good Children.* Only *Esplanade* and *Bagatelle,* among the French street
names of the city, seem to be commonly pronounced with any
approach to correctness.

avenue used to be reserved for wide streets in the suburbs. Thus Charles
street, on passing the old city boundary, became Charles *street-avenue.*
Further out it became the Charles *street-avenue-road*—probably a unique
triplication. But that was years ago. Of late many fifth-rate streets
in Baltimore have been changed into avenues.

Miscellanea

§ 1

Proverb and Platitude—No people, save perhaps the Spaniards, have a richer store of proverbial wisdom than the Americans, and surely none other make more diligent and deliberate efforts to augment its riches. The American literature of "inspirational" platitude is enormous and almost unique. There are half a dozen authors, *e. g.*, Dr. Orison Swett Marden and Dr. Frank Crane, who devote themselves exclusively, and to vast profit, to the composition of arresting and uplifting apothegms, and the fruits of their fancy are not only sold in books but also displayed upon an infinite variety of calendars, banners and wall-cards. It is rarely that one enters the office of an American business man without encountering at least one of these wall-cards. It may, on the one hand, show nothing save a succinct caution that time is money, say, "Do It Now," or "This Is My Busy Day"; on the other hand, it may embody a long and complex sentiment, ornately set forth. The taste for such canned sagacity seems to have arisen in America at a very early day. Benjamin Franklin's "Poor Richard's Almanac," begun in 1732, remained a great success for twenty-five years, and the annual sales reached 10,000. It had many imitators, and founded an aphoristic style of writing which culminated in the essays of Emerson, often mere strings of sonorous certainties, defectively articulated. The "Proverbial Philosophy" of Martin Farquhar Tupper, dawning upon the American public in the early 40's, was welcomed with enthusiasm; as Saintsbury says,[1] its success

---

[1] Cambridge History of English Literature, vol. xiii, p. 167.

on this side of the Atlantic even exceeded its success on the other.
But that was the last and perhaps the only importation of the
sage and mellifluous in bulk. In late years the American production of such merchandise has grown so large that the balance
of trade now flows in the other direction. Visiting Denmark,
Germany, Switzerland, France and Spain in the spring of 1917,
I found translations of the chief works of Dr. Marden on sale in
all those countries, and with them the masterpieces of such other
apostles of the New Thought as Ralph Waldo Trine and Elizabeth Towne. No other American books were half so well displayed.

The note of all such literature, and of the maxims that precipi-
tate themselves from it, is optimism. They "inspire" by voicing
and revoicing the New Thought doctrine that all things are possible to the man who thinks the right sort of thoughts—in the
national phrase, to the *right-thinker*. This right-thinker is indistinguishable from the *forward-looker,* whose belief in the con-
tinuity and benignity of the evolutionary process takes on the
virulence of a religious faith. Out of his confidence come the
innumerable saws, axioms and *geflügelte Worte* in the national
arsenal, ranging from the "It won't hurt none to try" of the
great masses of the plain people to such exhilarating confections
of the wall-card virtuosi as "The elevator to success is not running; take the stairs." Naturally enough, a grotesque humor
plays about this literature of hope; the folk, though it moves
them, prefer it with a dash of salt. "Smile, damn you, smile!"
is a typical specimen of this seasoned optimism. Many examples of it go back to the early part of the last century, for instance, "Don't monkey with the buzz-saw" and "It will never
get well if you pick it." Others are patently modern, *e. g.,*
"The Lord is my shepherd; I should worry" and "Roll over;
you're on your back." The national talent for extravagant and
pungent humor is well displayed in many of these maxims. It
would be difficult to match, in any other folk-literature, such
examples as "I'd rather have them say 'There he goes' than
'Here he lies,'" or "Don't spit: remember the Johnstown
flood," or "Shoot it in the arm; your leg's full," or "Cheer up;

there ain't no hell," or "If you want to cure homesickness, go
back home." Many very popular phrases and proverbs are
borrowings from above. "Few die and none resign" originated
with Thomas Jefferson; Bret Harte, I believe, was the author
of "No check-ee, no shirt-ee," General W. T. Sherman is commonly credited with "War is hell," and Mark Twain with "Life
is one damn thing after another." An elaborate and highly
characteristic proverb of the uplifting variety—"So live that
you can look any man in the eye and tell him to go to hell"—
was first given currency by one of the engineers of the Panama
Canal, a gentleman later retired, it would seem, for attempting
to execute his own counsel. From humor the transition to
cynicism is easy, and so many of the current sayings are at
war with the optimism of the majority. "Kick him again; he's
down" is a depressing example. "What's the use?" a rough
translation of the Latin "Cui bono?" is another. The same
spirit is visible in "Tell your troubles to a policeman," "How'd
you like to be the ice-man?" "Some say she do and some say
she don't," "Nobody loves a fat man," "I love my wife, but
O you kid," and "Would you for fifty cents?" The last originated in the ingenious mind of an advertisement writer and
was immediately adopted. In the course of time it acquired a
naughty significance, and helped to give a start to the amazing
button craze of ten or twelve years ago—a saturnalia of proverb
and phrase making which finally aroused the guardians of the
public morals and was put down by the police.

That neglect which marks the study of the vulgate generally
extends to the subject of popular proverb-making. The English
publisher, Frank Palmer, prints an excellent series of little volumes presenting the favorite proverbs of all civilized races, including the Chinese and Japanese, but there is no American
volume among them. Even such exhaustive collections as that
of Robert Christy [2] contain no American specimens—not even
"Don't monkey with the buzz-saw" or "Root, hog, or die."

[2] Proverbs, Maxims and Phrases of All Ages; New York, 1905. This
work extends to 1267 pages and contains about 30,000 proverbs, admirably
arranged.

§ 2

American Slang—This neglect of the national proverbial philosophy extends to the national slang. There is but one work, so far as I can discover, formally devoted to it,[3] and that work is extremely superficial. Moreover, it has been long out of date, and hence is of little save historical value. There are at least a dozen careful treatises on French slang,[4] half as many on English slang,[5] and a good many on German slang, but American slang, which is probably quite as rich as that of France and a good deal richer than that of any other country, is yet to be studied at length. Nor is there much discussion of it, of any interest or value, in the general philological literature. Fowler and all the other early native students of the language dismissed it with lofty gestures; down to the time of Whitney it was scarcely regarded as a seemly subject for the notice of a man of learning. Lounsbury, less pedantic, viewed its phenomena more hospitably, and even defined it as "the source from which the decaying energies of speech are constantly refreshed," and Brander Matthews, following him, has described its function as that of providing "substitutes for the good words and true which are worn out by hard service."[6] But that is about as far as the investigation has got. Krapp has some judicious paragraphs upon the matter in his "Modern English,"[7] there are a few scattered essays upon the underlying psychology,[8] and various uninforming magazine articles, but that is all. The practising authors of the country, like its philologians, have always shown

[3] James Maitland: The American Slang Dictionary; Chicago, 1891.

[4] For example, the works of Villatte, Virmaitre, Michel, Rigaud and Devau.

[5] The best of these, of course, is Farmer and Henley's monumental Slang and Its Analogues, in seven volumes.

[6] Matthews' essay, The Function of Slang, is reprinted in Clapin's Dictionary of Americanisms, pp. 565–581.

[7] P. 199 *et seq.*

[8] For example, The Psychology of Unconventional Language, by Frank K. Sechrist, *Pedagogical Seminary*, vol. xx, p. 413, Dec., 1913, and The Philosophy of Slang, by E. B. Taylor, reprinted in Clapin's Dictionary of Americanisms, pp. 541–563.

a gingery and suspicious attitude. "The use of slang," said Oliver Wendell Holmes, "is at once a sign and a cause of mental atrophy." "Slang," said Ambrose Bierce fifty years later, "is the speech of him who robs the literary garbage carts on their way to the dumps." Literature in America, as we have seen, remains aloof from the vulgate. Despite the contrary examples of Mark Twain and Howells, all the more pretentious American authors try to write chastely and elegantly; the typical literary product of the country is still a refined essay in the *Atlantic Monthly,* perhaps gently jocose but never rough—by Emerson, so to speak, out of Charles Lamb—the sort of thing one might look to be done by a somewhat advanced English curate. George Ade, undoubtedly one of the most adept anatomists of the American character and painters of the American scene that the national literature has yet developed, is neglected because his work is grounded firmly upon the national speech—not that he reports it literally, like Lardner and the hacks trailing after Lardner, but that he gets at and exhibits its very essence. It would stagger a candidate for a doctorate in philology, I daresay, to be told off by his professor to investigate the slang of Ade in the way that Bosson,[9] the Swede, has investigated that of Jerome K. Jerome, and yet, until something of the sort is undertaken, American philology will remain out of contact with the American language.

Most of the existing discussions of slang spend themselves upon efforts to define it, and, in particular, upon efforts to differentiate it from idiomatic neologisms of a more legitimate type. This effort is largely in vain; the border-line is too vague and wavering to be accurately mapped; words and phrases are constantly crossing it, and in both directions. There was a time, perhaps, when the familiar American counter-word, *proposition,* was slang; its use seems to have originated in the world of business, and it was soon afterward adopted by the sporting fraternity. But today it is employed without much feeling that it needs apology, and surely without any feeling that it is low.

[9] Olaf E. Bosson: Slang and Cant in Jerome K. Jerome's Works; Cambridge, 1911.

Nice, as an adjective of all work, was once in slang use only; today no one would question "a *nice* day," or "a *nice* time" or "a *nice* hotel." *Awful* seems to be going the same route. "*Awful* sweet" and "*awfully* dear" still seem slangy and school-girlish, but "*awful* children," "*awful* weather" and "an *awful* job" have entirely sound support, and no one save a pedant would hesitate to use them. Such insidious purifications and consecrations of slang are going on under our noses all the time. The use of *some* as a general adjective-adverb seems likely to make its way in the same manner. It is constantly forgotten by purists of defective philological equipment that a great many of our most respectable words and phrases originated in the plainest sort of slang. Thus, *quandary,* despite a fanciful etymology which would identify it with *wandreth* (= *evil*), is probably simply a composition form of the French phrase, *qu'en dirai-je?* Again, to turn to French itself, there is *tête,* a sound name for the human head for many centuries—though its origin was in the Latin *testa* (= *pot*), a favorite slang-word of the soldiers of the decaying empire, analogous to our own *block, nut* and *conch.* The word *slacker,* recently come into good usage in the United States as a designation for an unsuccessful shirker of conscription, is a substantive derived from the English verb *to slack,* which was born as university slang and remains so to this day. Brander Matthews, so recently as 1901, thought *to hold up* slang; it is now perfectly good American.

The contrary movement of words from the legitimate vocabulary into slang is constantly witnessed. Some one devises a new and intriguing trope or makes use of an old one under circumstances arresting the public attention, and at once it is adopted into slang, given a host of remote significances, and ding-donged *ad nauseam.* The Rooseveltian phrases, *muck-raker, Ananias Club, short and ugly word, nature-faker* and *big-stick,* offer examples. Not one of them was new and not one of them was of much pungency, but Roosevelt's vast talent for delighting the yokelry threw about them a charming air, and so they entered into current slang and were mouthed idiotically for months. Another example is to be found in *steam-roller.*

It was first heard of in June, 1908, when it was applied by Oswald F. Schuette, of the *Chicago Inter-Ocean,* to the methods employed by the Roosevelt-Taft majority in the Republican National Committee in over-riding the protests against seating Taft delegates from Alabama and Arkansas. At once it struck the popular fancy and was soon heard on all sides. All the usual derivatives appeared, *to steam-roller, steam-rollered,* and so on. Since then, curiously enough, the term has gradually forced its way back from slang to good usage, and even gone over to England. In the early days of the Great War it actually appeared in the most solemn English reviews, and once or twice, I believe, in state papers.

Much of the discussion of slang by popular etymologists is devoted to proofs that this or that locution is not really slang at all—that it is to be found in Shakespeare, in Milton, or in the Revised Version. These scientists, of course, overlook the plain fact that slang, like the folk-song, is not the creation of people in the mass, but of definite individuals, and that its character *as* slang depends entirely upon its adoption by the ignorant, who use its novelties too assiduously and with too little imagination, and so debase them to the estate of worn-out coins, smooth and valueless. It is this error, often shared by philologists of sounder information, that lies under the doctrine that the plays of Shakespeare are full of slang, and that the Bard showed but a feeble taste in language. Nothing could be more absurd. The business of writing English, in his day, was unharassed by the proscriptions of purists, and so the vocabulary could be enriched more facilely than today, but though Shakespeare and his fellow-dramatists quickly adopted such neologisms as *to bustle, to huddle, bump, hubbub* and *pat,* it goes without saying that they exercised a sound discretion and that the slang of the Bankside was full of words and phrases which they were never tempted to use. In our own day the same discrimination is exercised by all writers of sound taste. On the one hand they disregard the senseless prohibitions of school-masters, and on the other hand they draw the line with more or less watchfulness, according as they are of conservative or liberal habit. I find *the best of the bunch* and *joke-smith* in Saintsbury;[10] one could scarcely imagine either in Walter Pater. But by the same token one could not imagine *chicken* (for young girl),[11] *aber nit, to come across* or *to camouflage* in Saintsbury.

What slang actually consists of doesn't depend, in truth, upon intrinsic qualities, but upon the surrounding circumstances. It is the user that determines the matter, and particularly the user's habitual way of thinking. If he chooses words carefully, with a full understanding of their meaning and savor, then no word that he uses seriously will belong to slang, but if his speech is made up chiefly of terms poll-parroted, and he has no sense of their shades and limitations, then slang will bulk largely in his vocabulary. In its origin it is nearly always respectable; it is devised not by the stupid populace, but by individuals of wit and ingenuity; as Whitney says, it is a product of an "exuberance of mental activity, and the natural delight of language-making." But when its inventions happen to strike the popular fancy and are adopted by the mob, they are soon worn threadbare and so lose all piquancy and significance, and, in Whitney's words, become "incapable of expressing anything that is real."[12] This is the history of such slang phrases, often interrogative, as "How'd you like to be the ice-man?" "How's your poor feet?" "Merci pour la langouste," "Have a heart," "This is the life," "Where did you get that hat?" "Would you for fifty cents?" "Let her go, Gallegher," "Shoo-fly, don't bother me," "Don't wake him up" and "Let George do it." The last well exhibits the process. It originated in France, as "Laissez faire à Georges," during the fifteenth century, and at the start had satirical reference to the multiform activities of Cardinal Georges d'Amboise, prime minister to Louis XII.[13] It later

---

[10] Cambridge History of English Literature, vol. xii, p. 144.

[11] Curiously enough, the American language, usually so fertile in words to express shades of meaning, has no respectable synonym for *chicken*. In English there is *flapper*, in French there is *ingénue*, and in German there is *backfisch*. Usually either the English or the French word is borrowed.

[12] The Life and Growth of Language, New York, 1897, p. 113.

[13] *Cf.* Two Children in Old Paris, by Gertrude Slaughter; New York, 1918, p. 233. Another American popular saying, once embodied in a coon

became common slang, was translated into English, had a revival during the early days of David Lloyd-George's meteoric career, was adopted into American without any comprehension of either its first or its latest significance, and enjoyed the brief popularity of a year.

Krapp attempts to distinguish between slang and sound idiom by setting up the doctrine that the former is "more expressive than the situation demands." "It is," he says, "a kind of hyperesthesia in the use of language. *To laugh in your sleeve* is idiom because it arises out of a natural situation; it is a metaphor derived from the picture of one raising his sleeve to his face to hide a smile, a metaphor which arose naturally enough in early periods when sleeves were long and flowing; but *to talk through your hat* is slang, not only because it is new, but also because it is a grotesque exaggeration of the truth." [14] The theory, unluckily, is combated by many plain facts. *To hand it to him, to get away with it* and even *to hand him a lemon* are certainly not metaphors that transcend the practicable and probable, and yet all are undoubtedly slang. On the other hand, there is palpable exaggeration in such phrases as "he is not worth the powder it would take to kill him," in such adjectives as *break-bone* (fever), and in such compounds as *fire-eater,* and yet it would be absurd to dismiss them as slang. Between *block-head* and *bone-head* there is little to choose, but the former is sound English, whereas the latter is American slang. So with many familiar similes, *e. g., like greased lightning, as scarce as hen's teeth;* they are grotesque hyperboles, but surely not slang.

The true distinction between slang and more seemly idiom, in so far as any distinction exists at all, is that indicated by Whitney. Slang originates in an effort, always by ingenious individuals, to make the language more vivid and expressive. When in the form of single words it may appear as new metaphors,

song, may be traced to a sentence in the prayer of the Old Dessauer before the battle of Kesseldorf, Dec. 15, 1745: "Or if Thou wilt not help me, don't help those Hundvögte."
[14] Modern English, p. 211.

e. g., *bird* and *peach;* as back formations, *e. g.*, *beaut* and *flu;* as composition-forms, *e. g.*, *whatdyecallem;* as picturesque compounds, *e. g.*, *booze-foundry;* as onomatopes, *e. g.*, *biff* and *zowie;* or in any other of the shapes that new terms take. If, by the chances that condition language-making, it acquires a special and limited meaning, not served by any existing locution, it enters into sound idiom and is presently wholly legitimatized; if, on the contrary, it is adopted by the populace as a counter-word and employed with such banal imitativeness that it soon loses any definite significance whatever, then it remains slang and is avoided by the finical. An example of the former process is afforded by *Tommy-rot.* It first appeared as English school-boy slang, but its obvious utility soon brought it into good usage. In one of Jerome K. Jerome's books, ''Paul Kelver,'' there is the following dialogue:

''The wonderful songs that nobody ever sings, the wonderful pictures that nobody ever paints, and all the rest of it. It's *Tommy-rot!*''

''I wish you wouldn't use slang.''

''Well, you know what I mean. What is the proper word? Give it to me.''

''I suppose you mean *cant.* No, I don't. *Cant* is something that you don't believe in yourself. It's *Tommy-rot;* there isn't any other word.''

Nor was there any other word for *hubbub* and *to dwindle* in Shakespeare's time; he adopted and dignified them because they met genuine needs. Nor was there any other satisfactory word for *graft* when it came in, nor for *rowdy,* nor for *boom,* nor for *joy-ride,* nor for *omnibus-bill,* nor for *slacker,* nor for *trust-buster.* Such words often retain a humorous quality; they are used satirically and hence appear but seldom in wholly serious discourse. But they have standing in the language nevertheless, and only a prig would hesitate to use them as Saintsbury used *the best of the bunch* and *joke-smith.*

On the other hand, many an apt and ingenious neologism, by falling too quickly into the gaping maw of the proletariat, is spoiled forthwith. Once it becomes, in Oliver Wendell Holmes' phrase, ''a cheap generic term, a substitute for differentiated specific expressions," it quickly acquires such flatness that the fastidious flee it as a plague. One recalls many capital verb-phrases, thus ruined by unintelligent appreciation, *e. g., to hand him a lemon, to freeze on to, to have the goods, to fall for it,* and *to get by.* One recalls, too, some excellent substantives, *e. g., dope* and *dub,* and compounds, *e. g., come-on* and *easy-mark,* and verbs, *e. g., to vamp.* These are all quite as sound in structure as the great majority of our most familiar words, but their adoption by the ignorant and their endless use and misuse in all sorts of situations have left them tattered and obnoxious, and they will probably go the way, as Matthews says, of all the other "temporary phrases which spring up, one scarcely knows how, and flourish unaccountably for a few months, and then disappear forever, leaving no sign." Matthews is wrong in two particulars here. They do not arise by any mysterious parthenogenesis, but come from sources which, in many cases, may be determined. And they last, alas, a good deal more than a month. *Shoo-fly* afflicted the American people for at least two years, and "I *don't* think" and *aber nit* quite as long. Even "good-*night*" lasted a whole year.

A very large part of our current slang is propagated by the newspapers, and much of it is invented by newspaper writers. One needs but turn to the slang of baseball to find numerous examples. Such phrases as *to clout the sphere, the initial sack, to slam the pill* and *the dexter meadow* are obviously not of bleachers manufacture. There is not enough imagination in that depressing army to devise such things; more often than not, there is not even enough intelligence to comprehend them. The true place of their origin is the perch of the newspaper reporters, whose competence and compensation is largely estimated, at least on papers of wide circulation, by their capacity for inventing novelties. The supply is so large that connoisseurship has grown up; an extra-fecund slang-maker on the press has his following. During the summer of 1913 the *Chicago Record-Herald,* somewhat alarmed by the extravagant fancy of its baseball reporters, asked its readers if they would prefer a return to plain English. Such of them as were literate enough to send in their votes were almost unanimously against a change. As one of them said, "one is nearer the park when Schulte *slams the pill* than when he merely *hits the ball*." In all other fields the newspapers originate and propagate slang, particularly in politics. Most of our political slang-terms since the Civil War, from *pork-barrel* to *steam-roller*, have been their inventions. The English newspapers, with the exception of a few anomalies such as the *Pink-Un*, lean in the other direction; their fault is not slanginess, but an otiose ponderosity—in Dean Alford's words, "the insisting on calling common things by uncommon names; changing our ordinary short Saxon nouns and verbs for long words derived from the Latin." [15] The American newspapers, years ago, passed through such a stage of bombast, but since the invention of yellow journalism by the elder James Gordon Bennett—that is, the invention of journalism for the frankly ignorant and vulgar—they have gone to the other extreme. Edmund Clarence Stedman noted the change soon after the Civil War. "The whole country," he wrote to Bayard Taylor in 1873, "owing to the contagion of our newspaper 'exchange' system, is flooded, deluged, swamped beneath a muddy tide of slang." [16] A thousand alarmed watchmen have sought to stay it since, but in vain. The great majority of our newspapers, including all those of large circulation, are chiefly written, as one observer says, "not in English, but in a strange jargon of words that would have made Addison or Milton shudder in despair." [17]

§ 3

The Future of the Language—The great Jakob Grimm, the founder of comparative philology, hazarded the guess more than three-quarters of a century ago that English would one day be-

---

[15] A Plea for the Queen's English, p. 244.

[16] Life and Letters of E. C. Stedman, ed. by Laura Stedman and George M. Gould; New York, 1910, vol. i, p. 477.

[17] Governor M. R. Patterson, of Tennessee, in an address before the National Anti-Saloon League at Washington, Dec. 13, 1917.

come the chief language of the world, and perhaps crowd out several of the then principal idioms altogether. "In wealth, wisdom and strict economy," he said, "none of the other living languages can vie with it." At that time the guess was bold, for English was still in fifth place, with not only French and German ahead of it, but also Spanish and Russian. In 1801, according to Michael George Mulhall, the relative standing of the five, in the number of persons using them, was as follows:

French	31,450,000
Russian	30,770,000
German	30,320,000
Spanish	26,190,000
English	20,520,000

The population of the United States was then but little more than 5,000,000, but in twenty years it had nearly doubled, and thereafter it increased steadily and enormously, and by 1860 it was greater than that of the United Kingdom. Since that time the majority of English-speaking persons in the world have lived on this side of the water; today there are nearly three times as many as in the United Kingdom and nearly twice as many as in the whole British Empire. This great increase in the American population, beginning with the great immigrations of the 30's and 40's, quickly lifted English to fourth place among the languages, and then to third, to second and to first. When it took the lead the attention of philologists was actively directed to the matter, and in 1868 one of them, a German named Brackebusch, first seriously raised the question whether English was destined to obliterate certain of the older tongues.[18] Brackebusch decided against on various philological grounds,

[18] Long before this the general question of the relative superiority of various languages had been debated in Germany. In 1796 the Berlin Academy offered a prize for the best essay on The Ideal of a Perfect Language. It was won by one Jenisch with a treatise bearing the sonorous title of A Philosophico-Critical Comparison and Estimate of Fourteen of the Ancient and Modern Languages of Europe, viz., Greek, Latin, Italian, Spanish, Portuguese, French, German, Dutch, English, Danish, Swedish, Polish, Russian and Lithuanian.

none of them sound. His own figures, as the following table from his dissertation shows,[19] were against him:

English	60,000,000
German	52,000,000
Russian	45,000,000
French	45,000,000
Spanish	40,000,000

This in 1868. Before another generation had passed the lead of English, still because of the great growth of the United States, was yet more impressive, as the following figures for 1890 show:

English	111,100,000
German	75,200,000
Russian	75,000,000
French	51,200,000
Spanish	42,800,000
Italian	33,400,000
Portuguese	13,000,000 [20]

Today the figures exceed even these. They show that English is now spoken by two and a half times as many persons as spoke it at the close of the American Civil War and by nearly eight times as many as spoke it at the beginning of the nineteenth century. No other language has spread in any such proportions. Even German, which is next on the list, shows but a four-fold gain since 1801, or just half that of English. The number of persons speaking Russian, despite the vast extension of the Russian empire during the last century of the czars, has little more than tripled, and the number speaking French has less than doubled. But here are the figures for 1911:

English	160,000,000
German	130,000,000
Russian	100,000,000
French	70,000,000
Spanish	50,000,000

[19] Is English Destined to Become the Universal Language?, by W. Brackebusch; Göttingen, 1868.

[20] I take these figures from A Modern English Grammar, by H. G. Buehler; New York, 1900, p. 3.

| Italian | 50,000,000 |
| Portuguese | 25,000,000 [21] |

Japanese, perhaps, should follow French: it is spoken by 60,000,000 persons. But Chinese may be disregarded, for it is split into half a dozen mutually unintelligible dialects, and shows no sign of spreading beyond the limits of China. The same may be said of Hindustani, which is the language of 100,-000,000 inhabitants of British India; it shows wide dialectical variations and the people who speak it are not likely to spread. But English is the possession of a race that is still pushing in all directions, and wherever that race settles the existing languages tend to succumb. Thus French, despite the passionate resistance of the French-Canadians, is gradually decaying in Canada; in all the newly-settled regions English is universal. And thus Spanish is dying out in our own Southwest, and promises to meet with severe competition in some of the nearer parts of Latin-America. The English control of the sea has likewise carried the language into far places. There is scarcely a merchant ship-captain on deep water, of whatever nationality, who does not find some acquaintance with it necessary, and it has become, in debased forms, the *lingua franca* of Oceanica and the Far East generally. "Three-fourths of the world's mail matter," says E. H. Babbitt, "is now addressed in English," and "more than half of the world's newspapers are printed in English." [22]

Brackebusch, in the speculative paper just mentioned, came to the conclusion that the future domination of English would be prevented by its unphonetic spelling, its grammatical decay and the general difficulties that a foreigner encounters in seeking to master it. "The simplification of its grammar," he said, "is the commencement of dissolution, the beginning of the end, and its extraordinary tendency to degenerate into slang of

[21] *World* Almanac, 1914, p. 63.

[22] The Geography of Great Languages, *World's Work*, Feb., 1908, p. 9907. Babbitt predicts that by the year 2000 English will be spokne by 1,100,-000,000 persons, as against 500,000,000 speakers of Russian, 300,000,000 of Spanish, 160,000,000 of German and 60,000,000 of French.

every kind is the foreshadowing of its approaching dismember-
ment." But in the same breath he was forced to admit that
"the greater development it has obtained" was the result of
this very simplification of grammar, and an inspection of the
rest of his reasoning quickly shows its unsoundness, even without an appeal to the plain facts. The spelling of a language,
whether it be phonetic or not, has little to do with its spread.
Very few men learn it by studying books; they learn it by hearing it spoken. As for grammatical decay, it is not a sign of
dissolution, but a sign of active life and constantly renewed
strength. To the professional philologist, perhaps, it may sometimes appear otherwise. He is apt to estimate languages by
looking at their complexity; the Greek aorist elicits his admi-
ration because it presents enormous difficulties and is inordinately subtle. But the object of language is not to bemuse grammarians, but to convey ideas, and the more simply it accomplishes that object the more effectively it meets the needs of
an energetic and practical people and the larger its inherent
vitality. The history of every language of Europe, since the
earliest days of which we have record, is a history of simplifications. Even such languages as German, which still cling to a
great many exasperating inflections, including the absurd inflection of the article for gender, are less highly inflected than
they used to be, and are proceeding slowly but surely toward
analysis. The fact that English has gone further along that
road than any other civilized tongue is not a proof of its de-
crepitude, but a proof of its continued strength. Brought into
free competition with another language, say German or French
or Spanish, it is almost certain to prevail, if only because it is
vastly easier—that is, as a spoken language—to learn. The foreigner essaying it, indeed, finds his chief difficulty, not in mas-
tering its forms, but in grasping its lack of forms. He doesn't
have to learn a new and complex grammar; what he has to
do is to forget grammar.

Once he has done so, the rest is a mere matter of acquiring
a vocabulary. He can make himself understood, given a few
nouns, pronouns, verbs and numerals, without troubling him-

self in the slightest about accidence. "Me see she" is bad English, perhaps, but it would be absurd to say that it is obscure—and on some not too distant tomorrow it may be very fair American. Essaying an inflected language, the beginner must go into the matter far more deeply before he may hope to be understood. Bradley, in "The Making of English,"[23] shows clearly how German and English differ in this respect, and how great is the advantage of English. In the latter the verb *sing* has but eight forms, and of these three are entirely obsolete, one is obsolescent, and two more may be dropped out without damage to comprehension. In German the corresponding verb, *singen*, has no less than sixteen forms. How far English has proceeded toward the complete obliteration of inflections is shown by such barbarous forms of it as Pigeon English and Beach-la-Mar, in which the final step is taken without appreciable loss of clarity. The Pigeon English verb is identical in all tenses. *Go* stands for both *went* and *gone; makee* is both *make* and *made.* In the same way there is no declension of the pronoun for case. *My* is thus *I, me, mine* and our own *my.* "No belong *my*" is "it is not *mine*"—a crude construction, of course, but still clearly intelligible. Chinamen learn Pigeon English in a few months, and savages in the South Seas master Beach-la-Mar almost as quickly. And a white man, once he has accustomed himself to either, finds it strangely fluent and expressive. He cannot argue politics in it, nor dispute upon transubstantiation, but for all the business of every day it is perfectly satisfactory.

As we have seen in Chapters V and VI, the American dialect of English has gone further along the road thus opened ahead than the mother dialect, and is moving faster. For this reason, and because of the fact that it is already spoken by a far larger and more rapidly multiplying body of people than the latter, it seems to me very likely that it will determine the final form of the language. For the old control of English over American to be reasserted is now quite unthinkable; if the two dialects are not to drift apart entirely English must follow in American's tracks. This yielding seems to have begun; the exchanges from

[23] P. 5 *et seq.*

American into English grow steadily larger and more important than the exchanges from English into American. John Richard Green, the historian, discerning the inevitable half a century ago, expressed the opinion, amazing and unpalatable then, that the Americans were already "the main branch of the English people." It is not yet wholly true; a cultural timorousness yet shows itself; there is still a class which looks to England as the Romans long looked to Greece. But it is not the class that is shaping the national language, and it is not the class that is carrying it beyond the national borders. The Americanisms that flood the English of Canada are not borrowed from the dialects of New England Loyalists and fashionable New Yorkers, but from the common speech that has its sources in the native and immigrant proletariat and that displays its gaudiest freightage in the newspapers.

The impact of this flood is naturally most apparent in Canada, whose geographical proximity and common interests completely obliterate the effects of English political and social dominance. By an Order in Council, passed in 1890, the use of the redundant *u* in such words as *honor* and *labor* is official in Canada, but practically all the Canadian newspapers omit it. In the same way the American flat *a* has swept whole sections of the country, and American slang is everywhere used, and the American common speech prevails almost universally in the newer provinces. More remarkable is the influence that American has exerted upon the speech of Australia and upon the crude dialects of Oceanica and the Far East. One finds such obvious Americanisms as *tomahawk, boss, bush, canoe, go finish* (= to die) and *pickaninny* in Beach-la-Mar [24] and more of them in Pigeon English. And one observes a very large number of American words and phrases in the slang of Australia. The Australian common speech, in pronunciation and intonation, resembles Cockney English, and a great many Cockneyisms are in it, but despite the small number of Americans in the Anti-

[24] *Cf.* Beach-la-Mar, by William Churchill, former United States consul-general in Samoa and Tonga. The pamphlet is published by the Carnegie Institution of Washington.

podes it has adopted, of late, so many Americanisms that a Cockney visitor must often find it difficult. Among them are the
verb and verb-phrases, *to beef, to biff, to bluff, to boss, to break
away, to chase one's self, to chew the rag, to chip in, to fade
away, to get it in the neck, to back and fill, to plug along, to get
sore, to turn down* and *to get wise;* the substantives, *dope, boss,
fake, creek, knockout-drops* and *push* (in the sense of *crowd*);
the adjectives, *hitched* (in the sense of *married*) and *tough* (as
before *luck*), and the adverbial phrases, *for keeps* and *going
strong.*[25] Here, in direct competition with English locutions,
and with all the advantages on the side of the latter, American
is making steady progress.

"This American language," says a recent observer, "seems
to be much more of a pusher than the English. For instance,
after eight years' occupancy of the Philippines it was spoken
by 800,000, or 10 per cent, of the natives, while after an occupancy of 150 of India by the British, 3,000,000, or one per cent,
of the natives speak English."[26] I do vouch for the figures.
They may be inaccurate, in detail, but they at least state what
seems to be a fact. Behind that fact are phenomena which certainly deserve careful study, and, above all, study divested of
unintelligent prejudice. The attempt to make American uniform with English has failed ingloriously; the neglect of its investigation is an evidence of snobbishness that is a folly of the
same sort. It is useless to dismiss the growing peculiarities of
the American vocabulary and of grammar and syntax in the
common speech as vulgarisms beneath serious notice. Such vulgarisms have a way of intrenching themselves, and gathering
dignity as they grow familiar. "There are but few forms in
use," says Lounsbury, "which, judged by a standard previ-
ously existing, would not be regarded as gross barbarisms."[27]
Each language, in such matters, is a law unto itself, and each
vigorous dialect, particularly if it be spoken by millions, is a

[25] A glossary of latter-day Australian slang is in Doreen and the Sentimental Bloke, by C. J. Dennis; New York, 1916.
[26] The American Language, by J. F. Healy; Pittsburgh, 1910, p. 6.
[27] History of the English Language, p. 476.

law no less. "It would be as wrong," says Sayce, "to use *thou* for the nominative *thee* in the Somersetshire dialect as it is to say *thee art* instead of *you are* in the Queen's English." All the American dialect needs, in the long run, to make even pedagogues acutely aware of it, is a poet of genius to venture into it, as Chaucer ventured into the despised English of his day, and Dante into the Tuscan dialect, and Luther, in his translation of the Bible, into peasant German. Walt Whitman made a half attempt and then drew back; Lowell, perhaps, also heard the call, but too soon. The Irish dialect of English, vastly less important than the American, has already had its interpreters— Douglas Hyde, John Milington Synge and Augusta Gregory— and with what extraordinary results we all know. Here we have writing that is still indubitably English, but English rid of its artificial restraints and broken to the less self-conscious grammar and syntax of a simple and untutored folk. Synge, in his preface to "The Playboy of the Western World," [28] tells us how he got his gypsy phrases "through a chink in the floor of the old Wicklow house where I was staying, that let me hear what was being said by the servant girls in the kitchen." There is no doubt, he goes on, that "in the happy ages of literature striking and beautiful phrases were as ready to the story-teller's or the playwright's hand as the rich cloaks and dresses of his time. It is probable that when the Elizabethan dramatist took his ink-horn and sat down to his work he used many phrases that he had just heard, as he sat at dinner, from his mother or his children."

The result, in the case of the neo-Celts, is a dialect that stands incomparably above the tight English of the grammarians—a dialect so naïf, so pliant, so expressive, and, adeptly managed, so beautiful that even purists have begun to succumb to it, and it promises to leave lasting marks upon English style. The American dialect has not yet come to that stage. In so far as it is apprehended at all it is only in the sense that Irish-English was apprehended a generation ago—that is, as something un-

[28] Dublin, 1907. See also ch. ii of Ireland's Literary Renaissance, by Ernest A. Boyd; New York, 1916.

couth and comic. But that is the way that new dialects always come in—through a drum-fire of cackles. Given the poet, there may suddenly come a day when our *theirns* and *would'a hads* will take on the barbaric stateliness of the peasant locutions of old Maurya in "Riders to the Sea." They seem grotesque and absurd today because the folks who use them seem grotesque and absurd. But that is a too facile logic and under it is a false assumption. In all human beings, if only understanding be brought to the business, dignity will be found, and that dignity cannot fail to reveal itself, soon or late, in the words and phrases with which they make known their high hopes and aspirations and cry out against the intolerable meaninglessness of life.

Bibliography

(With a few exceptions, this bibliography is restricted to books and articles consulted by the author in preparing the present work. It embraces all the literature that he has found useful.)

Abeille, Luciano: El idioma national de los argentinos; Paris, 1900.

Alford, Henry: A Plea for the Queen's English; London, 1863.

Allen, E. A.: The Origin in Literature of Vulgarisms, *Chautauquan*, Nov., 1890.

Allen, Grant: Americanisms (in Chambers' Encyclopaedia, new ed.; Phila., 1906, vol. i).

American Medical Association: Style-book; Chicago, 1915.

Anon.: *Art.* Americanisms, Everyman Encyclopaedia, ed. by Andrew Boyle; London, n. d.

—— *Art.* Americanisms, New International Encyclopaedia, 2nd ed., ed. by F. M. Colby and Talcott Williams; New York, 1917.

—— Americanisms, *London Academy*, March 2, 1889.

—— Americanisms, *Southern Literary Messenger*, Oct., 1848.

—— British Struggles With Our Speech, *Literary Digest*, June 19, 1915.

—— Don't Shy at *Journalist, Editor and Publisher*, June 27, 1914.

—— Good Form in England; New York, 1888.

—— I Speak United States, *London Saturday Review*, Sept. 22, 1894.

—— The King's English, *Paterson's Magazine*, Jan., 1817.

—— Our Strange New Language, *Literary Digest*, Sept. 16, 1916.

—— Polyglot Kuntze: schnellste Erlernung jeder Sprache ohne Lehrer: Amerikanisch; Bonn am Rhein, n. d.

—— Progress of Refinement, *New York Organ*, May 29, 1847.

—— Quick Lunch Lingo, *Literary Digest*, March 18, 1916.

—— They Spake With Diverse Tongues, *Atlantic Monthly*, July, 1909.

—— To Teach the American Tongue in Britain, *Literary Digest*, Aug. 9, 1913.

—— Word-Coining and Slang, *Living Age*, July 13, 1907.

Archer, William: America and the English Language, *Pall Mall Magazine*, Oct., 1898.

—— The American Language; New York, 1899.

Arona, Juan de: Diccionario de peruanismos; Lima, 1882.

Arthur, William: An Etymological Dictionary of Family and Christian Names; New York, 1857.

Ayres, Leonard P.: The Spelling Vocabularies of Personal and Business Letters (Circular E126, Division of Education, Russell Sage Foundation); New York, n. d.

Babbitt, Eugene H.: College Words and Phrases, *Dialect Notes*, vol. ii, pt. i, 1900.

—— The English of the Lower Classes in New York City and Vicinity, *Dialect Notes*, vol. i, pt. ix, 1896.

—— The Geography of the Great Languages, *World's Work*, Feb., 1908.

Bache, Richard Meade: Vulgarisms and Other Errors of Speech, 2nd ed.; Philadelphia, 1869.

Baker, Franklin T.: The Vernacular (in Munro's Principles of Secondary Education; New York, 1915, ch. ix).

Bardsley, Charles W.: Curiosities of Puritan Nomenclature; London, 1880.

Barentz, A. E.: Woordenboek der Engelsche spreektaal . . . and Americanisms . . .; Amsterdam, 1894.

Baring-Gould, S.: Family Names and Their Story; London, 1910.

Barker, Henry: British Family Names; London, 1894.

Barr, Robert: *Shall* and *Will*, *Bookman*, Dec., 1895.

Barrère, Albert (and Chas. G. Leland): A Dictionary of Slang, Jargon and Cant, 2 vols.; New York, 1889.

Barringer, G. A.: Étude sur l'Anglais parlé aux États Unis (la Langue Américaine), *Actes de la Société Philologique de Paris*, March, 1874.

Barthelmess, Harriet: Determining the Achievement of Pupils in Letter Writing, Bull. xvi, Dept. of Educational Investigation and Measurement, Boston Public Schools (School Document No. 6), 1918.

Bartlett, John Russell: A Glossary of Words and Phrases Usually Regarded as Peculiar to the United States; New York, 1848; 2nd ed. enlarged, Boston, 1859; 3rd ed., 1860; 4th ed., 1877.

Baumann, H.: Londinismen (Slang und Cant); 2nd ed.; Berlin, 1902.

Bean, C. Homer: How English Grammar Has Been Taught in America, *Education*, vol. xiv, no. 8, April, 1914.

Beauchamp, Wm. M.: Aboriginal Places Names of New York; Albany, 1907.

—— Indian Names in New York; Fayetteville (N. Y.), 1893.

Beck, T. Romeyn: Notes on Mr. Pickering's Vocabulary. . . . *Transactions of the Albany Institute*, vol. i, 1830.

Beidelman, William: The Story of the Pennsylvania Germans . . . and Their Dialect; Easton (Pa.), 1898.

Bendelari, George: Curiosities of American Speech, *New York Sun*, Nov., 1895.

Benet, W. C.: Americanisms: English as Spoken and Written in the United States; Abbeville (S. C.), 1880.

Benton, Joel: The Webster Spelling-Book . . . , *Magazine of American History*, Oct., 1883.

Bergström, G. A.: On Blendings of Synonyms or Cognate Expressions in English; Lund (Sweden), 1906.

Bibaud, Maximilien: Le Mémorial des Vicissitudes et des Progrès de la Langue Française en Canada; Montreal, 1879.

Blackmar, F. W.: Spanish-American Words, *Modern Language Notes*, vol. vi.

Blattner, Karl: Metoula-Sprachführer: Englisch; Ausgabe für Amerika; Berlin-Schöneberg, 1912.

Blue, Rupert, ed.: Nomenclature of Diseases and Conditions, U. S. Public Health Service, Misc. Pub. No. 16; Washington, 1916.

Bonnell, J. W.: Etymological Derivation of the Names of the States, *Journal of Education*, vol. xlvii, p. 378.

Bosson, Olaf E.: Slang and Cant in Jerome K. Jerome's Works; Cambridge, 1911.

Bowen, Edwin W.: Questions at Issue in Our English Speech; New York, 1914.

Boyd, Stephen G.: Indian Local Names; York (Pa.), 1885.

Brackebusch, W.: Is English Destined to Become the Universal Language of the World?; Göttingen, 1868.

Bradley, Henry: The Making of English; London, 1904.

Bradley, W. A.: In Shakespeare's America, *Harper's Magazine*, Aug., 1915.

Brandenburg, George C.: Psychological Aspects of Language, *Journal of Educational Psychology*, June, 1918.

Bridges, Robert: A Tract on the Present State of English Pronunciation; Oxford, 1913.

Bristed, Charles A.: The English Language in America (in Cambridge Essays; London, 1855).

Buck, Gertrude: Make-Believe Grammar, *School Review*, vol. xxii, Jan., 1909.

Buehler, H. G.: A Modern English Grammar; New York, 1900.

Buies, Arthur: Anglicismes et Canadianismes; Quebec, 1888.

Burch, G. J.: The Pronunciation of English by Foreigners; Oxford, 1911.

Burke, William: The Anglo-Irish Dialect, *Irish Ecclesiastical Record*, 1896.

Burton, Richard: American English, (in Literary Likings: Boston, 1899).

Buttmann, Philipp Karl: Lexilogus; London, 1846.

Carpenter, George R.: The Principles of English Grammar For the Use of Schools; New York, 1898.

Carpenter, W. H.: Dutch Contributions to the Vocabulary of English in America, *Modern Philology*, July, 1908.

Carter, Alice P.: American English, *Critic*, vol. xiii.

Century Magazine: Style-sheet; New York, 1915.

Channing, William Ellery: Essay on American Language and Literature, *North American Review*, Sept. 1815.

Chapin, Florence A.: Spanish Words That Have Become Westernisms, *Editor*, July 25, 1917.

Charters, W. W. (and Edith Miller): A Course of Study in Grammar Based Upon the Grammatical Errors of School Children of Kansas City, Mo., *University of Missouri Bulletin*, vol. xvi, no. 2, Jan., 1915.

Chesterton, Cecil: British Struggles With Our Speech (summary of art. in *New Witness*), *Literary Digest*, June 19, 1915.

Chicago Daily News: Style-book . . . ; Chicago, 1908.

Chicago, University of: Manual of Style . . . 3rd ed.; Chicago, 1911.

Chubb, Percival: The Menace of Pedantry in the Teaching of English, *School Review*, vol. xx, Jan., 1912.

Churchill, William: Beach-la-mar: the Jargon or Trade Speech of the Western Pacific; Washington, 1911.

Clapin, Sylva: A New Dictionary of Americanisms . . . ; New York, (1902).

Clemens, Samuel L. (Mark Twain): Concerning the American Language (in The Stolen White Elephant: New York, 1888).

Cobb, Lyman: A Critical Review of the Orthography of Dr. Webster's Series of Books . . . ; New York, 1831.

—— New Spelling Book . . . ; New York, 1842.

Collins, F. Howard: Authors' & Printers' Dictionary, 4th ed., rev. by Horace Hart; London, 1912.

Combs, J. H.: Old, Early and Elizabethan English in the Southern Mountains, *Dialect Notes*, vol. iv, pt. iv, 1916.

Compton, A. G.: Some Common Errors of Speech; New York, 1898.

Coxe, A. Cleveland: Americanisms in England, *Forum*, Oct., 1886.

Crane, W. W.: The American Language, *Putnam's Monthly*, vol. xvi, p. 519.

—— Our Naturalized Names, *Lippincott's Magazine*, vol. lxiii, p. 575, April, 1899.

Crosland, T. W. H.: The Abounding American; London, 1907.

Cushing, J. S. Company: Preparation of Manuscript, Proof Reading, and Office Style at J. S. Cushing Company's; Norwood (Mass.), n. d.

Dana, Richard H., jun: A Dictionary of Sea Terms; London, 1841.

Dawson, A. H.: A Dictionary of English Slang and Colloquialisms; New York, 1913.

Dennis, C. J. Doreen and the Sentimental Bloke; New York, 1916.

Dialect Notes, vol. i, 1889–98; vol. ii, 1899–1904; vol. iii, 1905–12; vol. iv, 1913–16; vol. v, 1917–.

Douglas-Lithgow, R. A.: Dictionary of American Indian Place and Proper Names in New England; Salem (Mass.), 1909.

Dubbs, Joseph H.: A Study of Surnames; Lancaster (Pa.), 1886.

Dunlap, Fayette: A Tragedy of Surnames, *Dialect Notes,* vol. iv, pt. i, 1913.

Dunlap, Maurice P.: What Americans Talk in the Philippines, *American Review of Reviews,* Aug., 1913.

Dunn, Oscar: Glossaire Franco-Canadien; Quebec, 1880.

Dunstan, A. C.: Englische Phonetik; Berlin, 1912.

Earle, John: The Philology of the English Tongue; London, 1866; 5th ed., 1892.

—— A Simple Grammar of English Now in Use; London, 1898.

Eggleston, Edward: Wild Flowers of English Speech in America, *Century Magazine,* April, 1894.

Egli, Johann J.: Nomina Geographica, 2nd ed.; Zurich, 1893.

—— Der Völkergeist in den geographischen Namen; Zurich, 1894.

Elliott, A. M.: Speech-Mixture in French Canada: English and French, *American Journal of Philology,* vol. x, 1889, p. 133.

Elliott, John (and Samuel Johnson, Jr.): A Selected Pronouncing and Accented Dictionary . . . ; Suffield (Conn.), 1800.

Ellis, Alexander J.: On Early English Pronunciation, 4 vols.; London, 1869–89.

—— On Glosik, a Neu Sistem ov Inglish Spelling; London, 1870.

Elwyn, A. L.: A Glossary of Supposed Americanisms . . . ; Phila., 1859.

Emerson, Oliver Farrar: The Future of American Speech, *Dial,* vol. xiv.

—— A History of the English Language; New York, 1894.

English, Thomas Dunn: Irish in America, *New York Times,* Nov. 5, 1898.

Fallows, Samuel; Handbook of Briticisms, Americanisms, Colloquial and Provincial Words and Phrases; Chicago, 1883.

Farmer, John S.: Americanisms Old and New . . . ; London, 1889.

—— (and W. E. Henley): A Dictionary of Slang and Colloquial English; London, 1905.

—— (and W. E. Henley): Slang and its Analogues, 7 vols.; London, 1890–1904.

Ferguson, Robert: Surnames as a Science; London, 1883.

Fernald, F. A.: Ingglish az She iz Spelt; New York, 1885.

Ferraz, Juan Fernándes: Nahuatlismos de Costa Rica; San José de Costa Rica, 1892.

Field, Eugene: London letter in *Chicago News*, March 10, 1890.

Flaten, Nils: Notes on American-Norwegian, with a Vocabulary, *Dialect Notes*, vol. ii, pt. ii, 1900.

Flom, George T.: English Elements in Norse Dialects of Utica, Wisconsin, *Dialect Notes*, vol. ii, pt. iv, 1902.

Flügel, Felix: Die englische Philologie in Nordamerika, *Gersdorf's Repertorium*, 1852.

—— Die englische Sprache in Nordamerika, *Archiv für das Studium der neueren Sprachen und Literaturen*, band iv, heft i; Braunschweig, 1848.

Fowler, H. W. (and F. G. Fowler): The Concise Oxford Dictionary of Current English, 4th ed.; Oxford, 1914.

—— The King's English, 2nd ed.; Oxford, 1908.

Fowler, Wm. C.: The English Language . . . , 2nd ed.; New York, 1855.

Franklin, Benjamin: Scheme for a New Alphabet and a Reformed Mode of Spelling; Phila., 1768.

Franzmeyer, F.: Studien über den Konsonantismus und Vokalismus der neuenglischen Dialekte; Strassburg, 1906.

Freeman, Edward A.: Some Points in American Speech and Customs, *Longman's Magazine*, Nov., 1882.

Funk & Wagnalls Company: Style-card; New York, 1914.

Geikie, A. S.: Canadian English, *Canadian Journal*, vol. ii, 1857, p. 344.

Gentry, Thomas G.: Family Names from the Irish, Anglo-Saxon, Anglo-Norman and Scotch; Phila., 1892.

Gerek, William (and others): Is There Really Such a Thing as the American Language?, *New York Sun*, March 10, 1918.

Giles, Richard: Slang and Vulgar Phrases; New York, 1913.

Gould, Edwin S.: Good English . . . ; New York, 1867.

Grade, P.: Das neger Englisch, *Anglia*, vol. xiv.

Graham, G. F.: A Book About Words; London, 1869.

Grandgent, C. H.: English in America, *Die Neueren Sprachen*, vol. ii, pp. 443 and 520.

—— Fashion and the Broad *A*, *Nation*, Jan. 7, 1915.

—— From Franklin to Lowell: a Century of New England Prounciation, *Publications of the Modern Language Association*, vol. ii.

—— Notes on American Pronouns, *Modern Language Notes*, vol. vi, p. 82; *ibid.*, p. 458.

de la Grasserie, Raoul: Étude scientifique sur l'argot et le parler populaire; Paris, 1907.

Green, B. W.: Word-book of Virginia Folk-speech; Richmond, 1899.
Greenough, James B. (and George L. Kittredge): Words and Their Ways in English Speech; New York, 1902.
Haldeman, S. S.: Pennsylvania Dutch . . . ; London, 1872.
Hale, Horatio: The Origin of Languages, *Proc. American Association for the Advancement of Science*, 1886.
Hale, W. G. (and others): Report of the Joint Committee on Grammatical Nomenclature Appointed by the National Education Association, the Modern Language Association of America, and the American Philological Association; Chicago, 1918.
[Hall, B. H.]: A Collection of College Words and Customs; Cambridge (Mass.),.1851; 2nd ed., 1856.
Hall, Fitzedward: English, Rational and Irrational, *Nineteenth Century*, Sept., 1880.
—— Modern English; New York, 1873.
—— Recent Exemplifications of False Philology; New York, 1872.
Halliwell (-Phillips), J. O.: A Dictionary of Archaic and Provincial Words, Obsolete Phrases, Proverbs and Ancient Customs . . . , 2 vols.; London, 1847.
—— A Dictionary of Archaisms and Provincialisms, Containing Words Now Obsolete in England, All of Which are Familiar and in Common Use in America; 2nd ed., London, 1850.
Hancock, Elizabeth H.: Southern Speech, *Neale's Monthly*, Nov., 1913.
Hancock, T.: Newspaper English, *Academy*, Jan. 29, 1898.
Harrison, Henry: A Dictionary of the Surnames of the United Kingdom; London, 1912.
Harrison, James A.: Negro English, *Proc. American Philological Association*, 1885.
Hart, Horace: Rules for Compositors and Readers at the University Press, Oxford; 23rd ed.; London, 1914.
Hartt, Irene Widdemar: Americanisms, *Education*, vol. xiii.
Hastings, Basil MacDonald: More Americanisms (interview), *New York Tribune*, Jan. 19, 1913.
Hayden, Mary (and Marcus Hartog): The Irish Dialect of English: Its Origins and Vocabulary; *Fortnightly Review*, April and May, 1909.
Hays, H. M.: On the German Dialect Spoken in the Valley of Virginia, *Dialect Notes*, vol. iii, pt. iv, 1908.
Head, Edmund Walker: *Shall* and *Will*, or Two Chapters on Future Auxiliary Verbs; London, 1856.
Healy, J. F.: The American Language; Pittsburgh, 1910.
Helfenstein, James: A Comparative Grammar of the Teutonic Languages . . . ; London, 1870.

Hempl, George: Language Rivalry and Speech-Differentiation in the Case of Race-Mixture, *Tr. American Philological Assoc.*, vol. xxix, p. 31.

—— The Study of American English, *Chautauquan*, vol. xxii, p. 436.

Herrig, Ludwig: Die englische Sprache und Literatur in Nord-Amerika, *Der neueren Sprachen*, vol. xii, p. 24; vol. xiii, pp. 76 and 241; vol. xiv, p. 1.

Higginson, T. W.: American Flash Language in 1798, *Science*, May, 1885.

—— English and American Speech, *Harper's Bazar*, vol. xxx, p. 958.

Hill, Adams Sherman: Our English; New York, 1889.

Hodgins, Joseph L.: Our Common Speech, *New York Sun*, March 1, 1918.

Hoffman, C. F.: Philological Researches, *Literary World*, Aug. 21, 1847.

Holliday, Robert Cortes: Cann't Speak the Language (in Walking-Stick Papers; New York, 1918, p. 201).

Horn, W.: Historische neuenglische Grammatik; Strassburg, 1908.

—— Untersuchungen zur neuenglischen Lautgeschichte; Strassburg, 1905.

Hotten, John Camden: A Dictionary of Modern Slang, Cant and Vulgar Words . . . London, 1859.

Howells, William Dean: The Editor's Study, *Harper's Magazine*, Jan., 1886.

Hurd, Seth T.: A Grammatical Corrector or Vocabulary of the Common Errors of Speech . . . ; Phila., 1847.

Inman, Thomas: On the Origin of Certain Christian and Other Names; Liverpool, 1866.

J. D. J.: American Conversation, *English Journal*, April, 1913.

James, Henry: The Question of Our Speech; Boston and New York, 1905.

Jespersen, Jens O. H.: The Growth and Structure of the English Language; Leipzig, 1905; 2nd ed., 1912.

—— A Modern Grammar on Historical Principles; 2 vols.; Heidelberg, 1909–14.

Johnson, Burges: The Everyday Profanity of Our Best People, *Century Magazine*, June, 1916.

Johnson, Samuel, Jr.: A School Dictionary . . . ; New Haven, (1798?).

Jones, Daniel: The Pronunciation of English; Cambridge, 1909.

Joyce, P. W.: English as We Speak It in Ireland, 2nd ed.; London, 1910.

Kaluza, Max: Historische Grammatik der englischen Sprache, 2 vols.; Berlin, 1900–1.

Keijzer, M.: Woordenboek van Americanismen . . . ; Gorinchem (Holland), 1854.

Kellner, Leon: Historical Outlines of English Syntax; London, 1892.

Kelton, Dwight H.: Indian Names of Places Near the Great Lakes; Detroit, 1888.

Ker, Edmund T.: River and Lake Names in the United States; New York, 1911.

Kleuz, H.: Schelten-Wörterbuch; Strassburg, 1910.

Knortz, Karl: Amerikanische Redensarten und Volksgebräuche, Leipzig, 1907.

Knox, Alexander: Glossary of Geographical and Topographical Terms; London, 1904.

Koehler, F.: Worterbuch der Amerikanismen . . . ; Leipzig, 1866.

Koeppel, Emil: Spelling-Prounciation: Bemerkungen über den Einfluss des Schriftbildes auf den Laut in Englischen, *Quellen und Forschungen zur Sprach- und Culturgeschichte der Germanischen Völkes,* lxxxix; Strassburg, 1901.

Krapp, George Philip: Modern English; New York, 1910.

Krueger, G.: Was ist Slang, bezüglich Argot? (in Festschrift Adolf Taber; Braunschweig, 1905).

Kuhns, L. Oscar: The Origin of Pennsylvania Surnames, *Lippincott's Magazine,* vol. lix, p. 395, March, 1897.

Lacasse, R. P. Z.: Ces Jeunes-là, on ne les Comprend Plus (in Une Mine Produisant l'Or et l'Argent; Quebec, 1880, pp. 252–6).

Lang, Andrew: Americanisms, *London Academy,* March 2, 1895.

Lardner, Ring W.: You Know Me Al . . . New York, 1916.

Latham, Edward: A Dictionary of Names, Nicknames and Surnames; London, 1904.

Latham, Robert G.: The English Language; London, 1841.

Learned, Marion D.: The Pennsylvania German Dialect, Part I; Baltimore, 1889.

Letzner, Karl: Worterbuch der englischen Volksprache Australiens und der englischen Mischsprachen; Halle, 1891.

Lewis, Calvin L.: A Handbook of American Speech; Chicago, 1916.

Lienemann, Oskar: Eigentümlichkeiten des Engl. d. Vereinigten Staaten nebst wenig bekannten Amerikanismen; Zittau, 1886.

Lighthall, W. D.: Canadian English, *Week* (Toronto), Aug. 16, 1889.

Littman, Enno: *23* and Other Numerical Expressions, *Open Court,* vol. xxii, 1908.

Lloyd, R. J.: Northern English; Leipzig, 1908.

Lodge, Henry Cabot: The Origin of Certain Americanisms, *Scribner's Magazine,* June, 1907.

—— Shakespeare's Americanisms (in Certain Accepted Heroes; New York, 1897).

Long, Charles M.: Virginia County Names; New York, 1908.
Long, Percy W.: Semi-Secret Abbreviations, *Dialect Notes*, vol. iv, pt. iii, 1915.
Lounsbury, Thomas R.: Americanisms Real or Reputed, *Harper's Magazine*, Sept. 1913.
—— Differences in English and American Usage, *Harper's Magazine*, July 1913.
—— The English Language in America, *International Review*, vol. viii, p. 472.
—— English Spelling and Spelling Reform; New York, 1909.
—— A History of the English Language, revised ed.; New York, 1907.
—— Linguistic Causes of Americanisms, *Harper's Magazine*, June, 1913.
—— Scotticisms and Americanisms, *Harper's Magazine*, Feb., 1913.
—— The Standard of Pronunciation in English; New York and London, 1904.
—— The Standard of Usage in English; New York and London, n. d.
—— What Americanisms Are Not, *Harper's Magazine*, March, 1913.
Low, Sidney: Ought American to be Taught in Our Schools?, *Westminster Gazette*, July 18, 1913.
Low, W. H.: The English Language; Baltimore, 1917.
Lowell, James Russell: prefaces to The Biglow Papers, 1st and 2nd series; Cambridge, 1848–66.
Lower, M. A.: Patronymica Brittanica; London, 1860.
Luick, K.: Studien zur englischen Lautgeschichte; Vienna, 1903.
Mackay, Charles: The Ascertainment of English, *Nineteenth Century*, Jan., 1890.
McKenna, L. B.: Surnames, Their Origin and Nationality; Quincy (Ill.), 1913.
Mackintosh, Duncan: Essai Raissoné sur la Grammaire et la Prononciation Anglais . . . ; Boston, 1797.
McLean, John: Western Americanisms (in The Indians: Their Manners and Customs; Toronto, 1889, pp. 197–201).
Macmillan Co.: Notes for the Guidance of Authors; New York, 1918.
Maitland, James: The American Slang Dictionary . . . ; Chicago, 1891.
March, Francis A.: Spelling Reform; Washington, 1893.
Marsh, George P.: Lectures on the English Language; New York, 1859; 4th ed., enlarged, 1870.
—— The Origin and History of the English Language; New York, 1862; rev. ed., 1885.
Maspero, J.: Singularidades del español de Buenos Ayres, *Memorias de la Sociedad de lingüistica de Paris*, tome ii.

Matthews, Brander: Americanisms and Britticisms . . . ; New York, 1892.
—— Is the English Language Decadent? *Yale Review*, April, 1918.
—— Outskirts of the English Language, *Munsey's Magazine*, Nov., 1913.
—— Parts of Speech; New York, 1901.
—— The Standard of Spoken English, *North American Review*, June, 1916.
—— Why Not Speak Your Own Language?, *Delineator*, Nov., 1917.
Mätzner, Eduard A. F.: Englische Grammatik, 2 vols.; Leipzig, 1860–65, 3rd ed., 1880–85; tr. by C. J. Grece, 3 vols., London, 1874.
Mead, Theo. H.: Our Mother Tongue; New York, 1890.
Mearns, Hugh: Our Own, Our Native Speech, *McClure's Magazine*, Oct., 1916; reprinted, *Literary Digest*, Sept. 30, 1916.
Melville, A. H.: An Investigation of the Function and Use of Slang, *Pedagogical Seminary*, vol. xix, 1912.
Membreño, Alberto: Hondureñismos; Tegucigalpa, 1895.
Mencken, H. L.: The American: His Language, *Smart Set*, Aug., 1913.
—— The American Language Again, *New York Evening Mail*, Nov. 22, 1917.
—— American Pronouns, *Baltimore Evening Sun*, Oct. 25, 1910.
—— The Curse of Spelling, *New York Evening Mail*, April 11, 1918.
—— England's English, *Baltimore Evening Sun*, Sept. 22, 1910.
—— How They Say It "Over There," *New York Evening Mail*, Oct. 25, 1917.
—— More American, *Baltimore Evening Sun*, Oct. 20, 1910.
—— Moulding Our Speech, *Chicago Tribune*, Nov. 18, 1917.
—— The New Domesday Book, *New York Evening Mail*, April, 1918.
—— Nothing Dead About Language . . . , *New York Evening Mail*, Sept. 28, 1917.
—— Notes on the American Language, *Baltimore Evening Sun*, Sept. 7, 1916.
—— Spoken American, *Baltimore Evening Sun*, Oct. 19, 1910.
—— The Two Englishes, *Baltimore Evening Sun*, Sept. 15, 1910.
Menner, Robert J.: Common Sense in Pronunciation, *Atlantic Monthly*, Aug., 1913.
—— The Pronunciation of English in America, *Atlantic Monthly*, March, 1915.
Molee, Elias: nu tutonish, an international union language; tacoma, 1906.[1]
—— Plea for an American Language . . . ; Chicago, 1888.

[1] No capitals are used in the book. Even the title page is in lower case

Molee, Elias: Pure Saxon English; or, Americans to the Front; Chicago, 1890.

—— Tutonish; Tacoma, (Wash.), n. d.

—— Tutonish, or, Anglo-German Union Tongue; Chicago, 1902.

Montgomery, M.: Types of Standard Spoken English; Strassburg, 1910.

Moon, G. Washington: The Dean's English, 7th ed.; New York, 1884.

Morris, Edward E.: Austral English . . . ; London, 1898.

Morris, Richard: Historical Outlines of English Accidence; London, 1872; 2nd ed. rev., 1895.

Murison, W.: Changes in the Language Since Shakespeare's Time, (in The Cambridge History of English Literature, vol. xiv.; New York, 1917).

Murray, James A. H.: A New English Dictionary . . . ; Oxford, 1888, etc.

Newcomen, George: Americanisms and Archaisms, *Academy*, vol. xlvii, p. 317.

Norton, Chas. Ledyard: Political Americanisms . . . ; New York and London, 1890.

Oliphant, Samuel Grant: The Clan of Fire and Forge, or, The Ancient and Honorable Smiths; Olivet (Mich.), 1910.

—— Surnames in Baltimore, *Baltimore Sunday Sun*, 62 weekly articles, Dec. 2, 1906–Jan. 26, 1908 inc.; index, Feb. 2, 9, 16, 23, 1908.

Oliphant, W. Kingston: The New English; London, 1886.

Onions, C. T.: Advanced English Syntax; London, 1894.

Palmer, A. Smythe: The Folk and Their Word-Lore; London, 1904.

Paul, C. K.: The American Language, *Month*, vol. xciv.

Paul, Hermann O. T.: Grundriss der germanischen Philologie, rev. ed., 3 vols.; Strassburg, 1901–1909.

—— Prinzipien der Sprachgeschichte; Halle, 1886; 4th ed., 1909; tr. as Principles of the History of Language by H. A. Strong; London, 1888; rev. ed., 1891.

Payne, James E. (and others): Style Book: a Compilation of Rules Governing Executive, Congressional, and Departmental Printing, Including the *Congressional Record;* Washington, 1917.

Pearson, T. R.: The Origin of Surnames, *Good Words*, June, 1897.

Pettman, Charles: Africanderisms: a Glossary of South African Colloquial Words and Phrases; London, 1913.

Phipson, Evascutes A.: British vs. American English, *Dialect Notes*, vol. i, pt. i, 1889.

Pickering, John: A Vocabulary or Collection of Words and Phrases Which Have Been Supposed to be Peculiar to the United States of America . . . ; Boston, 1816.

Pound, Louise: British and American Pronunciation, *School Review*, June, 1915.

—— Domestication of the Suffix *-fest*, *Dialect Notes*, vol. iv, pt. v, 1916.

—— Vogue Affixes in Present-Day Word-Coinage, *Dialect Notes*, vol. v, pt. i, 1918.

—— Word-Coinage and Modern Trade Names, *Dialect Notes*, vol. iv, pt. i, 1913.

Poutsma, H.: A Grammar of Late Modern English, 2 vols.; Groningen, 1904–5.

Prince, J. Dyneley: The Jersey Dutch Dialect, *Dialect Notes*, vol. iii, pt. vi, 1910.

Proctor, Richard A.: Americanisms, *Knowledge*, vol. viii.

—— English and American-English, *New York Tribune*, Aug. 14, 1881.

—— "English as She is Spoke" in America, *Knowledge*, vol. vi.

Ralph, Julian: The Language of the Tenement-Folk, *Harper's Weekly*, vol. xli, p. 30.

Rambeau, A.: Amerikanisches, *Der neueren Sprachen*, vol. ii, p. 53.

Ramos y Duarte, Félis: Diccionario de mejicanismos . . . , 2nd ed.; Mexico, 1898.

Read, Richard P.: The American Language, *New York Sun*, March 7, 1918.

—— The American Tongue, *New York Sun*, Feb. 26, 1918.

Read, William A.: The Southern *R*, *Louisiana State University Bull.*, Feb. 1910.

—— Variant Pronunciations in the New South, *Dialect Notes*, vol. iii, pt. vii, 1911.

Rippmann, W.: The Sounds of Spoken English; London, 1906.

Riverside Press: Handbook of Style in Use at the Riverside Press, Cambridge, Mass.; Boston and New York, 1913.

Root, E.: American and British Enunciation, *Lippincott's*, Sept., 1911.

Rupp, Israel D.: A Collection of . . . Names of German, Swiss, Dutch, French and Other Immigrants in Pennsylvania from 1727 to 1776, 2nd rev. ed.; Phila., 1876.

Russell, T. Baron: Current Americanisms; London, 1893.

Salverte, Eusèbe: History of the Names of Men, Nations and Places, tr. by L. H. Mordacque, 2 vols.; London, 1862–4.

Sanchez, Jesus: Glosario de Voces Castellanas derivadas Nahüatl ó Mexicano; n. p., n. d.

Sanchez, Nellie van de Grift: Spanish and Indian Place Names of California; San Francisco, 1914.

Sanz, S. Monner: Notas al Castellano en America; Buenos Ayres, 1903.

Sayce, A. H.: Introduction to the Science of Language, 2 vols.; 4th ed., London, 1900.

Schele de Vere, M.: Americanisms: the English of the New World; New York, 1872.

—— Studies in English; New York, 1867.

Schulz, Carl B.: The King's English at Home, *New York Evening Mail*, Oct. 29, 1917.

Scott, Fred. N.: The Pronunciation of Spanish-American Words, *Modern Language Notes*, vol. vi.

—— Verbal Taboos, *School Review*, vol. xx, 1912, pp. 366–78.

Searle, William G.: Onomasticon Anglo-Saxonicum; Cambridge, 1897.

Sechrist, Frank K.: The Psychology of Unconventional Language, *Pedagogical Seminary*, vol. xx, Dec., 1913.

Seeman, B.: Die Volksnamen der amerikanischen Pflanzen; Hannover, 1851.

Shute, Samuel M.: A Manual of Anglo-Saxon; New York, 1867.

Skeat, W. W.: English Dialects From the Eighth Century to the Present Day; Cambridge, 1911.

—— An Etymological Dictionary of the English Language; Oxford, 1882; 4th ed., 1910.

—— A Primer of Classical and English Philology; Oxford, 1905.

Smalley, D. S.: American Phonetic Dictionary of the English Language; Cincinnati, 1855.

Smart, B. H.: A Practical Grammar of English Pronunciations; London, 1810.

Smith, Chas. Forster: Americanisms, *Southern Methodist Quarterly*, Jan., 1891.

—— On Southernisms, *Trans. American Philological Association*, 1883.

Soames, Laura: Introduction to English, French and German Phonetics; New York, 1899.

Sproull, Wm. O.: Hebrew and Rabbinical Words in Present Use, *Hebraica*, Oct., 1890.

Stearns, Edward J.: A Practical Guide to English Pronunciation for the Use of Schools; Boston, 1857.

Storm, J.: Englische Philologie; Leipzig, 1896.

Stratton, Clarence: Are You Uhmurican or American?, *New York Times*, July 22, 1917.

—— The New Emphasis of Oral English, *English Journal*, Sept., 1917.

Sunden, Karl: Contributions to the Study of Elliptical Words in Modern English; Upsala, 1904.

Sweet, Henry: A Handbook of Phonetics; London, 1877.
—— A History of English Sounds; London, 1876; Oxford, 1888.
—— The History of Language; London, 1900.
—— A New English Grammar, Logical and Historical, 2 vols.; Oxford, 1892–8; new ed., 1900–03.
—— The Practical Study of Languages; London, 1900.
—— A Primer of Spoken English; Oxford, 1900.
—— The Sounds of English; Oxford, 1908.
Swinton, William: Rambles Among Words; New York, n. d.
Tallichet, H.: A Contribution Towards a Vocabulary of Spanish and Mexican Words Used in Texas, *Dialect Notes*, vol. i, pt. iv.
Tamson, George J.: Word-Stress in English; Halle, 1898.
Tardivel, J. P.: L'Anglicisme: Voilà l'Ennemi; Quebec, 1880.
Taylor, Isaac: Words and Places, 3rd ed. rev.; London, 1873.
Thom, Wm. T.: Some Parallelisms Between Shakespeare's English and the Negro-English of the United States, *Shakespeariana*, vol. i, p. 129.
Thornton, Richard H.: An American Glossary . . . , 2 vols.; Phila. and London, 1912.
Toller, T. N.: Outlines of the History of the English Language; Cambridge, 1900.
Tooker, William W.: Indian Names of Places in the Borough of Brooklyn; New York, 1901.
Toro y Gisbert, Miguel de: Americanismos; Paris, n. d.
Trench, Richard C.: English Past and Present; London, 1855; rev. ed., 1905.
—— On the Study of Words; London, 1851; rev. ed., 1904.
Trumbull, J. Hammond: The Composition of Indian Geographical Names, *Collection of the Conn. Historical Society*, vol. ii.
Tucker, Gilbert M.: American English: *North American Review*, April, 1883.
—— American English, a Paper Read Before the Albany Institute, July 6, 1882, With Revision and Additions; Albany, 1883.
—— Our Common Speech; New York, 1895.
Van der Voort, J. H.: Hedendaagsche Amerikanismen; Gouda (Holland), 1894.
Vizetelly, Frank H.: A Desk-book of 25,000 Words Frequently Mispronounced; New York and London, 1917.
—— Essentials of English Speech, 2nd ed.; New York and London, (1917).
—— The Foreign Element in English, *New Age*, Oct., 1913.
Wagner, Leopold: Names and Their Meaning; London, 1892.
Walter, G. F.: Phillimore: Sporting Terms in Common Speech, *Monthly Review*, Nov., 1906.

Wardlaw, Patterson: Simpler English, *Bulletin of the University of South Carolina*, no. 38, pt. iii, July, 1914.

Ware, J. Redding: Passing English of the Victorian Era . . . ; London, n. d.

Warnock, Elsie L.: Terms of Approbation and Eulogy in American Dialect Speech, *Dialect Notes*, vol. iv, pt. i, 1913.

Warren, Arthur: Real Americanisms, *Boston Herald*, Nov. 20, 1892.

Watts, Harvey M.: Prof. Lounsbury and His Rout of the Dons on Americanisms, *Philadelphia Public Ledger*, April 16, 1915.

Webster, Noah: An American Dictionary of the English Language . . . 2 vols.; New York, 1828.

—— The American Spelling Book . . . Being the First Part of a Grammatical Institute of the English Language . . . Boston, 1783.

—— The American Spelling Book . . . revised ed.; Sandbornton (N. H.), 1835.

—— A Compendious Dictionary of the English Language; Hartford, 1806.

—— A Dictionary of the English Language Compiled for the Use of Common Schools in the United States; Boston, 1807.

—— A Dictionary of the English Language . . . for Common Schools . . . ; Hartford, 1817.

—— Dissertations on the English Language . . . ; Boston, 1789.

—— The Elementary Spelling Book . . . Phila., 1829.

—— The Elementary Spelling Book . . . revised ed.; New York, 1848.

—— A Grammatical Institute of the English Language . . . in Three Parts; Part 1, Containing a New and Accurate Standard of Pronunciation . . . ; Hartford, 1783.

—— A Letter to the Hon. John Pickering on the Subject of His Vocabulary; Boston, 1817.

—— The New American Spelling Book . . . ; New Haven, 1833.

Weekley, Ernest: Surnames; London, 1916.

Wetherill, Georgine N.: The American Language, *Anglo-Continental*, Jan., 1894.

Wheatley, Henry B.: Chronological Notices of the Dictionaries of the English Language, *Transactions of the Philological Society* (London), 1865.

White, D. S.: American Pronunciation, *Journal of Education*, July 13, 1916.

White, Richard Grant: Americanisms, parts i–viii, *Atlantic Monthly*, April, May, July, Sept., Nov., 1878; Jan., March, May, 1879.

—— British Americanisms, *Atlantic Monthly*, May, 1880.

—— Every-Day English . . . ; Boston, 1880.

—— Some Alleged Americanisms, *Atlantic Monthly*, Dec., 1883.

White, Richard Grant: Words and Their Uses, Past and Present; Boston, 1872; rev. ed., New York, 1876.

Whitman, Walt; Slang in America, *North American Review*, vol. cxli, p. 431.

Whitney, William D.: The Life and Growth of Language, New York, 1875.

—— Language and the Study of Language; New York, 1867.

Wilcox, W. H.: The Difficulties Created by the Grammarians are to be Ignored, *Atlantic Educational Journal*, Nov., 1912.

Williams, R. O.: Our Dictionaries; New York, 1890.

—— Some Questions of Good English; New York, 1897.

Wilson, A. J.: A Glossary of Colloquial Slang and Technical Terms in Use in the Stock Exchange and in the Money Market; London, 1895.

Wittmann, Elizabeth: Clipped Words, *Dialect Notes*, vol. iv, pt. ii, 1914.

Wright, Joseph: An English Dialect Dictionary, 6 vols.; London, 1896–1905.

—— The English Dialect Grammar; Oxford, 1905.

Wundt, W.: Die Sprache; Leipzig, 1900.

Wyld, H. C. K.: The Growth of English; London, 1907.

—— The Historical Study of the Mother Tongue; New York, 1906.

—— The Study of Living Popular Dialects and Its Place in the Modern Science of Language; London, 1904.

Yule, Henry (and A. C. Burnell). Hobson-Jobson: a Glossary of Anglo-Indian Words and Phrases, and of Kindred Terms, Etymological, Historical, Geographical and Discursive; new ed., ed. by Wm. Crooke; London, 1903.

List of Words and Phrases

The parts of speech are indicated only when it is desirable for clearness. The following abbreviations are used:

a.	adjective	*n.*	noun	*suf.*	suffix
adv.	adverb	*pref.*	prefix	*v.*	verb
art.	article	*pro.*	pronoun	*vp.*	verb-phrase.

a, *art.*, 62, 154, 267; *particle,* 207; *pref.*, 92.
a-*sound*, 11, 58–60, 94–5, 102, 173–4, 176.
Aarons, 280
aber nicht, 152.
aber nit, 152, 308, 311.
abgefaked, *v.*, 156.
aboard, 92.
abolitionist, 83.
above, 262.
Abraham, 280n.
absquatulate, *v.*, 82.
abuv, 262.
accept, 77n.
acceptum, 77n.
accommodation-train, 82.
accouchement, 127.
achtel, 118.
acre, 250, 252, 254.
acute, 160.
acy, *suf.*, 77.
ad, 142, 160.
Adamic, 73.
ad-card, 160.
addition, 50.
addressograph, 165.
ad-man, 160.
admitted to the bar, *vp.* 108.
adobe, 87.
ad-rate, 160.
advertisement, 160, 169, 176.
advertize, 262.
advocate, *v.*, 27, 48, 49, 51.
ad-writer, 160.
adze, 56.
aeon, 243.
aero, *a.*, 160.
acroplane, *a.*, 160.
aëroplane, *n.*, 263.
aëroplane, *n.*, 263n.
aesthetics, 257.
aetiology, 257.
affiliate, 77.

afoot, 97.
afterwards, 147, 148.
against, 91.
agenda, 100.
agent, 121.
ag'in, 91.
aggravate, 77.
a-going, 92.
Ahrens, 280.
ai-*sound*, 95, 96.
ain't, 145, 146, 204, 210.
air-line, 82, 105.
airplane, 263.
aisle-manager, 124.
aker, 250, 252, 254.
alabastine, 165.
alarm, 264.
alarmist, 33.
alarum, 264.
Albert, 275.
Albrecht, 275.
Albright, 275.
alderman, 47.
alfalfa, 109.
allay-foozee, 90.
Allegany, 296.
Alleghany, 296.
Allegheny, 296.
allez-fusil, 90.
all-fired, 129.
allot upon, 31.
allow, 33.
all right, 157.
allright, 263n.
allrightnick, 156.
ally, *n.*, 170.
almoner, 112.
alright, 27, 263.
also, 34.
altho, 262, 263.
aluminium, 264.
aluminum, 264.
always, 229.
am, 198, 209.

amachoor, 238.
amass, 95.
ambish, 160.
ambition, *n.*, 160; *v.*, 49.
Americanism, 38.
Americanize, 77.
Ames, 275.
amigo, 158.
am not, 210.
an, *art.*, 62, 95, 267.
anaemia, 242, 245, 257, 260.
a-fi-sice, 92.
Ananias club, 306.
anatomy, 95.
Anderson, 272.
andiron, 56.
and no mistake, 92.
André, 275.
Andrews, 275.
a-near, 92.
anemia, 242, 262.
aneurism, 242.
aneurysm, 242.
angry, 79, 99.
Anheuser, 153, 276.
anilin, 262.
Anne Arundel, 297.
annex, 242, 258n.
annexe, *n.*, 242, 245, 257, 258n, 260.
A No. 1, 161.
antagonize, 49, 136.
ante, *n.*, 87; *v.*, 202.
anteriour, 248n.
ante up, *v.*, 87, 111.
anti, 87.
anti-fogmatic, IR.
antmire, 126.
anxious-bench, 83, 84.
anxious-seat, 84.
any, 237.
anyways, 147, 229.
apartment, 110.
apern, 239.

340

prebendary, 112.
precinct, 83.
preelood, 240.
preferred, 171.
prelude, 240.
premeer, 240.
première, 240.
premiss, 260.
preparatory-school, 160.
prepaid, 100, 103.
prep-school, 104, 160.
presentation, 112.
president, 104, 119.
presidential, 30, 50, 51, 136.
prespiration, 238.
press, n., 100.
pressman, 99, 108.
pretence, 244.
pretense, 244.
pretty, 175.
pretzel, 88.
prickly-heat, 46.
primarily, 170.
primary, n., 83, 84.
primate, 112.
prime minister, 122.
primero, 94.
Prince Albert, 14.
principal, n., 104.
private-detective, 110.
private-enquiry-agent, 110.
prob'ly, 238.
procurer, 127.
professor, 33, 117, 118.
program(me), 100, 171, 244,
245, 260, 262, 263.
progress, v., 48, 51.
prolog, 262.
promenade, 98.
proof-reader, 100.
propaganda, 33.
proper, adv., 227.
property, 155.
proposition, 116.
prosit, 89, 89n.
prostitute, 127.
protectograph, 165.
protégé, 240, 264.
Protestant Episcopal, 113.
prove, 196.
proved, 196.
proven, 196.
provost, 104.
pub, 105, 139.
public-comfort-station, 127.
public-company, 106.
public-house, 100, 105, 124.
public-school, 100, 104.
public-servant, 27, 99, 105.
publishment, 31, 77.
pudding, 88n.
pudgy, 244, 246.

puerile, 174.
pull up stakes, vp., 78.
pull wool over his eyes, vp.,
78.
pumpernickel, 88.
pumpkin, 172.
pung, 48.
pungy, 47, 48, 111.
punster, 90n.
punt, n., 111.
Purgatoire, 292.
purae, 110.
push, n., 319.
pushed, 201.
pusht, 201.
put, 164, 196.
put a bug in his ear, vp., 78.
put it down, vp., 103.
put over, vp., 164.
pygmy, 244, 247.
pyjamas, 244, 252, 258, 259,
260.

Q-room, 264.
quadroon, 43.
quaff, 95.
quahaug, 30, 42.
quandary, 306.
quan'ity, 238.
quarantine-flag, 125.
quarter-day, 114.
quartette, 260.
quate, 236.
quaver, 113.
questionize, 77.
queue, 106.
quick, adv., 227.
quit, 196.
quite, 114, 116, 117.
quitter, 14.
quoit, 236.
quotation-marks, 100.

r, letter, 60.
r-sound, 61.
rabbit, 54.
Rabinovitch, 280.
raccoon, 40, 134n, 160.
racing-dope, 94.
radish, 237.
ragamuffin, 56.
rail, 82.
railroad, n., 100; v., 83.
railroad-man, 83, 100.
rails, 100.
railway, 100.
railway-guard, 118.
railway-man, 135.
railway-rug, 83.
railway-servant, 100.
railway-sub-office, 83.
Rain-in-the-Face, 86.

raise, n., 83, 156, v., 196.
raised, 196.
rake-off, 10.
Ralph, 286.
ram, 126.
rambunctious, 81, 82, 166.
ran, 196, 205.
ranch, n., 86; v., 87.
ranchero, 30.
ranchman, 87.
rancho, 30.
rancor, 244.
rancour, 244.
rang, 196.
range, 81.
rapides, 46n.
rapids, 40, 46, 86.
rare, a., 100, 104; v., 237.
rate-payer, 101, 105.
rates, 101.
rathskeller, 88, 240.
rational, 173.
rattler, 160.
rattlesnake, 160.
rattling, 116n.
Raymond, 283.
razor, 155.
razor-back, 45.
razor-strop, 237n.
re, suf., 252, 253, 256, 257,
259, 261.
read, 105, 196.
read for holy orders, vp.,
112.
ready-made, 124.
ready-tailored, 124.
ready-to-wear, 124.
real-estate agent, 18.
really, 228.
realm, 251.
rear, v., 236.
recall, n., 107.
receipts, 100.
recent, adv., 228.
reckon, 31.
reco'nize, 238.
rd, suf., 201.
reddish, 237.
red-eye, 85.
Red Indian, 99.
red-light-district, 127.
reed-bird, 45.
reel-of-cotton, 103.
reflexion, 260.
refresher, 108.
régime, 264.
regular, adv., 227; n., 83.
regularity, 84.
Reichman, 280.
Reiger, 274.
Reindollar, 277.
reit-evé, 155.

General Index

Aasen, Ivar, 5.
Abbreviations, 23, 161.
Actes de la Société Philologique de Paris, 18n.
Adams, Franklin P., 144n.
Adams, John. 50.
Adams, John Quincy, 49.
Ade, George, 16, 191, 305.
Addison, Joseph, 201n.
Adjective, American, 24, 27, 30, 33, 44, 48, 50, 56, 57, 76, 80–83, 230, 231.
Adverb, American, 24, 44, 76–80, 83, 146, 226–9.
Alford, Henry, 75, 76, 220, 312.
American Academy of Arts and Letters, 148.
American Dialect Society, 6, 7, 29, 235.
Americanism, definitions of; White's, 10; Lounsbury's, 10; Bartlett's, 30; Fowler's, 30; Farmer's, 32; Clapin's, 33; Thornton's, 33.
American Magazine, 185n.
American Philological Association, 261.
American Review of Reviews, 157n.
Ames, Nathaniel, 47.
Annual Review, 38.
Archer, William, 12, 28.
Archiv f. d. Studium d. neueren Sprachen, 18.
Aristophanes, 181n.
Arnold, Matthew, 3.
Arthur, T. S., 126n.
Athenaeum, 255.
Atlantic Educational Journal, 180n.
Atlantic Monthly, 9, 60n, 149, 305.
Australian English, 310.
Authors' and Printers' Dictionary, 256, 258.

Babbitt, Eugene H., 140n, 315.
Bache, Richard M., 95n, 126, 129n, 144n.
Baltimore street names, 300.
Baltimore Sun, 265n, 273n, 276n.
Bancroft, Aaron, 38, 253.
Bancroft, George, 71.
Bankhead, John H., 143n.
Bardsley, Charles W., 284n, 285n
Barentz, A. E., 18.
Barrère, Albert, 43, 94.
Barringer, G. A., 18.
Bartlett, John Russell, 10, 30, 34, 40, 44, 74, 87, 126.
Beach-la-Mar, 318.
Beecher, Henry Ward, 76.
Belknap, Jeremy, 39.
Bennett, Arnold, 13.
Beverley, Robert, 40, 45, 46.
Bierce, Ambrose, 305.
Bible, 56, 143, 198, 213, 226, 293, 307.
Billings, Josh, 190.
Blackwood's, 68.
Bonaparte, Prince, L.-L., 167.
Book of Common Prayer, 147.
Borland, Wm. P., 142n.
Bosson, O. E., 305.
Boston pronunciation, 58, 95, 173, 174.
Boucher, Jonathan, 38, 50, 160.
Boucicault, Dion, 93.
Boyd, E. A., 320n.
Boyd, Stephen G., 287n.
Brackebusch, W., 313, 314n.
Bradley, Henry, 209, 213n, 214, 257, 317.
Bremer, Otto, 5.
Bridges, Robert, 171n, 175, 237.
Bristed, Chas. A., 36, 75, 77n, 90, 116n, 133.
British Critic, 38, 50.

Lightning Source UK Ltd.
Milton Keynes UK
UKHW050954270921
391102UK00013B/179